Anatomy and Physiology

FOR ENGLISH LANGUAGE LEARNERS

Judy Meier Penn   Elizabeth Hanson

PEARSON
Longman

Anatomy and Physiology for English Language Learners

Pearson Education, 10 Bank Street, White Plains, NY 10606

Staff credits: The people who made up the *Anatomy and Physiology* team, representing editorial,
production, design, and manufacturing, are Pamela Fishman, Gosia Jaros-White, Sasha Kintzler, Melissa Leyva,
Edie Pullman, Debbie Sistino, and Patricia Wosczyk.
Cover design: Patricia Wosczyk
Text design: Patricia Wosczyk
Text composition: Integra
Text font: 11/13 Minion
Photo and illustration credits: Dorling Kindersley: **2** 1.1a, 1.1b, 1.1c, 1.1d, **4** 1.2a, 1.2b, 1.2c, 1.2d, **5** 1.3, 1.5, **7** 1.7, **12** 1.9, **14** 1.10, **16**
1.11a, 1.11b, 1.11c, 1.11d, **18** opener, **21** photo, **28** photo, **32** opener, **35** 3.4, **40** 3.9, 3.10, **45** 3.14, **46** 3.15, **59** opener, **84** opener, **85** 5.1, **87**
5.2, **88** 5.3, **91** 5.5, **96** 5.7, **99** 5.12, 5.13, **105** 5.17, **112** 6.5, **159** 8.4, **166** 8.6, **168** 8.7, **175** photo, **178** opener, **181** 9.4, **182** 9.5, **184** 9.6, **185**
9.8, **198** 9.11, **202** 9.15, **204** 9.16, **205** 9.17, **206** 9.18, **212** 10.4, **269** 12.12; EMG Education Management Group: **11** photo 1; Getty Images:
73 photo; Goodenough, Judith A; McGuire, Betty A; Wallace, Robert A, *Biology of Humans: Concepts, Applications, and Issues*, 1st Edition,
© 2005. Reprinted by permission of Pearson Education, Inc., Upper Saddle River, NJ: **7** 1.6, **19** 2.1, **20** 2.2, **30** 2.4, **33** 3.1, **44** 3.11, 3.12, **45**
3.13, **48** 3.16, **49** 3.17, **50** 3.18, 3.19, **52** 3.20, **53** 3.21, **56** 3.22, **60** 4.1, **64** 4.4, **68** 4.8, 4.9, 4.10, **70** 4.11, **71** 4.12, **73** 4.13, **75** 4.14, **76** 4.15, **82**
4.17, **92** 5.6, **98** 5.11, **100** 5.15, **108** 6.1, **109** 6.2, **110** 6.3, **111** 6.4, **113** 6.6, **114** 6.7, **136** 7.8, **138** 7.9, **142** 7.11, **155** 8.1, **157** 8.2, **168** 8.8, **173**
8.10, **176** 8.11, **181** 9.3, **185** 9.7, **187** 9.9, **199** 9.12, **209** 10.1, **211** 10.2, **212** 10.3, **214** 10.5, **215** 10.6, **227** 10.10, **230** 11.1, **232** 11.2, 11.3, **233**
11.4, **235** 11.5, 11.6, **237** 11.7, **243** 11.9, **244** 11.10, **247** 11.11, **248** 11.12, **251** 12.1, 12.2, **253** 12.3, 12.4, **256** 12.6, **257** 12.7, **263** 12.8, **265**
12.9, **266** 12.10, **268** 12.11, **279** 12.16, 12.17; Gunstream, Stanley E, *Biological Explorations: A Human Approach*, 5th Edition © 2005.
Reprinted by permission of Pearson Education, Inc., Upper Saddle River, NJ: **4** 1.4, **35** 3.2, **62** 4.2, **63** 4.3, **81** 4.16, **89** 5.4, **104** 5.16, **129** 7.1,
131 7.2, 7.3, **139** 7.10, **146** 7.14, **152** 7.15; Imagineering: **4** 1.2f, 1.2g, 1.2h, 1.2i, 1.2j, **22** 2.3, **26, 35**, 3.3, **37** 3.5, 3.6, **38, 39** 3.7, **40** 3.8, **65** 4.5,
66 4.6, **67** 4.7, **78, 97** 5.8, 5.9, **98** 5.10, **135** 7.7, **144** 7.12, 7.13, **161** 8.5, **171** 8.9, **181** 9.4, **194** 9.10, **219** 10.7, 10.8, 10.9, **254** 12.5, **272** 12.13,
274 12.14; Merrill Education: **128** opener, **154** opener; Pearson Education Custom Publishing: **132** 7.4, 7.5, **133** 7.6; Pearson Education/PH
College: **1** opener, **2** 1.1e, **4** 1.2e, **7** 1.8, **11** photo 2, **15** photo, **16** 1.11e, **54** photo, **55** photo, **100** 5.14, **102** photo, **107** opener, **115** 6.8, **117**
6.9, **118** 6.10, **123** photo, **126** 6.11, **169** photo, **179** 9.1, **180** 9.2, **188** photo, **190** photo, **191** photo 1, 2, **192** photo, **200** 9.13, **201** 9.14, **208**
opener, **229** opener, **238** photo, **250** opener, **274** photo; Stockbyte: **67** photo; Visuals Unlimited: **158** 8.3.
Photo Research: Director, Image Resource Center: Melinda Reo; Manager, Rights and Permissions:
Zina Arabia; Manager, Visual Research: Beth Brenzel; Manager, Cover Visual Research & Permissions:
Karen Sanatar; Image Permission Coordinator: Craig A. Jones

Library of Congress Cataloging-in-Publication Data
Penn, Judy Meier.
Anatomy and physiology for English language learners / Judy Meier Penn, Elizabeth Hanson.
    p. cm.
  Includes index.
  ISBN 0-13-195080-0
1. Readers—Medicine.   2. English language—Textbooks for foreign speakers.
3. Medicine—Vocabulary—Problems, exercises, etc.   4. English language—Medical English.
5. English language—Conversation and phrase books (for medical personnel)
6. Medicine—Language. I. Hanson, Elizabeth. II. Title.
PE1127.M4P44 2006
428.6'402461—dc22

2006000243

Printed in the United States of America
2 3 4 5 6 7 8 9 10–VHG–10 09 08 07

CONTENTS

Scope and Sequence ...... *iv*

Introduction ...... *vi*

CHAPTER 1 **Introduction to Anatomy and Physiology** *1*

CHAPTER 2 **The Integumentary System** *18*

CHAPTER 3 **The Skeletal System** *32*

CHAPTER 4 **The Muscular System** *59*

CHAPTER 5 **The Nervous System, Part 1** *84*

CHAPTER 6 **The Nervous System, Part 2** *107*

CHAPTER 7 **The Digestive System** *128*

CHAPTER 8 **Blood and Body Defenses** *154*

CHAPTER 9 **The Cardiovascular System** *178*

CHAPTER 10 **The Respiratory System** *208*

CHAPTER 11 **The Urinary System** *229*

CHAPTER 12 **The Reproductive System** *250*

Pronunciation Key *283*

Metric–English System Conversions *284*

Word Parts *285*

Achievement Test 1 (Chapters 1–3) *288*

Achievement Test 2 (Chapters 4–6) *291*

Achievement Test 3 (Chapters 7–9) *295*

Achievement Test 4 (Chapters 10–12) *298*

Answer Key *302*

Index *332*

Scope and Sequence

CHAPTER	CONTENT	LANGUAGE SKILLS	STUDY SKILLS	CULTURAL FOCUS
1 **Introduction to Anatomy and Physiology**	Building blocks of the body Homeostasis	Describing organization and function	Creating good study habits	Preparing for the future
2 **The Integumentary System**	Regions of the integument Accessory structures Common skin disorders Homeostasis: Maintaining body temperature	Asking for clarification	Using index cards	The use of touch to comfort
3 **The Skeletal System**	How a bone is organized The functions of bone Accessory structures of bone Major bones in the body Common bone disorders Homeostasis: Regulation of calcium	Stating degree of understanding	Studying with diagrams	Informality in forms of address
4 **The Muscular System**	Organization of a skeletal muscle How muscles move Types of muscles Major muscles in the body Common muscle disorders	Describing location	Mnemonic devices	Alternative healing
5 **The Nervous System, Part 1**	Organization of the nervous system How the nervous system works The peripheral nervous system Common neural disorders Homeostasis: reflex	Describing a sequence	Active reading	Folk medicine
6 **The Nervous System, Part 2**	Parts of the brain Parts of the spinal cord Autonomic nervous system Common CNS disorders	Stating and asking about differences	Forming a study group	Making progress in health care
7 **The Digestive System**	The path of food in the upper digestive tract Accessory organs The path of food in the lower digestive tract Common disorders of digestion Homeostasis: Regulating blood sugar, metabolism	Explaining cause and effect	Imagining a process	Direct communication

CHAPTER	CONTENT	LANGUAGE SKILLS	STUDY SKILLS	CULTURAL FOCUS
8 **Blood and Body Defenses**	The composition and functions of blood How infectious diseases occur Body defenses Blood disorders	Defining terms	Using reference sources	Spiritual forces in healing
9 **The Cardiovascular System**	The heart Measuring heart health The blood vessels and the lymphatic vessels Common cardiovascular disorders Homeostasis: Regulating heart functions	Describing relationships and connections	Concept map	The economy of health care
10 **The Respiratory System**	Organs of respiratory tract Breathing and gas exchange How the respiratory system stays healthy Common respiratory disorders Homeostasis: control of breathing	Describing a process	Summarizing information	Hierarchy of age and gender
11 **The Urinary System**	Anatomy and physiology of the kidneys Organs of urinary system Common urinary disorders Homeostasis: regulation of blood volume	Asking hypothetical questions	Categorizing information	Confidentiality and privacy
12 **The Reproductive System**	Male reproductive system Female reproductive system Fertilization and embryonic development Common reproductive disorders	Answering hypothetical questions	Putting it all together	Discussing the reproductive system with patients

INTRODUCTION

Anatomy and Physiology for English Language Learners is an introduction to basic anatomy and physiology. It presents science content and language skills necessary for success in academic science courses such as anatomy and physiology and human biology.

The textbook is designed for students at the high-intermediate level of English. Its goal is to prepare English language learners for success in future nursing and allied health prerequisite courses. It can also be used by students who already hold nursing or allied health degrees in their countries and are preparing to take certification examinations in the United States.

The textbook consists of twelve chapters, each focusing on a particular organ system. Every chapter contains:

- A brief introduction to the topic
- Anatomy and physiology content with level-appropriate readings
- Comprehension checks
- Building language and study skills sections
- Focus on culture section
- Workbook-type chapter review

At the end of the book, there are four achievement tests designed for in-class or self-testing; a pronunciation guide with phonetic symbols used in the text; conversion charts for metric and English systems; a word parts section that offers explanation of affixes that form scientific vocabulary; an answer key for comprehension checks and achievement tests; and a subject index.

Extensive Support to Engage Students in Content and Activate Prior Knowledge

Each chapter begins with a short overview of a particular organ system that introduces students to the chapter's overall goals. Warm-up exercises follow including: a body-system labeling activity, content questions to assess students' prior knowledge, and a fill-in exercise focusing on high-frequency verbs introduced in the chapter.

Motivating Anatomy and Physiology Content

The anatomy and physiology content is logically organized, and presented in a student-friendly tone. Level-appropriate readings and activities, with controlled vocabulary, offer students comprehensible content at a manageable level.

Comprehension Exercises Develop Critical Thinking

Throughout the chapters, there are periodic comprehension checks to ensure that students have understood what they have read. These feature a variety of exercises and sharpen students' critical reading and writing skills, such as skimming and scanning, summarizing, analyzing, categorizing, guessing meaning from context, defining, and comparing and contrasting.

Practical Pronunciation Practice

Phonetic transcriptions of difficult scientific vocabulary appear throughout the readings. These aid in understanding and reinforcing content and help students increase vocabulary. A pronunciation guide with phonetic symbols used in the text is included on page 283.

Functional Diagrams and Photographs Aid Comprehension

The abundance of diagrams and compelling art seizes students' interest, illustrates concepts, and guides students through processes.

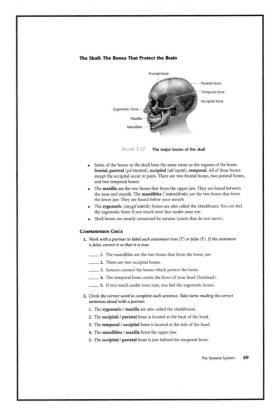

Building Language and Study Skills

Useful language and study skills strategies help students learn *how* to learn scientific content and *how* to talk and write about it. Building language sections include language functions commonly needed by students in science courses, including asking for clarification, describing cause and effect, and explaining a process. Study skills provide students with practical learning strategies, including writing summaries, mnemonic devices, concept maps, and active reading.

BUILDING LANGUAGE AND STUDY SKILLS

Describing Organization and Function

In the study of anatomy and physiology, it's important to be able to explain the organization and function of structures. You will have to do so in both your speaking and your writing.

When you describe organization, you'll often use the verbs *comprise* and *form*. These verbs mean the same thing.

EXAMPLE	FORM
A cell is comprised of molecules.	A bigger structure is comprised of or *formed by* smaller structures.
A cell is formed by molecules.	
Molecules comprise cells.	Smaller structures comprise or form larger structures.
Molecules form cells.	

In addition to describing the organization of a structure, you will often be asked to explain the *function* of a structure. When you describe a structure's purpose, you'll often use the word *function*.

EXAMPLE	FORM
The function of the heart is to pump blood.	The function of ____ is + innitive.
The heart's function is to pump blood.	The ____ 's function is + innitive.
The heart has the function of pumping blood.	The ____ has the function of + gerund.

PRACTICE

1. *Use the prompts below to write sentences that describe a structure's organization and function. The rst one is done for you. Pay attention to verb tense and subject / verb agreement. Then compare your answers with those of a partner.*

   1. Heart / muscle tissue / pump blood.
      The heart is formed by muscle tissue. Its function is to pump blood.
   2. The skin / epithelial tissue / protect the body.
   3. The stomach / muscle tissue / hold food.
   4. Muscles / muscle tissue / move.
   5. Bones / bone tissue / support the body.

---

2. *Work with two partners and take turns asking and answering these questions.*

   1. What is the function of the stomach?
   2. What kind of tissue comprises skin?
   3. What is the function of the heart?
   4. What kind of tissue forms the heart?

3. *These are authentic questions taken from an anatomy and physiology class. Use the vocabulary and grammar you know to answer the following questions. Ask your teacher to check your answers.*

   1. Describe the organization of the basic building blocks of the body, going from smallest to largest.
   2. Describe the parts of a cell and explain the function of each part.

Creating Good Study Habits

Everyone needs to study to learn anatomy and physiology. No one can learn all that there is to learn by just attending class. To study effectively outside of class, it is important to create good study habits for yourself. Good study habits include:

1. nding a quiet place to study
2. having a set time to study each day
3. studying often for shorter periods of time
4. making a study plan
5. making a commitment to yourself to study

PRACTICE

1. *Work in groups of three. Take turns asking and answering the questions on the chart below and record the answers. Share your answers with the class.*

	You	Classmate 1	Classmate 2
Where is a quiet place for you to study?			
What is your set time to study?			
How long do you study at one time?			
What do you need when you study?			

2. *Think about your daily schedule for tomorrow. Write down when and where you will study. Make a list of study tasks. Also, write down how spending time to study now will be important for your future. Share what you write with a partner.*

Up-to-Date Medical Information Prepares Students for Real-World Careers

Each chapter features a section called *Maintaining Homeostasis* that describes and illustrates the ways the particular body systems stay in balance.

Each chapter also contains numerous *Medical Alert* features. They describe illnesses and diseases that are associated with a particular body system.

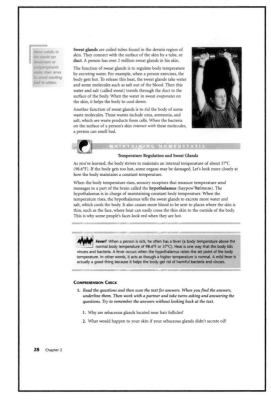

Sweat glands are coiled tubes found in the dermis region of skin. They connect with the surface of the skin by a tube, or duct. A person has over 2 million sweat glands in his skin.

The function of sweat glands is to regulate body temperature by *excreting* water. For example, when a person exercises, the body gets hot. To reduce this heat, the sweat glands take water and some molecules such as salt out of the blood. Then this water and salt (called *sweat*) travels through the duct to the surface of the body. When the water in sweat *evaporates* on the skin, it helps the body to cool down.

Another function of sweat glands is to rid the body of some waste molecules. These wastes include urea, ammonia, and salt, which are waste products from cells. When the bacteria on the surface of a person's skin *interact* with these molecules, a person can smell bad.

MAINTAINING HOMEOSTASIS

Temperature Regulation and Sweat Glands

As you've learned, the body strives to maintain an internal temperature of about 37°C (98.6°F). If the body gets too hot, some organs may be damaged. Let's look more closely at how the body maintains a constant temperature.

When the body temperature rises, sensory receptors that measure temperature send messages to a part of the brain called the **hypothalamus** (haypow'θɛlɑmɔs). The hypothalamus is in charge of maintaining constant body temperature. When the temperature rises, the hypothalamus tells the sweat glands to excrete more water and salt, which cools the body. It also causes more blood to be sent to places where the skin is thin, such as the face, where heat can easily cross the thin skin to the outside of the body. This is why some people's faces look red when they are hot.

Fever! When a person is sick, he often has a fever (a body temperature above the normal body temperature of 98.6°F or 37°C). Heat is one way that the body kills viruses and bacteria. A fever occurs when the hypothalamus raises the set point of the body temperature. In other words, it acts as though a higher temperature is normal. A mild fever is actually a good thing because it helps the body get rid of harmful bacteria and viruses.

COMPREHENSION CHECK

1. *Read the questions and then scan the text for answers. When you find the answers, underline them. Then work with a partner and take turns asking and answering the questions. Try to remember the answers without looking back at the text.*

   1. Why are sebaceous glands located near hair follicles?
   2. What would happen to your skin if your sebaceous glands didn't secrete oil?

Cross-Cultural Focus Promotes Cultural Awareness

Focus on Culture sections provide authentic cross-cultural conflicts common in health-care settings. The *Focus on Culture* feature is designed to familiarize students with potential cross-cultural misunderstandings and expand students' cultural competence. *Focus on Culture* includes engaging activities that highlight cultural diversity and provide opportunities for students to offer their own insights. *Culture Notes* throughout the chapter highlight interesting cultural facts related to a particular body system.

FOCUS ON CULTURE

Forms of Address

In many parts of the United States, it is common for people to call each other by their first names. They do this because it shows friendliness and comfort. In other cultures, it is more common for people to address each other using formal forms of address, such as Mr. or Mrs., especially when talking to someone who is not a member of the family or in their circle of friends. People who work in health care should be aware of this difference, so they won't offend anyone.

1. *The following story is about a cultural conflict that people may experience in a health-care setting. Read the story and then discuss the questions in small groups.*

   Mary, a nurse in her forties, is taking care of Mr. Cho, a man about her age. Mr. Cho, who was admitted to the hospital with severe back pain, has been under her care for three days. Mary has taken him to the bathroom, helped him to change clothes, checked his vital signs, and given him medication, including injections. In other words, Mary has been in close contact with Mr. Cho. To show him that she is friendly and cares about him, she has often joked with him and from the first day, she has called him by his first name—Chris—and not by his family name. Not being addressed as "Mister Cho" has upset Mr. Cho. He has felt disrespected and has felt that Mary has been treating him like a child. So after giving it a lot of thought, Mr. Cho decided to complain to Mary's supervisor.

   1. Why is Mr. Cho upset?
   2. When is it OK to call someone by their first name?
   3. Can you understand why Mary wants to call him by his first name?

2. *With a partner, choose one of the three following role plays. You may wish to write out the dialogue and practice it before performing it in front of the class.*

   Situation 1. Student A is Mr. Cho and Student B is the supervisor. Mr. Cho complains to the supervisor and the supervisor responds to his complaints.

   Situation 2. Student A is the nursing supervisor and Student B is Mary, the nurse. The nursing supervisor explains to Mary why Mr. Cho is upset. Mary reacts to what the supervisor is saying.

   Situation 3. Student A is Mary and Student B is Mr. Cho. Mary apologizes and Mr. Cho responds to the apology.

Chapter Reviews Provide Reinforcement and Encourage Critical Thinking

Chapter reviews include comprehension tests, labeling activities, a section with actual items from anatomy and physiology tests, and a section requiring students to synthesize information previously learned. A word bank is also included.

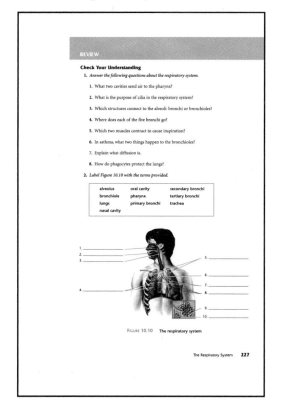

REVIEW

Check Your Understanding

1. *Answer the following questions about the respiratory system.*

   1. What two cavities send air to the pharynx?
   2. What is the purpose of cilia in the respiratory system?
   3. Which structures connect to the alveoli: bronchi or bronchioles?
   4. Where does each of the five bronchi go?
   5. Which two muscles contract to cause inspiration?
   6. In asthma, what two things happen to the bronchioles?
   7. Explain what diffusion is.
   8. How do phagocytes protect the lungs?

2. *Label Figure 10.10 with the terms provided.*

alveolus	oral cavity	secondary bronchi
bronchiole	pharynx	tertiary bronchi
lungs	primary bronchi	trachea
nasal cavity		

FIGURE 10.10 **The respiratory system**

The Respiratory System **227**

3. *Answer these typical anatomy and physiology quiz questions.*

   1. Which of these disorders involves the inability of alveoli to return to their original shape after inflation?
      a. Infant Respiratory Distress Syndrome   c. emphysema
      b. asthma   d. laryngitis
   2. When a person exercises, which of these will occur?
      a. dilation of bronchioles   b. constriction of bronchioles
   3. _____ Is this true or false? Your lungs inflate because air has filled them.
   4. Circle the correct word. When you speak, your vocal cords **contract / relax / vibrate.**
   5. Circle the correct words. Contraction of the **diaphragm / bronchioles** causes the thoracic cavity and lungs to **expand / get smaller.** This causes a difference in **weight / pressure** of the air inside the lungs as compared with outside. Air will **rush into / leave** the lungs.
   6. Circle the correct words. Inside the lungs, **oxygen / carbon dioxide** diffuses into the **alveoli / capillaries.**
   7. What is the function of the respiratory system?
   8. Where does incoming air go after it leaves the trachea?
   9. Describe three protective mechanisms in the respiratory system that prevent disease.
   10. Describe three ways in which colds differ from influenza.

Think More about It

   1. Where in the respiratory system do we find muscle? What type of muscle is it (smooth, cardiac, or skeletal)?
   2. In what ways is the nervous system involved with the respiratory system?
   3. How are the respiratory and cardiovascular systems linked?

Word Bank		
alveolus	expand	primary
breathe	expire, expiration	pulmonary
bronchiole	extend	respirator
bronchus	inhale	secondary
capture	inspire, inspiration	sinus
cartilage	larynx	surfactant
cellular respiration	lobe	tertiary
diffuse	macrophage	trachea
epiglottis	nasal cavity	vibrate
exhale	pharynx	vocal cords

228 Chapter 10

Assessments Measure Student Progress

Achievement tests for in-class or self-testing assess students' mastery of anatomy and physiology content and build test-taking confidence. Tests are designed to be taken after every three chapters.

Achievement Test 1
CHAPTERS 1–3
(50 points total)

A. *Answer the questions below, using complete sentences.* *(2 points)*
   1. What is homeostasis?
   2. What is the function of hormones?

B. *Match each item with the building block that describes it.* *(5 points)*
   ____ 1. the femur bone   a. tissue
   ____ 2. the epidermis   b. molecule
   ____ 3. all the bones in the body   c. cell
   ____ 4. osteocyte   d. organ system
   ____ 5. keratin   e. organ

C. *Circle the correct word(s) to complete each sentence.* *(5 points)*
   1. When a bone has a crack or break, this is called a **dislocation / fracture.**
   2. Bones are connected to other bones by **tendons / ligaments.**
   3. In flat and long bones, the outermost layer of bone is **spongy / compact.**
   4. Nerves and blood vessels are found inside the **dermis / epidermis** of the skin.
   5. When the cartilage at a joint becomes worn away, the person may experience **rheumatoid arthritis / osteoarthritis.**

D. *Label each statement true (T) or false (F).* *(6 points)*
   ____ 1. The hypodermis is the outermost layer of skin.
   ____ 2. The sebaceous glands are the glands in the skin that help to control body temperature.
   ____ 3. Some of the cells in the epidermis are dead.
   ____ 4. Blood vessels can be found inside bones.
   ____ 5. The cell membrane is permeable.
   ____ 6. Calcitonin is a hormone that causes calcium in the blood to be stored in the bones.

E. *Complete the sentences with the correct word(s).* *(6 points)*
   1. Bone matrix is made of two molecules: _____ and _____.
   2. Bone cells are called _____.
   3. One function of the skin is to _____.
   4. Another name for a joint is a(n) _____.
   5. Another name for the kneecap is the _____.
   6. Physiology is the study of the _____ of body parts.

288 Achievement Test 1

TEACHER'S NOTES

Content-Based Instruction

Content-based instruction means learning *about* something rather than learning *about* language. (Stephen Davies, *Internet TESL Journal*, Vol. IX, No. 2, February 2003). It is based on the premise that students learn language more successfully and are more motivated when language is used as a vehicle to learn meaningful and relevant content. A content-based teaching approach integrates cognitive, academic, and language skills. Students using *Anatomy and Physiology for English Language Learners* will benefit because they are learning anatomy and physiology in one course. The knowledge they gain will meet their direct goals. Students practice typical tasks they will encounter in their content courses while they are developing both receptive and productive language skills. Students listen, read, discuss, and write about anatomy and physiology topics, check comprehension, build study skills, and participate in regular assessments.

A Typical Teaching Sequence Using *Anatomy and Physiology for English Language Learners*

1. Review the previous lesson.
2. Build background knowledge before teaching a new lesson. Complete the warm-up exercises.
3. Pre-teach new information (draw on the board, bring in models, use diagrams, tell stories).
4. Pronounce all new terms; have students repeat.
5. Have students read silently, aloud, or in small groups.
6. Have students answer questions or summarize information.
7. Check comprehension.

Planning Lessons and Teaching Tips

- Make a list of your expectations (objectives) for each unit. Include language skills as well as content mastery. Prioritize the objectives. Decide what can be sacrificed if you run out of time. The goal is to give students a solid foundation. Remember, this will not be the only anatomy and physiology course they will take.
- Be specific in describing your expectations to students. For instance, do you expect students to be on time for class? To turn in assignments on time? Do you expect students to work on assignments individually or in pairs and groups? What are your expectations of their language skills? What are your expectations of their mastery of the content?
- In early units, focus on building language and study skills.
- Assess students' comprehension and skills regularly. Assessment is not just exams and quizzes. Assess listening, reading, speaking, and writing skills on a continuous basis.
- Do not lecture all of the time. Use a variety of teaching styles: hands-on demonstrations, practice with anatomical models, storytelling to illustrate a process, small group work, pronunciation practice, reading/listening exercises.
- Monitor your speaking. Speak at a normal pace, but simplify language, eliminate additional, non-essential information and enunciate clearly. Use visuals whenever possible.
- Write difficult words on the board as you pronounce them. Write the steps in a process on the board as you discuss it.

- Encourage students to participate and ask for clarification. Have students summarize information they have heard or read and state what is not clear. Be aware of cultural differences and be creative about finding ways students can respond without losing dignity. For example, have them list things that are confusing on the board or on slips of paper (anonymously) before class.
- Look for places in each unit where you can ask students to share information and stories about their cultures. This is particularly important if you have a class with students from many different cultures.

Notes for the ESL Teacher

Even though your language background is probably stronger than your science background, you can still successfully teach anatomy and physiology (A&P) to your ESL students. In fact, this content-based approach requires that you use the skills you already possess. You already know that you need to present information in manageable, comprehensible chunks and provide numerous practice opportunities. You also know how to present content and explain language rules in simple and creative ways. However, you will need to study some A&P content prior to teaching your students. Plan to spend some time reading and becoming comfortable with A&P concepts and vocabulary. To prepare, read this text before teaching it. This will give you an understanding of how the body systems interact with one another. You may also want to read an entry level A&P text for native speakers. Additionally, it may be beneficial to observe a few human biology and A&P classes. As you teach, keep in mind that you may have students in class who already know A&P in their native language at a level much deeper than yours. Don't let this intimidate you. These students can be valuable assets to you. Enlist their help in answering questions you may not be able to answer.

Notes for the Anatomy and Physiology Teacher

The biggest challenge for the content teacher is to be realistic about the amount of material you can cover. In a way, the exercise of deciding what is essential at this level is liberating. In fact, teaching students good skills for learning anatomy and physiology is much more productive than teaching infinite amounts of information. The goal of a course like this is to help students to become good learners of biology and to become more comfortable with communicating in the English language. Later courses in anatomy and physiology will provide them with plenty of content! As an A&P teacher, you may want to add more detail about exceptions to concepts or more complex examples, but this will simply confuse an English language learner who is focusing on learning the content. You will find that, in this text, many details you think are important for college-level A&P have been omitted. However, if students are given a good foundation, they will easily absorb those details in future courses.

To prepare to teach this course it may be beneficial to observe an ESL class and discuss ESL teaching strategies with the teacher. Ask ESL students in your other courses about the challenges they have faced. What was hardest for them as English language learners in a biology class? What cultural differences have they noticed that make it more difficult for them to communicate with or collaborate with native English speakers, both teachers and students? For instance, is it considered acceptable to admit in front of the class that you don't understand something? Or is it taboo in their culture to touch human bones or other human tissues in a laboratory? Finally, enjoy the opportunity to help your students learn about the human body while also learning English and becoming more aware of different cultures.

A Note from the Authors

I was asked to take on this project after nearly 20 years of teaching biology at the college level. It took no effort to convince me! I have taught students from all over the world. Many of my fondest memories have involved working with students who have English as their

second language. I have enjoyed learning more about their cultures. I have also admired their determination and passion for learning in a language that is new to them. These students' experiences and input has greatly influenced this book. My goal is to give English language learners the proper tools to become the valuable health-care professionals I know they can be.
Judy Meier Penn

I found that teaching anatomy and physiology to ESL students was not much different from teaching regular ESL. The only requirement is that you learn basic A&P. I hadn't known much A&P prior to teaching it to my ESL students. It might be a bit of a learning curve for you, as it was for me, to learn A&P content as well as vocabulary. I spent approximately 80 hours studying A&P prior to feeling comfortable teaching it at a basic level to my students. To prepare for teaching, I observed A&P classes several times and read a regular entry-level A&P textbook. I can safely say that I have learned basic A&P, but even more from my A&P students. Teaching this subject matter has been and continues to be a rewarding and positive experience.
Elizabeth Hanson

Acknowledgments

The authors wish to thank the following reviewers who helped to shape this book: **Virginia Gayle Blease**, Medical University of South Carolina, Charleston, SC; **Eleanor Brown**, Livingston Adult School, Livingston, NJ; **Gail Gaffney**, Algonquin College Language Institute, Ottawa, Ontario, Canada; **Steve Goetz**, Shoreline Community College, Seattle, WA; **Patricia Larson**, North Seattle Community College, Seattle, WA; **Kathleen Lundgren**, Southern New Hampshire University, Manchester, NH; **John McCormick**, North Shore Community College, Danvers, MA; **Geraldine Mulligan**, NCC Hispanic Development Corporation, Newark, NJ; **Carol Pineiro**, CELOP Boston University, Boston, MA.

In addition, the authors would like to thank Development Editor, Debbie Sistino; Associate Development Editor, Gosia Jaros-White; Senior Production Editor, Sasha Kintzler; and Editorial Director, Pam Fishman.

The authors wish to thank the following colleagues at Shoreline Community College: Steve Goetz (for initial editing and encouragement), Jo McEntire (for her advice on publishing and recommendation to Pearson), Josie Saldin and Donna Wilde (for their expertise in content-based instruction), and Donna Miller-Parker (for her tireless efforts in creating bridges to success for ESL students).

From Elizabeth Hanson: I wish to give a special thanks to my ESL students who come to the United States seeking a better life for themselves and their families. Your hard work, vision, and perseverance help us all realize that dreams do come true. Next, I must thank my 13-year-old son Christopher. Between your sports, music, schoolwork, and social life, and my regular job, I don't know how I found the time to write, but I did. You encouraged me and took on extra responsibilities doing what you knew had to be done. You are an amazingly perceptive, kind, and talented young man. Finally, Judy Penn. You and I make a great writing team. When we wrote together, I think we shared a brain because we often could finish each other's thoughts. What a wonderful experience that was!

From Judy Meier Penn: My special thanks to my husband Phil for his encouragement, patience, advice, and editing skills. Catlin Star Penn ("cat" is her first language) was the silent third author of this book, always purring softly on my lap through countless hours at the computer. I would never have become a biology educator without the early influences of my parents, Ray and Vera Meier, who taught me about living things around me and showed me the joys of teaching. I thank my sister and best friend, Karen, for her sense of humor and for helping me to remember what's important. And special thanks to Lai Hin Saetern, who educated me about what it is like to be an English language learner in a biology class. Finally, I wish to thank my coauthor, Elizabeth, for making this a truly fun project!

CHAPTER 1

Introduction to Anatomy and Physiology

In this chapter you will learn:

ANATOMY AND PHYSIOLOGY

- *The building blocks of the body*
- *Homeostasis—how the body controls conditions*

ENGLISH

- *Describing organization and function*

STUDY SKILLS

- *Creating good study habits*

CULTURE

- *Preparing for the future*

DID YOU KNOW *that 60 percent of the body's weight consists of water?*

INTRODUCTION

Welcome to the study of anatomy and physiology. **Anatomy** (ə′nætəmi) is the study of the parts of the body. The study of anatomy includes the names of the parts of the body and where they are located. For example, you will learn the names for the different parts of the heart and where they are located in the heart. **Physiology** (fɪziy′ɑlədʒi) is the study of the function, or purpose, of body parts. For example, in this book, you will learn how blood travels through the heart and how each part of the heart works to make blood move.

The human body is an amazing machine with many parts that work together to keep you alive and healthy. In this chapter, you will learn about the body's building blocks: molecules, cells, tissues, organs, and organ systems. You will also learn about homeostasis, the way your body maintains balance.

1. *Work with a partner. Look at the diagram of the body's building blocks. Try to label the parts with the words in the box. Look at Figure 1.2 on page 4 to check your answers.*

| cell | molecule | organ | organ system | tissue |

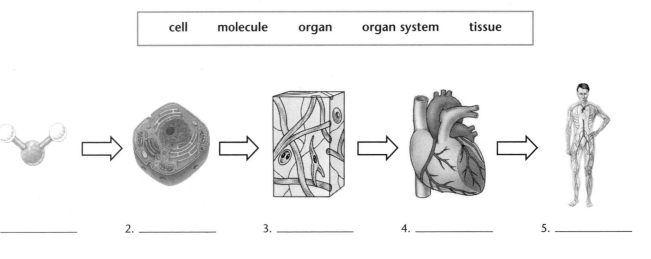

1. _____   2. _____   3. _____   4. _____   5. _____

FIGURE 1.1 **The body's building blocks**

2. *With your partner, try to answer these questions. If you do not know the answers, do not worry. You will find the answers as you read through this chapter.*

   1. What does the word *anatomy* mean?

   2. Which is larger: a cell or a molecule?

   3. Name two organs in your body.

   4. What does your body do if it gets too hot?

   5. What is a hormone?

3. *Read each verb, its simple definition, and its passive voice form. Then fill in the verbs in the sentences that follow. Pay attention to verb tense and subject / verb agreement. Compare your answers with those of another student.*

BASE FORM	PASSIVE VOICE FORM	MEANING
arrange	be arranged	to organize
comprise	be comprised of	to make / form
form	be formed	to make / comprise
give off	be given off	to send out / exit
interpret	be interpreted	to figure out
maintain	be maintained	to keep the same
monitor	be monitored	to watch
perform	be performed	to do
secrete	be secreted	to send to another place
take in	be taken in	to go in

1. You _____ food through your mouth.

2. Your body is _____ of many organs.

3. Your body wants to _____ its temperature.

4. Your brain _____ the information it receives.

5. Your cells _____ wastes such as carbon dioxide.

6. Every organ in your body _____ a specific task.

7. Some organs _____ molecules into the bloodstream.

8. A group of organs _____ an organ system.

9. In an organ system, the organs _____ in a specific way.

10. Your skin _____ the air for temperature changes.

THE BUILDING BLOCKS OF THE BODY

There are five basic building blocks of the body. Going from smallest to largest they are: molecules, cells, tissues, organs, and organ systems. Each building block *forms* the next. Molecules form cells. Cells form tissues. Tissues form organs and organs form organ systems.

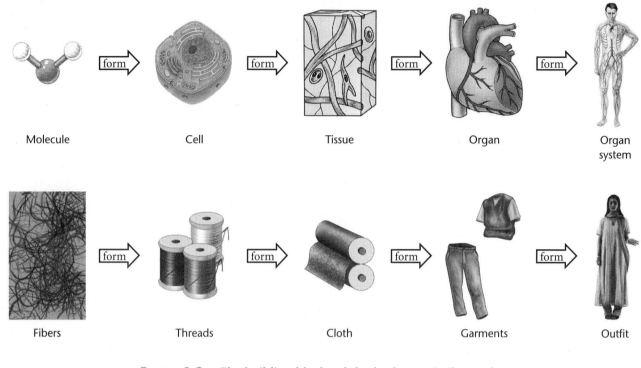

Molecule   Cell   Tissue   Organ   Organ system

Fibers   Threads   Cloth   Garments   Outfit

FIGURE 1.2   **The building blocks of the body are similar to the building blocks of an outfit (a set of clothes).**

Molecules and Cells

Molecules ('mɑlıkyulz) are the basic building block of all things, living and nonliving. Everything on Earth is *comprised of* molecules: paper, air, trees, soil, food, water, and the human body. Sugar, fat, water, oxygen, and carbon dioxide are all examples of molecules found in the body.

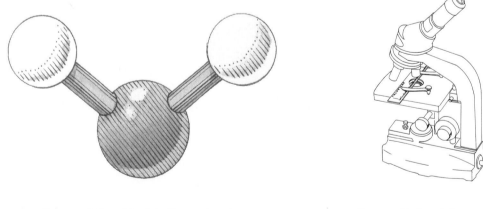

FIGURE 1.3   **Model of a molecule**

FIGURE 1.4   **Microscope**

Cells are found in all living things. Nonliving things do not contain cells. Cells are comprised of groups of molecules. Most cells are too small for you to see with just your eyes; you need a microscope to see cells.

There are many different kinds of cells in the body: fat cells, muscle cells, blood cells, bone cells. What makes one cell different from another is that they are made of different kinds of molecules *arranged* in unique ways. Even though these cells have different functions in the body and look different from each other under a microscope, they all contain the same parts.

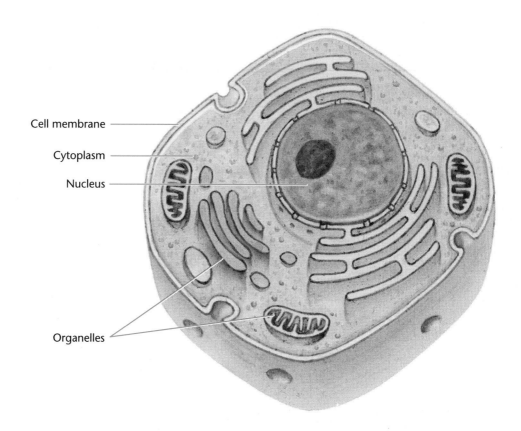

Cell membrane

Cytoplasm

Nucleus

Organelles

FIGURE 1.5 **Diagram of a cell and its parts**

All cells are filled with **cytoplasm** (ˈsaytəplæzəm), a jelly-like material. Cytoplasm holds many small cell parts, or **organelles** (ɔrgəˈnɛlz). All cells *take in* nutrients, such as sugar and oxygen and *give off* wastes, such as carbon dioxide. All nutrients and wastes pass easily through the cell membrane, the "skin" of the cell. When it is easy for things to pass through a membrane, that membrane is called **permeable** (ˈpɛrmiyəbəl).

Finally, each cell, except for a red blood cell, has a **nucleus** (ˈnuwkliyəs). The nucleus controls the cell. It is like the cell's brain. Molecules called DNA (deoxyribonucleic acid) are located in the nucleus. DNA contains information that tells the cell how to do its job, such as breaking apart a sugar or storing fat. DNA is also the genetic material that makes one person different from another. In effect, DNA is the cell's instruction book.

Remember that a cell is the basic unit of all living organisms, and that each type of cell has a different job to do within the body.

1. *Answer the questions below. Then compare your answers with those of a partner.*

   1. Where do you find molecules?

   2. Where DON'T you find cells?

   3. What do you use to see cells?

   4. What is the function of cytoplasm?

   5. What does the word *permeable* mean?

   6. Does a red blood cell have a nucleus?

   7. Where do you find DNA?

   8. What is DNA?

2. *Match the terms with their definitions by writing the letters in the correct blanks. Then compare your answers with those of a partner.*

   _____ 1. cell   **a.** the basic building block of all living and nonliving things

   _____ 2. cytoplasm   **b.** the "skin" of a cell

   _____ 3. DNA   **c.** the cell's "brain"

   _____ 4. membrane   **d.** a basic building block of all living things

   _____ 5. molecule   **e.** cell parts

   _____ 6. nucleus   **f.** the jelly-like material which holds cell parts in place

   _____ 7. organelles   **g.** easy to pass through

   _____ 8. permeable   **h.** the cell's instruction book located inside the nucleus

Tissues, Organs, and Organ Systems

Cells that look alike and have the same function join together to form a **tissue** ('tɪʃuw). For example, muscle cells comprise muscle tissue. Other examples of tissues include fat tissue, blood tissue, nerve tissue, and bone tissue.

When a group of different tissues join together to carry out a specific function within the body, they form an **organ**. The heart is an organ comprised of muscle tissue, connective tissue, blood tissue, and epithelial tissue. These tissues join together to carry out the function of pumping blood. The small intestine is another organ. It is comprised of epithelial tissue, connective tissue, nerve tissue, and muscle tissue. Its function is to absorb nutrients from food.

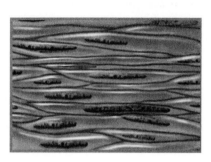

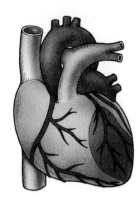

FIGURE 1.6   Smooth muscle tissue

FIGURE 1.7   The heart is an organ

Just as a group of tissues join together to comprise an organ, a group of organs join together to comprise an **organ system**. An organ system is a group of different organs that *perform* related functions in the body. For example, the heart and blood vessels comprise the **circulatory** (ˈsɛrkyələtɔriy) **system**. Likewise, the mouth, stomach, and intestines are parts of the **digestive** (dayˈdʒɛstɪv) **system**.

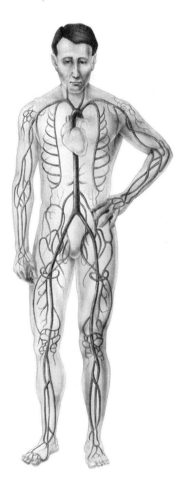

FIGURE 1.8   The circulatory system

1. *Read the questions and then scan the text for the answers. When you find the answers, underline them. Then work with a partner and take turns asking and answering the questions. Try to remember the answers without looking back at the text.*

    1. What are tissues comprised of?

    2. Name three different types of tissue.

    3. What kinds of tissues comprise the heart?

    4. Name three different organs.

    5. What is the definition of an organ system?

2. *Number each of the body's building blocks 1 to 5 from smallest to largest. Compare your answers with the class.*

    _____ cell

    _____ organ system

    _____ organ

    _____ molecule

    _____ tissue

3. *Fill in the blanks with the correct terms. Make sure to use the correct word form.*

organ	organ system	tissue

    1. A _____ is comprised of like cells.

    2. A group of _____ form an organ system.

    3. An _____ is a group of organs that work together to carry out a function.

Describing Organization and Function

In the study of anatomy and physiology, it's important to be able to explain the organization and function of structures. You will have to do so in both your speaking and your writing.

When you describe organization, you'll often use the verbs *comprise* and *form*. These verbs mean the same thing.

EXAMPLE	FORM
A cell is comprised of molecules.	A bigger structure *is comprised of*
A cell is formed by molecules.	or *formed by* smaller structures.
Molecules comprise cells.	Smaller structures *comprise* or *form*
Molecules form cells.	larger structures.

In addition to describing the organization of a structure, you will often be asked to explain the *function* of a structure. When you describe a structure's purpose, you'll often use the word *function*.

EXAMPLE	FORM
The function of the heart is to pump blood.	The function of _____ is + infinitive.
The heart's function is to pump blood.	The _____ 's function is + infinitive.
The heart has the function of pumping blood.	The _____ has the function of + gerund.

Practice

1. *Use the prompts below to write sentences that describe a structure's organization and function. The first one is done for you. Pay attention to verb tense and subject / verb agreement. Then compare your answers with those of a partner.*

   1. Heart / muscle tissue / pump blood.

      The heart is formed by muscle tissue. Its function is to pump blood.

   2. The skin / epithelial tissue / protect the body.

   3. The stomach / muscle tissue / hold food.

   4. Muscles / muscle tissue / move.

   5. Bones / bone tissue / support the body.

2. *Work with two partners and take turns asking and answering these questions.*

1. What is the function of the stomach?
2. What kind of tissue comprises skin?
3. What is the function of the heart?
4. What kind of tissue forms the heart?

3. *These are authentic questions taken from an anatomy and physiology class. Use the vocabulary and grammar you know to answer the following questions. Ask your teacher to check your answers.*

1. Describe the organization of the basic building blocks of the body, going from smallest to largest.
2. Describe the parts of a cell and explain the function of each part.

Creating Good Study Habits

Everyone needs to study to learn anatomy and physiology. No one can learn all that there is to learn by just attending class. To study effectively outside of class, it is important to create good study habits for yourself. Good study habits include:

1. finding a quiet place to study
2. having a set time to study each day
3. studying often for shorter periods of time
4. making a study plan
5. making a commitment to yourself to study

PRACTICE

1. *Work in groups of three. Take turns asking and answering the questions on the chart below and record the answers. Share your answers with the class.*

	You	Classmate 1	Classmate 2
Where is a quiet place for you to study?			
What is your set time to study?			
How long do you study at one time?			
What do you need when you study?			

2. *Think about your daily schedule for tomorrow. Write down when and where you will study. Make a list of study tasks. Also, write down how spending time to study now will be important for your future. Share what you write with a partner.*

HOMEOSTASIS

Your body works hard to keep itself in balance. In fact, one of the most amazing things about the human body is how it manages to work properly most of the time. Thankfully, most of us spend much more time feeling healthy than we do feeling sick.

Homeostasis (howmiyow´steysɪs) is the way the body keeps in balance. The body needs to keep constant levels of things like body temperature, water, and blood pressure. *Homeo-* means *same* and *-stasis* means *condition*. Therefore, the word *homeostasis* means *to keep the same condition*. In the study of anatomy and physiology, you'll hear the phrase "maintain homeostasis," which is another way to say "keep in balance" or "maintain the same condition."

An example of homeostasis is how your body wants to keep the same internal temperature (98.6°F or 37°C) all the time. This "ideal" temperature is called the "set point." If your body gets too hot, what happens? You **sweat** (´swɛt). When you sweat, water leaves your body. As the sweat dries on your skin, it cools your body down to its proper temperature. Likewise, if your body gets too cold, you shiver. The shivering movement of your body produces heat. This heat causes your body temperature to rise until you reach the set point temperature (98.6°F or 37°C).

We can compare homeostasis of body temperature to the way that temperature is maintained in a house. Many homes have a furnace. A person sets the furnace to a particular temperature so that the house always maintains that temperature. For example, the person may want the inside of his house to always be at 70°F (21°C). However, when it gets cold outside, the house starts to cool. When the furnace detects that the temperature in the house is less than 70°, the furnace turns on and the house starts to warm up. When the house reaches its set point of 70° again, the furnace turns off.

COMPREHENSION CHECK

Read the questions and then scan the text for the answers. When you find the answers, underline them. Then work with a partner and take turns asking and answering the questions. Try to remember the answers without looking back at the text.

1. What are three things that the body wants to keep constant?

2. Define the word *homeostasis*.

3. What does the body do when it gets too hot?

4. What is a set point?

5. How is a house's furnace similar to a human body?

Maintaining Homeostasis: Negative Feedback and Reflexes

Recall how your body keeps its temperature constant. You sweat when you are too hot and shiver when you are too cold. Homeostasis of body temperature is maintained by using a **negative feedback** process. The word *negative* means *bad* and the word *feedback* means *information*.

Your body also uses negative feedback when it senses other imbalances in your body. For example, when you exercise, your body might notice that you don't have enough oxygen to keep going. Not having enough oxygen is an example of negative feedback. When the body senses that it doesn't have enough of something, a homeostatic process occurs to improve the situation. In the case of exercising, you start to breathe faster and your heart beats faster to provide your cells with more oxygen.

No matter what aspect of your body is being *monitored*, homeostasis is usually maintained by negative feedback in the form of a **reflex** ('riyflɛks). A reflex is a series of events in the body that help to maintain homeostasis. A reflex occurs when the body makes a change without your having to think about it. Reflexes are automatic.

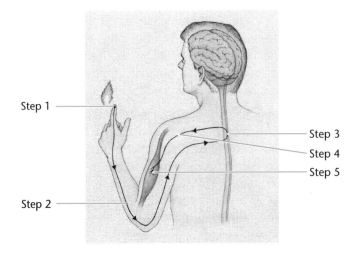

Step 1
Step 2
Step 3
Step 4
Step 5

FIGURE 1.9   **Steps in a reflex**

Let's look at how homeostasis is maintained by negative feedback and a reflex when your finger touches fire. Figure 1.9 shows the steps involved in this homeostatic process.

1. Sensors in your finger feel the pain and heat of fire. Too much heat and pain! This is a "negative condition" and the part of the body that can fix this problem must be notified. Homeostasis is maintained when the body corrects this negative condition.

2. To start to correct this condition, nerves in your finger send a message about the pain and heat to your spinal cord.

3. Your spinal cord *interprets* the message ("A finger is feeling pain and heat"). It makes the decision to move the finger away from the fire.

4. The spinal cord sends a message ("Make the finger move"). The message is carried along a nerve to the muscle that can cause the finger to move.

5. Muscles receive the message ("Make the finger move"). They contract and the finger moves away from the fire.

Homeostasis is restored! Your finger moved away from the negative situation. All reflexes follow this five-step process automatically. Again, reflexes are one way that the body responds to negative feedback and maintains homeostasis.

The body also uses negative feedback to keep other things constant, such as amounts of nutrients (sugar, oxygen, salts), amounts of hormones (insulin, growth hormone), blood pressure, heart rate, and breathing rate.

COMPREHENSION CHECK

1. *Work with a partner to label each statement true (T) or false (F). If the statement is false, correct it so that it is true.*

   _____ **1.** A reflex takes a long time.

   _____ **2.** The spinal cord can make reflex decisions.

   _____ **3.** Nerves send messages to muscles so the muscles can move.

   _____ **4.** Homeostasis is usually maintained with positive feedback.

   _____ **5.** Sensors are the first part of a reflex.

   _____ **6.** Negative feedback gives information that something is not right.

2. *Complete the sentences using the words in the box. Take turns reading the correct sentences aloud with a partner.*

muscle	negative feedback	nerves	reflex	spinal cord

   1. A very fast homeostatic reaction is called a _____.

   2. The _____ is a part of the body that makes decisions.

   3. A part of the body that receives neural messages and then moves is called a _____.

   4. When the body notices that there is a problem, _____ occurs.

   5. _____ send messages.

Homeostatic Messengers

The body has two ways to send messages to correct negative situations. One of the two ways that the body can send messages is along a nerve. How did the body send a message to the finger to make it move away from the fire? It sent a message along nerves. **Nerves** (nɛrvz) are organs that quickly send messages to and from the spinal cord or the brain. The muscles received a neural message. The muscles moved the finger and then the negative situation of being burned was corrected. Thankfully, neural messages are very fast.

The other way the body can send messages is in the form of hormones. **Hormones** (ˈhɔrmownz) are molecules produced by organs called **endocrine glands** (ˈɛndəkrɪn ˈglændz). Endocrine glands *secrete* hormones into the bloodstream when the body notices a situation that can be balanced by hormones. Blood carries hormones to their destination.

For example, when the body notices that there is too much sugar in the blood, the pancreas (an endocrine gland) secretes the hormone insulin into the bloodstream. Insulin corrects the sugar imbalance by causing sugar to be taken out of the blood and stored in the liver.

Thus, the two tools the body uses to maintain homeostasis are hormones and neural messages. Hormonal messages are not as fast as neural messages, but their effects last much longer. For example, when insulin is released into the bloodstream, the insulin doesn't just send a message and then disappear. Insulin stays in the blood and continues to stimulate the liver and other cells to store sugar for over an hour. Compare this process to a neural message—its effect lasts less than a second!

We can compare the speed of neural and hormonal messages to sending mail. Nerves are fast, like e-mail. Messages are received almost instantly, like when you feel heat and move your hand away from fire. Hormonal messages are slow, like sending a letter by ground mail. They get to where they need to go, but take a lot longer.

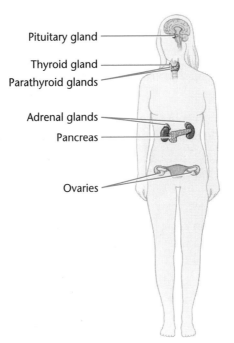

Pituitary gland

Thyroid gland
Parathyroid glands

Adrenal glands
Pancreas

Ovaries

Figure 1.10   Endocrine glands

COMPREHENSION CHECK

Circle the correct word(s) to complete each sentence. Take turns reading the correct sentences aloud with a partner.

1. A **hormonal / neural** message is faster.

2. The effects of a **hormonal / neural** message last longer.

3. Endocrine glands secrete **hormones / neural messages**.

4. Hormones travel in the **nerves / bloodstream**.

5. If the situation is an emergency, the messages will probably be sent by a **hormone / nerve**.

Preparing for the Future

In some cultures, it is customary for people to prepare for the future. These people usually anticipate what is going to happen in their lives and plan accordingly. For example, before many women give birth to a baby, they make sure that they have the necessary clothes, a place for the baby to sleep, and arrange for family or friends to help to take care of the newborn. In other cultures, people hesitate to plan for the future.

1. *Read this story about a cultural conflict that people may experience in a health-care setting.*

A young woman is eight months pregnant. She goes to the doctor for a check-up. The nurse at the health-care clinic cheerfully asks her about preparations for the baby.

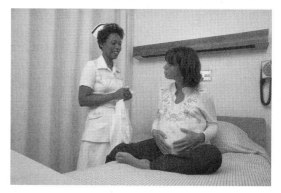

"Do you have a car seat, a crib, bottles, and diapers?" The young woman looks down and says no. She replies that she and her husband don't have a car seat or any other supplies for the baby. The nurse is surprised and wonders if the family is poor and needs money. She asks, "Do you need money to get those things?" The pregnant woman replies, "Everything will be supplied when the time comes."

2. *Work in groups of three. Take turns asking and answering the questions on the chart below and record the answers. Share your answers with the class.*

	You	Classmate 1	Classmate 2
Why do you think the pregnant woman isn't prepared?			
If you (or your partner) were pregnant, how early would you prepare for the baby?			
What are the advantages of being prepared for the future? What are the advantages of letting the future take care of itself?			

Check Your Understanding

1. *Answer the following questions about the building blocks of the body and homeostasis.*

    1. What does the word *anatomy* mean?

    2. What does the word *physiology* mean?

    3. What are the five basic building blocks of the body?

    4. Which is larger, a cell or a molecule? An organ or a tissue?

    5. Name two organs in your body.

    6. What is the name of the process that maintains conditions in your body?

    7. Give an example of a reflex that helps you to maintain homeostasis.

    8. How does your body adjust if it gets too hot?

    9. Name two ways that messages are sent in the body.

2. *Label Figure 1.11 with the terms provided.*

cell	molecule	organ	organ system	tissue

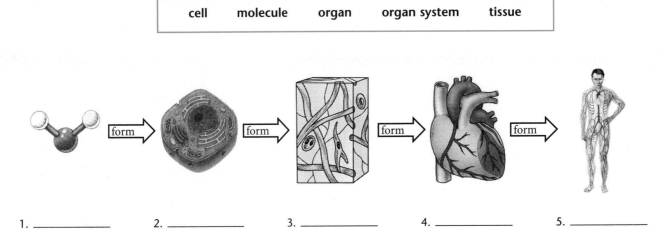

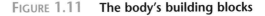

1. _____ 2. _____ 3. _____ 4. _____ 5. _____

FIGURE 1.11   The body's building blocks

3. *Answer these typical anatomy and physiology quiz questions.*

    1. Tissues are made of many _____.

       a. organs   **b.** molecules   **c.** cells   **d.** bones

    2. Water, sugar, and oxygen are examples of _____.

       a. organs   **b.** molecules   **c.** cells   **d.** tissues

3. Number each of the body's building blocks 1 to 5 from smallest to largest.

_____ organ systems

_____ tissues

_____ cells

_____ organs

_____ molecules

4. Describe the function of each of the following in a reflex:

sensors   nerves   spinal cord

5. What are the two types of messengers that are used in maintaining homeostasis? Which is the fastest? The longest lasting?

Think More about It

1. Name as many different organ systems in the body as you can.

2. What parts of your body change when you exercise vigorously?

Word Bank		
arrange	interpret	organelles
cell	maintain	perform
comprise	membrane	permeable
control	molecule	reflex
cytoplasm	monitor	secrete
DNA	negative feedback	sensors
endocrine glands	nerves	set point
form	neural message	sweat
give off	nucleus	take in
homeostasis	organ	tissue
hormones	organ system	

CHAPTER 2

The Integumentary System

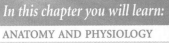
In this chapter you will learn:

ANATOMY AND PHYSIOLOGY

- *The regions of the integument*
- *Accessory structures in the integument*
- *Common skin disorders*

ENGLISH

- *Asking for clarification*

STUDY SKILLS

- *Using index cards*

CULTURE

- *The use of touch to comfort*

DID YOU KNOW *that the average person's skin weighs 4–5 kilograms (8.8–11 pounds)? If you could lay all of a person's skin flat, it would make a square 2 meters by 2 meters (79 inches by 79 inches).*

INTRODUCTION

Integument (ɪnˈtɛgyəmənt) is the word used within the medical profession for skin. The integument is the outer covering of the body. It holds all of the parts of the body inside and prevents unwanted things from getting into the body from the outside. The integument has three layers, or regions: epidermis, dermis, and hypodermis (fat). The integument also contains accessory structures such as blood vessels, nerves, nails, hair, oil glands, and sweat glands.

1. *Work with a partner. Look at this diagram of the integument. Try to label the regions and structures of the skin with the words in the box. Look at Figure 2.2 on page 20 to check your answers.*

blood vessels	epidermis	hypodermis	oil gland
dermis	hair	nerve	sweat gland

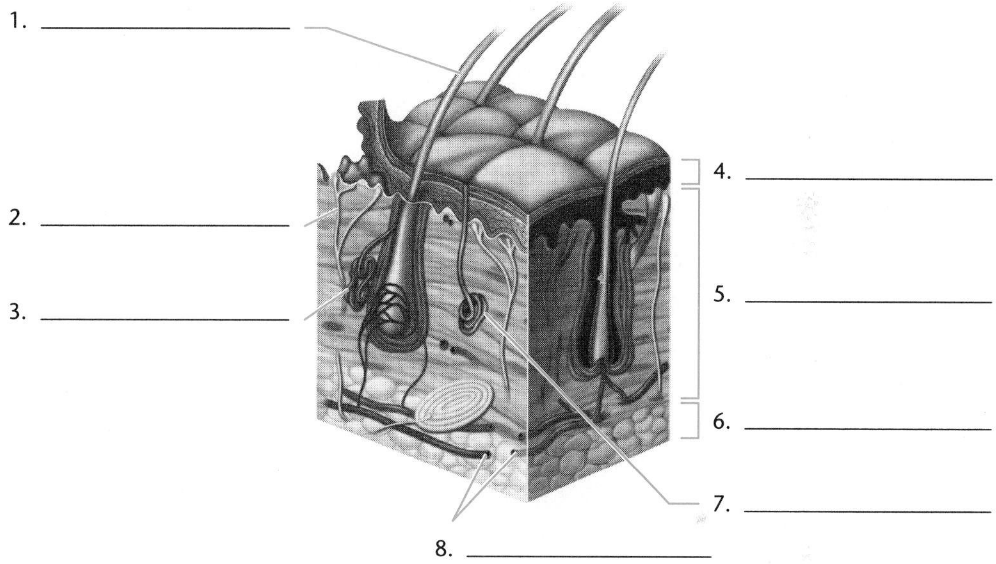

1. _____

2. _____

3. _____

4. _____

5. _____

6. _____

7. _____

8. _____

FIGURE 2.1   **Section through the integument**

2. *With your partner, try to answer these questions. If you do not know the answers, do not worry. You will find the answers as you read through this chapter.*

1. What is the function of the skin?

2. Why do some people have darker skin than others?

3. Can skin stretch?

4. What is the purpose of having hair?

5. How can sweating help maintain a person's health?

3. *Read each verb, its simple definition, and its passive voice form. Then fill in the verbs in the sentences that follow. Pay attention to verb tense and subject / verb agreement. Compare your answers with those of another student.*

BASE FORM	PASSIVE VOICE FORM	MEANING
evaporate	be evaporated	change from liquid to gas, go into the air
excrete	be excreted	send out of body
insulate	be insulated	protect from change
interact	—	work with, communicate with
invade	be invaded	enter unwelcome
moisturize	be moisturized	make wet or moist
vary	be varied	be different

1. Wastes _____ when you use the bathroom.

2. Water _____ from your skin when you sweat.

3. Germs sometimes _____ the skin through a wound.

4. Fat helps to _____ the body.

5. Bacteria _____ with sweat to produce an odor.

6. The amount of fat people have _____ from person to person.

7. Some people with dry skin use lotion to _____ their skin.

THE REGIONS OF THE INTEGUMENT

The skin or integument has three major regions. The **epidermis** (ɛpɪˈdɛrməs) is the outer region of the integument. The **dermis** is the second region of the integument that lies beneath the epidermis. The **hypodermis** (haypəˈdɛrməs) is located below the dermis region of skin.

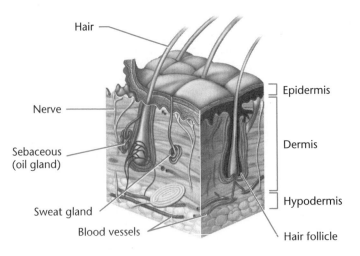

FIGURE 2.2   Section through the integument

The Epidermis

The epidermis is the outer region of the integument. *Epi-* means *upon* and *derm-* means *skin*. So, the epidermis is the upper region of skin.

The epidermis is comprised of many layers of flattened cells that form a tissue called **epithelial** (ɛpɪˈθiyliyəl) **tissue**. Two important molecules are found in epithelial tissue: keratin and melanin.

Keratin (ˈkɛrətɪn) is a molecule found in the top layers of the epidermis. The upper layers of the epidermis are comprised of dead cells that contain keratin. Keratin makes your skin tough and waterproof. When you swim or bathe, the keratin keeps water from entering your body through the skin.

Some people like to lie in the sun to make their skin darker. This is called "getting a tan."

Melanin (ˈmɛlənɪn) molecules are also located in the epidermis. Melanin is found in both living and dead cells in the epidermis. The function of melanin is to give color to a person's skin and to protect the skin from the sun. People with darker skin have more melanin in their skin than people with lighter skin. How much melanin a person has in her skin depends on genetics. People whose ancestors came from hot climates near the equator have more melanin than people whose ancestors came from the far north or far south. Sunlight contains ultraviolet (UV) rays that can cause skin cancer.

Skin Cancer! A **tumor** is a group of cells that are multiplying in a rapid and uncontrolled way. **Skin cancer** occurs when something (usually too much exposure to UV rays, the harmful rays in sunlight) causes the cells in the skin to multiply too fast. Sometimes, the tumor develops from a **mole** (an area where melanin is concentrated). Moles look like dark brown or black spots on the skin. If a person sees that a mole has changed, he or she should see a doctor to learn if it is skin cancer. If skin cancer is detected early, it can be treated. If not, it can spread to the rest of the body and may cause death.

The epidermis also has a group of **resident bacteria** living on its surface. These bacteria are helpful because they have the job of fighting bad bacteria and viruses that are trying to *invade* your body. Resident bacteria also secrete molecules that poison invading bacteria.

COMPREHENSION CHECK

1. *Answer the questions below. Then compare your answers with those of a partner.*

   1. What molecule gives the epidermis its strength?

   2. What molecule makes skin waterproof?

   3. What are two ways that the epidermis helps to maintain your health?

   4. Why do some people have darker skin than others?

   5. How might a person know if he had skin cancer?

2. *Match the terms with their definitions by writing the letters in the correct blanks. Then compare your answers with those of a partner.*

_____ 1. epidermis

_____ 2. epithelial

_____ 3. invade

_____ 4. keratin

_____ 5. melanin

_____ 6. mole

_____ 7. resident bacteria

_____ 8. secrete

_____ 9. tumor

_____ 10. UV rays

a. when something bad enters your body

b. the harmful rays from the sun which cause skin cancer

c. to send outside of a cell

d. the top layer of skin

e. helpful bacteria that kill the bad bacteria

f. small dark area on the skin where melanin is concentrated

g. a molecule that keeps your skin tough and waterproof

h. gives color to a person's skin

i. the tissue that comprises the epidermis

j. a group of cells that multiply in an uncontrolled way

The Dermis and the Hypodermis

The dermis is the second region of the integument. It lies beneath the epidermis and is thicker than the epidermis. Locate the dermis in Figure 2.2 on page 20. The dermis contains mostly connective tissue. The function of this connective tissue is to hold the epidermis to the tissues below it such as muscle and fat. In effect, the dermis holds the epidermis in place so that it doesn't fall off the body.

The **connective tissue** within the dermis contains cells and three kinds of **protein fibers**. However, each type of fiber has a unique purpose. They are:

- **Collagen** (ˈkɑlədʒən) fibers—give the skin strength, make it flexible, and hold water to moisturize the skin

- **Elastin** (ɪˈlæstən) fibers—allow the skin to stretch

- **Reticular** (rɪˈtɪkyələr) fibers—act like a net to hold connective tissue together

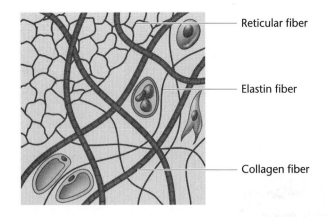

Reticular fiber

Elastin fiber

Collagen fiber

FIGURE 2.3 **Connective tissue**

Blisters and Calluses! When damage occurs in the dermis (such as a burn), the dermis may separate from the epidermis. The space between the dermis and epidermis then fills with fluid. This is called a **blister**. If a particular area of the skin is constantly rubbed against a hard object, like a shoe or garden tool, it can cause that area of the epidermis to thicken over time and become hard. This is called a **callus** (ˈkæləs).

The hypodermis is located below the dermis region of skin. *Hypo-* means *under*. Look for the hypodermis in Figure 2.2 on page 20. The hypodermis is comprised of fat. This fat is called **adipose** (ˈædɪpows) tissue. The function of adipose tissue is to provide protection for the organs and to *insulate* the body from cold. Adipose tissue *varies* in thickness among people. Some people whose ancestors came from colder regions have more fat than people whose ancestors came from tropical regions. This is because people in colder regions need more body fat to stay warm.

COMPREHENSION CHECK

1. *Complete the sentences below using the words in the box. Take turns reading the correct sentences aloud with a partner.*

adipose	callus	cells	connective	elastin	protein

1. The dermis is made of _____ tissue, and the hypodermis is made of _____ tissue.

2. Connective tissue contains _____ and _____ fibers.

3. _____ fibers allow the skin to stretch.

4. An area of the epidermis that is thickened is called a _____.

2. *Circle the correct word to complete each sentence. Take turns reading the correct sentences aloud with a partner.*

   1. **Reticular / Elastin** fibers act like a net to hold connective tissue together.

   2. **Hypodermis / Adipose** is another word for fat.

   3. Collagen fibers are found within the **epidermis / dermis**.

   4. **Collagen / Elastin** fibers are able to stretch.

   5. The **hypodermal / epithelial** layer of skin contains dead skin cells.

BUILDING LANGUAGE AND STUDY SKILLS

Asking for Clarification

In the study of anatomy and physiology, it's important to be able to ask clarifying questions when you don't understand something. For example, suppose the teacher is explaining to the class how too much sun can lead to skin cancer. However, while you are listening to your teacher, you don't understand exactly why the sun is dangerous. You need to be able to ask your teacher a clarification question to better understand the lecture such as: "Could you explain again why the sun is so bad for the skin?"

When you ask clarification questions, you'll often use words such as *can* and *could* and the verbs *explain*, and *give me an example*. Sometimes, you'll simply ask, "*What does the word _____ mean?*" Usually, your teachers will be happy to stop their lecture to answer your questions.

Other common verbs used with clarification questions include *show* and *tell*.

EXAMPLE	FORM
What does the word *callus* mean?	What does the word _____ mean?
Can you explain how melanin protects the skin?	Could / Can you explain + noun / noun clause?
Could you give me an example of a skin disorder?	Could / Can you give me an example of + noun / noun clause?
Could you tell me what a blister is again?	Could you show / tell me + noun / noun clause?

PRACTICE

1. *Work with a partner. Take turns asking for and giving clarification of the following terms:*

adipose	blister	collagen	dermis	keratin	UV rays

2. *On an index card, write down a new word or concept from this chapter. Work with a partner.*
   - Ask your partner to clarify the word or concept on your card.
   - Then have your partner ask you to clarify the word or concept on his or her card.
   - Finally, exchange cards with your partner.
   - Repeat this process six more times with new partners.

3. *You were absent from class for two days because you were sick. When you ask your teacher what you should do to catch up, your teacher asks you to read pages 18–23 in this chapter and write her a note asking for clarification of two or more words or concepts in the reading that you do not understand well.*

Using Index Cards

Using index cards is a good way to learn new vocabulary. On one side of the card, write the new word. On the other side, write the definition of the word, or a translation of the word in your native language. Keep the cards with you and study the words for ten minutes every day.

PRACTICE

1. *Write each of the words below on one side of an index card and write its definition on the opposite side. Look through this chapter to find the definitions. Work with a partner. Take turns showing each other the words and asking for the definitions.*

collagen fibers	elastin fibers	hypodermis	keratin	reticular fibers
dermis	epidermis	integument	melanin	

2. *Play a game called "concentration."*

- Write the words from Exercise 1 on index cards.
- Write the definitions on separate index cards.
- Spread all of the cards out facedown (so you cannot read the words or the definitions).
- Put the cards with the words in one row and the cards with the definitions in another row.
- Play with a partner.
- One partner turns over two cards, one word and one definition.
- If the word "matches" the definition, the student takes the two cards and goes again. If the cards don't match, turn the cards over facedown and the next student continues.
- Play until all matches have been made. The student with the most cards at the end of the game is the winner.

ACCESSORY STRUCTURES IN THE INTEGUMENT

The integument has several important **accessory structures** within its layers. The word *accessory* means *extra* or *in addition*. Accessory structures are the extra things inside the skin. They can be located in one or more regions of the skin. Accessory structures include: blood vessels, nerves, nails, hair, oil glands, and sweat glands.

Blood Vessels and Nerves

Locate the blood vessels and nerves in Figure 2.2 on page 20. **Blood vessels** bring nutrients (food and oxygen) to the cells of the integument. They also get rid of waste products. Blood vessels are located in the hypodermis and dermis regions, but not in the epidermis. In places where the epidermis is very thin, like the inside of your wrist, you can actually see the larger blood vessels located in the dermis.

Nerves are another accessory structure in the integument. Nerves allow us to have feeling in our skin. The tips of nerves that come closest to the surface of the skin are called **sensory receptors**. Each sensory receptor is specialized to feel a specific stimulus. Some receptors feel heat, some feel pain, and some feel pressure. When sensory receptors are stimulated, they cause electrical signals to be sent along the nerves to the brain or spinal cord. When electrical signals reach the brain, we realize that we feel cold or pain.

COMPREHENSION CHECK

1. *Work with a partner. Decide if the information is true about nerves or true about blood vessels. Put a check mark (✓) in the appropriate box.*

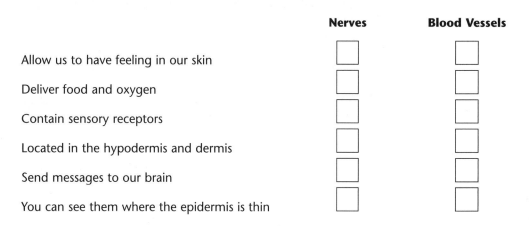

	Nerves	Blood Vessels
Allow us to have feeling in our skin	☐	☐
Deliver food and oxygen	☐	☐
Contain sensory receptors	☐	☐
Located in the hypodermis and dermis	☐	☐
Send messages to our brain	☐	☐
You can see them where the epidermis is thin	☐	☐

2. *Match the terms with their definitions by writing the letters in the correct blanks. Then compare your answers with those of a partner.*

_____ 1. blood vessels

_____ 2. nerves

_____ 3. nutrients

_____ 4. sensory receptors

a. Oxygen and food are examples of these.

b. These feel such things as heat and pressure.

c. These carry blood.

d. These carry electrical messages to and from the brain.

Nails and Hair

Nails are extensions of the epidermis found on the fingers and toes. Nails feel harder than skin because they contain large amounts of a special kind of keratin called hard keratin. Because our nails are strong, we use nails to pick up small things and scratch our skin. That's why our nails become dirty very easily. It's very important to keep your nails clean. Bacteria and fungi can live under the nail and in the nail bed, the place where the nails begin their growth. Fungi are larger than bacteria and include yeasts and molds.

Nail Fungus! Sometimes, people get an infection underneath their nails that is caused by a fungus. An infection caused by a fungus is called a **mycosis** (may′kowsəs). These infections can be very difficult to cure because it is hard to get the medication to the place where the fungus is growing underneath the nails. Sometimes, the entire nail has to be removed. Mycoses (plural of mycosis) are also difficult to cure because the cells of the fungus are similar to our own cells. This makes it hard to take an antibiotic or antifungal that doesn't also harm our own cells. To avoid fungal infections, it is very important to use very clean tools when doing a manicure and to keep nails clean.

We often think about the hair on our head and want it to look good. Actually, hair has several functions. For example, the hairs in your nose filter the air as you breathe and trap bacteria and viruses before they can get into your lungs. Also, hair helps to protect you from getting hurt. A man who shaves all his hair off feels a hit on his head more than a person who has a full head of hair. Finally, hair helps with sensation because sensory receptors are found near where hair begins its growth. Recall that sensory receptors are nerve endings. As a result, when something brushes against or touches a hair, you feel it.

Hair is made from keratin similar to the keratin found in the layers of the epidermis. Keratin in our hair makes it waterproof and strong. Like the epidermis, hair also contains melanin. People with dark hair have more melanin in their hair than people with blond hair.

Hair begins its growth in the dermis inside little pockets called **follicles** (′fɑlɪkəlz). It then grows up through the dermis and epidermis until it reaches the outside of the body.

People need to go to school to get a license to cut hair in many countries.

Dandruff! Those little white flakes that you sometimes find on your shoulders after combing your hair are called dandruff. Dandruff is actually a natural part of your skin's growth. The white flakes are the dead layers of epidermis that fall off the skin naturally. Dandruff is caused by oil glands that are either too active or not active enough. Scientists also think that some dandruff may occur when a normal skin fungus that lives on the scalp grows out of control.

COMPREHENSION CHECK

1. *Work with a partner to label each statement true* (T) *or false* (F). *If the statement is false, correct it so that it is true.*

   _____ 1. Nails grow out of the epidermis of the skin.

   _____ 2. Nails get their hardness from melanin.

   _____ 3. Hair contains keratin.

   _____ 4. Everyone has the same amount of melanin in their hair.

   _____ 5. Hair starts growing in the epidermis.

2. *Match the terms with their definitions by writing the letters in the correct blanks. Then compare your answers with those of a partner.*

   _____ 1. dandruff   **a.** nerve endings that help you to feel things

   _____ 2. follicles   **b.** little white flakes that are dead layers of the epidermis

   _____ 3. mycosis   **c.** the little pockets that hair grows out of

   _____ 4. sensory receptors   **d.** a fungal infection that often occurs under the nails

Sebaceous (Oil) Glands and Sweat Glands

Sometimes, when you look at yourself in the mirror, you'll see that your skin or hair looks oily. This oil comes from oil glands, also known as **sebaceous** (sə′beyʃəs) **glands**. These glands are usually found close to hair follicles. Locate the sebaceous gland in Figure 2.2 on page 20. Sebaceous glands secrete an oily substance which is called **sebum** (′siybəm). Sebum has three purposes:

- To soften the skin
- To prevent too much water from leaving the skin
- To kill bacteria

 Acne! Acne is an active **inflammation** (irritation, swelling) of the sebaceous glands. This results in **pimples** on the skin. Bacteria cause acne and acne can get worse due to an excess of hormones (as in the teenage years). Stress can also worsen acne.

Sweat glands are coiled tubes found in the dermis region of skin. They connect with the surface of the skin by a tube, or **duct**. A person has over 2 million sweat glands in his skin.

The function of sweat glands is to regulate body temperature by *excreting* water. For example, when a person exercises, the body gets hot. To release this heat, the sweat glands take water and some molecules such as salt out of the blood. Then this water and salt (called sweat) travels through the duct to the surface of the body. When the water in sweat *evaporates* on the skin, it helps the body to cool down.

Another function of sweat glands is to rid the body of some waste molecules. These wastes include urea, ammonia, and salt, which are waste products from cells. When the bacteria on the surface of a person's skin *interact with* these molecules, a person can smell bad.

MAINTAINING HOMEOSTASIS

Temperature Regulation and Sweat Glands

As you've learned, the body strives to maintain an internal temperature of about 37°C (98.6°F). If the body gets too hot, some organs may be damaged. Let's look more closely at how the body maintains a constant temperature.

When the body temperature rises, sensory receptors that measure temperature send messages to a part of the brain called the **hypothalamus** (haypow′θæləməs). The hypothalamus is in charge of maintaining constant body temperature. When the temperature rises, the hypothalamus tells the sweat glands to excrete more water and salt, which cools the body. It also causes more blood to be sent to places where the skin is thin, such as the face, where heat can easily cross the thin skin to the outside of the body. This is why some people's faces look red when they are hot.

Fever! When a person is sick, he often has a fever (a body temperature above the normal body temperature of 98.6°F or 37°C). Heat is one way that the body kills viruses and bacteria. A fever occurs when the hypothalamus raises the set point of the body temperature. In other words, it acts as though a higher temperature is normal. A mild fever is actually a good thing because it helps the body get rid of harmful bacteria and viruses.

COMPREHENSION CHECK

1. *Read the questions and then scan the text for answers. When you find the answers, underline them. Then work with a partner and take turns asking and answering the questions. Try to remember the answers without looking back at the text.*

   1. Why are sebaceous glands located near hair follicles?

   2. What would happen to your skin if your sebaceous glands didn't secrete oil?

3. Why do people sweat?

4. In what region of the integument are the sweat glands located?

5. Describe two ways that the skin helps to maintain body temperature?

2. *Circle the correct word(s) to complete each sentence. Take turns reading the correct sentences aloud with a partner.*

1. Acne occurs due to inflammation of the **sebaceous / sweat** glands.

2. The hypothalamus helps in regulating the body's **temperature / inflammation**.

3. **Sebum / Pimples** soften the skin, kill bacteria, and prevent too much water from leaving the skin.

4. Having **a fever / sweat glands** is one way that the body kills viruses and bacteria.

FOCUS ON CULTURE

The Use of Touch to Comfort

Touch is perceived differently in different cultures. In certain cultures, touching a person outside of the family is judged as inappropriate. In fact, it is sometimes believed that if you are touched by an inappropriate person, it could bring you bad luck. Also, in certain cultures, men are not permitted to shake hands with women. However, in other cultures, touch is seen as a means of bringing comfort, showing concern, and in many situations, it's even expected.

The following two stories are about cultural conflicts people may experience in a health-care setting. Read each story and then discuss the questions in small groups.

A nurse receives an angry call from a woman who brought her baby in the day before for a check-up. The baby was healthy. As the woman was leaving with her baby, the nurse touched the baby's face, smiled at the baby and the mother, and commented how cute the baby was. The next morning, the baby woke up crying and had a fever. The mother called the nurse and yelled at her for making the baby sick.

1. Do you think it is possible that the nurse made the baby sick?

2. How do you feel about strangers touching and complimenting children?

A young nursing assistant in a nursing home feels badly because an elderly woman patient is in great pain. She wishes to comfort the woman, so she gives her a hug. The patient's family sees this and becomes angry. They demand that the nursing supervisor remove the nursing assistant from their mother's care. They think the young nursing assistant is being disrespectful.

1. How would you comfort an older person who was in pain if you were the nursing assistant?

2. When is it OK to touch another person?

Check Your Understanding

1. *Answer the following questions about the integumentary system.*

   1. Name the three regions of the skin.

   2. What region of integument contains sweat glands?

   3. What is the homeostatic function of sweat glands?

   4. What sorts of molecules are found in the skin?

   5. What sorts of tissues are found in the skin?

   6. Why do some people have darker skin than others?

   7. Can skin stretch?

   8. What are the three purposes of sebum?

   9. Where in the skin do you find protein fibers?

   10. What are the three kinds of protein fibers and their purpose?

   11. What is the purpose of having hair?

   12. What is the name of the little pocket from which hair grows?

   13. What molecule do both nails and skin share?

2. *Label Figure 2.4 with the terms provided.*

blood vessel	hair	nerve
dermis	hair follicle	sensory receptor
epidermis	hypodermis	sweat gland

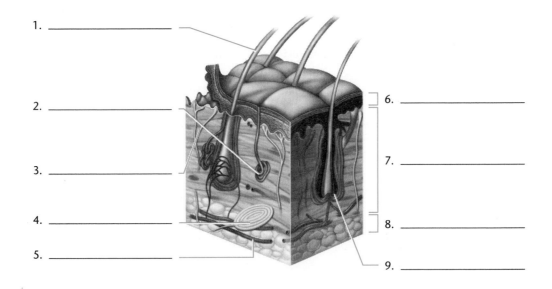

1. _____

2. _____

3. _____

4. _____

5. _____

6. _____

7. _____

8. _____

9. _____

FIGURE 2.4   Section through the integument

3. *Answer these typical anatomy and physiology quiz questions.*

1. Which of these has the job of excreting waste molecules?
   a. the hair follicles
   b. the sweat glands
   c. the sebaceous glands
   d. the nails

2. The skin stays soft and moist because of _____.
   a. the secretions of the sweat glands
   b. keratin in the epidermis
   c. the secretions of the sebaceous glands
   d. melanin in the epidermis

3. Describe the appearance of a sweat gland.

4. Explain how the skin is involved in maintaining a constant body temperature.

5. What is the purpose of melanin?

6. The integument has many functions. Name as many as you can.

Think More about It

1. Give two suggestions for keeping skin healthy.

2. Do you think people with lighter skin would get skin cancer more often than those with darker skin? Why or why not?

Word Bank		
acne	epithelial tissue	melanin
adipose	evaporate	moisturize
blister	excrete	mole
callus	follicle	sebaceous gland
collagen	hypodermis	sebum
connective tissue	insulate	sweat gland
dermis	integument	UV rays
duct	interact with	vary
elastin	invade	
epidermis	keratin	

CHAPTER **3**

The Skeletal System

In this chapter you will learn:

ANATOMY AND PHYSIOLOGY

- *How a bone is organized*
- *The functions of bone*
- *Accessory structures of bone*
- *Major bones in the body*
- *Common bone disorders*

ENGLISH

- *Stating degree of understanding*

STUDY SKILLS

- *Studying diagrams*

CULTURE

- *Informality in forms of address*

DID YOU KNOW *that adults have 206 bones? Babies are born with over 300 bones, but many of these bones grow together to form single bones.*

INTRODUCTION

The skeleton is *constructed of* bones. Bone is important in five ways. First, bones are the main *support* for the body; they give your body shape. Without bones, your body would lie flat, like a puddle of water. For example, the bones that make up your spine allow you to sit up straight. The bones in your legs support the weight of your body so that you can stand up. Another function of your skeleton is movement. Muscles are *attached* to bones and when muscles move, bones move. Third, bones protect the organs beneath them. The ribs provide protection for the lungs and heart. The skull protects the brain. Fourth, bone is a storage place for calcium and fat. Finally, bones are the location where blood cells are made.

1. *Work with a partner. Look at the diagram of the skeleton. Try to label the parts with the words in the box. Look at Figure 3.16 on page 48 to check your answers.*

clavicle	humerus	pubis	sternum
femur	mandible	ribs	

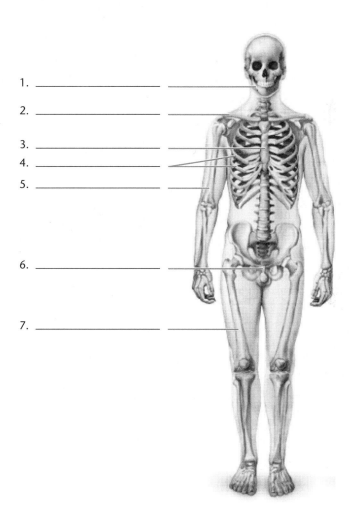

1. _____ _____

2. _____ _____

3. _____ _____
4. _____ _____

5. _____ _____

6. _____ _____

7. _____ _____

FIGURE 3.1   **The skeleton**

2. *With your partner, try to answer these questions. If you do not know the answers, do not worry. You will find the answers as you read through this chapter.*

1. What is the function of the skeleton?

2. What is bone made of?

3. What happens when bones don't get the right nutrients?

4. What holds bones to one another?

5. What holds bones to muscles?

3. *Read each verb, its simple definition, and its passive voice form. Then fill in the verbs in the sentences that follow. Pay attention to verb tense and subject / verb agreement. Compare your answers with those of another student.*

BASE FORM	PASSIVE VOICE FORM	MEANING
attach	be attached to	to connect
classified	be classified	to be organized into like groups
construct	be constructed of	to build
cure	be cured	to make a condition better
embed	be embedded	to be buried in
fuse	be fused	to connect strongly
locate	be located	to find or to be placed
relieve	be relieved	to take away pain
store	be stored	to contain / keep
support	be supported	to hold weight

1. The skeleton _____ of bones.

2. Some diseases cannot be _____.

3. One bone _____ to another with ligaments.

4. Some bones _____ together so you can't separate them.

5. Calcium _____ in bones.

6. Bones can be _____ according to where they are in the body.

7. Your legs _____ your weight when you stand.

8. The humerus is the bone _____ in your upper arm.

9. Sometimes, headaches can _____ by aspirin.

10. Bone cells _____ within the solid part of a bone.

Bones are actually organs. Recall that an organ is comprised of different tissues and carries out specific functions.

Bone Tissue

Bones are made mostly of bone tissue. Bone tissue resembles a chocolate chip cookie. The bone cells, known as **osteocytes** ('astiyəsayts), are like the chocolate chips. They are *embedded* in a hard substance called **matrix** ('meytrıks). The matrix is like the cookie. Bone tissue is mostly matrix. Matrix contains calcium salts and collagen fibers. Calcium salts give strength to bone while the collagen gives bone some flexibility.

Blood vessel

Matrix

Osteocyte

FIGURE 3.3 **Osteocytes embedded in matrix look like chocolate chips in a chocolate chip cookie.**

FIGURE 3.2 **Bone tissue. Osteocytes embedded in matrix.**

There are two different ways that bone tissue can appear.

1. The tissue in **compact bone** is arranged in circular layers around a blood vessel. A slice of compact bone looks like several slices of onion.
2. The tissue in **spongy bone** is arranged so that it looks like a sponge. There are many holes in spongy bone and blood vessels are *located* in these holes.

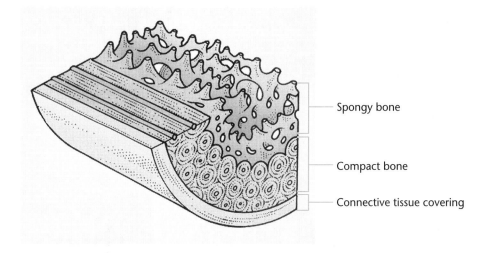

Spongy bone

Compact bone

Connective tissue covering

FIGURE 3.4 **Section of human bone showing the arrangement of compact and spongy types of bone tissue**

The Skeletal System **35**

1. *Read the questions and then scan the text for the answers. When you find the answers, underline them. Then work with a partner and take turns asking and answering the questions. Try to remember the answers without looking back at the text.*

   1. What is the name of a bone cell?

   2. What two molecules comprise bone matrix?

   3. What do calcium salts give to bones?

   4. What are the two different ways that bone tissue can appear?

   5. How is compact bone arranged?

   6. What is in the holes of spongy bone?

2. *Complete the paragraph using the words in the box.*

calcium salts	compact bone	osteocytes
collagen	matrix	spongy bone

   There are two types of bone tissue: (1) _____ and

(2) _____. Both types of bone tissue are comprised of

bone cells called (3) _____. These bone cells are embedded

in a hard material called (4) _____. Protein fibers called

(5) _____ give bone some flexibility. Bone gets its strength

from (6) _____.

Types of Bone

In every bone of the body, you will find both compact and spongy bone. Compact and spongy areas are arranged in different ways in bones of different shapes. If the bone is a **flat bone**, such as the bones in the skull, the compact and spongy bone are arranged like a sandwich.

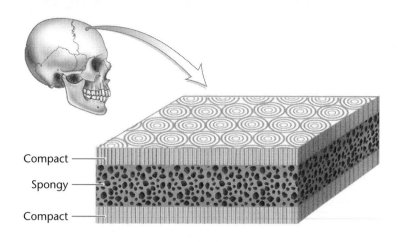

FIGURE 3.5 A flat bone, showing arrangement of compact and spongy bone

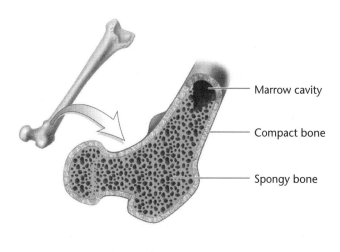

FIGURE 3.6 A long bone, showing arrangement of compact and spongy bone

If the bone is a **long bone**, like the bones in your arm, the compact bone is on the outside and the spongy bone is on the inside. The innermost part of a long bone is hollow (empty). This cavity is called the **marrow cavity**. Cavity means *hole* or *empty space*. The marrow cavity is where **bone marrow** is *stored*. There are two types of bone marrow: red and yellow. Red bone marrow makes blood cells. Yellow bone marrow stores fat.

COMPREHENSION CHECK

Work with a partner to label each statement true (T) *or false* (F). *If the statement is false, correct it so that it is true.*

_____ **1.** Both flat and long bones are comprised of spongy bone and compact bone.

_____ **2.** The inside of flat bones is hollow.

_____ **3.** The outer part of both flat bones and long bones is comprised of spongy bone.

_____ **4.** Flat bone has bone tissue arranged like a sandwich.

_____ **5.** Bone marrow is found in the marrow cavity of long bones.

You have already learned that the skeleton is important as support for the body, in movement of the body, and as protection for the organs beneath. In addition, the bones have two other important functions: blood cell production and storage of fat and calcium.

Production of Blood Cells

The red bone marrow is the site of blood cell production. Cells within this bone marrow produce all of the types of blood cells. These immature blood cells move into the blood vessels and travel to other locations in the body where they mature. We will learn more about blood cells in Chapter 8.

Bone as a Storage Organ

As mentioned earlier, fat is stored in the yellow bone marrow. Fat is a reserve source of energy for the bone tissue. In addition, the bone matrix is a storage location for calcium. Although calcium gives the bone matrix its strength, calcium is also necessary for proper function of muscles and nerves. Muscles and nerves get their calcium from the blood. If there is not enough calcium in the blood, then it is possible to remove calcium from the bone matrix and put it into the bloodstream. So bone is an extra source of calcium if there is not enough calcium in a person's diet. Shown below are some dietary sources of calcium. What kind of food do you eat that contains calcium? Is there a calcium-rich food shown that you have never eaten?

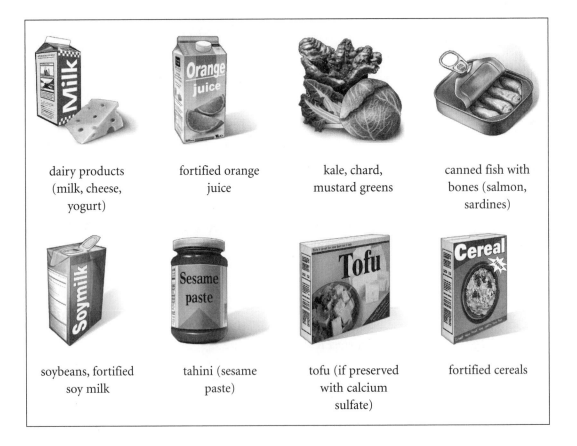

dairy products (milk, cheese, yogurt)

fortified orange juice

kale, chard, mustard greens

canned fish with bones (salmon, sardines)

soybeans, fortified soy milk

tahini (sesame paste)

tofu (if preserved with calcium sulfate)

fortified cereals

Dietary Sources of Calcium

Homeostasis of Calcium

If your body has extra calcium, it is stored in the bone matrix. When your body needs more calcium, it takes calcium out of the bone matrix and puts it into the bloodstream.

Homeostasis of calcium levels is controlled by two hormones.

- **Calcitonin** (kælsə′townən) is a hormone made in the **thyroid gland**. When calcitonin is released into the bloodstream, it causes the extra calcium in the blood to be taken out and added to the bone matrix. It is then stored in the matrix until needed.

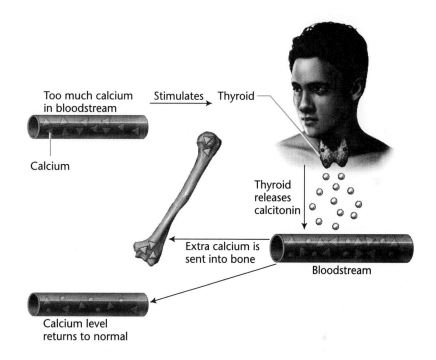

Too much calcium in bloodstream

Stimulates

Thyroid

Calcium

Thyroid releases calcitonin

Extra calcium is sent into bone

Bloodstream

Calcium level returns to normal

FIGURE 3.7   **Homeostasis of calcium. If there is too much calcium in the blood, the thyroid gland secretes calcitonin. Calcitonin causes the bone to take calcium out of the blood and store it in the matrix.**

- **Parathyroid** (pærə′θayəroyd) **hormone (PTH)** is made in the **parathyroid glands**. These glands are located just behind the thyroid gland in your neck (see Figure 1.10 on page 14). When your body needs calcium, PTH causes it to be taken out of bone matrix and put into the bloodstream.

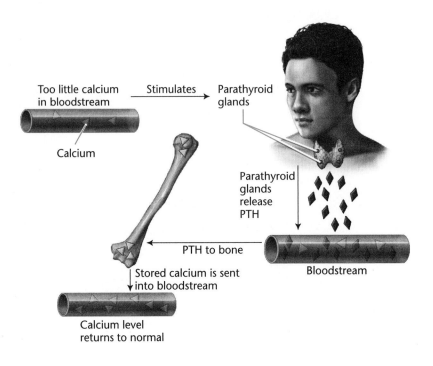

Too little calcium in bloodstream — Stimulates → Parathyroid glands

Calcium

Parathyroid glands release PTH

PTH to bone

Bloodstream

Stored calcium is sent into bloodstream

Calcium level returns to normal

FIGURE 3.8 **Homeostasis of calcium. If there is too little calcium in the blood, the parathyroid glands secrete PTH. PTH causes bone to release calcium into the blood.**

Osteoporosis! Osteoporosis (ɑstiyowpə′rowsəs) is a disorder that most commonly occurs in adults over 50 years old. Too little calcium causes the density (strength) of bone to decrease. Too little calcium makes it easier for bones to break. To decrease the chance of having osteoporosis, you should be sure your diet has the recommended amount of calcium. Regular exercise also helps to prevent osteoporosis.

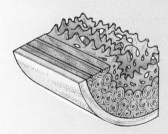 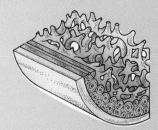

FIGURE 3.9 **Healthy bone**   **FIGURE 3.10** **Bone of a person with osteoporosis. Note the larger openings and thinner areas of matrix**

1. *Circle the correct word(s) to complete each sentence. Take turns reading the correct sentences aloud with a partner.*

   1. Calcium is stored in bone **marrow / matrix**.

   2. **Beef / Milk** contains more calcium.

   3. Calcitonin causes calcium to be **released from / stored in** bone.

   4. PTH stands for **parathyroid hormone / parathyroid glands**.

   5. If your body needs calcium, **parathyroid hormone / calcitonin** is released.

   6. Osteoporosis means that bone density is **strong / weak**.

2. *Complete the sentences below using the words in the box. Take turns reading the correct sentences aloud with a partner.*

calcitonin	osteoporosis	PTH
calcium	parathyroid gland	thyroid gland

   1. A molecule you need for strong bones is called _____.

   2. _____ is the hormone that sends calcium to bones.

   3. A disorder where your bones are weak due to a lack of calcium is called _____.

   4. The hormone which causes calcium to be released from bones is called _____.

   5. _____ is the gland that secretes PTH.

   6. The gland that secretes calcitonin is called the _____.

BUILDING LANGUAGE AND STUDY SKILLS

Stating Degree of Understanding

In Chapter 2, you learned how to ask for clarification. You learned to ask questions such as: "*Could you show me the epithelial layer again?*" In addition to being able to ask for clarification, it is equally important for you to be able to speak up when you don't understand something. If you don't understand something and you don't speak up, your teacher will think you have understood the material.

On the job, it can be very dangerous for someone to think you've understood something when you haven't. For example, you could give someone the wrong medication. Many problems at school and outside of school can be avoided if you speak up when you don't understand what someone has said.

Read the examples of responses students gave their professor about his lecture on bone tissue. The examples are listed in order of degree of certainty.

	EXAMPLE	FORM
Very Sure	I understand how the arrangement of spongy bone and compact bone differ.	*I understand* + noun / noun clause. This sentence means that you understand something completely.
	I think I understand the difference between bone marrow and red marrow.	*I think I understand* + noun / noun clause. Putting *I think* at the beginning of the sentence means that you *may* not understand completely.
	I'm not sure about the sources of calcium. I'm not sure why calcium is important for your body.	*I'm not sure about* + noun / noun clause. Saying *I'm not sure* means that you *do not* understand completely and you need more explanation.
Not Sure	I don't understand how calcium levels are maintained.	*I don't understand* + noun / noun clause. Saying *I don't understand* means that you do not understand at all.

PRACTICE

1. *Work in small groups. Write each of the questions below on an index card. Turn the cards facedown in a pile. Take turns choosing a card and asking and answering the questions. Answer the questions as completely as you can. If no one in the group knows the answer, ask your teacher.*

For example:

A: Do you understand the difference between yellow bone marrow and red bone marrow?

B: No, I don't understand the difference.

A: Red bone marrow makes blood cells. Yellow bone marrow stores fat.

Questions

Do you know . . .?

- where calcitonin is secreted
- the difference between the arrangement of a long bone and a flat bone
- what causes osteoporosis
- the function of bone marrow
- how hard matrix is
- [your own question]

2. *Your teacher was absent for two days. So she asked you to study pages 35–37 in this chapter and write her a note explaining what you understood and what you did not understand about the reading. In the note, include at least three things you understood and two things you did not understand well.*

Studying Diagrams

When you study anatomy and physiology, you need to look at diagrams. In many textbooks, diagrams are called figures. Some of these diagrams illustrate the location of parts of the body. Some diagrams show you the structure of body parts, such as the structure of bone tissue (Figure 3.2 on page 35). Other diagrams explain processes such as maintaining homeostasis of calcium in the body (Figure 3.7 on page 39). It is important that you are able to interpret diagrams and learn from them.

To make the task of interpreting and learning from diagrams easier, follow these steps:

1. Read the short description (caption) that accompanies the diagram.

2. Make sure that you understand the purpose of the diagram. The purpose might be to describe the location of several related structures, or it might be to describe the steps in a process that occurs within the body.

3. Finally, spend some time studying the diagram. Ask yourself these questions:

   - What do colors in the diagram mean?

   - Are letters, symbols, or abbreviations used? If so, what do they mean?

   - Are there numbered steps in the diagram?

   - Is the diagram explained in the reading?

   - Would you be able to explain this diagram to someone else?

   - Is there something about the diagram that you don't understand?

PRACTICE

1. *Look at Figure 3.2 on page 35 and follow the steps listed above. Write your answers on a piece of paper. When you are done, compare your answers with those of a partner.*

2. *Look at Figure 3.7 on page 39 and follow the steps listed above. Write your answers on a piece of paper. When you are done, compare your answers with a partner and ask your partner these questions:*

   - What is the hardest part of studying diagrams for you?

   - How long did it take for you to interpret the diagram?

   - What did you learn about spending time with diagrams?

BONE: ACCESSORY STRUCTURES

There are several accessory structures that are associated with bone. These include cartilage, ligaments, tendons, and joints.

Cartilage

Your skeleton is made of more than just bone tissue. It also has **cartilage** ('kɑrtəlɪdʒ). Cartilage is more flexible than bone and can be found in areas where bones connect (such as in the knee or elbow). It is also found in areas that need some support but require more flexibility for movement (such as the ear or nose). Like bone, cartilage tissue is made of cells, collagen fibers, and matrix.

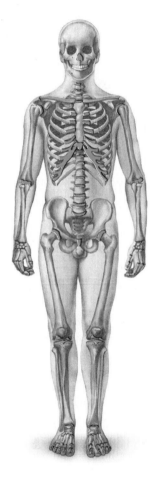

Figure 3.11   The skeletal system with cartilage shaded in blue

Ligaments and Tendons

Bones are connected to one another with connective tissue called **ligaments** ('lɪgəmənts). Ligaments are comprised of collagen and some elastin fibers. Recall from Chapter 2 that collagen fibers give strength, while elastin fibers allow for stretching. Elastin fibers make the connection between the bones flexible. Ligaments *fuse* with the outer covering of one bone and then connect it to the outer covering of another bone.

For bones to move, they need to be connected to muscles. **Tendons** (ˈtɛndənz) are the strands of connective tissue that connect bones to muscles. Tendons are organized in much the same way as ligaments.

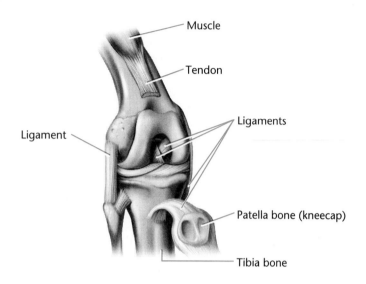

FIGURE 3.12   **Tendons and ligaments in the knee joint**

Joints

A **joint** or **articulation** (ɑrtɪkyəˈleyʃən) is the name given to the place where two or more bones come together. Joints can be *classified* according to the amount of movement they provide at their location. They are:

Sutures (ˈsuwtʃərz) are joints where there is little or no movement between bones. These are most commonly found in the skull.

Slightly moveable joints can be found where there is some movement between bones, such as in the spine.

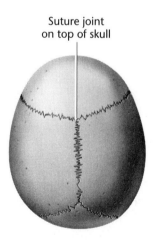

FIGURE 3.13   **Sutures in the skull**

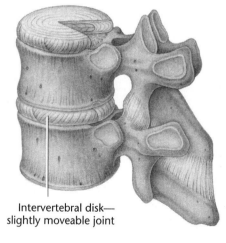

FIGURE 3.14   **Intervertebral disks, the articulations in the spine**

Synovial (sɪ'nowviyəl) **joints** allow for a great deal of movement between bones. In synovial joints there is a special type of space (called the *synovial cavity*) between the bones. This space contains **synovial fluid**, which acts as a cushion for the bones when the joint is moved. Without synovial fluid, movement would be very painful. The bones in synovial joints also have cartilage on the surfaces to make movement smoother.

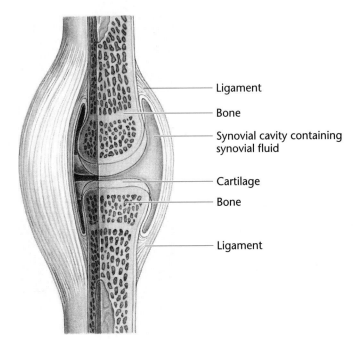

Ligament

Bone

Synovial cavity containing synovial fluid

Cartilage

Bone

Ligament

FIGURE 3.15   **A synovial joint**

Osteoarthritis! Osteoarthritis (ɑstiyowɑr'θraytəs) occurs when synovial articulations become worn. Often, the cartilage wears down and the bones rub against one another. This is very painful. Osteoarthritis is most common in people over 60 years old.

Rheumatoid arthritis! Rheumatoid arthritis ('ruwmətoyd ɑr'θraytəs) occurs when extra synovial fluid builds up in the synovial cavity. This happens because the body mistakenly makes chemicals that identify the joint tissue as "foreign." This type of disorder is called *autoimmune*, which means defense against self. The body begins the process of destroying the joint, which it mistakenly recognizes as foreign. In rheumatoid arthritis, this attack causes synovial fluid to build up in the joint. The build-up of fluid is called *inflammation*. Rheumatoid arthritis can occur at any age and can *be relieved* (but not *cured*) by using anti-inflammatory medications such as aspirin.

1. *Answer the questions below. Then compare your answers with those of a partner.*

    1. How does cartilage differ from bones in terms of flexibility?
    2. What connective tissue structure connects bones to bones? Bones to muscles?
    3. What is another word for *joint*?
    4. What are the three types of joints?
    5. How do synovial joints differ from the other two kinds of joints?
    6. What is the function of synovial fluid?
    7. What causes people who have osteoarthritis to feel pain?
    8. What does the term *autoimmune* mean?
    9. If you have an inflammation, what is happening in your body?

2. *Complete the sentences below using the following words and phrases. Take turns reading the correct sentences aloud with a partner.*

    a. more flexible than bone
    b. provide flexibility
    c. a joint
    d. where two bones connect
    e. bone to muscle
    f. a painful condition when synovial joints become worn
    g. acts like a cushion for bones when the joint is moved

    h. a painful condition when extra synovial fluid builds up
    i. the build-up of fluid
    j. bones to bones
    k. joints where there is little or no movement
    l. when the body attacks itself
    m. can be found in the spine

    1. An articulation is another term for _____.
    2. An autoimmune disorder is _____.
    3. Cartilage is _____.
    4. A tendon connects _____.
    5. Collagen fibers _____.
    6. Inflammation causes _____.
    7. An articulation is found _____.
    8. Osteoarthritis is _____.
    9. A ligament connects _____.
    10. Rheumatoid arthritis is _____.
    11. Slightly moveable joints _____.
    12. Sutures are _____.
    13. Synovial fluid _____.

MAJOR BONES IN THE BODY

The skeleton can be divided into three basic parts: skull, axial skeleton, and appendicular skeleton. The bones in the skull surround the head. The axial skeleton is comprised of the bones that support the main axis or trunk of the body. The appendicular skeleton consists of the bones of the arms and legs, along with the bones that attach them to the axial skeleton.

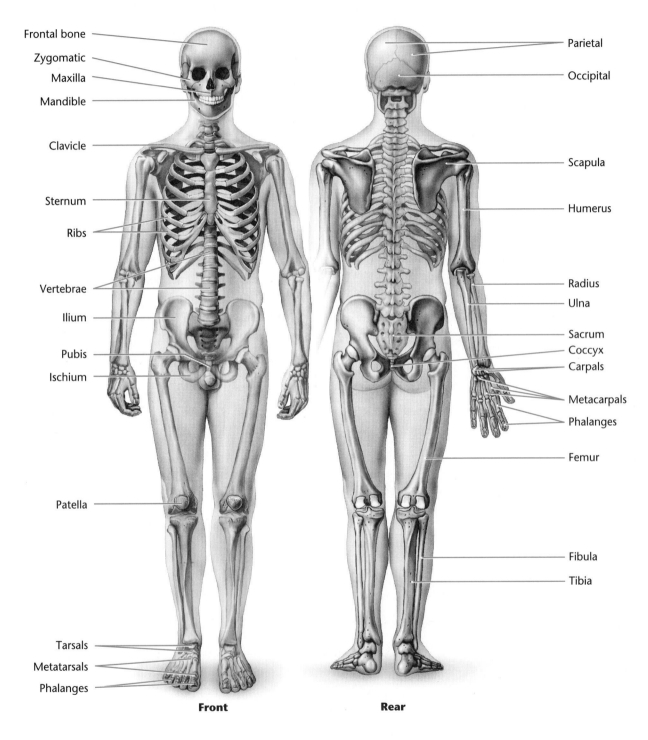

Frontal bone
Zygomatic
Maxilla
Mandible
Clavicle
Sternum
Ribs
Vertebrae
Ilium
Pubis
Ischium
Patella
Tarsals
Metatarsals
Phalanges

Parietal
Occipital
Scapula
Humerus
Radius
Ulna
Sacrum
Coccyx
Carpals
Metacarpals
Phalanges
Femur
Fibula
Tibia

Front

Rear

FIGURE 3.16   **The skeleton**

The Skull: The Bones That Protect the Brain

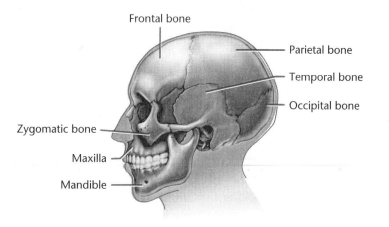

FIGURE 3.17   **The major bones of the skull**

- Some of the bones in the skull have the same name as the regions of the brain: **frontal**, **parietal** (pǝ'rayǝtǝl), **occipital** (ɑk'sɪpǝtl), **temporal**. All of these bones except the occipital occur in pairs. There are two frontal bones, two parietal bones, and two temporal bones.

- The **maxilla** are the two bones that form the upper jaw. They are found between the nose and mouth. The **mandibles** ('mændɪbǝlz) are the two bones that form the lower jaw. They are found below your mouth.

- The **zygomatic** (zaygǝ'mætɪk) bones are also called the cheekbones. You can feel the zygomatic bone if you touch your face under your eye.

- Skull bones are mostly connected by sutures (joints that do not move).

COMPREHENSION CHECK

1. *Work with a partner to label each statement true (T) or false (F). If the statement is false, correct it so that it is true.*

   _____ **1.** The mandibles are the two bones that form the lower jaw.

   _____ **2.** There are two occipital bones.

   _____ **3.** Sutures connect the bones which protect the brain.

   _____ **4.** The temporal bone covers the front of your head (forehead).

   _____ **5.** If you touch under your eyes, you feel the zygomatic bones.

2. *Circle the correct word to complete each sentence. Take turns reading the correct sentences aloud with a partner.*

   1. The **zygomatic / maxilla** are also called the cheekbones.

   2. The **occipital / parietal** bone is located at the back of the head.

   3. The **temporal / occipital** bone is located at the side of the head.

   4. The **mandibles / maxilla** form the upper jaw.

   5. The **occipital / parietal** bone is just behind the temporal bone.

The Axial Skeleton

The next part of the skeleton is the **axial** (ˈæksiyəl) **skeleton**. The axial skeleton supports the body in the following ways:

- The "backbone" or spine supports the "trunk" (main part) by keeping you upright. It consists of 33 bones called **vertebrae** (ˈvɛrtɪbrey). Vertebrae (plural of vertebra) have different shapes and names, depending on their location in the spine.

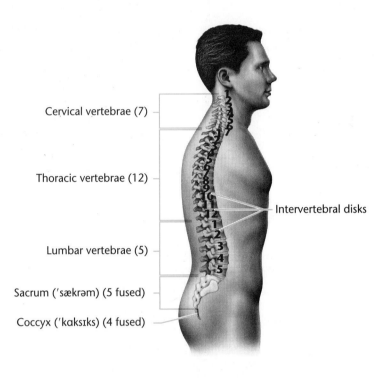

Cervical vertebrae (7)

Thoracic vertebrae (12)

Intervertebral disks

Lumbar vertebrae (5)

Sacrum (ˈsækrəm) (5 fused)

Coccyx (ˈkɑksɪks) (4 fused)

FIGURE 3.18   **The vertebrae**

- The **ribs** protect the heart and lungs. There are 12 pairs of ribs. Cartilage connects the ribs to the **sternum**.

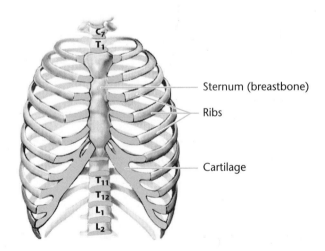

Sternum (breastbone)

Ribs

Cartilage

FIGURE 3.19   **Sternum and ribs**

1. *Read the questions and then scan the text for answers. When you find the answers, underline them. Then work with a partner and take turns asking and answering the questions. Try to remember the answers without looking back at the text.*

    1. What is the function of the axial skeleton?

    2. What is the common name for the spine?

    3. How many vertebrae do you have?

    4. How many different regions of the spine are there?

    5. What organs do the ribs protect?

    6. How many pairs of ribs do you have?

    7. What connects the ribs to the sternum?

2. *Complete the sentences below using the words in the box. Take turns reading the correct sentences aloud with a partner.*

ribs	sternum	vertebra	vertebrae

    1. The spine is comprised of 33 _____. One of them is called a _____.

    2. There are 12 pairs of _____.

    3. Ribs connect to the _____ in the middle of the chest.

3. *Put the spinal regions in order with 1 the region closest to the head and 5 the region closest to the chair when you sit.*

    _____ coccyx

    _____ cervical

    _____ lumbar

    _____ sacrum

    _____ thoracic

The Appendicular Skeleton

The **appendicular** (æpən'dɪkyələr) **skeleton** is used for movement: walking, reaching for things, sitting down. The bones of the arms, hands, legs, and feet, plus the bones that attach them to the axial skeleton are included in the appendicular skeleton.

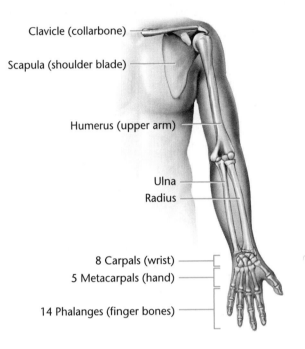

Clavicle (collarbone)

Scapula (shoulder blade)

Humerus (upper arm)

Ulna
Radius

8 Carpals (wrist)
5 Metacarpals (hand)

14 Phalanges (finger bones)

FIGURE 3.20   Bones of the arm and shoulder

Each arm has three bones: the **humerus** ('hyuwmərəs), the **radius** ('reydiyəs), and the **ulna** ('ɑlnə). The humerus makes up the upper arm, and the radius and ulna connect it to the hand.

The humerus attaches to two bones in the shoulder region: the **clavicle** (or collarbone) in the front and the **scapula** ('skæpyələ) (or shoulder blade) in the back. The clavicle also attaches to the sternum.

The radius and ulna connect to the bones of the wrist called **carpals.** Carpals connect to **metacarpals,** the main long bones of the hand. Each finger consists of three bones called **phalanges** ('fælændʒɪz), except for the thumb which has two.

Look at Figure 3.21. It shows the bones of the leg and pelvis. The upper leg bone is called the **femur** ('fiymər). It connects to the pelvis at the hip joint. The pelvis consists of a pair of **hip bones** that connect with the lower vertebrae. Each hip bone actually is made of three separate bones that have fused. Those bones are the **ilium** ('ɪliyəm), **ischium** ('ɪskiyəm), and **pubis** ('pyuwbɪs).

The femur connects with the tibia and fibula at the knee joint. The **patella** (pə'tɛlə) (kneecap) is located on the front side of the knee joint. The **tibia** ('tɪbiyə) is the larger of the lower leg bones. The **fibula** ('fɪbiyələ) is more slender and delicate.

The bones of the ankle are called **tarsals**. Tarsals connect to **metatarsals**, the long bones of the foot. Each toe has three **phalanges**, except for the "big toe" which has two.

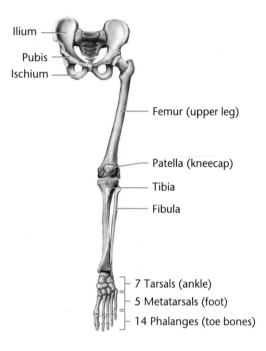

Ilium

Pubis

Ischium

Femur (upper leg)

Patella (kneecap)

Tibia

Fibula

7 Tarsals (ankle)

5 Metatarsals (foot)

14 Phalanges (toe bones)

FIGURE 3.21   **Bones of the leg and pelvis**

A **break** in a bone is called a *fracture*. Fractures usually heal quite easily because of the good blood supply to the bones. A **dislocation** occurs when a bone is moved out of its normal position within a joint.

COMPREHENSION CHECK

1. *Read the questions and then scan the text for answers. When you find the answers, underline them. Then work with a partner and take turns asking and answering the questions. Try to remember the answers without looking back at the text.*

   1. How many bones are in one arm (not including the hand)?

   2. The humerus attaches to what two lower arm bones?

   3. What are wrist bones called?

   4. What are the longest bones in the hand called?

   5. How many phalanges does the thumb have?

   6. How many bones are there in all ten of your fingers?

2. *Circle the correct word to complete each sentence. Take turns reading the correct sentences aloud with a partner.*

1. The upper leg bone is called the **femur / tibia**.

2. The **ischium / ilium** is the upper bone of the pelvis.

3. The **patella / fibula** is another name for the kneecap.

4. The toe bones are called the **tarsals / phalanges**.

5. The **tarsals / metatarsals** are the anklebones.

3. *Where are the following bones in the body? Work with a partner and check the correct column below. Then compare your answers with the class.*

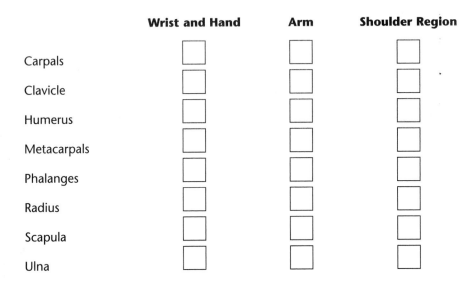

	Wrist and Hand	Arm	Shoulder Region
Carpals	☐	☐	☐
Clavicle	☐	☐	☐
Humerus	☐	☐	☐
Metacarpals	☐	☐	☐
Phalanges	☐	☐	☐
Radius	☐	☐	☐
Scapula	☐	☐	☐
Ulna	☐	☐	☐

4. *Match the bones to their location by writing the letters in the correct blanks. Then compare your answers with those of a partner.*

_____ 1. carpals   **a.** upper arm bone

_____ 2. fibula   **b.** bones of hand connecting to phalanges

_____ 3. ulna   **c.** foot bones connecting to phalanges

_____ 4. ischium   **d.** collarbone

_____ 5. metatarsals   **e.** wrist bones

_____ 6. humerus   **f.** in the lower leg, beside the tibia

_____ 7. clavicle   **g.** pelvic bone that lies above the ischium

_____ 8. pubis   **h.** the largest of the two lower leg bones

_____ 9. metacarpals   **i.** lower arm bone

_____ 10. tibia   **j.** below the ilium

Forms of Address

In many parts of the United States, it is common for people to call each other by their first names. They do this because it shows friendliness and comfort. In other cultures, it is more common for people to address each other using formal forms of address, such as Mr. or Mrs., especially when talking to someone who is not a member of the family or in their circle of friends. People who work in health care should be aware of this difference, so they won't offend anyone.

1. *The following story is about a cultural conflict that people may experience in a health-care setting. Read the story and then discuss the questions in small groups.*

Mary, a nurse in her forties, is taking care of Mr. Cho, a man about her age. Mr. Cho, who was admitted to the hospital with severe back pain, has been under her care for three days. Mary has taken him to the bathroom, helped him to change clothes, checked his vital signs, and given him medication, including injections. In other words, Mary has been in close contact with Mr. Cho. To show him that she is friendly and cares about him, she has often joked with him and from the first day, she has called him by his first name—Chris—and not by his family name. Not being addressed as "Mister Cho" has upset Mr. Cho. He has felt disrespected and has felt that Mary has been treating him like a child. So after giving it a lot of thought, Mr. Cho decided to complain to Mary's supervisor.

1. Why is Mr. Cho upset?

2. When is it OK to call someone by their first name?

3. Can you understand why Mary wants to call him by his first name?

2. *With a partner, choose one of the three following role plays. You may wish to write out the dialogue and practice it before performing it in front of the class.*

Situation 1. Student A is Mr. Cho and Student B is the supervisor. Mr. Cho complains to the supervisor and the supervisor responds to his complaints.

Situation 2. Student A is the nursing supervisor and Student B is Mary, the nurse. The nursing supervisor explains to Mary why Mr. Cho is upset. Mary reacts to what the supervisor is saying.

Situation 3. Student A is Mary and Student B is Mr. Cho. Mary apologizes and Mr. Cho responds to the apology.

Check Your Understanding

1. *Answer the following questions about the skeletal system.*

    1. Name three functions of bone.

    2. What is the matrix of bone made of?

    3. What are the two types of bone tissue? Are they made of the same molecules and cells?

    4. Where does your body store extra calcium? What hormone helps with this? Which gland makes this hormone?

    5. If your body needs more calcium, how does it get more? What hormone is involved? Which gland makes this hormone?

    6. What happens when bones get too little calcium?

    7. Where would you find cartilage in your body?

    8. What holds bones to one another? What holds bones to muscles?

    9. Where would you find suture joints? Where would you find synovial joints?

    10. Explain the difference between osteoarthritis and rheumatoid arthritis.

2. *Label Figure 3.22 with the terms provided. One term is used twice.*

carpals	ilium	patella	scapula
clavicle	ischium	parietal	sternum
coccyx	mandible	phalanges	tarsals
femur	maxilla	pubis	tibia
fibula	metacarpals	radius	ulna
frontal	metatarsals	ribs	vertebra
humerus	occipital	sacrum	zygomatic

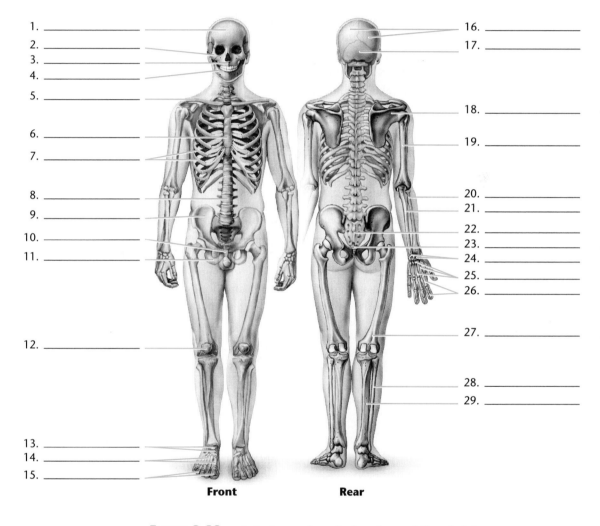

1. _____
2. _____
3. _____
4. _____
5. _____
6. _____
7. _____
8. _____
9. _____
10. _____
11. _____
12. _____
13. _____
14. _____
15. _____

16. _____
17. _____
18. _____
19. _____
20. _____
21. _____
22. _____
23. _____
24. _____
25. _____
26. _____
27. _____
28. _____
29. _____

Front   **Rear**

FIGURE 3.22   Anterior and posterior views of the skeleton

INTRODUCTION

Muscles are organs that help your body move. We use muscles for all body movements, including walking, standing, typing on a keyboard, and chewing food. Even the beating of the heart is caused by muscles. In this chapter, you will learn how muscles are organized, how they contract, and the names of some of the muscles of the body.

1. **Work with a partner. Look at this diagram of the muscles of the front of the body. Try to label the parts with the words in the box. Look at Figures 4.12, 4.13, and 4.14 on pages 71, 73, and 75 to check your answers.**

biceps brachii	quadriceps	triceps brachii
pectoralis	tibialis anterior	

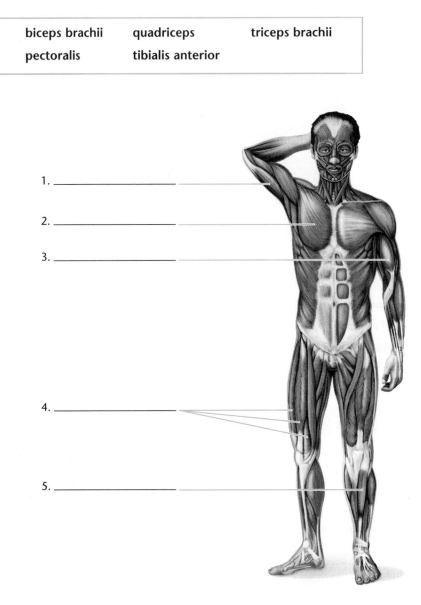

1. _____

2. _____

3. _____

4. _____

5. _____

FIGURE 4.1   Muscular system

2. *With your partner, try to answer these questions. If you do not know the answers, do not worry. You will find the answers as you read through this chapter.*

1. What is the function of skeletal muscle?

2. How are muscle cells organized within muscles?

3. What kinds of molecules are muscles made of?

4. What part of the body tells muscles to move?

5. What organs in the body contain muscle tissue?

3. *Read each verb, its simple definition, and its passive voice form. Then fill in the verbs in the sentences that follow. Pay attention to verb tense and subject / verb agreement. Compare your answers with those of another student.*

BASE FORM	PASSIVE VOICE FORM	MEANING
bend	be bent	to move forward or back
contract	be contracted	to get shorter
extend	be extended	to lengthen or straighten
flex	be flexed	to pull toward you, to bend
inherit	be inherited	to get traits from your parents
transmit	be transmitted	to carry or send
stimulate	be stimulated	to excite

1. You _____ your muscles to show someone how strong you are.

2. Can you _____ your arm to reach the ceiling?

3. A molecule can _____ a message from one location in the body to another.

4. The doctor wants to see if you can _____ down to touch your toes.

5. When you move, your muscles get shorter, or _____.

6. My teacher has _____ my interest in learning anatomy.

7. I _____ my height from my father.

ORGANIZATION OF SKELETAL MUSCLE

Muscles are very interesting structures because they are highly organized. To understand how they are organized, it is important to first understand the concept of "bundle."

Gather eight pencils, and organize them to make sure that they are even with each other. Put them in your hand and hold on to them. That's a bundle, a bundle of pencils. Muscle cells, muscle tissue, and whole muscles are all comprised of bundles. We'll begin our study of muscle organization by moving from the organization of a single muscle cell to the organization of muscle tissue to the organization of a whole muscle.

Look at Figure 4.2. As you read about how a muscle is organized, locate the parts on the figure. A single muscle cell is called a **fiber**. A fiber is comprised of bundles called **myofibrils** (mayow′faybrəlz). *Myo-* means *muscle*; *fibril* means *small fiber*. One single muscle cell might be comprised of hundreds or thousands of myofibrils.

Similarly, each myofibril is also formed by bundles. The bundles that comprise a myofibril are made of **myofilaments** (mayə′filəmənt). *Filament* means *thread*. A myofibril contains many myofilaments.

Finally, a single myofilament is **not** comprised of bundles. Instead, it is comprised of one of two kinds of protein molecules: **actin** or **myosin**. In other words, there are actin myofilaments and myosin myofilaments. Actin and myosin are what make a muscle move. You'll learn more about how actin and myosin function later in the chapter.

Muscle fibers join together to form muscle tissue. A bundle of fibers is called a **fascicle** (′fæsɪkəl). A single skeletal muscle is comprised of bundles of fascicles held together by connective tissue.

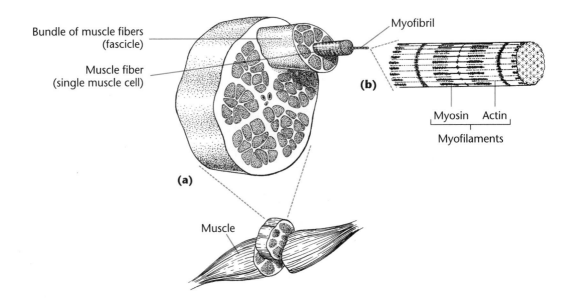

FIGURE 4.2   **Diagram of whole muscle. A muscle is made of fascicles (bundles) of muscle fibers. Each muscle fiber is comprised of myofibrils, which are bundles of myofilaments. Myofilaments are comprised of either actin or myosin.**

In summary, a skeletal muscle is comprised of bundles of fascicles, a fascicle is comprised of bundles of fibers, a fiber is comprised of bundles of myofibrils, and a myofibril is comprised of bundles of myofilaments. Finally, a myofilament is not comprised of bundles. It is comprised of either actin or myosin protein molecules.

COMPREHENSION CHECK

1. *Answer the questions below. Then compare your answers with those of a partner.*

    1. What kind of bundles comprise a fiber?

    2. Where do you find myofilaments?

    3. What are the two types of myofilament?

    4. Which is the smallest: fiber, myofilament, or myofibril?

    5. Do fascicles comprise fibers or do fibers comprise fascicles?

    6. Name all of the structures of a muscle, going from smallest to largest.

2. *Match the terms with their definitions by writing the letters in the correct blanks. Then compare your answers with those of a partner.*

    _____ 1. actin and myosin   **a.** means "muscle"

    _____ 2. bundle   **b.** a group of these comprise a myofibril

    _____ 3. fiber   **c.** protein molecules

    _____ 4. myo-   **d.** a group

    _____ 5. myofibril   **e.** a group of these comprise a fiber

    _____ 6. myofilament   **f.** a muscle cell

    _____ 7. protein   **g.** comprised of many fascicles

    _____ 8. muscle   **h.** actin and myosin are this kind of molecule

3. *Label Figure 4.3 with the terms in the box. Look at Figure 4.2 on page 62 to check your answers.*

fascicle	fiber	myofilaments	myofibril

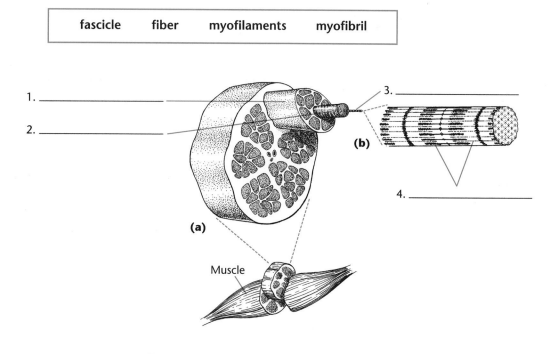

1. _____

2. _____

3. _____

4. _____

(b)

(a)

Muscle

FIGURE 4.3   **Organization of a whole muscle**

From Brain to Muscle

When you need to get a drink of water, you've made a decision to move muscles. You have to move muscles to stand up, to walk to the sink, and to pour a glass of water. When you make a decision to move, messages are sent from your brain along **motor neurons** to muscle fibers. *Motor* means *movement*. *Neuron* means *nerve cell*. A motor neuron is a neuron that sends messages about movement to muscles in your body. You can move when fibers in your skeletal muscles receive messages from motor neurons.

However, the end of a motor neuron and a skeletal muscle fiber do not touch. When the message to move reaches the end of the motor neuron, a molecule is released from the motor neuron and this molecule jumps, or is *transmitted*, to the muscle fiber. This molecule is called a **neurotransmitter**. *Neuro-* means *nerve*. *Transmit* means *to carry* or *to send*.

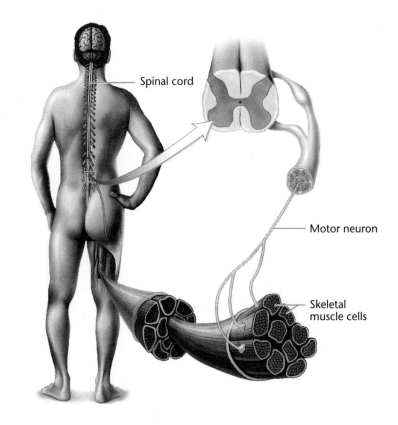

FIGURE 4.4   **A message from the spinal cord travels along a motor neuron to the skeletal muscle.**

In many cultures, acupuncture is a common technique for relieving pain. The acupuncturist uses thin needles to stimulate certain places in the body. The purpose is to relieve pain and to stimulate repair of damaged tissues. Techniques such as acupuncture are called "alternative medicine" because they are not part of the traditional methods of healing. However, acupuncture is becoming more popular for pain relief throughout the world.

There are many different types of neurotransmitters. The neurotransmitter that transmits a message to a skeletal muscle fiber to begin the movement process is called **acetylcholine** (əsiytəl′kowliyn), commonly called ACh. When ACh leaves the neuron and jumps to a muscle fiber, the muscle fiber produces an electrical signal. This electrical signal causes the actin and myosin (which comprise the myofilaments) to move. When actin and myosin move, the muscle moves.

COMPREHENSION CHECK

1. *Work with a partner to label each statement true (T) or false (F). If the statement is false, correct it so that it is true.*

_____ **1.** Motor neurons touch skeletal muscle fibers.

_____ **2.** Neurotransmitters are molecules that are sent from the muscle fiber to the motor neuron.

_____ **3.** ACh causes the muscle fiber to produce an electrical signal.

_____ **4.** Actin and myosin are the molecules that move in order to cause the muscle to move.

_____ **5.** Motor neurons send messages from the muscle to the brain.

2. *Circle the correct word to complete each sentence. Take turns reading the correct sentences aloud with a partner.*

1. The word "motor" means _____.
   a. nerve   **b.** move   **c.** signal   **d.** tissue

2. A neuron is a(n) _____.
   a. molecule   **b.** tissue   **c.** cell   **d.** organ

3. A neurotransmitter is a(n) _____.
   a. molecule   **b.** tissue   **c.** cell   **d.** organ

Myofibril at Rest

To move a muscle, actin and myosin, the protein molecules that comprise a myofilament, must move. To more clearly understand how they move, let's first look at how these myofilaments are organized to form a myofibril at rest. We'll then look at how the actin and myosin change position after they receive a message to move.

Look at Figure 4.5 below. It is a diagram of a portion of a single myofibril at rest. The muscle fiber that contains this myofibril has not received a message to move. This diagram will look different after ACh attaches to the muscle fiber.

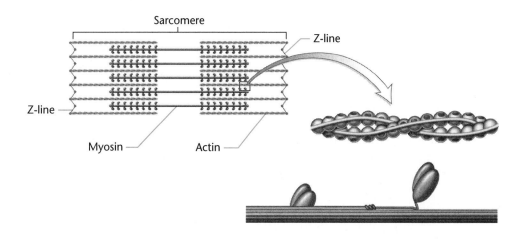

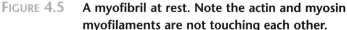

FIGURE 4.5   **A myofibril at rest. Note the actin and myosin myofilaments are not touching each other.**

Notice that there are thin vertical lines all along the myofibril. These are called **Z-lines**. The space between the Z-lines is called a **sarcomere** (ˈsɑrkowmiyər). Notice that there are many sarcomeres in a myofibril. How many sarcomeres can you see in the myofibril in Figure 4.5? Now look again at the myofibril to find the actin and myosin. You can see that actin is attached to the Z-lines and that myosin lies in the center of the sarcomere. Notice that the myosin does not touch the Z-line or the actin. Now look at the actin. The actin looks like a twisted pearl necklace. Look again at the myosin. The myosin looks like golf clubs. Notice that the myosin heads are *bent* back. This means that they are in the "cocked" position. Figure 4.5 is a diagram of how actin and myosin look at rest *before* they receive the signal to move. After the actin and myosin receive the signal to move, the diagram will look different.

COMPREHENSION CHECK

1. *Read the questions and then scan the text for answers. When you find the answers, underline them. Then work with a partner and take turns asking and answering the questions. Try to remember the answers without looking back at the text.*

   1. What are the vertical lines in the myofibril called?

   2. What does actin look like?

   3. What is actin attached to?

   4. What does myosin look like?

   5. Where is myosin located in the sarcomere?

   6. Are the myosin heads "cocked" or "uncocked" in Figure 4.6?

2. *Label Figure 4.6 with the terms in the box. One term is used twice. Look at Figure 4.5 on page 65 to check your answers.*

actin	myosin	sarcomere	Z-line

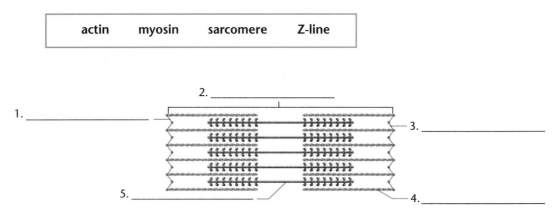

FIGURE 4.6   **A myofibril at rest**

Contraction in the Myofibril

Now that you understand what a myofibril looks like at rest, let's look at how actin and myosin change when the muscle has been signaled to move. Below is a diagram of a myofibril that has been stimulated to move by ACh.

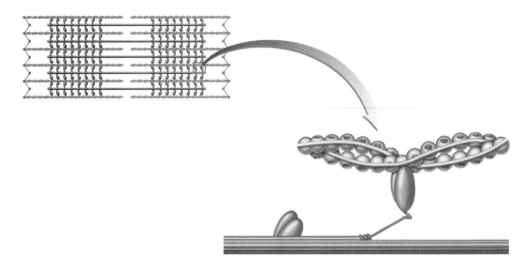

FIGURE 4.7   **A myofibril during contraction. Note the myosin has pushed the actin toward the center of the sarcomere. The sarcomere has shortened when compared with the one in Figure 4.5.**

When signaled to move, notice how the myosin attaches to the actin and pushes the actin toward the center of the sarcomere. The Z-lines move with the actin, and this causes the sarcomeres to become shorter. When sarcomeres shorten, the muscle fiber shortens. Another word for shorten is *contract*. When the muscle fibers contract, the entire muscle contracts. In turn, when muscles contract, they cause bones to move. When certain muscles in your arm contract, you are able to reach for the glass of water.

After the muscle contraction occurs (you have finished reaching for your drink of water), your muscle needs to return to a relaxed state. To return to a relaxed state, the myosin heads become cocked again. Myosin heads can't return to the cocked position without first getting energy from a molecule called **ATP** (adenosine tri-phosphate). ATP is made by organelles (cell parts) inside of muscle fibers. These organelles are called **mitochondria** (maytow′kɑndriyə). Mitochondria make ATP by breaking apart food molecules (sugar, fats, carbohydrates, and proteins).

Circle the correct word(s) to complete each sentence. Take turns reading the correct sentences aloud with a partner.

1. When muscles contract, they **shorten / lengthen**.

2. After ATP attaches to the myosin head, it becomes **cocked / uncocked**.

3. ATP is made in the **mitochondria / nucleus** of the muscle fiber.

4. The energy in ATP comes from **oxygen / food molecules**.

5. When contraction occurs, **actin pushes myosin / myosin pushes actin**.

∿∿∿ Muscular Dystrophy! Some people *inherit* a disease that destroys the muscle fibers and replaces them with fat and connective tissue. People who have muscular dystrophy are unable to move their muscles very well. Their movements seem clumsy and they fall down a lot. Eventually, the disease affects the muscles that control breathing and the person dies of respiratory failure. In the most common form of muscular dystrophy, the individual dies very young.

TYPES OF MUSCLE

This chapter has focused on skeletal muscle. You now know that when skeletal muscles contract, bones move. You also know that skeletal muscles contract when they receive messages from motor neurons. Usually, these messages come from the brain and are **voluntary**, meaning that you are aware of making the decision to move the muscle. Most of the body's skeletal muscles are voluntary. Only a few skeletal muscles are **involuntary**, meaning that they contract without you thinking about it. These muscles are the diaphragm and intercostal muscles. These muscles make it possible for you to breathe.

There are two other types of muscle in the human body. Both of these muscle types are involuntary. One type is **smooth muscle**. Smooth muscle can be found in the lining of many organs. For example, smooth muscle is found in digestive organs such as the stomach and intestines, as well as in the passageways leading to the lungs, the urinary bladder, some blood vessels, and the uterus. Smooth muscle gets its name from the fact that the muscle fibers have a more uniform appearance, not striped as in the skeletal muscle. The second type is **cardiac muscle**. Cardiac muscle is found exclusively in the heart. Cardiac muscle fibers are similar in organization to skeletal muscle fibers, except the fibers are branched. Another difference between skeletal and cardiac muscle is that cardiac muscle fibers contract on their own without any neural stimulation. They don't need messages from the brain or spinal cord to move.

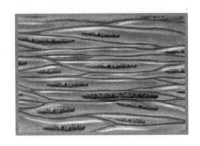
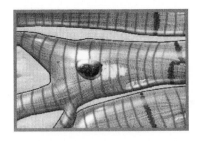

FIGURE 4.8   **Skeletal muscle**   FIGURE 4.9   **Smooth muscle**   FIGURE 4.10   **Cardiac muscle**

Check the type of muscle (smooth, cardiac, or skeletal) that would be involved in each of the following activities or processes.

	Smooth	Cardiac	Skeletal
1. Mixing and breaking apart food in the stomach	☐	☐	☐
2. Running to catch the bus	☐	☐	☐
3. Making the heart beat	☐	☐	☐
4. Chewing food	☐	☐	☐
5. Making the blood vessels narrower	☐	☐	☐
6. Contracting the uterus during childbirth	☐	☐	☐

THE SKELETAL MUSCLES OF THE BODY

The human body has over 600 skeletal muscles. Many of these muscles exist in pairs. For example, there are two **biceps brachii** (ˈbaysɛps ˈbreykiyay) muscles, one on each arm. There are two **temporalis** (tɛmpəˈrælǝs) muscles, one on each side of the head. There are two **rectus femoris** (ˈrɛktǝs ˈfɛmǝrǝs) muscles, one on each thigh.

Muscles are often named for the areas in which they are located. For instance, the **tibialis anterior** (tɪˈbiyælǝs ænˈtɪriyǝr) muscle is located on the front ("anterior") of the **tibia**, a bone of the lower leg. Muscles are also named for the bones they connect. For instance, the **sternocleidomastoid** (stɛrnowklaydowmæsˈtoyd) connects the sternum ("sterno"), the clavicle ("cleido"), and the mastoid area of the temporal bone.

Learning the skeletal muscles can seem hard at first, but there are ways to help you learn them.

- Divide the body into areas and learn each area separately. For example, choose the head and learn all of its muscles.

- Remember that the name of a muscle often gives you a hint about its location, shape, or what it does. For example, the rectus *abdominis* is located in the *abdomen* (stomach area).

- Learning word parts will help! For example, if you know that *anterior* means *front*, then every time you see the word *anterior*, you will know that the muscle is in the front of something. The word part *ante-* means *before* or *front*.

This book lists only the major muscles. You will learn more muscles as you advance in your study of anatomy. The number you'll see in parentheses indicates how many of those muscles exist in the body.

The Muscles of the Head

Temporalis (tɛmpəˈrælǝs) (2): located beneath the temporal bone. English speakers often refer to the side of the head near the eye as the "temple." The temporalis muscles help you to close your mouth.

Frontalis (frɑntˈaylɪs) (2): located beneath the frontal bone, at the "front" of the head, on the forehead. The frontalis muscles contract when you raise your eyebrows.

Orbicularis oculi (ɔrbɪkyə′lɛrəs ′ɑkyalay) (2): around the eye. *Orb* means *circle* and *oculi* refers to the eye. The orbicularis oculi muscles are used to blink your eyes.

Masseter (mæ′sɪtər) (2): located between the side of the mouth and the ear—in the cheek. The masseter muscles raise your lower jaw and are important in chewing. In fact, *masseter* means *chewer*.

Orbicularis oris (ɔrbɪkyə′lɛrəs ɔrəs) (2): around the mouth. *Orb* means *circle* and *oris* means *mouth*. The orbicularis oris are the muscles used to close the lips. You use these muscles when you whistle and talk.

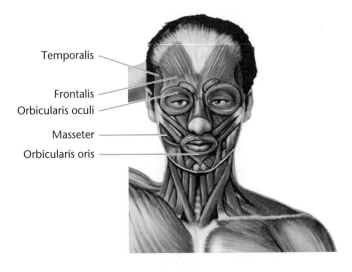

Temporalis
Frontalis
Orbicularis oculi
Masseter
Orbicularis oris

FIGURE 4.11   **Facial muscles**

COMPREHENSION CHECK

1. *Match the name of the muscle with the description of its location by writing the letters in the correct blanks. Then compare your answers with those of a partner.*

   _____ 1. frontalis

   _____ 2. masseter

   _____ 3. orbicularis oculi

   _____ 4. orbicularis oris

   _____ 5. temporalis

   a. This muscle circles your mouth.

   b. This muscle circles each of your eyes.

   c. This muscle is on your forehead.

   d. This muscle is on either side of your head, next to your eyes.

   e. This muscle is located on either side of your mouth and *extends* up to either ear.

2. *Answer the questions below. Then compare your answers with those of a partner.*

   1. What does the name "frontalis" tell you about the location of the muscle with that name?

   2. There are two "orbicularis" muscles. What does the term "orbicularis" mean?

   3. What body part does "oculi" refer to?

   4. What body part does "oris" refer to?

Muscles of the Anterior Trunk and Upper Arm

Anterior is the term used to describe the front of the body. All of these muscles are visible from the front of the body.

Sternocleidomastoid (stɛrnowklaydowmæsʹtoyd) (2): connects the sternum, the clavicle, and the temporal bone (on the head). The sternocleidomastoid muscles are important in *flexing* the neck. For example, these muscles contract when you are lying down and begin to raise your head.

Biceps brachii (ʹbaysɛps ʹbreykiyay) (2): These muscles are located on the front of the arm. They are the ones you see when you "show your muscles." *Bi-* means *two*. These muscles have two places where they attach to the shoulder. The biceps brachii help you to bend your arms at the elbows.

Pectoralis major (pɛktəʹræləs ʹmeydʒər) (2): large muscles across the chest. *Pecto-* means *chest*; *major* means *bigger*. The pectoralis major is an important muscle for flexing the arm and pulling the rib cage upward. You use this muscle when pushing and throwing.

Deltoid (ʹdɛltoyd) (2): The deltoid muscles have a triangular shape and rest on the shoulder. The name comes from the Greek letter "delta" which looks like a triangle. The deltoids are used when moving your arms away from the body.

Intercostals (ɪntərʹkowstəlz) (many): The intercostals are found between the ribs. *Inter-* means *between*; *cost-* means *rib*. The intercostals assist with breathing.

Diaphragm (ʹdayəfræm) (1): This broad muscle divides the interior of the body trunk into two sections: the chest cavity and the abdominal cavity. *Dia-* means *across*; *-phragm* means *partition* or *wall*. The diaphragm is essential for breathing.

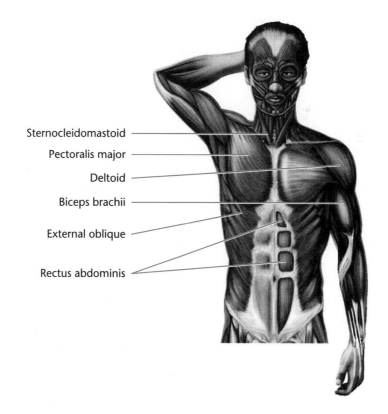

Sternocleidomastoid

Pectoralis major

Deltoid

Biceps brachii

External oblique

Rectus abdominis

FIGURE 4.12   **Muscles of the anterior body trunk and arm**

Rectus abdominis (ˈrɛktəs æbˈdɑmənəs) (2): Two vertical (up-and-down) muscles that extend from the chest down to the bottom of the trunk. In the United States, body builders sometimes call these muscles the "six-pack" because there are three divisions to the muscle on either side of the midline, just like there are three divisions on each side of a six-pack of soda. *Rectus* means *upright* or *straight*; *abdominis* refers to the abdomen.

External oblique (ɪkˈstɛrnəl əˈbliyk) (2): sheets of muscle that go from the rectus abdominis over to the side of the body. They are arranged so that the fibers run at a diagonal (45° angle). *Oblique* means *side-to-side*. The external oblique and the rectus abdominis are important in supporting and protecting the internal organs of the abdomen, such as the liver, the intestines, and the stomach. These areas of muscle are very strong because the fibers go in different directions.

Six-pack of soda

COMPREHENSION CHECK

1. *Work with a partner to label each statement true (T) or false (F). If the statement is false, correct it so that it is true.*

   _____ 1. Intercostal muscles are located between your ribs.

   _____ 2. The diaphragm is necessary for breathing.

   _____ 3. The deltoid muscle covers your abdomen.

   _____ 4. The sternocleidomastoid goes from your sternum to your pelvis.

   _____ 5. The external oblique is located in the center of your abdomen.

   _____ 6. The pectoralis major is located on your chest.

   _____ 7. The rectus abdominus is located on your abdomen.

2. *Match the words or word parts with their definitions by writing the letters in the correct blanks. Then compare your answers with those of a partner.*

   _____ 1. inter-   **a.** across

   _____ 2. pecto-   **b.** ribs

   _____ 3. external   **c.** vertical (up and down)

   _____ 4. costal   **d.** between

   _____ 5. oblique   **e.** on the abdomen

   _____ 6. dia-   **f.** two attachments

   _____ 7. rectus   **g.** front

   _____ 8. abdominis   **h.** side to side

   _____ 9. anterior   **i.** chest

   _____ 10. bi-   **j.** outside

Muscles of the Posterior of the Trunk and Upper Arm

Posterior is the term used to describe the back side of the body. All of these muscles can be viewed on the back of the body.

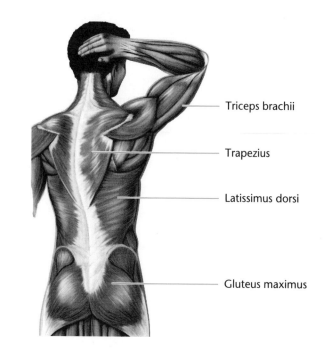

— Triceps brachii

— Trapezius

— Latissimus dorsi

— Gluteus maximus

FIGURE 4.13   Muscles of the posterior body trunk and arm

Trapezius (trə′piyziyəs) (2): a sheet of muscle that extends from the neck across the back shoulder. The trapezius helps to move the scapula (shoulder blade). You might guess that this muscle is used when holding on to a trapeze!

Triceps brachii (′traysɛps ′breykiyay) (2): This muscle is located on the back of the upper arm. *Tri-* means three; this muscle has three places where it attaches to the shoulder. *Brach-* refers to branches. The arm can be considered a branch off the main body trunk, so the main muscles in the arm are called brachii. The triceps brachii helps you to extend your forearm.

Latissimus dorsi (lə′tɪsəməs ′dɔrsay) (2): a muscle that extends from the side of the body across the back. *Lat-* means *side*; *dorsi* refers to the back. The latissimus dorsi helps you to extend your arms from the body. It is important when you play tennis or swim.

Gluteus maximus (′gluwtiyəs ′mæksɪməs) (2): muscles that form the buttocks (you sit on this muscle). *Glutos-* means *buttock*, and *maximus* means *the biggest*. The gluteus maximus muscle extends the thigh, and therefore is important in running and climbing.

1. *Circle the correct answer. Then compare your answers with those of a partner.*

   1. This muscle extends from the neck across the back shoulder. It helps to move the scapula.

      a. trapezius   **b.** latissimus dorsi   **c.** gluteus maximus

   2. This muscle extends from the side of the body across the back. It is important when you swim or play tennis.

      a. trapezius   **b.** latissimus dorsi   **c.** gluteus maximus

   3. This muscle forms the buttocks and you sit on it. It is important for running and climbing.

      a. trapezius   **b.** latissimus dorsi   **c.** gluteus maximus

   4. The triceps brachii attaches to the _____.

      a. neck   **b.** shoulder   **c.** leg

2. *What do the following word parts tell us about the muscle? If you need to, refer back to your reading.*

   1. Tri- (as in triceps brachii) _____

   2. Dorsi (as in latissimus dorsi) _____

   3. Lat- (as in latissimus dorsi) _____

   4. Maximus (as in gluteus maximus) _____

   5. Brachii (as in biceps or triceps brachii) _____

Muscles of the Leg

The **quadriceps femoris** (′kwɑdrɪsɛps ′fɛmərəs) is sometimes called "quads" by body-builders. (*Quad-* means *four.*) The quadriceps femoris is actually four muscles that form the front of the upper leg. The quadriceps femoris helps to extend the knee and is important for running, climbing, and getting up from your chair. The four muscles on each leg that make up this group are:

- **Vastus lateralis** (′væstəs lætər′ɑləs) (2): *vastus* means *large, lateralis* means *on the side.*

- **Vastus medialis** (′væstəs mə′dæləs) (2): *vastus* means *large, medialis* means *middle.*

- **Rectus femoris** (′rɛktəs ′fɛmərəs) (2): *rectus* means *upright* or *straight, femoris* means it lies on top of the *femur.*

- **Vastus intermedius** (′væstəs ɪntər′miydiyəs) (2): *vastus* means *large, intermedius* means *in between.* Because the vastus intermedius muscle is actually beneath the rectus femoris, deeper in the leg, it is not seen in the diagram.

Sartorius (sar′tɔriyǝs) (2): an S-shaped muscle that extends diagonally across each thigh. If you use your imagination, it almost has an S-shape ("S" for "Sartorius"). The sartorius helps to flex the thigh.

Tibialis anterior (tɪ′biyælǝs æn′tɪriyǝr) (2): This muscle is on the front of each tibia (lower leg). *Anterior* means *front*. The tibialis anterior helps to keep you from tripping when you are walking.

Biceps femoris (′baysɛps ′fɛmǝrǝs): The large muscle on the back of the femur, toward the side of the body. *Bi-* means *two*; it has two places where it attaches to the femur. *Femoris* means it is attached to the *femur*. The biceps femoris muscle is part of a group of muscles on the back of each thigh known as "hamstrings." The hamstring group is important in flexing the knee and extending the thigh.

Gastrocnemius (gæstrɔk′niymiyǝs) (2): This muscle is typically called the calf muscle. It is the large muscle that makes up the back of each lower leg. *Gaster* means *belly* (round stomach); *kneme* means *leg*. The gastrocnemius is important in walking, running, and standing on tiptoe.

Important tendon: The **Achilles** (ǝ′kɪliyz) or **calcaneal** (kæl′kɛniyǝl) **tendon** (2) connects the lower part of the gastrocnemius with the bones of the heel. If this tendon is severed (cut) or injured, it is very painful and it may be impossible to walk. Remember, a tendon is a tissue that connects a muscle to bone.

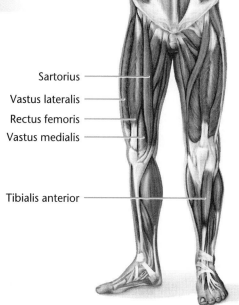

Sartorius
Vastus lateralis
Rectus femoris
Vastus medialis

Tibialis anterior

FIGURE 4.14 **Muscles of the anterior leg**

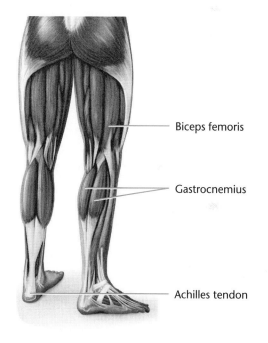

Biceps femoris

Gastrocnemius

Achilles tendon

FIGURE 4.15 **Muscles of the posterior leg**

Sprains! Sprains are the tearing or overstretching of ligaments. Recall that a ligament is a tissue that connects bones to bones. When ligaments tear or overstretch, this causes pain at the joint, and sometimes prevents movement at that joint.

Hamstring Pull! A hamstring pull is a type of muscle strain (overstretching of the muscle) that involves one of the hamstring muscles on the back of the thigh.

COMPREHENSION CHECK

1. *Write the name of the leg muscle next to the correct description.*

   1. This muscle is very large and is beneath the rectus femoris. You can't see it on the diagram. _____

   2. These four muscles are called *quads* by bodybuilders.

      a. _____

      b. _____

      c. _____

      d. _____

   3. This is the top middle muscle on the upper leg. _____

   4. This muscle lies on the tibia. _____

2. *Match the terms with their definitions by writing the letters in the correct blanks. Then compare your answers with those of a partner.*

_____ 1. femoris	**a.**	on the side
_____ 2. intermedius	**b.**	large
_____ 3. lateralis	**c.**	middle
_____ 4. medialis	**d.**	four
_____ 5. quad-	**e.**	on top of the femur
_____ 6. rectus	**f.**	upright, straight
_____ 7. vastus	**g.**	in between

Describing Location

Your anatomy and physiology teacher will often show you a diagram or a model of an organ or an organ system to explain the location of various structures. For example, she will show you a diagram of the muscles in the anterior of the body to explain each muscle's location. She will likely use the same diagram or model to ask you questions about the location of each muscle. When you aren't sure of a structure's location, such as where the rectus abdominus is, you will need to ask questions to find out its location. Otherwise, you will probably misunderstand a lecture and make mistakes on tests.

Read the following dialogue between a teacher (T) and student (S). The teacher is explaining the location of muscles of the anterior (front) body. Then look on page 78 to note the common vocabulary used to describe location.

T: The large muscle located **across the** chest is the pectoralis major.

S: What muscles **are located near** the pectoralis major?

T: The deltoid muscles **lie on** the shoulders and **are lateral to** the pectoralis major.

S: Right, I remember. And isn't the rectus abdominus **located near** the pectoralis major?

T: Exactly. The rectus abdominus **is inferior to** the pectoralis major and **extends from** the pectoralis major down to the bottom of the trunk. Do you remember what muscle **extends laterally from** the rectus abdominus?

S: I think it's the external oblique.

T: You've got it! I think you understand the location of the muscles now.

Look at the illustration of the human body below and read the examples that describe the locations of body structures on page 78. Pay attention to the phrases of location.

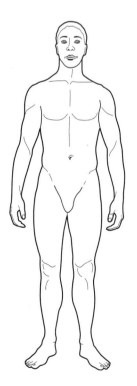

be superior to	The head <u>is superior to</u> the body trunk.
be inferior to	The body trunk <u>is inferior to</u> the head.
be anterior to	The nose <u>is anterior to</u> the ears.
be posterior to	The vertebrae <u>are posterior to</u> the sternum.
be medial to	The sternum <u>is medial to</u> the ribs.
be lateral to	The ribs <u>are lateral to</u> the sternum.
extend from ____ to ____	The arm <u>extends from</u> the shoulder <u>to</u> the hand.
lie between ____ and ____	The nose <u>lies between</u> the mouth <u>and</u> the eyes.
lie beneath	The muscles <u>lie beneath</u> the skin.
encircles	The eyelashes <u>encircle</u> the eyes.

PRACTICE

1. *Look at Figure 4.12 of the body's anterior muscles on page 71. Write questions asking about location. Walk around the classroom and ask at least two classmates your questions. For example:*

   Where are the pectoralis muscles located?

   Which muscle extends from behind the ear to the clavicle bone?

2. *Look again at the muscles on page 71. Work with a partner. Take turns touching each muscle with a pencil and stating its name and location. For example:*

   This is the rectus abdominus. It is in the medial part of the abdomen and extends from

   the ____ to the ____.

3. *These are authentic questions taken from an anatomy and physiology class. Use the vocabulary and grammar you know to answer the following questions. Ask your teacher to check your answers.*

   1. Describe the location of the frontalis muscle.
   2. Describe the location of the tibialis anterior muscle.
   3. Describe the location of the trapezius muscle.
   4. Describe the location of the biceps brachii muscle.
   5. Describe the location of the sternocleidomastoid muscle.

Using Mnemonics

All of the systems you study in anatomy and physiology contain many terms to memorize. Using mnemonics is a helpful way to memorize words that occur in groups. A common mnemonic technique is to take the first letters of the more difficult words you want to learn and from those letters create words that are easier to remember. For example, many people remember the names of the planets (Mercury, Venus, Earth, Mars, Jupiter, Saturn, Uranus, Neptune, Pluto), by creating this sentence: **M**y **V**ery **E**ducated **M**other **J**ust **S**erved **U**s **N**ine **P**izzas.

Suppose you want to memorize the names of the muscles in the anterior of the body. First, list the muscles. For example, going from the neck to the pelvis, the muscles are: sternocleidomastoid, deltoid, pectoralis major, intercostals, rectus abdominis, and external oblique. The first letters of each muscle are: s, d, p, i, r, e. To help you to remember the names of these muscles, you can make an amusing sentence, such as: Some (sternocleidomastoid) Ducks (deltoid) Produce (pectoralis major) Interesting (intercostals) Round (rectus abdominis) Eggs (external oblique). Your mnemonic sentence for remembering this muscle group is: Some Ducks Produce Interesting Round Eggs. Using the first letter of important terms like this to make an amusing sentence is a mnemonic device and makes learning fun.

PRACTICE

You have studied the muscles of the legs, head, anterior trunk and upper arm, and posterior trunk. Look at Figure 4.1 on page 60. Then follow these steps.

- Choose a group of muscles in an area of the body.

- Write down the muscles you need to learn in that area.

- Take the first letter of each muscle you've written down and develop a mnemonic.

- When you've finished your mnemonic, stand up and share it with four people in the class.

- After everyone sits down, your teacher will have several students write their mnemonic on the board. Then everyone in the class can vote for the funniest one, the strangest one, and the one that would be the easiest to remember.

FOCUS ON CULTURE

Alternative Medicine

Alternative medicine is becoming more popular in the United States. Many people, concerned with the high cost of prescription drugs and surgery, are turning to the medicine of other cultures for help. In Seattle, Washington, for example, Bastyr University trains people to become specialists in naturopathic medicine, acupuncture, and herbal medicine. Scientists at the university also do research to determine the effectiveness of such treatments, so these treatments will become more acceptable to American doctors and insurance companies.

The following story is about a cultural conflict that people may experience in a health-care setting. Read the story and then discuss the questions in small groups.

A woman in her early fifties was diagnosed with cancer. Instead of going to a medical doctor, she decided to heal her cancer by going to an herbalist. This particular herbalist told the woman to eat very large amounts of carrots, broccoli, and cabbage and to take large doses of vitamins. He also instructed her to sit quietly each day and imagine that the cancer was leaving her body. The woman believed in this treatment regime for her cancer. However, her daughter was very upset by her mother's treatment choice and pushed her to see an oncologist, a medical doctor specializing in cancer treatment.

1. What do you think about the mother's approach to treating her cancer?

2. What are some differences between an alternative doctor's training and a medical doctor's training? How many years does it take to become a medical doctor?

3. What kinds of alternative healers can be found in your country?

4. How does one become a healer?

Check Your Understanding

1. *Answer the following questions about the muscular system.*

   1. What is the function of skeletal muscle?
   2. Describe how a muscle is organized. Use the terms myofibril, muscle, myofilament, actin, myosin, fiber, and fascicle.
   3. Name the two types of proteins that comprise myofilaments and describe the appearance of each.
   4. How do skeletal muscles get the signal to move?
   5. Describe what happens within a myofibril when it gets the signal to contract.
   6. What is the name of the molecule that provides energy for muscle contraction?
   7. What is the difference (in terms of function) between cardiac muscle and skeletal muscle?
   8. What kinds of organs in the body contain smooth muscle tissue?
   9. What are two differences between cardiac muscles and skeletal muscles?
   10. Give an example of a skeletal muscle that is involuntary.
   11. Name three muscles in the leg.
   12. Name two muscles in the head.

2. *Label Figures 4.16 and 4.17 with the terms provided. One term will be used twice.*

actin	fiber	myofilaments	sarcomere
fascicle	myofibril	myosin	Z-line

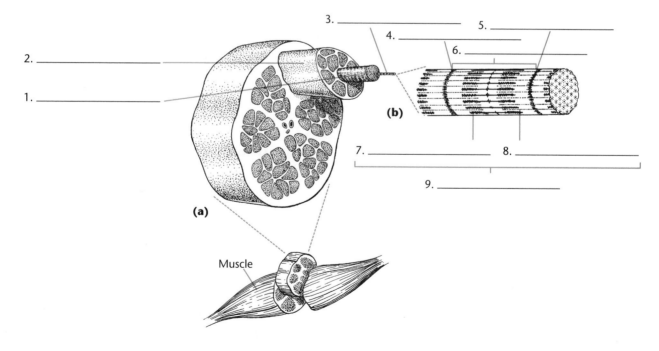

3. _____ 5. _____
4. _____ 6. _____
2. _____
1. _____
   (b)
7. _____ 8. _____
9. _____
(a)

Muscle

FIGURE 4.16   **Anatomy of muscle**

Achilles tendon	gastrocnemius	rectus femoris
biceps brachii	gluteus maximus	sartorius
biceps femoris	latissimus dorsi	temporalis
deltoid	masseter	tibialis anterior
external oblique	pectoralis major	trapezius
frontalis	rectus abdominis	triceps brachii

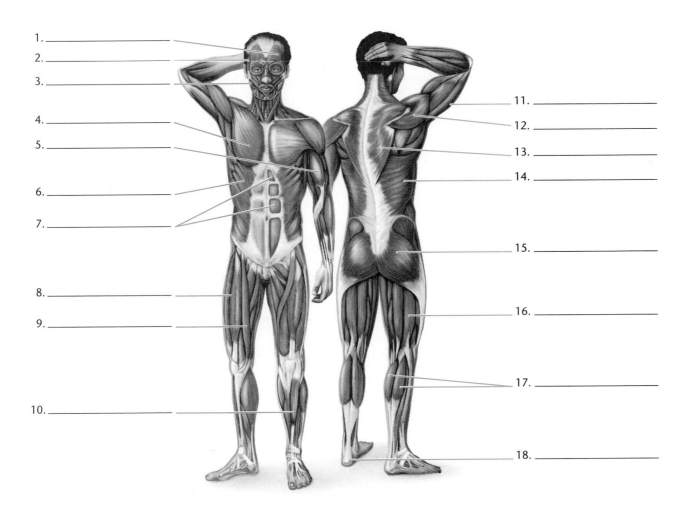

1. _____
2. _____
3. _____
4. _____
5. _____
6. _____
7. _____
8. _____
9. _____
10. _____

11. _____
12. _____
13. _____
14. _____
15. _____
16. _____
17. _____
18. _____

FIGURE 4.17   Muscular system

3. *Answer these typical anatomy and physiology quiz questions.*

1. Which muscle type is voluntary?
   a. skeletal   **b.** skeletal and cardiac   **c.** smooth

2. Which sequence lists the parts of a skeletal muscle in correct order from smallest to largest?
   a. muscle, myofilament, myofibril, fiber, fascicle
   b. fascicle, fiber, myofilament, myofibril, muscle
   c. myofilament, myofibril, fiber, fascicle, muscle
   d. myofibril, myofilament, fiber, fascicle, muscle

3. Explain the role of ATP in skeletal muscle contraction. What would happen if there were no ATP available?

4. What is the difference between a strain and a sprain?

5. What is ACh? Where is it made? What is its role in skeletal muscle contraction?

Think More about It

1. What part does muscle play when we eat and digest food?

2. What part does muscle play in the circulatory system?

3. Name three organ systems that seem to require muscles in order to function properly.

Word Bank		
acetylcholine	fiber	neurotransmitter
actin	flex	sarcomere
adenosine triphosphate	hamstring pull	skeletal muscle
bundle	inherit	smooth muscle
bend	motor neuron	sprain
cardiac muscle	muscular dystrophy	stimulate
contract	myofibril	transmit
extend	myofilament	Z-line
fascicle	myosin	

CHAPTER 5

The Nervous System, Part 1

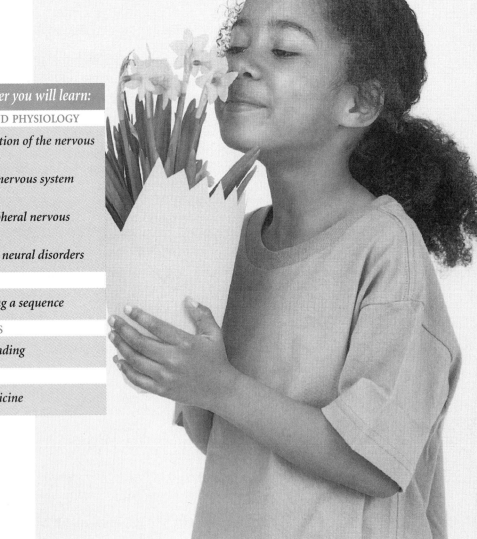

In this chapter you will learn:

ANATOMY AND PHYSIOLOGY

- *Organization of the nervous system*
- *How the nervous system works*
- *The peripheral nervous system*
- *Common neural disorders*

ENGLISH

- *Describing a sequence*

STUDY SKILLS

- *Active reading*

CULTURE

- *Folk medicine*

DID YOU KNOW *that messages sent along nerves may travel at speeds of up to 150 meters (492 feet) per second?*

INTRODUCTION

The nervous system is the main communication and decision-making system of the body. The brain, spinal cord, nerves, and sensory organs are all part of the nervous system. This chapter will discuss the organization of the nervous system, how a reflex occurs, and how neurons and nerves function. Chapter 6 will deal with the brain, spinal cord, and the autonomic nervous system.

1. *Work with a partner. Look at the diagram of the nervous system. Try to label the parts with the words in the box. Look at Figure 5.2 on page 87 to check your answers.*

> brain   nerves   spinal cord

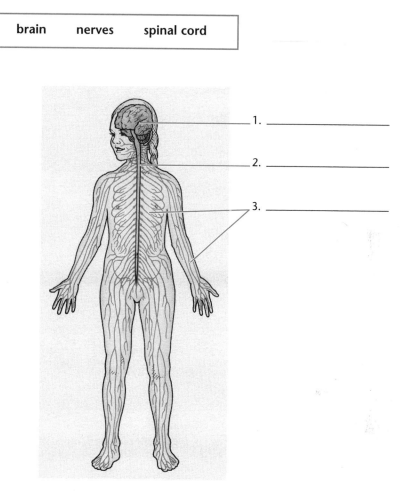

1. _____

2. _____

3. _____

FIGURE 5.1   **The nervous system**

2. *With your partner, try to answer these questions. If you do not know the answers, do not worry. You will find the answers as you read through this chapter.*

1. What is the function of the nervous system?

2. What are nerves and what is their function?

3. What do sensory organs do? Can you name one?

4. What is the name of the major cell type in the nervous system?

5. What happens in a reflex?

3. *Read each verb, its simple definition, and its passive voice form. Then fill in the verbs in the sentences that follow. Pay attention to verb tense and subject / verb agreement. Compare your answers with those of another student.*

BASE FORM	PASSIVE VOICE FORM	MEANING
deaden	be deadened	to cause to have no feeling
detect	be detected	to find or locate
excite	be excited	to stimulate

1. The body has methods to _____ when something is not working.

2. Neurotransmitters _____ muscles so that they contract.

3. Dentists _____ the tissue around a tooth before they drill.

THE ORGANIZATION OF THE NERVOUS SYSTEM

The nervous system is divided into two major areas, the central nervous system (CNS) and the peripheral nervous system (PNS).

The CNS and the PNS

The **central nervous system** (CNS) contains the brain and the spinal cord. The brain and spinal cord are the control centers of the body. The brain is in charge when you make decisions like where to go on vacation or what to eat for dinner. The spinal cord is in charge of most reflex decisions. Recall that a reflex is an automatic movement. For example, if your hand touches a hot stove, you automatically pull away from it.

The **peripheral** (pə′rɪfərəl) **nervous system** (PNS) contains the nerves that carry messages to and from the CNS. The PNS also contains sensory receptors. Sensory receptors are cells or parts of cells that feel things such as pain, heat, and pressure. For example, your fingers contain many sensory receptors. The PNS also contains sensory organs such as the ears, eyes, and nose. Your sensory receptors and sensory organs gather information and then send it along nerves to your brain and spinal cord.

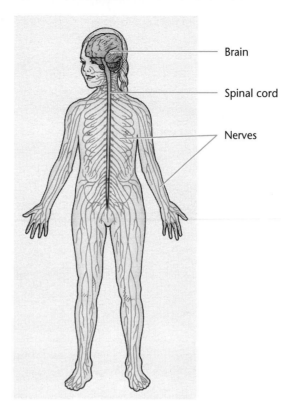

Brain

Spinal cord

Nerves

FIGURE 5.2   **The nervous system**

COMPREHENSION CHECK

Circle the correct word(s) to complete each sentence. Take turns reading the correct sentences aloud with a partner.

1. The central nervous system is comprised of the brain and **nerves / spinal cord**.

2. The part of the nervous system that makes decisions is the **CNS / PNS**.

3. **Nerves / Sensory receptors** carry messages to the CNS.

4. A **sensory receptor / sensory organ** is comprised of a single cell or part of a cell.

5. Nerves are part of the **CNS / PNS**.

The CNS and the PNS: A Story

The central nervous system (CNS) and the peripheral nervous system (PNS) have different jobs to do. The following story will show these differences.

One day, a man named Joe was cooking when his hand accidentally touched the stove. "Ouch!" he yelled. The sensory receptors (ends of the nerves) in Joe's finger felt pain and heat. These sensory receptors sent a message along a nerve to Joe's spinal cord. The spinal cord interpreted the message to mean: "Joe's hand felt pain and heat." The spinal cord then made a decision for Joe to move his hand away from the stove. The spinal cord sent that message along a nerve to the muscles in Joe's hand and arm, making those muscles contract. Joe had already moved his hand before realizing he was getting burned. This is an example of a spinal cord decision. The experience made Joe think about what had happened. "That was dumb. I'll be more careful next time." The decision to be more careful was made by the brain. Usually, automatic movements come from the spinal cord, while ideas are produced by the brain.

Remember, the spinal cord is often in charge of making reflex decisions. Obviously, Joe didn't have to think about removing his hand from the stove. Let's look at the steps of Joe's reflex.

1. Sensory receptors in his hand felt heat and pain. (PNS)
2. A message was sent along nerves (PNS) to the spinal cord (CNS).
3. The spinal cord (CNS) interpreted the message about the heat and pain in his hand and decided what to do.
4. After the spinal cord decided what to do, it sent a message along a nerve (PNS) to his hand and arm.
5. Muscles in his hand and arm contracted to move away from the stove.

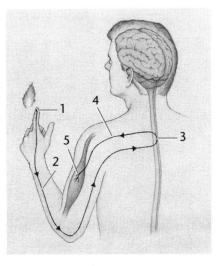

FIGURE 5.3   **A reflex. Sensory receptors in the finger detect pain and heat. A message is sent along nerves to the spinal cord, which decides to send a message along a nerve to the muscle that moves the hand away from the fire.**

The brain differs from the spinal cord in function. The brain is in charge of remembering information. A message about pain and heat went to Joe's brain. The message went to at least two places in his brain, the memory center (to remember not to touch the hot stove again) and the speech center (to direct him to say "Ouch!"). You will be learning more about the parts of the brain later.

COMPREHENSION CHECK

Circle the correct word(s) to complete each sentence. Take turns reading the correct sentences aloud with a partner.

1. The **sensory organs / sensory receptors** in Joe's hand felt pain and heat.
2. A message was sent along Joe's nerve to his **PNS / CNS**.
3. The **spinal cord / brain** made the reflex decision for Joe's hand to move.
4. Joe's **spinal cord / brain** will remind Joe to be more careful next time.
5. Only the brain is in charge of **reflexes / memory**.

HOW THE NERVOUS SYSTEM WORKS

To completely understand how the PNS and CNS function, it is necessary to first understand how the cells of the nervous system function.

Cells of the Nervous System

The major cell of the nervous system is the **neuron** ('nuwrɑn). There are many different kinds of neurons. **Motor neurons** send messages from the CNS to move muscles. **Sensory neurons** send messages to the CNS about what you see, smell, touch, taste, or hear. Most neurons have three parts.

1. The **cell body** is the widest part of the neuron. It contains most of the cell parts needed for the neuron to do its job. It is the decision-making part of the neuron.

2. The **dendrites** ('dɛndrayts) are short branches at one end of the cell body. Dendrites receive messages from other neurons and send these messages to the cell body.

3. The **axon** ('æksɑn) is a single long extension at the other end of the cell body. An axon can be as long as your arm or your leg! At the end of the axon, there are branches. These axon branches send messages from the axon to other neurons or to muscles.

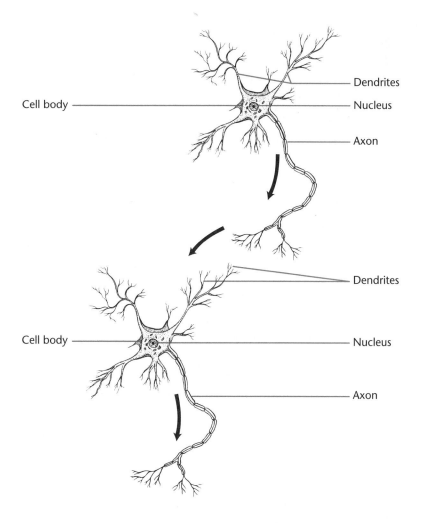

FIGURE 5.4   Neurons, with the cell parts and direction of message illustrated

Circle the letter of the correct word(s) to complete each sentence. Check your answers with those of a partner.

1. Motor neurons send messages from the CNS to _____.
   a. see   **b.** move muscles   **c.** smell   **d.** hear

2. Neurons are _____.
   a. molecules   **b.** organs   **c.** cells   **d.** tissues

3. The _____ of a neuron receives messages from other neurons.
   a. axon   **b.** cell body   **c.** dendrite   **d.** nucleus

4. You find neurons in the _____.
   a. brain   **b.** spinal cord   **c.** PNS   **d.** a, b, and c

5. There is usually only one _____ in the neuron, and it has branches at the end.
   a. axon   **b.** cell body   **c.** dendrite   **d.** nucleus

How a Neuron Sends a Message

Right now, you are reading. Sensory neurons in your eyes are sending messages to your brain. The neurons in your brain are interpreting what you are reading. Later, you might feel hungry. You feel hungry when neurons in your stomach send messages to your brain that the stomach is empty. Our neurons are always sending and receiving messages twenty-four hours a day, seven days a week.

To send a message, a neuron becomes *excited*. When a neuron gets excited, two molecules, sodium and potassium, move in and out of the neuron. Sodium and potassium cause an electrical current to form in the area between the neuron's cell body and axon. This area is like the fuse on a firecracker. Once you have enough flame to light the fuse, the fire burns all the way down the fuse to the firecracker. Likewise, in the area of the neuron where the cell body and axon connect, if enough sodium and potassium move, the "fuse is lit" and the electrical current is sent all the way down to the end of the neuron's axon.

When the electrical current reaches the end of the axon, it is in an area of the axon called the **synaptic** (sɪ′næptɪk) **end bulb**. In the synaptic end bulb, there are small sacs called **vesicles**. When the electrical current reaches the synaptic end bulb, it stimulates the vesicles to release a molecule called a **neurotransmitter**. It is interesting to note that neurons don't touch each other. (See Figure 5.5.) Therefore, the neurotransmitter must jump from the synaptic end bulb across this space to the dendrite of the next neuron. This space between the axon of one neuron and the dendrite of another is called a **synapse** (′sɪnæps).

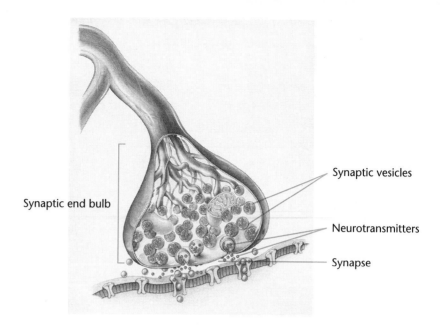

Synaptic end bulb

Synaptic vesicles

Neurotransmitters

Synapse

FIGURE 5.5   **A synapse. At the synaptic end bulb of the first neuron, synaptic vesicles are stimulated to release their neurotransmitters into the synapse. These neurotransmitters attach to receptors on the cell membrane of the second neuron below.**

There are **receptor molecules** on the dendrite of the second neuron and these receptors are waiting for the neurotransmitters. When the neurotransmitters attach to these receptors, another electrical signal is produced.

COMPREHENSION CHECK

1. *Put the steps of how a message is sent in order from 1 to 6. The first thing that happens is 1, and it is already done for you.*

    _____ An electrical current forms.

    __1__ Sodium and potassium move in and out of the neuron.

    _____ The vesicles release a neurotransmitter.

    _____ An electrical current is sent to the end of the neuron's axon.

    _____ The neurotransmitter jumps across the synapse and attaches to the receptor molecules of the next neuron.

    _____ The electrical current stimulates the vesicles.

2. *Complete the sentences using the words in the box. Take turns reading the correct sentences aloud with a partner.*

axon	receptor molecules	synaptic end bulb
dendrites	sodium and potassium	vesicles
neurotransmitter	synapse	

1. The end of an axon is called the _____.

2. A/An _____ is the space between neurons.

3. The two molecules that cause a neuron to get excited are _____.

4. _____ release a chemical that jumps to the next neuron.

5. The chemical that is sent from one neuron to the next is the _____.

6. The long branch of a neuron which messages travel down is called the _____.

7. Neurotransmitters attach to _____ after they jump the synapse.

8. The short branches of a neuron that receive messages are called _____.

Speed of Neural Messages

Not all neural messages move at the same speed. Some messages like those of a reflex (Joe taking his hand away from the hot stove), need to move more quickly than other messages (such as a message to tell your hand to reach for a book).

To help messages move more quickly, some neurons have a fatty insulation covering their axons (like a jacket). This fatty insulation is called a **myelin sheath** (ˈmayəlɪn ʃiyθ). These axons are called **myelinated** (insulated) though small areas of the axons are not insulated. Thus, these axons look like they are padded in parts. See the figure below.

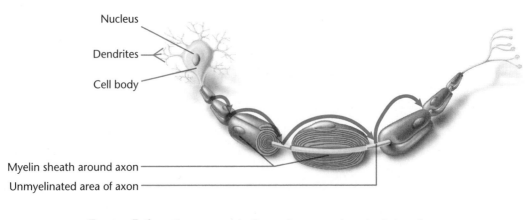

Nucleus

Dendrites

Cell body

Myelin sheath around axon

Unmyelinated area of axon

FIGURE 5.6   **The arrows indicate how an electrical signal is conducted along a myelinated axon.**

Messages move more quickly along myelinated axons because electricity can't travel on or in the myelin sheath. When an electrical message is traveling down an axon and comes into contact with a myelin sheath, it skips over it and lands on the next **unmyelinated** part of the axon. The message is thus able to move more quickly than if it had to travel down the whole axon.

To better understand the concept of myelination, imagine you are on a bus during rush hour driving on an unmyelinated street. Your bus has to stay on the street as it goes from stop to stop, picking up and dropping off passengers. It takes a long time before some passengers get home. Suddenly, however, the street becomes myelinated. The bus is then able to jump from stop to stop without having to travel on the street between the stops. It simply jumps over all of the traffic between the stops. You are able to get home very quickly because the street is myelinated between the bus stops.

Multiple Sclerosis (MS)! Sometimes, the body's defense cells begin to attack and destroy healthy cells without any clear reason. When this attack occurs on the myelin sheath around axons, it is called **multiple sclerosis** or **MS**. People with MS are losing the myelin sheaths around their axons, thus causing the speed of messages in the nervous system to slow down. This may make it harder for the person to move. Eventually, the signal is so slow that it results in **paralysis** (not able to move muscles) and even death if the diaphragm is paralyzed.

COMPREHENSION CHECK

Answer the questions below. Then compare your answers with those of a partner.

1. Do all neural messages move at the same speed?

2. What helps some messages move faster than others?

3. What is the fatty insulation called?

4. Are there areas on the myelinated axon that aren't insulated?

5. What do messages do when they come into contact with the myelin sheath?

6. What happens to someone with multiple sclerosis?

BUILDING LANGUAGE AND STUDY SKILLS

Describing a Sequence

In your study of anatomy and physiology, you will be asked to describe processes to show that you understand them. For example, you have learned the steps involved in a reflex. Look at this example of how a reflex process is described.

First, sensory receptors detect a **stimulus**. **After** detecting a **stimulus**, a message is sent along a neuron to the **spinal cord**. **The spinal cord then** interprets the message and decides what to do. **After** making a decision, **the spinal cord** sends its decision along another neuron to an **organ**. **When the organ** receives the message, it carries it out. The reflex is completed.

Notice how key words in the above paragraph are repeated in the next sentence. Also notice the time-sequencing words (first, after, next, then, finally). Repeating key words and using time-sequencing words is commonly done when describing a process.

1. *You have learned in this chapter how one neuron sends a message to another neuron. Below, the steps of how one neuron sends a message to another are out of order. Work in pairs to put the steps in order. After you have put the steps in order, practice using the sequencing language that you have learned. Be sure to repeat key words of one sentence in the next sentence and to use transition words.*

   _____ The vesicles release a neurotransmitter.

   _____ An electrical current forms.

   _____ The neurotransmitter jumps across the synapse and attaches to the receptor molecules of the next neuron.

   _____ An electrical current stimulates the vesicles.

   _____ Sodium and potassium move in and out of the neuron.

   _____ An electrical current is sent to the end of the axon.

2. *Recall the steps involved in a reflex. Write those steps out of order. Hand them to a partner. When you receive a list of steps from your partner, put them in order and write down the step-by-step process. Be sure to repeat key words of one sentence in the next sentence and to use transition words.*

3. *Exchange your writing with a partner. Take turns asking questions to make sure that you have understood the step-by-step process. These questions might include:*

   1. What happens first?

   2. What happens after _____?

   3. What happens after that?

   4. What happens next?

4. *These are authentic questions taken from an anatomy and physiology class. Use the vocabulary and grammar you know to answer these questions. Ask your teacher to check your answers.*

   1. When an electrical current reaches the end of the axon, what happens next?

   2. After the spinal cord makes a decision in a reflex, what happens next?

   3. What is the first step in a reflex pathway?

   4. List the steps in a reflex pathway.

Active Reading

There are several reading techniques you can learn to help you remember important information. They include: highlighting, note taking, and reading and reciting.

1. **Highlighting**

   Highlighting means to underline or highlight important information in a text with a highlighting pen. Highlighting pens come in a variety of colors such as pink, orange, and yellow. With your pen, you highlight the information that you need to learn. You should highlight important information the second time you read your text. That way you are sure what information is important. When you go back to study the text, you can then pay closest attention to the highlighted information rather than having to reread the entire text.

2. **Note taking**

   A good way to begin note taking is to read the selection once, then take notes as you read it a second time. Write your notes on a separate piece of paper. The notes should include the main points you want to learn. When you go back to study the text, you can then pay closest attention to the information that you have written in your notes.

3. **Reading and reciting**

   Reading and reciting means that you first read a section of text. For example, you might read a few sentences or a paragraph. You then look away and recite (say) aloud what you have read. To recite means to say again. It's always helpful to reread your text after you've recited it to make sure that you are able to remember all of the important points.

PRACTICE

Use the text below to practice each of the study techniques. Then, in small groups, discuss which of the three reading techniques you liked the best and why.

To send a message, a neuron becomes excited. When a neuron gets excited, two molecules, sodium and potassium, move in and out of the neuron. Sodium and potassium cause an electrical current to form in the area between the neuron's cell body and axon. If enough sodium and potassium are present, an electrical current is sent all the way down to the end of the axon.

When the electrical current reaches the end of the axon, it is in an area of the axon called the **synaptic end bulb**. In the synaptic end bulb, there are small sacs called **vesicles**. When the electrical current reaches the synaptic end bulb, it stimulates the vesicles to release a chemical called a **neurotransmitter**. It is interesting to note that neurons don't touch each other. (See Figure 5.5.) Therefore, the neurotransmitter must jump from the synaptic end bulb across this space to the dendrites of the next neuron. This space between the axon of one neuron and the dendrites of another is called a **synapse**.

THE PERIPHERAL NERVOUS SYSTEM

The peripheral nervous system (PNS) contains all of the nervous system components outside the brain and spinal cord. Recall that the PNS is comprised of nerves, sensory receptors, and sensory organs.

Nerves

Neurons are organized into larger structures called **nerves**. Neurons are cells; nerves are organs. Nerves are organized in a similar way to muscles. Recall that muscles are comprised of fascicles that are, in turn, comprised of bundles of muscle fibers. Nerves are also comprised of fascicles. The fascicles in nerves are comprised of dendrites and/or axons.

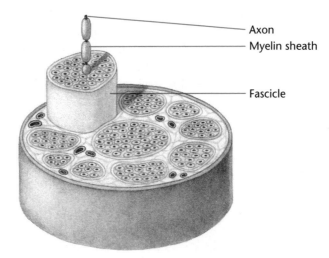

FIGURE 5.7   **This cross section of a nerve illustrates fascicles (bundles) of myelinated axons.**

Nerves are found in the peripheral nervous system (PNS). They form the connection between sensory receptors (for example, in the finger tip), the central nervous system (CNS), and organs. There are two major categories of nerves in the PNS: cranial nerves and spinal nerves.

Cranial ('kreyniyəl) **nerves** travel between the brain and other areas in the head. Even though these nerves are found in the head, they are still part of the PNS. All nerves are part of the PNS. There are twelve pairs of cranial nerves. These can be classified into three different types of nerves: sensory, motor, and mixed.

- **Sensory nerves** travel from a sensory receptor to the brain. For example, the optic nerve sends messages from the eye to the brain when you are reading. Sensory nerves carry "one-way" messages only. Another term for a sensory nerve is an **afferent** ('æfərənt) **nerve**. It is important to remember that <u>a</u>fferent nerves <u>a</u>pproach the CNS. Look at Figure 5.8 to see a sensory nerve.

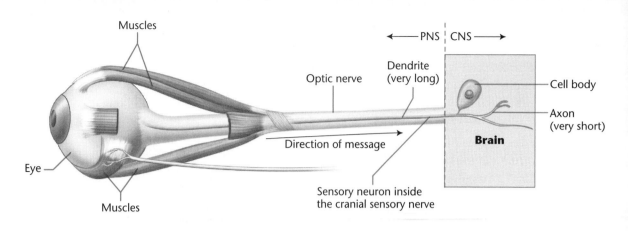

FIGURE 5.8   Sensory nerves, such as the optic nerve, carry "one-way" messages to the CNS. The cell body and axon of the sensory neuron are located in the CNS, while the dendrite is located in the PNS.

- **Motor nerves** travel from the brain to a muscle or gland in the head. Messages are also "one-way" but travel in the opposite direction of sensory nerves. For example, the oculomotor nerve sends messages from the brain to the muscles of the eye. It contains motor neurons and is important in controlling eye movement (directing your eye to look at something). Another term for a motor nerve is an **efferent** ('ɛfərənt) **nerve**. It is important to remember that <u>e</u>fferent nerves <u>e</u>xit the CNS.

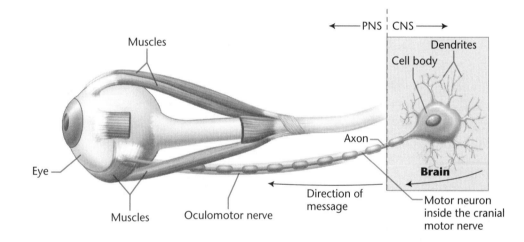

FIGURE 5.9   Motor nerves, such as the oculomotor nerve, carry "one-way" messages from the CNS. The cell body and dendrites of the motor neuron are located in the CNS, while the axon is located in the PNS.

- **Mixed nerves** (see Figure 5.10) carry messages in both directions. This means that some of the neurons in the nerve carry messages from the brain to the muscles (efferent motor neurons), while other neurons in the same nerve carry messages from sensory receptors to the brain (afferent sensory neurons). The facial nerve is an example of this type of nerve. The facial nerve sends messages about what you taste to the brain. The facial nerve also carries messages from the brain to skeletal muscles of the face telling you to smile (when you like the food). The facial nerve has both afferent and efferent neurons, so it's a mixed nerve.

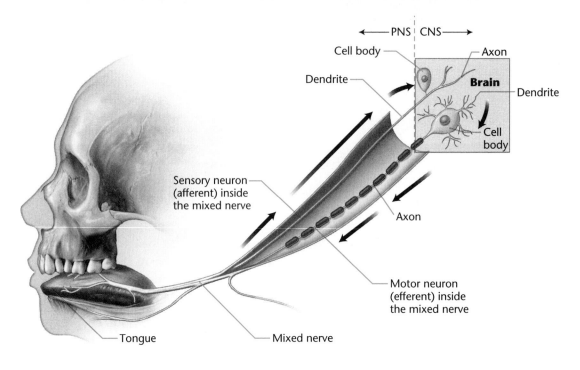

FIGURE 5.10 Mixed nerves carry "two-way" messages, both to the CNS (along sensory neurons) and from the CNS (along motor neurons).

Spinal nerves travel between the spinal cord and the rest of the body. There are 31 pairs of spinal nerves that attach to the spinal cord. Spinal nerves are always mixed nerves. Recall that mixed nerves send messages both to and from the CNS. A particular spinal nerve carries messages from a specific area of the body to the spinal cord. It also carries messages from the spinal cord to the muscles in that area of the body. For example, branches of three spinal nerves join together to form the femoral nerve. When you touch the front of your thigh, this nerve has afferent neurons sending messages to the brain. The femoral nerve also has efferent neurons that send messages from the brain to the quadriceps muscles so that you can walk.

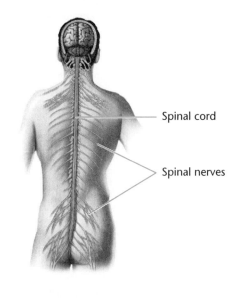

FIGURE 5.11 Spinal nerves travel between the spinal cord and various areas of the body.

COMPREHENSION CHECK

1. *Circle the correct word(s) to complete each sentence. Take turns reading the correct sentences aloud with a partner.*

   1. There are **31 / 12** pairs of cranial nerves.

   2. All cranial nerves connect the brain with places in the **head / body trunk**.

   3. Another term for a sensory nerve is **efferent / afferent**.

   4. All sensory nerves carry messages **to / from** the brain.

   5. Motor nerves send messages **to / from** the brain.

   6. Another term for a motor nerve is **afferent / efferent**.

   7. Both motor nerves and sensory nerves carry messages **one way / two ways**.

   8. Mixed nerves carry messages **one way / two ways**.

   9. Efferent nerves **approach / exit** the CNS.

   10. All **cranial / spinal** nerves are mixed nerves.

   11. Spinal nerves carry **afferent / efferent / two-way** messages.

   12. The brain connects directly with **cranial / spinal** nerves.

2. *Match the terms with their definitions by writing the letters in the correct blanks. Then compare your answers with those of a partner.*

   _____ 1. afferent nerves   **a.** travel away from CNS

   _____ 2. cranial nerves   **b.** are found in the head

   _____ 3. efferent nerves   **c.** travel both to and from CNS

   _____ 4. mixed nerves   **d.** connect with the spinal cord

   _____ 5. spinal nerves   **e.** travel to the CNS

Sensory Receptors and Organs

In order for a nerve to send a message to the CNS, something must first stimulate a sensory receptor. There are two types of **sensory receptors**. Sensory receptors can be the ends of neurons (for example, pain receptors in your finger), or they can be entire cells that are part of a sensory organ (for example, cells in the eye or ear). The role of sensory receptors is to detect a stimulus, such as heat, pain, chemicals (as in taste or smell), light rays, sound waves, or pressure. The following are some examples of sensory organs and their receptors.

The **eye** is a sensory organ. In the eye, there are two types of sensory receptor cells. They are the rods and cones, found in the layer of cells called the **retina** (ˈrɛtənə). **Rods** are primarily for sharpness of vision while **cones** are important in color vision, your ability to see in color.

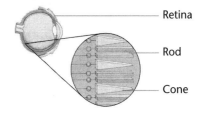

Retina

Rod

Cone

FIGURE 5.12   **The eye**

FIGURE 5.13   **The retina contains rods and cones, the sensory receptor cells for vision.**

Children in many countries have their hearing and vision checked at school every year.

The **ear** is another sensory organ. In the ear, there are two basic types of sensory receptors. The **cochlea** (ˈkowkliyə) is an area inside the ear that looks like a snail. The cochlea contains the sensory receptors for hearing. Another area inside the ear is called the **vestibular apparatus** (vɛˈstɪbyələr æpəˈrætəs). The vestibular apparatus contains sensory receptors for position and balance. These cells detect the position of your head and the direction your body is moving. For example, the vestibular apparatus detects when you are walking forward, when you stop, and when you spin around in a circle.

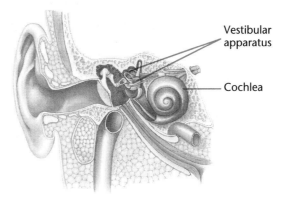

FIGURE 5.14   **The ear**

The **skin** is also considered a sensory organ. In the skin, there are many different types of sensory receptors. These sensory receptors are the tips of neurons. They are labeled in Figure 5.15. Not all sensory receptors in the skin can sense the same thing. Some sense pressure, some sense heat, some sense pain, and others sense position.

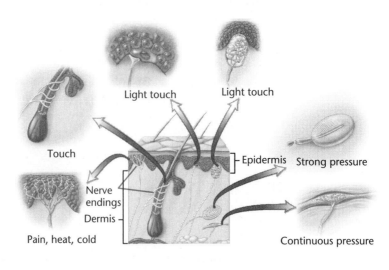

FIGURE 5.15   **Sensory receptors in the skin**

Anesthesia! During surgery, **anesthesia** (ænəs'θiyʒə) is often used to prevent the patient from feeling any pain. The chemicals used in anesthesia usually prevent the sensory receptors from sending messages to the CNS. When the CNS doesn't receive any messages from these receptors, no pain is felt. There are two types of anesthesia. One type of anesthesia is called **local anesthesia**. A local anesthetic is used to *deaden* the pain over a small area such as having a cavity filled in your tooth or if you are getting stitches for a cut on your finger. **General anesthesia** is used when the doctor wants to "put you to sleep," so no pain is felt anywhere in the body. In this case, the anesthetic is put into the bloodstream where it works to prevent most messages from being sent. The person loses consciousness, basically falling into a deep sleep.

COMPREHENSION CHECK

1. *Read the questions and then scan the text for answers. When you find the answers underline them. Then work with a partner and take turns asking and answering the questions. Try to remember the answers without looking back at the text.*

    1. What are three examples of a stimulus?

    2. What are the two forms that sensory receptors can take?

    3. Where are the rods and cones located in the eyes?

    4. Are rods and cones cells or the tips of neurons?

    5. How many basic types of sensory receptors are in the ears?

    6. What is the function of the cells in the cochlea?

    7. What is the name of the area in the ear which has the function of sensing position and balance?

    8. In the skin, do all sensory receptors detect the same type of stimulus?

    9. Are sensory receptors in the skin cells or the end of neurons?

    10. What is the difference between general and local anesthesia?

2. *Complete the sentences using the words in the box. Take turns reading the correct sentences aloud with a partner.*

---

cochlea	**sensory receptors**	**vestibular apparatus**
rods and cones	**stimulus**	

---

1. This structure helps you to keep your balance. _____

2. These are the sensory receptors in your eyes. _____

3. Heat, pain, and pressure are examples of this. _____

4. They are either in the form of cells or the tips of neurons.
   _____

5. This is the structure in the ear where hearing takes place.
   _____

Folk Medicine

Folk medicine was the way people remained healthy and overcame illness long before the beginning of modern medicine. Today, in many parts of the world, many people still prefer to take folk remedies to remain healthy or to treat illness. Some folk medicine developed thousands of years ago based on human experiences with the natural environment. Folk remedies include different forms of touch or heat, contacting spiritual forces, and herbal medicines (medicines from plants).

Traditionally in China, health is defined as a state of physical and spiritual harmony with nature. In ancient China, doctors had two tasks. The first task was to keep their patients healthy. In fact, patients paid their doctor to keep them healthy. However, when patients got sick, the doctor wasn't paid and the doctor actually had to provide treatment for free and pay for the patient's medication until the patient got well. Also in traditional Chinese medicine, an illness in one organ is not just examined in that organ. Other organs and parts of the body are treated as well. For example, an illness in the kidneys is thought to be controlled by the heart. Also, like most people in the world, many Chinese don't like the idea of having surgery. They feel that surgery is too invasive. They also don't like tests that involve drawing blood because they believe that blood means life and to lose blood means to lose a bit of one's life force.

1. *The following story is about a cultural conflict that people may experience in a health-care setting. Read the story and then discuss the questions in small groups.*

Mr. Yu went to a Western doctor complaining about pain in his kidneys. The doctor ordered many tests that included blood and urine tests, which made Mr. Yu very uncomfortable and upset. The doctor was confused by Mr. Yu's reaction to these tests. After diagnosing Mr. Yu with kidney stones, the doctor suggested that he would need surgery. Mr. Yu refused the surgery, and instead, decided to go to a traditional Chinese doctor. The Chinese doctor treated Mr. Yu with acupuncture, moxibustion (using cups which provide suction on various parts of the body), and some special herbs.

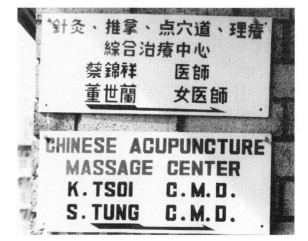

1. Why do you think Mr. Yu was upset about the tests and refused the surgery?

2. How would you react to Mr. Yu if you were the Western doctor?

3. Do you think that folk medicine works?

2. *The table on page 103 shows some common folk remedies for certain illnesses. These remedies are common in many parts of the world. For example, the concept of illnesses being caused by fate or bad luck is common among many Native Americans as well as certain religious groups. Work in groups of three. Take turns reading the table aloud and then discuss the questions that follow.*

FOLK REMEDY	BELIEVED CAUSE OF THE ILLNESS	EXAMPLE
Acupuncture: Needles are used to stimulate lines going from place to place in the body.	There's an imbalance in the "chi." Chi is the body's life force energy. A person can have strong chi or weak chi.	A person suffering from a kidney disorder might receive 20 needles inserted in locations from his toes to the top of his head.
Hot / cold / wet / dry balance: To restore health, the balance among these elements must be restored.	One of the four elements is stronger than the others.	After a woman has a baby (a hot experience), she can't eat pork (a hot food).
Strong emotional states: To restore health, people visit folk healers, shrines, or offer prayers.	A strong emotional state can cause the soul to leave the body and wander freely. This may result in depression, lack of interest in one's appearance, and lack of sleep.	A person who is suffering from depression is instructed to visit a shrine, light candles, and make promises to saints.
"The evil eye": The person who caused the illness cares for the person he or she made ill.	Too much admiration from another person can cause an illness.	A baby is overly admired by a stranger and becomes sick.
Resignation: The person is still cared for by friends and family, and may see a folk healer.	Illness is the result of something that has happened in the past or something that will happen in the future.	A person gets sick after causing a friend to get a divorce.

1. Do you or people in your culture believe in any of these folk remedies?

2. How would you react if a person came to you for treatment and had a belief in something from the table above that you didn't agree with?

3. Do any of these folk remedies seem like they should be integrated into Western medicine?

Check Your Understanding

1. *Answer the following questions about the nervous system.*

    1. What is the function of the nervous system?

    2. Which organs are part of the CNS? Which organs are part of the PNS?

    3. Name the five steps in a reflex.

    4. Is a neuron part of a nerve, or is a nerve part of a neuron?

    5. Name three parts of a neuron and explain what each part does.

    6. How do messages travel between two neurons?

    7. How does myelin affect messages traveling in the nervous system?

    8. What is the difference between cranial and spinal nerves?

    9. What type of nerve is always mixed?

    10. Name the two forms that sensory receptors can take.

    11. Do sensory receptors stimulate efferent or afferent neurons?

2. *Label Figures 5.16 and 5.17 with the terms provided.*

axon	cell body	dendrite	nucleus

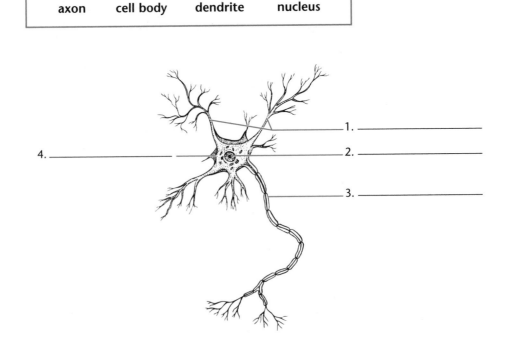

1. _____

2. _____

3. _____

4. _____

FIGURE 5.16   **A neuron**

neurotransmitter	synapse	synaptic end bulb	vesicle

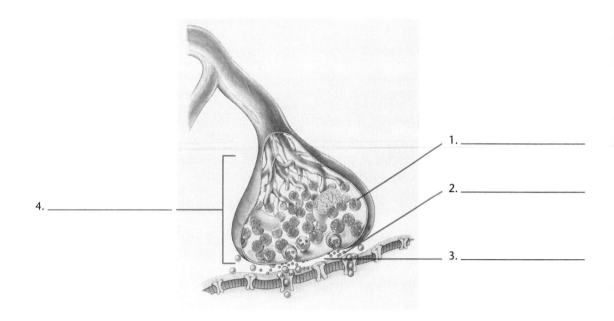

4. _____

1. _____

2. _____

3. _____

Figure 5.17   A synapse

3. *Answer these typical anatomy and physiology quiz questions.*

_____ **1.** Is this true or false? Sensory nerves carry efferent messages.

_____ **2.** Is this true or false? Unmyelinated axons transmit messages more slowly than myelinated axons.

3. Circle the correct term. A **sensory / motor** neuron tells a skeletal muscle fiber to contract.

4. In a typical nervous system pathway, the afferent neuron would send a message to:
   a. the motor neuron   **c.** the effector organ
   b. the sensory receptor   **d.** the CNS

5. Which of these is the sensory receptor in the eye?
   a. taste buds   **b.** rods and cones   **c.** vesicles   **d.** neurons

6. A particular cranial nerve only sends messages from the ear to the brain. It is a
_____ nerve.
   a. sensory   **b.** motor   **c.** mixed

7. Number the structures in the order in which a reflex message is sent. The place where the reflex begins should be numbered 1.

_____ CNS   _____ skeletal muscle fiber   _____ motor neuron

_____ sensory receptor   _____ sensory neuron

Think More about It

1. What kind of things would the nervous system control in the digestive system?

2. What kind of things would the nervous system control in the muscular system?

3. What kind of things would the nervous system control in the cardiovascular system?

Word Bank		
axon	mixed nerve	process
cell body	motor nerve	reflex
central nervous system	myelin sheath	sensory nerve
deaden	nerve	sensory receptor
dendrites	neuron	synapse
detect	neurotransmitter	synaptic end bulb
excite	peripheral nervous system	vesicles

CHAPTER 6

The Nervous System, Part 2

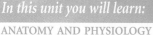
In this unit you will learn:

ANATOMY AND PHYSIOLOGY

- *The central nervous system: parts of the brain and the spinal cord*
- *The autonomic nervous system*
- *Common CNS disorders*

ENGLISH

- *Stating and asking about differences*

STUDY SKILLS

- *Forming a study group*

CULTURE

- *Making progress in health care*

DID YOU KNOW *that the human brain weighs about 1.4 kilograms (3 pounds) and that the neurons in your brain must have oxygen and glucose (a simple sugar) to survive?*

INTRODUCTION

In Chapter 5, you learned about the organization of the nervous system. You learned that neurons are the main cells of the nervous system, and their axons are bundled together to form nerves. Recall that nerves, along with sensory receptors, are part of the peripheral nervous system. The central nervous system consists of the brain and spinal cord. In this chapter, you will learn more about the parts of the brain and spinal cord, and how the nervous system controls the function of organs.

1. *Look at the diagram of the brain. Then answer the questions that follow.*

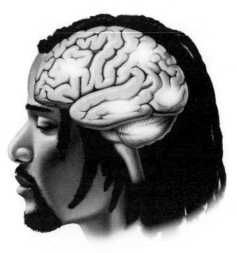

FIGURE 6.1   The human brain

1. Name one part of the brain.

2. The brain connects at its lower end to the _____.

3. Point to the part of the brain that you think will help you interpret what you hear.

2. *With a partner, try to answer these questions. If you do not know the answers, do not worry. You will find the answers as you read through this chapter.*

1. What are some of the functions of the brain?

2. What are some of the functions of the spinal cord?

3. What protects the brain?

4. How does the nervous system help to control your heart rate and your digestion?

3. *Some of the verbs you will see in this unit have been introduced in Chapter 5 and some are new. Use the verbs in the box to complete the sentences that follow. Pay attention to verb tense and subject / verb agreement. Compare your answers with those of another student.*

deaden	detect	excite	sort out

1. Sensory receptors _____ a stimulus.

2. When an electrical current forms on a neuron, it is said to be _____.

3. Anesthetics are used to _____ sensation in an area of the body.

4. Parts of the CNS _____ neural messages that come from all over the body and send them to the correct areas of the brain for interpretation.

THE CNS

Recall from Chapter 5 that the central nervous system contains the brain and the spinal cord. The job of both the brain and the spinal cord is to receive messages and make decisions. When Joe touched the hot stove, the sensory neurons in his hand sent a message to his spinal cord. His spinal cord then made the decision for him to pull his hand away from the stove. Another message was sent to Joe's brain for him to remember to be more careful next time. Recall that both parts of the central nervous system receive messages, but they react to the messages differently. The spinal cord is mostly in charge of reflexes. The brain is mostly in charge of things like thinking, language, and memory.

The Spinal Cord

The spinal cord rests inside the vertebral column (spine). The spinal cord extends from the back of your head all the way to your tailbone. If the spinal cord is damaged, a person can become paralyzed because messages won't be able to be sent from the spinal cord to the rest of the body. Therefore, the spinal cord needs to be protected. The spinal cord is protected by several layers of connective tissue, some of which are as tough as leather, and by the bony vertebrae that make up the vertebral column.

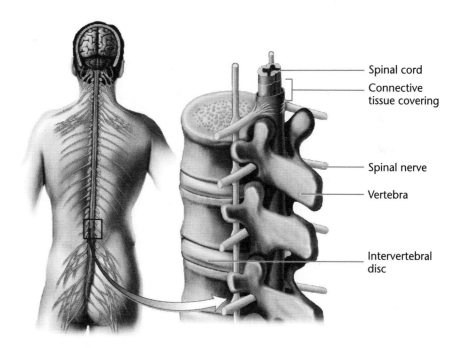

FIGURE 6.2   **The spinal cord travels through central openings in the vertebrae, with spinal nerves exiting through holes at the sides between the vertebrae.**

The spinal cord has two main functions. First, the spinal cord is just like a freeway. Neural messages travel along the spinal cord from the body to the brain and from the brain to the body. The other function of the spinal cord is to make reflex decisions.

A cross section of the spinal cord is shown in the center of Figure 6.3. It looks like a piece of bread cut from a loaf.

There are two different areas in the cross section of the spinal cord. Look at Figure 6.3. The darker, butterfly-shaped area of the spinal cord is the **gray matter**. Gray matter is where decision-making occurs.

In the area outside the butterfly-shaped region is the **white matter**. It is white because its myelinated axons contain fat which is white. The white matter is the freeway going up and down the spinal cord to the brain and the peripheral nerves. Recall that myelinated axons make the messages travel quickly.

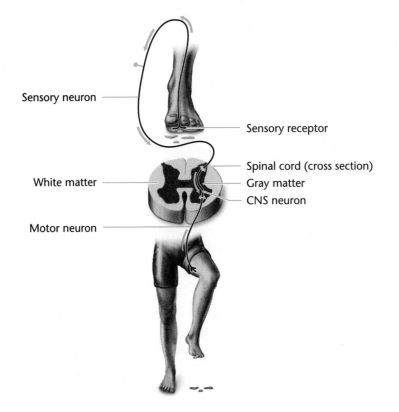

Sensory neuron

Sensory receptor

Spinal cord (cross section)
White matter
Gray matter
CNS neuron

Motor neuron

FIGURE 6.3 **A cross section through the spinal cord illustrating a reflex pathway. A sensory receptor detects pain when the foot steps on glass. This causes a message to be sent along the sensory neuron to the spinal cord. The CNS neuron in the spinal cord interprets the message and causes a message to be sent along a motor neuron to the muscles in the leg. The person lifts his foot.**

COMPREHENSION CHECK

1. *Answer the questions below. Then compare your answers with those of partner.*

   1. Where is your spinal cord located?

   2. What are the two main functions of the spinal cord?

   3. Why can damage to your spinal cord cause paralysis?

   4. How strong is the connective tissue that protects the spinal cord?

   5. Why are many reflex decisions made in the spinal cord and not in the brain?

   6. Are reflex decisions made in the white matter or in the gray matter?

   7. What makes the white matter white?

   8. How does the function of white matter differ from gray matter?

2. *Label Figure 6.4 with the following structures. Try not to look at Figure 6.3 on page 110.*

CNS neuron	motor neuron	sensory receptor
gray matter	sensory neuron	white matter

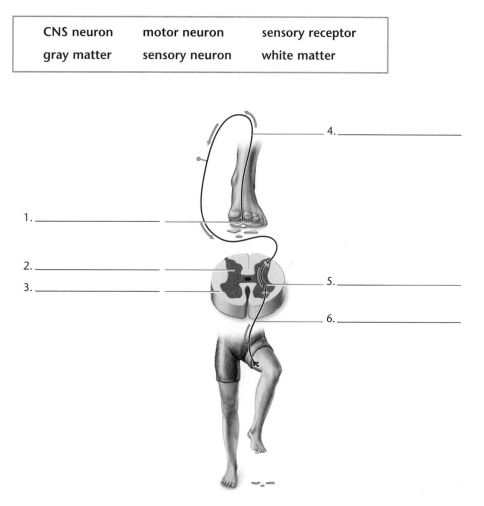

1. _____

2. _____

3. _____

4. _____

5. _____

6. _____

FIGURE 6.4   The reflex pathway

The Brain

The other portion of the CNS is the brain. Like the spinal cord, the brain also needs protection. It is protected by the skull and tough connective tissue layers located between the skull and the brain tissue.

As in the spinal cord, gray and white matter are also present in the brain. Gray matter is the outer layer of brain tissue. Gray matter contains neurons. It is where interpretation, thought, and conscious decision-making occurs. A conscious decision is when you know what you are thinking, like when you decide to get a glass of water.

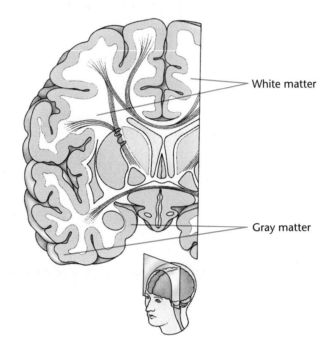

White matter

Gray matter

FIGURE 6.5 **Section of brain tissue showing the gray matter on the outside and white matter on the inside**

Beneath the gray matter is white matter. White matter contains only myelinated axons. These axons carry messages to and from all of the different areas of the brain, just like the white matter in the spinal cord carries messages up and down the spinal cord. These axons are myelinated, so messages can travel quickly throughout the brain.

The brain is a more complex organ than the spinal cord. It has more anatomical structures and complex functions than the spinal cord. There are two large regions in the brain, the **cerebrum** (sə′riybrəm) and the **cerebellum** (sɛrə′bɛləm).

The Cerebrum

The biggest region of the brain is called the cerebrum. It contains billions of neurons. The cerebrum is where conscious thought occurs. Remember, conscious thought is when you are aware of what you are thinking. For example, right now you are aware that you are reading about the brain. Other functions of the cerebrum include interpreting information from your senses (such as recognizing a person's face) or feeling emotions (such as happiness or fear).

The cerebrum is divided into separate areas called lobes. Each lobe in the cerebrum has specific functions. Note that each lobe is named for the bone under which it is located.

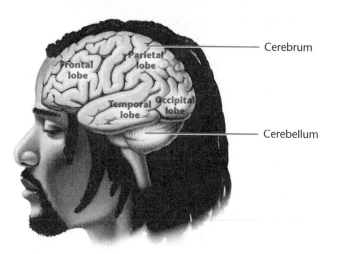

FIGURE 6.6   The cerebrum and cerebellum. The four different lobes of the cerebrum are labeled.

- **The frontal lobe** controls motor (skeletal muscle) activity. The frontal lobe has other roles as well, such as controlling motivation (wanting to do something) and judgment.

- **The temporal** (′tɛmpərəl) **lobe** is important in memory. It also interprets messages that come from your ears. Notice that it is the lobe closest to your ears.

- **The parietal** (pə′rɑyətəl) lobe interprets most of the sensory information that comes from the skin and internal organs. It also interprets information about pain and the position of your body.

- **The occipital** (ɑk′sɪpətl) **lobe** is important in interpreting information that you see. Notice how far this lobe is from your eyes.

> **Alzheimer's Disease!** A person with Alzheimer's (′ɑltshaymərz) disease has a gradual loss of memory, especially about recent events. Alzheimer's patients can also have changeable moods and a short attention span. It is not yet known exactly what causes this to occur, but there is definitely damage to the neurons in the brain.

The Cerebellum

The other large region of the brain is the cerebellum. The cerebellum is important in maintaining balance. You need balance to climb stairs or to walk on an icy sidewalk. The cerebellum receives messages about your body's muscle positions. After interpreting those messages, it communicates with the frontal lobe of the cerebrum to help you make decisions about movement. For example, if you are walking on an icy sidewalk and you want to be careful, the cerebrum tells your muscles to make small strong steps. But it does so only after interpreting information sent from the cerebellum about muscle position.

1. *Each lobe of the cerebrum carries out specific functions. Work with a partner. Put a check mark (✓) in the correct column.*

Function	Frontal Lobe	Temporal Lobe	Parietal Lobe	Occipital Lobe
Interpret touch	☐	☐	☐	☐
Control skeletal muscles	☐	☐	☐	☐
Interpret what you hear	☐	☐	☐	☐
Interpret what you see	☐	☐	☐	☐

2. *Label Figure 6.7 with the following structures. Try not to look at Figure 6.6 on page 113.*

cerebellum	occipital lobe	temporal lobe
frontal lobe	parietal lobe	

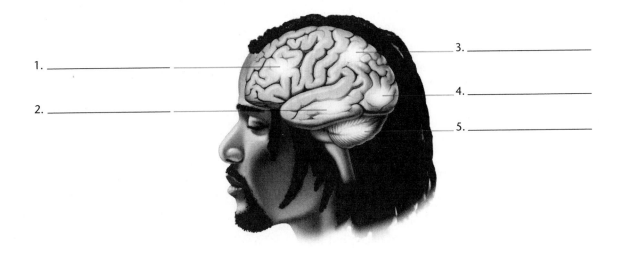

1. _____

2. _____

3. _____

4. _____

5. _____

FIGURE 6.7   **The human brain**

The Diencephalon

The brain is a very complex organ. In addition to the two large regions of the brain (the cerebrum and the cerebellum), there are other regions that are equally important.

The **diencephalon** (dayɛn'sɛfələn) is the name given to an area in the brain that contains four major parts. Each part has a distinct function and is very important for your survival. Damage to the diencephalon could result in death.

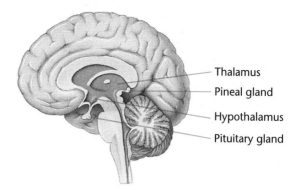

FIGURE 6.8 **The parts of the diencephalon**

- The **thalamus** ('θæləməs) is a central brain region that is important as a relay station for sensory messages arriving from all over the body. A relay station is like a big train station. Trains arrive at the station from different places and later, when these trains depart, they all travel to different destinations. Sensory messages arrive at the thalamus from sensory organs and receptors. The thalamus helps to send these messages to where they need to go in the cerebrum. For instance, when the sensory message is from the ear, the thalamus makes sure it goes to the part of the temporal lobe that interprets what you hear. When a sensory message comes from the eye, the thalamus makes sure it goes to the occipital lobe. Without the thalamus, the sensory messages wouldn't get *sorted out* and sent to the correct place for interpretation.

- The **hypothalamus** (haypow'θæləməs) lies just below the thalamus. The hypothalamus regulates body temperature, food and water intake, and helps to control heart rate, blood pressure, breathing rate, and digestion. The hypothalamus helps to control many of the processes we consider automatic. Without the hypothalamus, a person would die.

- The **pituitary** (pɪ'tuwətɛriy) **gland** makes many essential hormones. These hormones include growth hormone (controls bone growth) and hormones that regulate other glands (for example, thyroid, ovaries, testes, adrenal). The pituitary gland also plays a role in secreting hormones made in the hypothalamus that are important in childbirth and water homeostasis. If a person did not have a pituitary gland, he would have to take all of the hormones it makes as separate drugs.

- The **pineal** ('pɪniyəl) **gland** is thought to maintain the body's awareness of the passage of time (the "body clock"). Scientists suggest that the pineal gland produces a hormone called **melatonin** (mɛlə'townɪn) which helps to regulate the body's sense of time. Not many people get injuries to the pineal gland because it is so deep within the brain; therefore, scientists don't know much about what the pineal gland does. Studying the effect of injuries to a particular part of the brain often tells scientists what that area does. Thus, the function of the pineal gland is still part mystery today.

Jet Lag! When a person flies to a different part of the world, it often takes a few days to adjust to the different time in that new location. Some people take melatonin as a way to help the body clock adjust to the new time more easily. However, scientists are still not sure whether this remedy really works.

1. *Circle the letter of the correct answer. Check your answers with those of a partner.*

1. When sensory messages go to the thalamus, what happens?
   a. The thalamus sends the messages to the spinal cord.
   b. The thalamus sends the messages to the correct part of the cerebrum.
   c. The thalamus interprets them and makes decisions.
   d. The thalamus sends all of the messages to the cerebellum.

2. What are two things that the hypothalamus regulates?
   a. walking and sleeping
   b. heart rate and body temperature
   c. heart rate and posture
   d. body clock and balance

3. The pituitary gland _____.
   a. makes hormones that control bone growth and regulate other glands
   b. controls breathing and heart rate
   c. tells muscles when to move
   d. controls food and water balance

4. The pineal gland seems to help with _____.
   a. maintaining the body's water balance
   b. sorting out sensory messages
   c. awareness of time
   d. regulating heart rate and breathing

2. *Each area of the diencephalon is different. Work with a partner to write the correct information in the chart below. (Only two of the four structures secrete hormones.)*

	Thalamus	**Hypothalamus**	**Pituitary gland**	**Pineal gland**
Location				
Function				
Hormone(s) secreted				

The Brainstem

The other smaller region of the brain is called the **brainstem**. The brainstem is a "superhighway" that connects the brain and the spinal cord. Nearly all messages going to and from the brain must go through the brainstem. All parts of the brainstem are important for your survival.

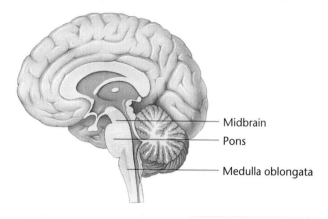

Midbrain

Pons

Medulla oblongata

FIGURE 6.9   **The parts of the brainstem**

The brainstem has three parts.

- The **midbrain** lies just below / behind the thalamus. The midbrain controls reflexes relating to sight and hearing. For instance, if someone throws a ball at your face, you blink your eyes. This is a visual reflex. While the spinal cord is responsible for almost all reflexes, the reflex decision to blink your eyes came from the midbrain.

- The **pons** (pɑnz) lies below the midbrain. The pons helps to make sure that you breathe very smoothly.

- The **medulla oblongata** (mɛ′duwlə ɑblɑŋ′gɑtə) (or just **medulla**) lies between the pons and the spinal cord. The medulla is extremely important in maintaining homeostasis of heart rate, blood pressure, breathing, as well as coughing, sneezing, swallowing, and vomiting.

Brainstem Injury! An injury to the brainstem is usually quite serious because the brainstem is so important in maintaining proper cardiovascular and respiratory function. Such an injury can result in death.

COMPREHENSION CHECK

1. *Work with a partner to label each statement true (T) or false (F). If the statement is false, correct it so that it is true.*

_____ **1.** The brainstem connects the brain and the spinal cord.

_____ **2.** All messages going to the brain pass through the brainstem.

_____ **3.** A brainstem injury can make it harder to control the heart.

_____ **4.** The midbrain is a relay station for sensory messages.

_____ **5.** The medulla maintains homeostasis of many body functions.

_____ **6.** The pons is located above the midbrain.

2. *Label Figure 6.10 with the following structures. Try not to look at Figures 6.8 and 6.9 on pages 115 and 117.*

hypothalamus	midbrain	pituitary gland	thalamus
medulla	pineal gland	pons	

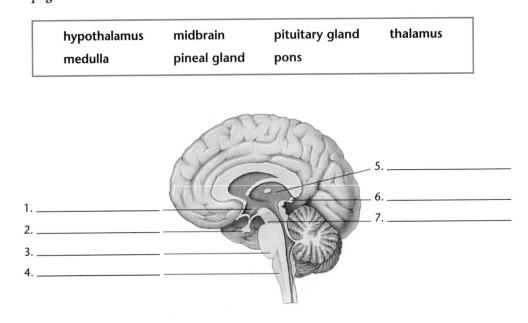

1. _____
2. _____
3. _____
4. _____

5. _____
6. _____
7. _____

FIGURE 6.10   **The human brain**

The Limbic System and the Reticular Formation

Deep inside the brain is the **limbic** (ˈlɪmbɪc) **system**. It is made up of small groups of neurons located in many areas of the brain. The neurons in all of these areas work together to cause our emotions, such as fear and love.

The **reticular formation** is another collection of small areas, primarily in the brainstem, that works to keep the brain alert. If the reticular formation is damaged, a person may go into a **coma** (ˈkowmə), which means they are no longer conscious.

COMPREHENSION CHECK

Answer the questions below. Then compare your answers with those of a partner.

1. What is the function of the limbic system?

2. What is the function of the reticular formation?

3. What happens when a person goes into a coma?

BUILDING LANGUAGE AND STUDY SKILLS

Stating and Asking about Differences

Your anatomy and physiology teacher will often explain various structures to you that seem quite similar. For example, the pons and the medulla are similar in that they both control breathing. However, these structures are also different. The pons helps to make sure that you breathe smoothly while the medulla decides how fast and how deeply you breathe. Being able to ask questions will help you to understand differences between two similar structures or concepts. Also, you will be required to explain differences between similar structures and concepts on examinations and in class.

Read the following sentences that state differences. Notice how the statements can be made in four different ways.

EXAMPLE	FORM
Gray matter and white matter differ.	_____ and _____ differ.
Gray matter and white matter have different functions	_____ and _____ have different _____.
Gray matter and white matter are different.	_____ and _____ are different.
There are differences between gray matter and white matter.	There are differences between _____ and _____.

Read the following questions about differences. Notice how the questions can be formed in four different ways.

EXAMPLE	FORM
How do gray matter and white matter differ?	How do _____ and _____ differ?
What are the different functions of gray matter and white matter?	What are the different _____ of _____ and _____?
How are gray matter and white matter different?	How are _____ and _____ different?
Are there differences between gray matter and white matter?	Are there differences between _____ and _____?

PRACTICE

1. *Use the following prompts to write questions. Use the words* differ, different, *and* difference *in your questions. When you have finished writing your questions, look back at what you have learned in this chapter so far to be sure that you can answer the questions. Take turns asking and answering questions with your partner.*

Example: cerebrum / cerebellum
How are the cerebrum and cerebellum different?

1. limbic system / reticular formation

2. white matter / gray matter

3. conscious thought / subconscious thought

4. the frontal lobe / the temporal lobe

5. thalamus / hypothalamus

6. the parietal lobe / the frontal lobe

2. *These are authentic questions taken from an anatomy and physiology class. Use the vocabulary and grammar you know to answer these questions. Ask your teacher to check your answers.*

   1. Both the cerebrum and cerebellum are important in helping you to move your body. How do their roles differ with respect to body movement?

   2. Most reflexes are controlled by the spinal cord. However, the midbrain is also important in reflex control. How do these structures differ regarding reflexes?

Forming a Study Group

As you progress in your study of anatomy and physiology, you'll likely come into contact with people who want to form a study group. A study group usually consists of two to six students taking the same class who meet together on a regular basis to study course information. Some study groups meet once or twice a week for one or two hours. Others might meet only to study for major exams. Study groups provide opportunities for students to share information and learn from each other, and thus reinforce the concepts they are learning in class. Study groups support your regular classes and can be fun, too.

If you are interested in starting a study group you can ask a few classmates to join you, or, you can ask your professor to suggest a few students who might benefit from forming a study group with you.

After you have your group organized, decide together how you want to proceed.

Here are two study methods:

   1. All the members bring questions that they have about the course content. For example, if a person isn't sure how the central nervous system works, he or she might bring in questions about the CNS to ask the group. The focus here is to clear up each others' misunderstandings and to find clarification on difficult concepts.

   2. Alternatively, members of a study group can divide up content and come prepared to present information to the other members of the group on a particular topic. For example, in the case of the nervous system one person might take common disorders, another person might take the function of the spinal cord, someone else might take the function of the brain, and someone else takes the anatomy of the whole system. The group members listen to the presentations and ask questions to clear up their misunderstandings and to find clarification on difficult concepts.

PRACTICE

Form a study group to study the information you have learned so far about the spinal cord. First, your group will study the information for one hour using the first method as outlined above. Then your group will study the brain using the second method of studying in a group. Again, you'll meet for one hour.

Each way of studying in a group may have its pros (good points) and cons (bad points). After you have completed your two study group experiences, complete the pro-con chart on page 121 and share your findings with the class. Is there one way of studying in a group that most of your classmates prefer?

	Study Group One	Study Group Two
Pros		
Cons		

THE AUTONOMIC NERVOUS SYSTEM

Motor neurons that originate in the CNS tell muscles to move. The CNS also stimulates cardiac and smooth muscles and some glands to function. Neurons that tell the body what to do without your conscious decision are part of the **autonomic** (αtə′nαmɪk) **nervous system (ANS)**. The ANS carries out involuntary responses to help maintain homeostasis of many conditions in the body, such as breathing rate, heart rate, and body temperature. There are two divisions of the ANS: the sympathetic division and the parasympathetic division.

The Sympathetic Division

The sympathetic division is used to respond to "fight or flight" situations. "Fight or flight" situations are scary situations. For example, if you see a rat, you'll either run from it (flight) or hit it (fight). When something scary puts the body on alert or stresses it, the sympathetic division takes over. Results include increased heart rate, decreased digestive activity, increased breathing rate, dilation of pupils (widening) of the eyes, sweating, and increased blood pressure.

For example: A woman sees a mouse and is frightened. How does her body respond?

1. The **sensory receptors** in her eyes detect the stimulus (a mouse).

2. A message is sent along **sensory (afferent) neurons** to the spinal cord and several places in the brain. Afferent means that messages approach (go toward) the CNS.

3. The message is interpreted in the **CNS**. The spinal cord makes the decision for the woman to jump on a chair (beginning a reflex response). Different parts of her brain make decisions for her to scream and to increase her heart rate, breathing rate, and blood pressure.

4. To carry out the decisions of the brain and spinal cord, messages are sent along **efferent (motor or ANS) neurons** to the different organs needed to respond to the mouse. Efferent means that messages exit or leave the CNS.

5. The **organs** carry out the responses. For instance, the woman's heart muscle beats faster, her blood vessels constrict (get smaller), her breathing muscles contract faster, her leg muscles cause her to jump on the chair, and muscles in her face cause her to scream.

Many people throughout the world are instinctively afraid of snakes, insects, and rodents. When people see animals they are afraid of, their bodies begin this autonomic response.

In our example, the pathway looks like this:

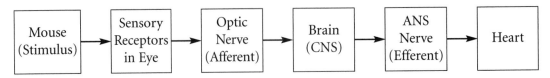

COMPREHENSION CHECK

1. *Answer the questions below. Then compare your answers with those of a partner.*

   1. Give an example of a fight or flight situation.

   2. When you are scared, what are three ways your body reacts?

2. *What happens when a woman sees a rat? Put the steps in order from 1 (what happens first) through 5 (what happens last).*

   _____ A message is sent along afferent neurons to the CNS.

   _____ The organs carry out the response. The woman jumps on a chair and screams.

   _____ Messages are sent along efferent neurons to the different organs needed for a reaction.

   _____ Sensory receptors in the eyes see a rat.

   _____ The message is interpreted in the CNS and decisions are made regarding how the woman should react.

Parasympathetic Division

The **parasympathetic division** is used for responses carried out in a "rest and digest" situation. "Rest and digest" means that there is no stress in your environment. In other words, when the body is relaxed, has just eaten a meal, or is sleeping, this division becomes dominant. Results include slower heart and breathing rates, decreased blood pressure, constriction (opening) of pupils, and increased activity in the digestive system.

For example: Grandfather just finished eating his dinner. He is relaxing in his chair.

1. **Sensory receptors** in the stomach detect the presence of food. Other sensory receptors in his muscles detect lack of muscle activity.

2. Messages about Grandfather's relaxed condition and the food in his stomach are sent along **sensory (afferent) neurons** to the spinal cord and brain.

3. The **CNS** interprets the messages. The spinal cord and brain decide to prepare the digestive system to digest the food. Since there is little need for oxygen, the CNS also decides to slow the heart and breathing rate.

4. Messages are sent from the CNS along **efferent (motor or ANS) neurons** to the appropriate organs: the digestive organs, and the heart and breathing muscles.

5. The **organs** carry out the response. The heart slows down, breathing muscles slow down, and muscles and glands in the digestive system are activated.

The same five parts are present in the parasympathetic response as in the sympathetic response.

> **∿∿∿** **Stroke!** A stroke, or cerebrovascular accident (CVA), occurs when blood vessels to a particular area of the brain are blocked. The blockage can have many causes: a blood clot, swelling of brain tissue, or build-up of fatty material inside blood vessels. This blockage of blood vessels prevents nutrients from getting to the neurons and the neurons begin to die. Depending upon which area of the brain is affected, the person may lose the ability to talk, move muscles, or even breathe! Luckily, patients can often recover from the stroke when undamaged neurons grow new branches into that area and take over the functions that have been lost.

COMPREHENSION CHECK

1. *Answer the questions below. Then compare your answers with those of a partner.*

    1. What time of day are you in the "rest and digest" situation?

    2. When you are relaxing, what are three ways your body reacts?

2. *What happens when Grandfather falls asleep after eating dinner? Put the steps in order from 1 (what happens first) through 5 (what happens last).*

_____ The digestive organs begin the digestive process.

_____ Sensory receptors in his stomach detect the presence of food.

_____ Messages are sent along efferent neurons to the different digestive organs.

_____ Messages about the food are sent along afferent neurons to the CNS.

_____ The message is interpreted in the CNS and decisions are made to start the digestive process.

FOCUS ON CULTURE

Making Progress in Health Care

In 1999, the life expectancy for white males in the United States was 74.6 years. For black males, it was 67.8 years. In 1999, African-Americans also had a 38 percent higher chance of dying from a stroke than white Americans and a 27 percent higher chance of dying from cancer. As a result of such differences in health among people of different races and socioeconomic levels, the U.S. government came up with a program called "Healthy People 2010." The goal of this program is to improve the health of all American people, including increasing the life span of people of color and other minority groups. This program has goals of improving access to good medical care and increasing access to illness prevention information, such as information about diet and smoking cessation programs. (U.S. Department of Health and Human Services [2000], *Healthy People 2010: Understanding and Improving Health*, Second Edition, Portland: Book News, Inc.)

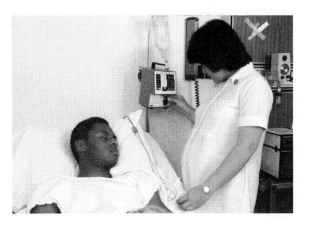

The following story is about the differences in accessing health care. Read the story and then discuss the questions in small groups.

Mr. Jones, an African-American, was diagnosed with lung cancer at the local hospital in his farming community. He'd had a bad cough for six months before deciding to go to the doctor. By the time Mr. Jones was diagnosed, his cancer was widespread. Mr. Jones had very little health insurance and didn't have much money, so he had very few options for health care. He got treatment at his local hospital. If he'd had more money and better insurance, he'd have been able to go to a hospital that has all of the up-to-date technologies. He could've seen doctors who had greater knowledge about treating his form of cancer. Due to Mr. Jones's lack of financial resources, his chance of recovering was much lower.

1. Is the same level of health care equally available to all people in your home country? Why or why not?

2. What would you do if you were Mr. Jones?

3. If you could choose three ways to improve the health of people in your country, what three ways would you choose?

4. In your opinion, what is the biggest problem facing people's health today in your country?

5. What can be done to increase people's life expectancy? By whom?

Check Your Understanding

1. *Answer the following questions about the nervous system.*

    1. Which two structures comprise the CNS?

    2. What are the two major functions of the spinal cord?

    3. What are the four major regions of the brain?

    4. How do gray matter and white matter differ in function?

    5. In what part of the brain are each of the four lobes located?

    6. How did each lobe get its name?

    7. What is the name of each lobe and one of its major functions?

    8. Which of the structures listed below are found in the diencephalon? In the brainstem?

	In the diencephalon	In the brainstem
Hypothalamus	☐	☐
Medulla oblongata	☐	☐
Midbrain	☐	☐
Pineal gland	☐	☐
Pituitary gland	☐	☐
Pons	☐	☐
Thalamus	☐	☐

    9. What is the function of the limbic system?

    10. Which structure helps to keep the brain alert and if damaged, could result in a person going into a coma?

    11. What are the two divisions of the autonomic nervous system?

    12. Is the ANS under your conscious control?

    13. Which division of the ANS is in charge if you are stressed?

    14. What is the difference between an afferent neuron and an efferent neuron?

    15. Describe the five steps your body would undergo if you saw a snake at your feet right now.

2. *Label Figure 6.11 with the terms provided.*

cerebellum	medulla	pons
cerebrum	midbrain	spinal cord
hypothalamus	pituitary gland	thalamus

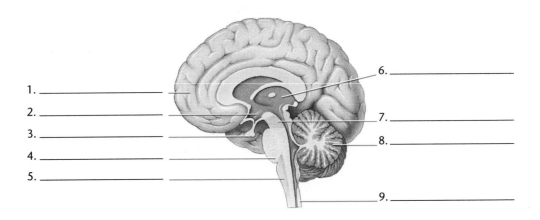

1. _____

2. _____

3. _____

4. _____

5. _____

6. _____

7. _____

8. _____

9. _____

FIGURE 6.11   **The brain**

3. *Answer these typical anatomy and physiology quiz questions.*

_____ **1.** Is this true or false? The area of the brain that interprets hearing is the occipital lobe of the cerebrum.

_____ **2.** Is this true or false? Messages from the eyes are sorted out in the thalamus and then sent mostly to the occipital lobe.

3. What part of the brain is responsible for maintaining many homeostatic processes, including body temperature and food and water intake?
a. pons   **b.** frontal lobe   **c.** hypothalamus   **d.** midbrain

4. Which is NOT true about the medulla?
a. It is located below the pons but above the spinal cord.
b. It helps to maintain homeostasis of blood pressure and heart rate.
c. It plays a role in breathing.
d. It is responsible for keeping track of the passage of time.

5. Which of the following would be characteristic of the parasympathetic division of the autonomic nervous system? Choose all that are correct.
a. heart rate and breathing rate rise
b. stimulated by resting or eating
c. sweating
d. constriction of the pupils of the eye

6. Circle the correct term. The **pineal / pituitary** gland makes melatonin.

7. Circle the correct term. The **temporal / occipital** lobe is the part of the brain that does all of the interpretation of visual messages.

8. Which part of the brain interprets sensory messages that originate when you burn your hand?
   a. frontal lobe
   b. midbrain
   c. hypothalamus
   d. parietal lobe

Think More about It

Now that you know more about the nervous system, see if you can add to your answers to this section in Chapter 5 on page 106.

Word Bank		
brain	medulla oblongata	sorted out
brainstem	midbrain	spinal cord
cerebellum	occipital lobe	sympathetic division
cerebrum	parasympathetic division	temporal lobe
diencephalon	parietal lobe	thalamus
frontal lobe	pineal gland	white matter
gray matter	pituitary gland	
hypothalamus	pons	
limbic system	reticular formation	

4. Where does food go after it leaves the stomach?

5. What are some common digestive problems?

3. *Read each verb, its simple definition, and its passive voice form. Then fill in the verbs in the sentences that follow. Pay attention to verb tense and subject / verb agreement. Compare your answers with those of another student.*

BASE FORM	PASSIVE VOICE FORM	MEANING
absorb	be absorbed	to move from one area to another
accumulate	be accumulated	to collect
convert	be converted	to change from one form into another
digest	be digested	to break into smaller molecules
dissolve	be dissolved	to make a solid disappear in a liquid
eliminate	be eliminated	to get rid of, remove from body
grind	be ground	to crush with a hard object
liquefy	be liquefied	to turn into a fluid or liquid
neutralize	be neutralized	to make not acidic or alkaline
regulate	be regulated	to control, keep the same

1. Just as a sponge removes water from a table, the bloodstream _____ water from the intestines.

2. Because the small intestine works best at a neutral pH, the acid from the stomach must be _____ when it reaches the small intestine.

3. Food waste is _____ from the body through the anus.

4. Water in saliva helps to turn food into a liquid, or _____ the food in the mouth.

5. Hormones control or _____ how fast your body breaks down food.

6. Your back teeth are useful for _____ food.

7. When you eat lots of candy, sugar _____ on your teeth.

8. If you stir sugar in water, it will _____.

9. Food is _____ from large molecules into smaller molecules during digestion.

10. Food is broken down into small molecules, or _____, in the small intestine.

THE PATH OF FOOD: UPPER DIGESTIVE TRACT

The upper digestive tract is the region extending from the mouth (oral cavity) to the stomach. It includes the oral cavity and its contents (teeth, tongue), the pharynx, the esophagus, and the stomach.

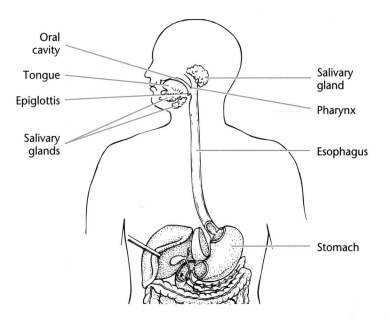

Oral cavity
Tongue
Epiglottis
Salivary glands

Salivary gland
Pharynx
Esophagus
Stomach

FIGURE 7.2   **Upper digestive tract**

The Oral Cavity

The sight, smell, taste, and thought of food stimulates the production of **saliva** (sə′layvə). Saliva is the name of the watery liquid in the mouth. Saliva is made by six sac-like organs called **salivary glands**. The salivary glands are located between the mouth and ear, at the base of the tongue and on the sides of the mouth. These glands secrete saliva. Saliva has three functions. First, saliva contains a molecule that helps to kill bacteria in the mouth. You will learn more about this bacteria-fighting molecule in the next chapter. Second, saliva contains molecules that begin to digest starches found in foods such as rice, bread, or potatoes. The digestion of starch must begin in the mouth because starch molecules are quite large. Third, saliva *liquefies* food, *dissolving* food molecules. When food molecules are dissolved, we are able to taste food.

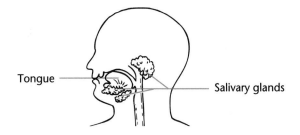

Tongue
Salivary glands

FIGURE 7.3   **Location of salivary glands**

Different foods have different tastes. Some food, such as candy, is sweet. Potato chips and French fries are salty. You can taste your food because of the tiny bumps on your tongue. These bumps contain **taste buds**. Each taste bud is stimulated by one of five basic flavors: sweet, sour, salty, umami (a taste like beef or chicken), and bitter. Different regions of the tongue have concentrations of different taste buds.

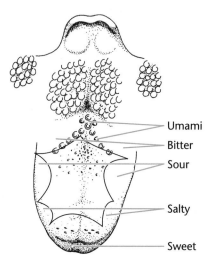

FIGURE 7.4   **Different regions of the tongue specialize in detecting different tastes**

In addition to enabling you to taste food, the tongue along with the muscles of the mouth move the food as you chew it with your teeth. Chewing breaks the large pieces of food into smaller ones so that the food can be easily swallowed. Humans have 32 teeth as adults. There are four different types of teeth:

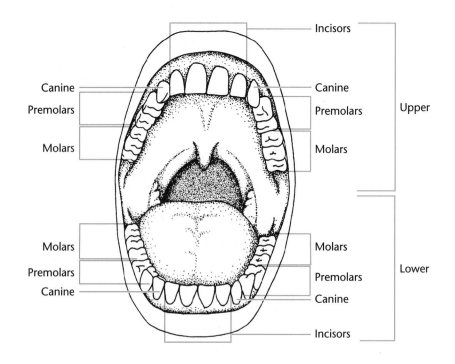

FIGURE 7.5   **Oral cavity with four different types of teeth**

When a "baby tooth" falls out, children in the United States usually put it under their pillows at night, waiting for a "tooth fairy" to bring them coins for their tooth. Do people in your culture have any traditions associated with the loss of "baby teeth?"

1. **Incisors** (ɪnˈsayzərz) are teeth that are located at the front of the mouth. There are eight incisors, four on the upper jaw and four on the lower. Incisors are used for cutting and biting.

2. **Canines** (ˈkeynaynz) are fang-like teeth that are to the side of the incisors. There are two canines on the upper jaw and two on the lower. Canine teeth are used for tearing food.

3. **Premolars** (priyˈmowlərz) are teeth located to the side of each canine. There are four premolars on the upper jaw and four on the lower. Premolars are used for chewing and *grinding* food.

4. **Molars** (ˈmowlərz) are teeth located at the very back of the mouth. There are six molars on the upper jaw and six on the lower. Molars are used for grinding food. The last molars that are in the very back on each side are sometimes called *wisdom teeth*. The word *wisdom* means *knowledge gained through learning and experience*. These last molars got this name because they do not appear until a person nears adulthood. Many people have their wisdom teeth removed if there is not enough room in their mouth for them to grow correctly. If a wisdom tooth grows under one of the other molars, this may cause pain as the other molar is pushed upward.

Each tooth has three main layers:

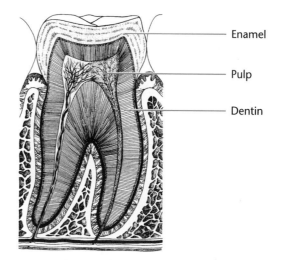

FIGURE 7.6   **Section through a molar, illustrating the three layers of a tooth**

1. The outer layer of a tooth is called **enamel** (ɪˈnæməl). Enamel is a hard, protective white coating.

2. Beneath the enamel is the **dentin** (ˈdɛntən). Dentin is made of calcium salts and protein, and comprises the largest part of the tooth.

3. The inner area of a tooth is called the **pulp** (pɑlp). The pulp is the only area of a tooth that contains living cells. This is where the tooth's nerve and blood supply is located. If you have a toothache, the pain you feel is the result of sensory receptors in the pulp area. The sensory receptors send messages about pain along sensory neurons to the sensory regions of the brain.

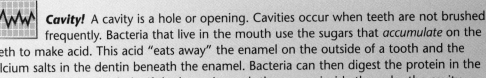 **Cavity!** A cavity is a hole or opening. Cavities occur when teeth are not brushed frequently. Bacteria that live in the mouth use the sugars that *accumulate* on the teeth to make acid. This acid "eats away" the enamel on the outside of a tooth and the calcium salts in the dentin beneath the enamel. Bacteria can then digest the protein in the dentin. This results in a hole. If the bacteria reach the nerves inside the pulp, the cavity becomes painful. A dentist can fix the cavity by filling the hole. The best way to avoid cavities is to brush and floss teeth after each meal to keep the sugars away from the bacteria that live in your mouth.

COMPREHENSION CHECK

1. *Answer the questions below. Then compare your answers with those of a partner.*

    1. What molecule does saliva start to digest? Why is it important to begin digestion of this molecule in the oral cavity?

    2. What are the five basic flavors that stimulate taste buds?

    3. What does saliva do to food molecules so that you are able to taste them?

    4. How many teeth should an adult have?

    5. Name the four types of teeth and describe their location in the mouth.

    6. Name the three layers in a tooth from the outside to the inside.

    7. What causes cavities? What can you do to prevent cavities?

2. *Circle the correct answer to complete each sentence. Take turns reading the correct sentences aloud with a partner.*

    1. You can tell if a food is sweet or salty because you have _____ in your mouth.
        a. saliva
        b. salivary glands
        c. taste buds
        d. molars

    2. _____ liquefies food and begins to digest starch molecules.
        a. Milk
        b. Saliva
        c. Cavities
        d. Salivary glands

    3. _____ teeth are used for tearing food.
        a. Molar
        b. Premolar
        c. Incisor
        d. Canine

4. The teeth at the very back of the mouth are called _____.
   a. molars
   b. premolars
   c. incisors
   d. canines

5. The inner part of a tooth that contains nerve endings is called _____.
   a. dentin
   b. enamel
   c. pulp
   d. a taste bud

6. The outermost layer of a tooth, called _____, is very hard and protects the tooth.
   a. dentin
   b. enamel
   c. pulp
   d. taste buds

The Path to the Stomach

After food is chewed, it is swallowed. To swallow, the tongue pushes the food to the back of the mouth and into the **pharynx** (ˈfærɪŋks), commonly called the throat. At the end of the pharynx there are two tubes. One tube consists of the **larynx** (ˈlærɪŋks), also called the voice box. The larynx connects with the **trachea** (ˈtreykiyə), which is the path for air to the lungs. When you breathe, the air goes into your larynx and trachea.

The other tube at the end of the pharynx is the **esophagus** (ɪˈsɑfəgəs), a long muscular tube that leads to the stomach. When you swallow, food moves first into the pharynx, then into the esophagus, and then down to the stomach.

When you swallow, you want food to enter the esophagus, not the larynx. As you swallow, a flap of tissue called the **epiglottis** (ɛpɪˈglɑtɪs) covers the larynx. The epiglottis covers the larynx when you swallow to prevent food from entering the trachea. Figure 7.7 shows how the larynx, esophagus, and epiglottis are positioned when breathing and swallowing.

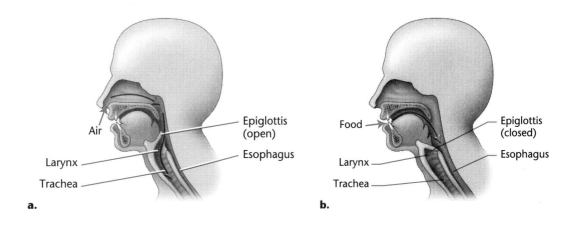

FIGURE 7.7 **When breathing, the epiglottis is raised, allowing air to enter the larynx (a). When swallowing, the epiglottis covers the opening to the larynx, preventing food from entering the airway (b).**

Many Americans are trained to help people who are choking. The method used to help a choking person is called the Heimlich maneuver. Fire departments offer this training as part of first aid courses to the general public.

 **Choking!** If food enters the larynx and trachea, a **cough reflex** called **choking** occurs. You choke when sensory receptors on the walls of the larynx and trachea sense that something is there that shouldn't be there. Food can enter your trachea if someone makes you laugh or scares you after you have begun to swallow. If you breathe in air at the same time you are swallowing, this causes the epiglottis to open, and the food may enter the larynx instead of the esophagus, causing the cough reflex to occur. This is called choking. People sometimes say "the food went down the wrong tube." Muscles in the walls of the trachea and larynx usually propel (push) the food back up into the mouth where it can then be swallowed down the esophagus.

Let's turn now to what happens when food enters the esophagus. The esophagus has muscle tissue around it. When the esophagus senses food at its top, the muscle tissue begins to contract. The contractions move in waves from the top of the esophagus to the bottom. These waves of contraction are called **peristalsis** (pɛrɪ'stɑlsəs). Peristalsis squeezes the food down the esophagus to your stomach.

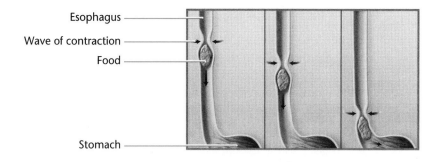

Esophagus

Wave of contraction

Food

Stomach

FIGURE 7.8   **Peristalsis**

At the end of the esophagus, there is a small ring of smooth muscle which relaxes to allow food to enter the stomach. The ring of muscle is called the **gastroesophageal sphincter** (gæstrowiysɑfə'dʒiyəl 'sfɪŋktər). After the food is in the stomach, the gastroesophageal sphincter closes to prevent food from being pushed upward into the esophagus.

 **Heartburn!** If you lie down shortly after eating a big meal or if the gastroesophageal sphincter doesn't close completely, the acid from the stomach can move back into the esophagus. This causes inflammation (a burning feeling) in the lining of the esophagus. This inflammation is commonly known as heartburn.

COMPREHENSION CHECK

1. *Read the questions and then scan the text for answers. When you find the answers, underline them. Then work with a partner and take turns asking and answering the questions. Try to remember the answers without looking back at the text.*

   1. What is the job of the epiglottis?

   2. Where does the trachea go? What does it carry?

3. Where does the esophagus go? What does it carry?

4. What is another word for "cough reflex"?

5. How does food move down the esophagus?

6. What kind of tissue comprises the gastroesophageal sphincter?

2. *Complete the sentences using the words in the box. Take turns reading the correct sentences aloud with a partner.*

epiglottis	heartburn	peristalsis	trachea
esophagus	larynx	sphincter	

1. The tube that leads to the stomach is called the _____.

2. The _____ is a flap of tissue that covers the trachea when you swallow.

3. _____ is a special type of muscle contraction that propels food down the esophagus to the stomach.

4. When stomach acid is pushed back up into the esophagus, this disorder is called _____.

5. When air moves toward the lungs, it moves from the pharynx to the _____ and then down the tube called the _____.

6. A ring of muscle that separates two organs is called a _____.

The Stomach

The stomach is a muscular sac. Inside the stomach, food is further liquefied by acid secreted by tiny glands in the stomach walls. This acid is strong and can "eat away" almost anything: meat, carrots, cake, and any other kind of food. Because stomach acid is so strong, it can hurt the stomach. To protect itself from damage, the stomach lining contains cells that constantly produce **alkaline mucus**. Alkaline is the opposite of acid. Alkaline mucus *neutralizes* acid, making it less harmful to the stomach lining. This mucus basically coats the stomach lining to prevent acid from "eating" it.

Peptic ulcers! Lesions (sores) in the wall of the stomach are called **peptic ulcers**. People used to believe that peptic ulcers were caused by stress, too much acid, or eating spicy food. We now know that these lesions are actually caused by a bacterium that lives in the stomach. This bacterium causes certain areas of the stomach wall to become irritated. This irritation leads to secretion of more acid than normal and increases the damage to the stomach wall. Peptic ulcers feel like someone pouring vinegar onto an open wound. Peptic ulcers are now successfully treated with antibiotics that kill the bacteria. Medicines can also be given to decrease the amount of acid present in the stomach.

Protein digestion begins in the stomach with the help of **enzymes** (′ɛnzaymz) made by the stomach. Enzymes are molecules that help chemical reactions to go faster. These enzymes help to break down protein molecules into smaller molecules. Smaller molecules are able to move more easily into the bloodstream when they reach the small intestine. Although some protein digestion occurs in the stomach, most digestion of food occurs in the small intestine.

The stomach wall has three layers of muscle. This muscle is arranged so that when it contracts, the food in the stomach is squeezed in all directions. Imagine that you are washing a shirt by hand. You add soap and water to the shirt and squeeze it in all directions. That's just what your stomach does to food. Its muscles contract in different directions, allowing the stomach juices to mix well with the food. When this mixing is completed, the food and juices have become a thick liquid, like a milkshake.

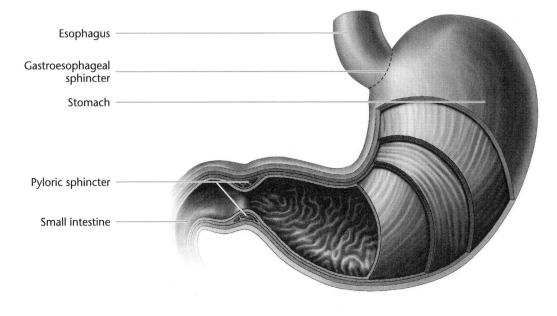

Esophagus

Gastroesophageal sphincter

Stomach

Pyloric sphincter

Small intestine

FIGURE 7.9   **The stomach. Note the three layers of muscle in the wall.**

When the small intestine is ready to receive food from the stomach, another ring of smooth muscle connecting the stomach and small intestine relaxes. This ring of muscle is called the **pyloric** (pay′lɔrɪk) **sphincter**. As a rule, the pyloric sphincter allows only small amounts of food to enter the small intestine at a time so that the small intestine can fully digest the food and *absorb* the nutrients.

1. *Label Figure 7.10 with the terms in the box. Look at Figures 7.2 and 7.9 on pages 131 and 138 to check your answers.*

esophagus	pharynx	small intestine
gastroesophageal sphincter	pyloric sphincter	stomach
oral cavity	salivary glands	

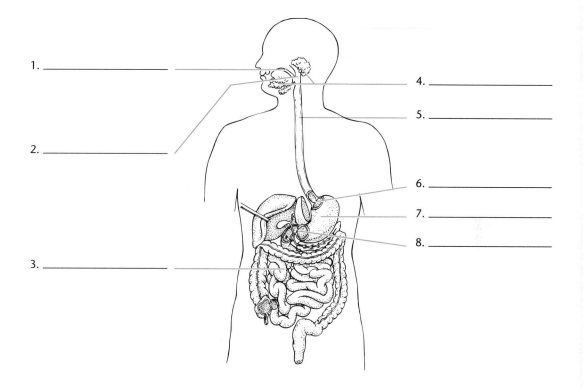

1. _____

2. _____

3. _____

4. _____

5. _____

6. _____

7. _____

8. _____

FIGURE 7.10   **The upper digestive tract**

2. *Circle the correct word(s) to complete each sentence. Take turns reading the correct sentences aloud with a partner.*

1. **Starch / Protein** is first digested in the stomach.

2. The **pyloric / gastroesophageal** sphincter separates the stomach from the small intestine.

3. Peptic ulcers are caused by **spicy food / a bacterium.**

4. **Enzymes / Mucus** help to protect the lining of the stomach from acid.

5. Mucus is **acidic / alkaline.**

Explaining Cause and Effect

As you learn about physiological processes and disorders associated with body systems, you will need to explain what causes disorders and how disorders affect the body.

For example, your teacher might ask:

What causes a choke reflex?

(or *Why do people have a choke reflex?* or *What is the reason that people have a choke reflex?*)

You might answer:

When food goes down the trachea, a choke reflex occurs.

You would give the reason, or **cause**, in this case: *when food goes down the trachea*, and the result, or **effect**: *a choke reflex occurs.*

This type of structure is called a **cause and effect sentence**. Each cause and effect sentence consists of one cause clause and one effect clause. The **cause clause** tells you why something happens. The **effect clause** explains the result.

CAUSE AND EFFECT STRUCTURE WORDS

- Use the words **because**, **since**, and **when** to introduce the cause clause. In writing, if you begin a sentence with a cause clause, you must use a comma (,) before the effect clause.

  When you don't brush your teeth, *you get cavities.*

- If you end a sentence with a cause clause, you do not use a comma.

  *You get cavities **when you don't brush your teeth**.*

- Use the words **as a result of, for this reason, so, therefore, thus**, and **consequently** to introduce the effect clause. Notice the punctuation in the following sentences.

  You didn't brush your teeth; ***consequently, you have cavities now**.*
  His pyloric sphincter doesn't close properly, ***so he gets frequent heartburn**.*

- You can also separate cause and effect into two separate sentences.

  You didn't brush your teeth. ***Consequently, you have cavities now**.*

- Remember that you cannot use the words that introduce the cause clause and the effect clause together in the same sentence. Read this sentence and guess why it is wrong.

  **Because his pyloric sphincter doesn't close properly, so he gets frequent heartburn.*

1. *Complete the chart with cause and effect clauses. Then compare your answers with those of a partner. Be sure to use correct punctuation.*

CAUSE	EFFECT
1. Because I didn't brush my teeth	*I have a big cavity now.*
2.	as a result, a stomach lesion appears.
3. When you smell or think about food,	
4.	so you can taste food.
5. Saliva liquefies food	
6. The gastroesophageal sphincter closes	
7.	therefore, the dentist has to remove your wisdom teeth.
8. There isn't enough alkaline mucus in the stomach	

2. *These are authentic questions taken from an anatomy and physiology class. Use cause and effect structures to answer these questions.*

1. What causes cavities?

2. Why do people get peptic ulcers?

3. What causes peristalsis?

Imagining a Process

Students of anatomy and physiology are often able to remember physiological processes much better when they can imagine what it's like to be part of a process. For example, in the case of the digestive system, many anatomy and physiology students find it very helpful to imagine that they are actually a piece of food traveling through the digestive tract. This may seem at first to be a strange way to learn. However, by actively involving yourself in the learning process, you are utilizing more of your mind, such as your senses of vision and touch, your imagination, and even your humor.

Look at this example of how one student used his imagination to learn the path of food in the upper digestive tract.

I am a piece of cake. Incisors take a bite of me. I am in the mouth. Saliva is getting me wet and the tongue is pushing me around the mouth. I'm getting soft.

You'll be able to use this learning strategy in the following ways in later chapters:

- Immune system—imagine you're a virus or bacterium entering the body
- Cardiovascular system—imagine you are a blood cell traveling through the blood vessels
- Respiratory—imagine you are an oxygen molecule
- Urinary—imagine you are a water molecule moving through the urinary system
- Reproduction—imagine you are a sperm

Imagine you are a piece of food; for example, "I am a piece of chicken." Starting with taking a bite, describe your journey through the digestive system. Where do you go? What happens to you? What do the walls of the places you travel through look like? Stop when you get to the small intestine. Share what you've written with a classmate. Continue the story of your adventure through the digestive system after you finish reading the chapter.

ACCESSORY ORGANS HELP WITH DIGESTION

After the food leaves your stomach, it goes to the small intestine. Most digestion takes place in the small intestine with the help of **accessory organs**. *Accessory* means *extra*. Your body needs extra organs to help with digestion, but food doesn't go to those organs. Instead, these organs send molecules to the small intestine to aid in the digestion of certain food molecules.

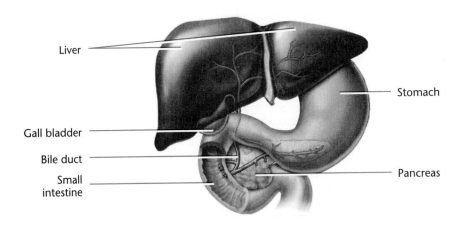

FIGURE 7.11   **Accessory organs of the digestive system**

The Liver

The **liver** is a large, brown organ that lies under the diaphragm and on top of the stomach. The liver performs many different functions. One of its important functions is the production of **bile**. Bile is a greenish liquid that separates fat into small droplets. Without bile, fats tend to float as one big layer. The fact that the droplets are smaller makes digestion easier. If this layer were not broken into smaller pieces, the enzymes that digest fat would take too long to digest all the fat.

To better understand the function of bile, imagine a greasy layer of fat that coats a cooking pan. You add dishwashing soap to the water to break up and wash away the greasy layer. Bile acts just like soap by breaking up fat into small pieces.

The Gall Bladder

The liver doesn't actually send bile directly to the small intestine. Instead, after the liver makes bile, the bile is sent to the **gall bladder**. The gall bladder is a small organ located under the liver. The gall bladder concentrates (takes extra water out of) the bile and stores it until it's needed. When food is present in the small intestine, the gall bladder contracts and sends bile along a **duct** (a small tube) to the small intestine. In the small intestine, the bile helps to break fat into smaller droplets to be digested and absorbed more easily.

Gallstones! Gallstones are like big salt **crystals** that may lodge (get stuck) in the bile duct or accumulate in the gall bladder. They often form when a person has too much **cholesterol** in their diet. Cholesterol is a fat-like molecule that is found in foods such as meat, butter, and eggs. Bile contains cholesterol. Gallstones can be very painful because the crystals have sharp edges and irritate the wall of the bile duct. The gallstones can also block or prevent bile from going to the small intestine, preventing proper fat digestion. A doctor may choose to break gallstones apart using **ultrasound** or, in more serious cases, a person's gall bladder may be removed. If that happens, the person must be careful not to eat too much fat at one time because there won't be as much bile going into the small intestine to help with fat digestion.

The Pancreas

Another accessory organ that sends important molecules to the small intestine to aid in digestion is the **pancreas** ('pæŋkriyəs). The pancreas is located near the first portion of the small intestine and just beneath the stomach. The pancreas produces digestive enzymes that are used in the small intestine to break down sugars, proteins, and fats. These enzymes travel from the pancreas to the small intestine in a watery liquid that contains **sodium bicarbonate** (bay'kɑrbəneyt). Sodium bicarbonate is important because it neutralizes acid in the food entering the small intestine from the stomach. Sodium bicarbonate protects the small intestine from stomach acid, just like mucus protects the stomach. The neutralization of acid by sodium bicarbonate also creates an optimal (perfect) environment for digestion in the small intestine. Digestion there works best when conditions are not acidic.

COMPREHENSION CHECK

1. *Work with a partner to fill out the chart below.*

Molecule	Where is it made?	Where does it go?	Function
Sodium bicarbonate			
Digestive enzymes			
Bile			

2. *Circle the correct word(s) to complete each sentence. Take turns reading the correct sentences aloud with a partner.*

   1. The gall bladder **makes / stores** bile.

   2. A duct is a **cavity / small tube**.

   3. Gallstones are caused by too much **water / cholesterol** in the diet.

   4. Gallstones can be destroyed with **ultrasound / water**.

   5. When a person's gall bladder is removed, he must watch the amount of **fat / protein** in his diet.

Regulation of Blood Sugar

In addition to making enzymes and sodium bicarbonate, the pancreas is also important as an **endocrine gland**. Recall from Chapter 1 that endocrine glands make **hormones** that are important in maintaining homeostasis. The pancreas makes two important hormones, insulin and glucagon. Both are important in maintaining blood sugar homeostasis.

1. **Insulin** (′ɪnsələn) is a hormone produced by the pancreas. After you've eaten a meal, blood sugar (glucose) levels begin to rise, causing the pancreas to secrete insulin. Insulin causes the cells to take the sugar out of the blood and use it for energy. If the cells do not need all the sugar, the cells *convert* the sugar to fat.

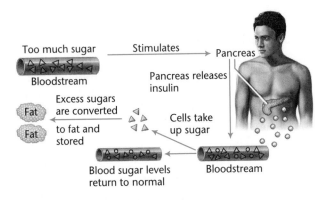

FIGURE 7.12   **When blood sugar levels are high, the pancreas releases insulin. Insulin causes cells of the body to take up sugar and store it as fat. The blood sugar levels then return to normal.**

2. **Glucagon** (′gluwkəgɑn) is another hormone produced by the pancreas. Your blood sugar levels decrease if you go several hours without eating a meal. This is because insulin has told cells to take sugar out of the blood. However, organs like the brain still need to get sugar from the blood to function properly. The low level of glucose in your blood causes the pancreas to stop secreting insulin and to secrete glucagon instead. Glucagon causes more sugar to enter the blood from the cells that have stored it as fat.

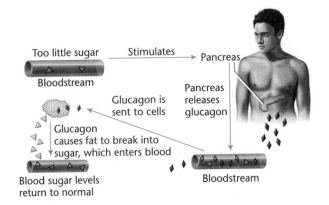

FIGURE 7.13   **When blood sugar levels are low, the pancreas releases glucagon. Glucagon causes cells to convert fat into sugar, which enter the bloodstream. The blood sugar levels then return to normal.**

Diabetes mellitus! When blood sugar homeostasis is not properly maintained a person may have **diabetes mellitus** (daγə'biytəs mə'laytəs). There are two categories:

- **Type I (Insulin-Dependent) Diabetes** most often begins at adolescence (ages 11–13) and is sometimes called "juvenile diabetes." In Type I diabetes, the pancreas is not able to make insulin. Therefore, the body often has too much glucose in the blood. People with Type I diabetes must monitor their glucose levels during the day and inject insulin as needed to maintain adequate blood sugar levels.

- **Type II (Non-Insulin Dependent) Diabetes** most often begins in late adulthood (50–70 years). People who are overweight and have a family history of this disorder are more likely to get it. In this case, insulin may be produced in adequate amounts, but the body's cells do not respond to the insulin correctly. These individuals may be able to control their diabetes with medication and proper diet and exercise.

COMPREHENSION CHECK

1. *Work with a partner to label each statement true* (T) *or false* (F). *If the statement is false, correct it so that it is true.*

   _____ 1. The pancreas is an endocrine gland.

   _____ 2. Insulin causes sugar to be taken out of the blood and stored as fat.

   _____ 3. Glucagon causes the liver and other cells to release sugar into the blood.

   _____ 4. Right after a big meal, the pancreas is releasing glucagon.

   _____ 5. If someone has not eaten in 8 hours, their blood sugar levels will be low.

2. *Circle the correct answers. Take turns reading the correct sentences aloud with a partner.*

   1. The job of this organ is to secrete hormones.
      a. liver
      b. gall bladder
      c. endocrine gland

   2. This condition starts at a young age and requires injection of insulin.
      a. Type I diabetes
      b. Type II diabetes

   3. This substance helps to reduce acid in the small intestine.
      a. insulin
      b. sodium bicarbonate
      c. glucagon

   4. This hormone causes an increase in the amount of sugar in the bloodstream.
      a. insulin
      b. glucagon

   5. This condition occurs most often in late adulthood and is more likely in people who are overweight.
      a. Type I diabetes
      b. Type II diabetes

The Small Intestine

The **small intestine** is six meters (19.7 feet) long. When liquefied food leaves the stomach and enters the small intestine, bile and pancreatic juices follow. Enzymes in the wall of the small intestine and pancreatic enzymes digest food, breaking it into smaller molecules. The majority of food digestion occurs in the small intestine. The only exceptions are the partial digestion of starch in the mouth by saliva and the partial digestion of proteins in the stomach.

Most of the smaller food molecules pass through cells that line the small intestine and enter the bloodstream. This process is called **absorption**. Because the membrane of the intestinal cells only allows smaller food molecules to pass in and out of the cell, food must be digested first before it can be absorbed.

Once the food molecules pass through the cells that line the small intestine, they enter capillaries, which are small blood vessels that lie just beneath the intestinal cells. These capillaries transport the molecules to larger vessels that eventually lead to the liver. In the liver, some of the food molecules are stored for later use, while others remain in the blood for immediate use by the body's cells. For example, if there is a lot of sugar in the blood after eating, insulin tells the liver to store it. In addition to making bile and storing food molecules, the liver also takes poisons (for example, alcohol or drugs) out of the food.

When digestion and absorption is complete in the small intestine, peristalsis occurs to push the food waste forward into the large intestine.

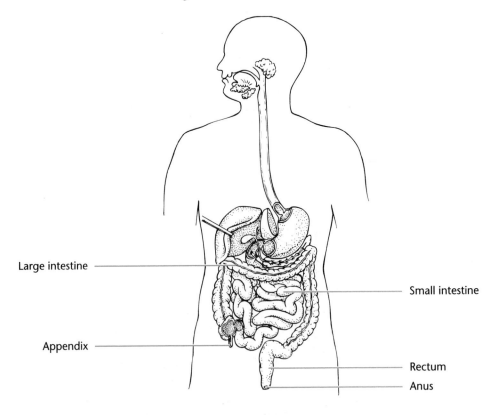

FIGURE 7.14   **The lower digestive tract**

Diarrhea! If something causes food to move too quickly through the small intestine, very little of the water is absorbed. This causes feces (waste) to become liquid, a condition called **diarrhea** (dayə′riyə). Diarrhea may be caused by bacteria or viruses or by a food allergy.

COMPREHENSION CHECK

1. *Circle the correct answer to complete each sentence. Take turns reading the correct sentences aloud with a partner.*

   1. The small intestine is the location where _____.
      a. most foods are digested
      b. most foods are absorbed
      c. most foods are digested and absorbed
      d. very little food is digested or absorbed

   2. After food is digested, it _____.
      a. enters the blood immediately
      b. enters intestinal cells and then passes into capillaries
      c. passes immediately into the large intestine
      d. is eliminated

   3. Blood containing food molecules goes from the small intestine to the _____.
      a. pancreas
      b. stomach
      c. liver
      d. large intestine

   4. The liver _____.
      a. makes bile
      b. stores excess sugar
      c. takes toxins out of food
      d. all of the above

2. *Match the terms with their definitions by writing the letters in the correct blanks. Then compare your answers with those of a partner.*

   _____ 1. absorption   a. breaking up food into small molecules
   _____ 2. bile   b. a substance that breaks down food into smaller molecules
   _____ 3. capillaries   c. food moves too fast through the small intestine
   _____ 4. digestion   d. when molecules cross cells to get to the blood
   _____ 5. enzyme   e. small blood vessels that food molecules first enter
   _____ 6. diarrhea   f. a substance that breaks up fat

Regulation of Cellular Metabolism

When cells use energy in food molecules, this is called **metabolism** (mə'tæbəlizəm). The cell either converts the food molecule to a stored form of energy (such as fat) or uses the energy to do its work (such as muscle contraction).

Thyroid hormone, made by the thyroid gland in the neck, helps to *regulate* cellular metabolism. The amount of thyroid hormone in the body is monitored by the pituitary gland. If there is too little thyroid hormone, the pituitary gland releases **Thyroid Stimulating Hormone (or TSH)**. TSH causes the thyroid gland to release more thyroid hormone. When there is enough thyroid hormone in the blood, the pituitary gland stops releasing TSH. This is a form of negative feedback. Recall that negative feedback is a method to maintain homeostasis by returning a condition to normal.

The countries with the highest frequency of iodine deficiency are in central Africa and central Asia (including India). The World Health Organization estimates that 740 million people in the world have disorders caused by iodine deficiencies.

 Hypothyroidism! Hypothyroidism (*hypo* means *below*) is a condition in which the person makes too little thyroid hormone. As a result, his metabolic rate is below normal. In infants, this condition leads to cretinism, which means that the child has poor skeletal and nervous system development (mental retardation). Adults with hypothyroidism are often weak, tired, and feel cold. They may also experience weight gain. Hypothyroidism may be caused by inadequate iodine in the diet, pituitary or thyroid malfunction (not working properly).

Hyperthyroidism! Hyperthyroidism (*hyper* means *above*) is a condition in which the person makes too much thyroid hormone. These individuals have a high metabolic rate. A high metabolic rate leads to increases in blood pressure, restlessness, weight loss, and irregular heart rate. Hyperthyroidism may be caused by tumors in the pituitary or thyroid gland, or by the body mistakenly stimulating the thyroid to produce its hormone.

Goiter! An enlargement of the thyroid gland that is not caused by cancer is called a **goiter**. Sometimes, the thyroid becomes so large that the goiter is visible as a large lump at the front of the neck. Goiter can be caused by too much TSH or by deficient (too little) iodine. Iodine is required for thyroid hormone to be produced. Iodine deficiencies occur most often when people live in areas that have too little iodine in the soil or are not near the ocean.

COMPREHENSION CHECK

Work with a partner to label each statement true (T) *or false* (F). *If the statement is false, correct it so that it is true.*

_____ 1. Thyroid hormone regulates cellular metabolism.

_____ 2. TSH causes less thyroid hormone to be secreted.

_____ 3. Someone with hypothyroidism has too much thyroid hormone.

_____ 4. Someone with hyperthyroidism would tend to lose weight.

_____ 5. An infant who has hyperthyroidism would have a condition called cretinism.

_____ 6. A goiter can be caused by too little iodine in the diet.

Direct Communication

Doctors in the United States usually communicate in a very direct manner with their patients. They tell them what is causing their health problems, even when it may mean that the patient is dying. Doctors often give their patients lots of written information about their illness as well.

However, in some cultures, it may be considered inappropriate to give bad news to someone, so the doctor doesn't always talk to the patient directly about his or her illnesses. Instead, the doctor will communicate with the patient's family.

The following story is about a cultural conflict that people may experience in a health-care setting. Read the story and then discuss the questions in small groups.

Jane, a 65-year-old woman, had tests done a week ago to see if she had cancer. After receiving the test results, the doctor's office called Jane to make an appointment for her to meet with the doctor. Jane entered the doctor's office nervously. The doctor showed her a variety of lab results which included numbers corresponding to her blood tests as well as X-rays of her spleen. He told her that she had Stage IV cancer of the blood. He added that she had a 40 percent chance of recovery. Jane felt like crying. The doctor went on to say that if she did recover, there would be an 80 percent chance of the cancer returning within five years. She was also given lots of written information which discussed the treatment plan and was then sent home. When Jane's son visited her that evening, he found his mother at the kitchen table reading the information and crying.

1. Do you think that knowing all this information is helping Jane or hurting her?

2. Do doctors usually speak openly to patients about their illnesses in your home country?

3. What are the good points about doctors speaking openly to their patients? What are the bad points about doctors speaking openly to their patients?

The Large Intestine

After the food leaves your small intestine, it goes to the large intestine. The large intest[ine]
1.5 meters (4.9 feet) long. Its job is to absorb the water, sodium, and potassium from t[he]
food. These molecules are sent into the bloodstream which takes them to many organs
the body. For example, sodium and potassium are sent to neurons. Recall that sodium
potassium are necessary for neurons to send messages. The sodium and potassium hel[p]
create the electrical current that flows along the axons. Sodium and potassium are also
important in muscle contractions.

After sodium, water, and potassium are removed from the food, what's left is known as
('fiysiyz). One third of the weight of the feces is bacteria that occur naturally in the lar[ge]
intestine. That's why it is important for people to wash their hands with soap and wate[r]
after going to the bathroom. People generally have a bowel movement every 1–3 days t[o]
eliminate this food waste. When you study anatomy and physiology, you will often hea[r the]
term "BM" for bowel movement.

After the absorption of water, sodium, and potassium has been completed, muscle
contractions in the large intestine squeeze the feces down into the **rectum** ('rɛktəm), t[he]
lower portion of the large intestine. There are two sphincters at the bottom of the rectu[m.]
The **internal anal sphincter** relaxes when feces push against it. We do not consciously
control this sphincter. The internal anal sphincter is controlled by the spinal cord. Fror[n the]
internal anal sphincter, the feces are moved to the external anal sphincter. We consciou[sly]
control this muscle. When the external anal sphincter relaxes, **defecation** (dɛfə'keyʃən[)]
movement of the feces out of the body, occurs.

 Constipation! If defecation doesn't occur regularly, more water is absorbed
from the fecal matter than normal. This results in **constipation** (kɑnstɪ'peyʃə[n])
which is a difficulty in removal of feces because they are too solid. Constipation can resu[lt]
in serious problems such as **appendicitis** (apɛndə'saytəs). The appendix is a small pouc[h]
or sac that attaches near the beginning of the large intestine. The job of the appendix is
unknown. Constipation can eventually push feces backward into this area. The bacteria i[n]
the feces cause fluid to accumulate near the appendix. If the appendix bursts, the inside
the abdominal cavity can become infected with these bacteria, resulting in a serious
disease called **peritonitis** (pɛrətən'aytəs).

COMPREHENSION CHECK

*Circle the correct word to complete each sentence. Take turns reading the correct
sentences aloud with a partner.*

1. **Diarrhea / Constipation** is a condition where the feces have become hard, maki[ng]
   a bowel movement difficult.

2. The place where feces exit the body is the **anus / rectum**.

3. The **external / internal** anal sphincter is under a person's conscious control.

4. **Feces / Peritonitis** is the bacterial infection of the abdominal cavity caused by
   constipation.

5. **Appendicitis / Peritonitis** is a bacterial infection of the small sac at the beginnin[g]
   of the large intestine.

6. The **rectum / anus** is the last section of the large intestine.

7. The large intestine absorbs **water / glucose**.

Blood and Body Defenses

pter you will learn:

AND PHYSIOLOGY

*mposition and
ns of blood*

fectious diseases

*e body defends itself
 disease*

ng terms

LLS

reference sources

al forces in healing

KNOW *that your body contains about 5 liters of blood? This blood contains about
ed blood cells!*

Check Your Understanding

1. *Answer the following questions about the digestive system.*

   1. What are two purposes of saliva?

   2. What two cavities lead to the pharynx?

   3. What is the difference between the esophagus and the trachea?

   4. Does the epiglottis close to cover the larynx or the esophagus?

   5. How many layers of muscle are in the stomach?

   6. Why does the stomach need alkaline mucus?

   7. What is the purpose of bile? Where is it made and stored?

   8. What are the two important hormones that the pancreas produces?

   9. Where does the absorption of food molecules take place?

  10. If someone says that they have a high metabolism, what does that mean?

  11. What is the purpose of thyroid hormone?

  12. What three things are absorbed in the large intestine?

2. *Label Figure 7.15 with the terms provided.*

appendix	gall bladder	liver	pyloric sphincter	small intestine
esophagus	large intestine	pancreas	rectum	

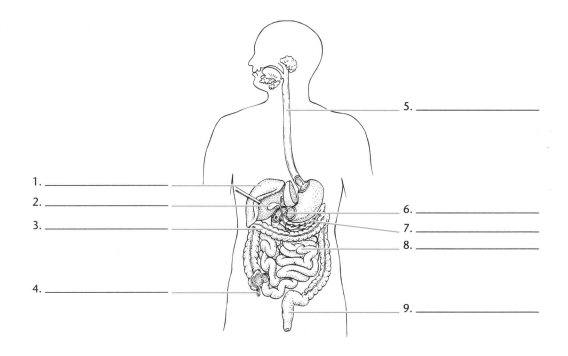

1. _____
2. _____
3. _____
4. _____
5. _____
6. _____
7. _____
8. _____
9. _____

FIGURE 7.15 **The digestive tract**

The Digestive System   **151**

3. *Answer these typical anatomy and physiology quiz questions.*

1. Circle the correct word. The **esophagus / epiglottis** is the structure that covers the larynx when you swallow food.

2. _____ Is it true or false? Peristalsis means that all the muscle in an organ contracts at the same time.

3. Which statement about hormones is NOT true?
   a. Glucagon is the hormone that helps your brain get sugar when you are starving.
   b. Insulin is the hormone that controls metabolic rate in the cells.
   c. Hypothyroidism is when the thyroid gland doesn't make enough thyroid hormone.

4. Which organ does most of the digestion and absorption of food?
   a. liver
   b. small intestine
   c. stomach
   d. large intestine

5. Circle the letter(s) of the disorders that are correctly matched with their description.
   a. Diarrhea: food moves too slowly through the small intestine.
   b. Heartburn: food and acid pushed into the esophagus from stomach.
   c. Constipation: too much water is absorbed from the feces.
   d. Ulcers: caused by eating too much spicy food.

6. Why is mucus so important in the stomach?

Think More about It

1. How does the nervous system interact with the digestive system?

2. Is there any muscle tissue in the digestive system? Where? What kind of muscle is present?

3. What hormones are important in regulating how our bodies manage food?

Word Bank	
absorb	eliminate
accessory organs	enamel
accumulate	endocrine gland
acid	enzymes
alkaline mucus	epiglottis
anus	esophagus
canines	feces
cavity	gall bladder
constipation	glucagon
convert	grind
dentin	incisors
diabetes	insulin
diarrhea	intestines
digest	larynx
digestion	liquefy
digestive tract	liver
duct	molars

CHAP

In this c

ANATOM
- *The*
  func
- *Hov*
  occu
- *Hov*
  aga

ENGLISH
- *Def*

STUDY
- *Usi*

CULTUR
- *Spi*

DID YO
25 trilli

INTRODUCTION

Blood is the red liquid that flows within the blood vessels of your body. It is the main method of transport for nutrients, water, oxygen, hormones, and waste products. In this chapter, you will learn about the composition of blood and its function. You will also learn how the body defends itself against infectious diseases.

1. *Work with a partner. Look at the diagram of the tube of blood. Try to label the two main parts of blood—plasma and cells. Look at Figure 8.2 on page 157 to check your answers.*

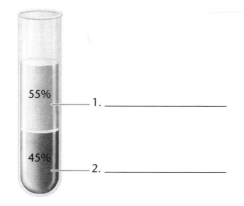

55% — 1. _____

45% — 2. _____

FIGURE 8.1   **A tube of human blood, separated into plasma and cells**

2. *With your partner, try to answer these questions. If you do not know the answers, do not worry. You will find the answers as you read through this chapter.*

   1. What are some functions of blood?

   2. What sorts of things would you find in blood?

   3. Do you think blood is a tissue?

   4. Name some diseases that one person can give to another person.

3. *Read each verb, its simple definition, and its passive voice form. Then fill in the verbs in the sentences that follow. Pay attention to verb tense and subject / verb agreement. Compare your answers with those of another student.*

BASE FORM	PASSIVE VOICE FORM	MEANING
activate	be activated	to cause to come alive, to start
burst	be burst	to explode
centrifuge	be centrifuged	to spin until a liquid breaks into its parts
coagulate	be coagulated	to become thick
line	be lined	to cover the inside
overwhelm	be overwhelmed	to make unbearable, to weaken
penetrate	be penetrated	to enter through a barrier such as skin
recycle	be recycled	to use again
tag	be tagged	to label, identify or name

1. Blood is _____ to separate it into its components.

2. It is difficult for bacteria to _____ the skin.

3. After you cut yourself, blood begins to thicken, or _____, at the location of the cut.

4. To protect the stomach from acid, an alkaline mucus _____ the stomach.

5. Instead of allowing bacteria to live, the body causes them to _____.

6. To know which viruses to destroy, the body has to _____ them before it can destroy them.

7. Your immune system becomes _____ when it detects a harmful virus or bacterium.

8. Instead of being destroyed, the iron in old blood cells is _____.

9. When you are sick, your body defenses are _____ by all the germs.

BLOOD

Blood is the liquid that flows within the blood vessels throughout your body. Blood carries nutrients, hormones, oxygen, and water to all areas of the body. If blood is prevented from bringing these things to a certain part of the body, the cells in that body part could die.

Look at Figure 8.2. It shows how blood is collected, processed and separated.

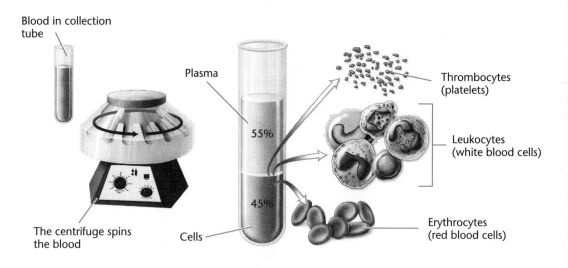

FIGURE 8.2 **In the laboratory, blood collected in tubes is centrifuged. The centrifuge spins the blood until it separates into its two main parts: plasma and cells. There are three types of cells: erythrocytes, leukocytes, and platelets.**

When blood is *centrifuged* (ˈsɛntrɪfyuwdʒd), it separates into its two major components: plasma and cells. The liquid portion of blood is called **plasma**. Plasma is mostly water but also contains molecules such as sugar, hormones, sodium, potassium, and salts dissolved in the water. These molecules give plasma its yellow color. The main job of plasma is to provide a solution, a liquid, in which to carry nutrients, hormones, and blood cells through the blood vessels.

The solid portion of blood is comprised of cells. Blood is actually considered to be a tissue because it contains many different types of cells that are organized to do particular jobs. There are three major types of cells: **erythrocytes** (ɪˈrɪθrəsayts), **leukocytes** (ˈluwkəsayts), and **platelets** (ˈpleytləts). Platelets are sometimes called **thrombocytes** (ˈθrɑmbowsayts).

Erythrocytes, one of the major types of blood cells, are also known as red blood cells. *Erythro-* means *red*; *-cyte* means *cell*. Erythrocytes are shaped like a cough lozenge—medicine you take when you have a bad cough. Like a cough lozenge, erythrocytes are round with an indented central region.

The function of erythrocytes in the blood is to carry oxygen throughout the body. To carry oxygen, each erythrocyte contains an important molecule called **hemoglobin** (ˈhiyməglowbən). Hemoglobin is a protein that attaches to and holds oxygen. Each erythrocyte contains about 250 million hemoglobin molecules. Each hemoglobin molecule can hold four oxygen molecules. When oxygen attaches to hemoglobin, it causes the erythrocyte to turn red. It is the erythrocytes in your blood that make it look red.

In the United States, people often donate blood to places called "blood banks." This blood goes to hospitals where it is given as a transfusion. A transfusion is when new blood is given to a person who has lost a lot of his own blood.

Anemia! **Anemia** (əˈniymniyə) is a condition in which the patient feels very tired and cold, and looks pale. In anemia, the blood is not carrying enough oxygen. There are many different kinds of anemia, depending on the cause. Anemia can be caused by a lack of iron or vitamin B_{12} in the diet, severe blood loss, an infection, or abnormal hemoglobin molecules.

Sickle cell anemia is a type of anemia that is inherited. Patients with sickle-cell anemia have abnormally shaped hemoglobin and this causes their red blood cells to have an unusual sickle (or crescent) shape (see Figure 8.3). When these cells pass through blood vessels, they tend to cluster together and block blood flow. This leads to extreme pain and a lack of oxygen for a normal day's activity. There is no cure at this time for this disease.

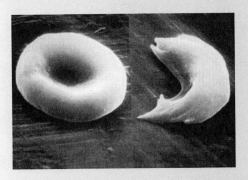

FIGURE 8.3 **A healthy red blood cell (left) and a sickled red blood cell (right)**

Another major type of cell found in the blood is the **leukocyte**. Leukocytes are also known as white blood cells. *Leuko-* means *white*; *-cyte* means *cell*. The job of leukocytes is to defend the body against diseases. There are five types of leukocyte: **basophils, eosinophils, lymphocytes, neutrophils**, and **monocytes**. Blood carries these cells to injured or infected areas of the body where they do specific tasks to help you recover from disease.

- **Basophils** (ˈbeysəfɪlz) and **eosinophils** (iyəˈsɪnəfɪlz) release chemicals that trigger inflammation. Inflammation is the heat and swelling process that is important in healing injuries and fighting infections.

- **Lymphocytes** (ˈlɪmfəsayts) are important in producing **antibodies** (ˈæntiybɑdiyz). Antibodies are proteins that *tag* bacteria and viruses as dangerous. After the bacteria and viruses are tagged, neutrophils and monocytes can remove them.

- **Neutrophils** (ˈnuwtrəfɪlz) and **monocytes** (ˈmɑnəsayts) "eat" bacteria and other foreign substances.

Leukemia! **Leukemia** (luw'kiymiyə) is a cancer of the white blood cells. There are many types of leukemia and they are named by the type of white blood cell that is multiplying in an uncontrolled way. For instance, **lymphocytic** (lɪmfə'sɪtɪk) leukemia occurs when lymphocytes are produced in too large a quantity and do not mature. These cancerous cells *overwhelm* the bloodstream and the bone marrow preventing normal production of blood cells. This makes the patient more susceptible to disease and anemia.

The best solution for lymphocytic leukemia is a **bone marrow transplant**. In this treatment, radiation is used to destroy the patient's bone marrow (and thus the cells that would make blood cells). Then bone marrow cells from a donor are placed into the patient to take the place of the destroyed bone marrow. Since the cancerous cells have been destroyed, this treatment usually cures the individual.

The last of the three major types of cells found in blood is the **platelet**. Platelets play an important role in stopping bleeding. To stop bleeding, blood *coagulates*, which means that platelets come to the area and cause fibers to form across the cut. These fibers help to catch blood cells and a clot then forms which eventually stops the bleeding.

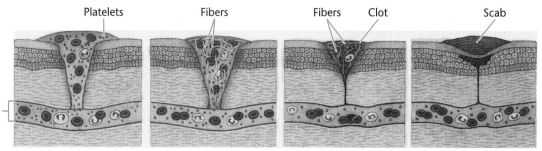

FIGURE 8.4 **When the skin is broken, platelets move to the area and cause fibers to form. Blood cells accumulate in this area, forming a clot. This blocks the opening and prevents loss of more blood.**

 Hemophilia! There are several molecules involved in coagulation. These molecules are called "coagulation factors." If a person lacks the ability to make one or more of these molecules, his blood will not be able to coagulate properly. This condition is called **hemophilia** (hiymə'fɪliyə) and it is an inherited disease. There are several types of hemophilia; each type is named for the coagulation factor that is missing. People with hemophilia must take an artificially produced coagulation factor so they don't bleed to death when they are injured.

1. *Answer the questions below. Then compare your answers with those of a partner.*

   1. What are the two main components of blood?

   2. Name the three major types of blood cells.

   3. What is the function of an erythrocyte?

   4. How many oxygen molecules can one hemoglobin molecule carry?

   5. What is the function of platelets?

   6. Why is sickle cell anemia so painful?

   7. What happens if a person with hemophilia is injured and starts bleeding?

   8. How do people get hemophilia?

2. *What is the function of each leukocyte? Work with a partner. Put a check mark (✓) in the box under each leukocyte's function.*

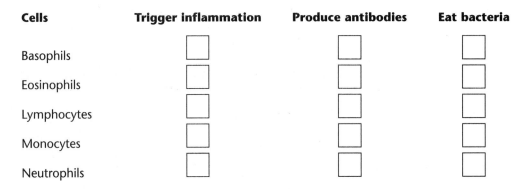

Cells	Trigger inflammation	Produce antibodies	Eat bacteria
Basophils	☐	☐	☐
Eosinophils	☐	☐	☐
Lymphocytes	☐	☐	☐
Monocytes	☐	☐	☐
Neutrophils	☐	☐	☐

INFECTIOUS DISEASE

Many people get a vaccine (væk'siynz) to avoid getting the flu during the winter. A vaccine is made from weaker forms of the pathogen. The vaccine stimulates the body to build defenses against that pathogen.

Disease is a change in a person's health caused by a **microorganism** (maykrow'ɔrgənizəm), a living thing that is too small to see without a microscope. Common diseases throughout the world include AIDS, malaria, and hepatitis. Microorganisms that cause diseases are called **pathogens** ('pæθədʒənz).

When microorganisms invade the body, a person is said to have an **infection**. Two of the most common types of microorganisms are **viruses** ('vayrəsɪz) and **bacteria** (bæk'tɪriyə). Viruses and bacteria are found all around you: in the air, in water, and on things you touch. They are also found on you, even when you are not sick!

A **virus** is very small. Examples of viruses include HIV, influenza (flu), hepatitis, and polio. A virus is a tiny particle made of protein and a nucleic acid. A nucleic acid is the molecule that contains instructions that tell a cell how to do various things. For example, a nucleic acid tells cells how to make a protein. Some scientists don't think viruses are alive because they can't reproduce on their own. When a virus enters your body, it needs to use the organelles of your cells to reproduce. Recall that organelles are the parts of your cells.

A **bacterium** is usually larger than a virus. The plural form of bacterium is bacteria. A bacterium is a simple single-celled organism that can reproduce on its own, like human cells. So bacteria are considered to be alive. However, they are different from most cells because they do not have a nucleus though they do contain nucleic acid. Bacteria only contain a few simple parts. Some examples of bacteria include *E. coli* and *Salmonella*.

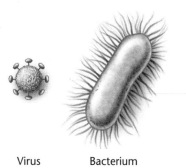

Virus   Bacterium

FIGURE 8.5   **A virus and a bacterium**

Cholera! **Cholera** ('kɑlərə) is a disease that is caused by a bacterium called *Vibrio cholerae*. These bacteria are often found in water that is not clean. When people drink this water, cholera may develop. People may also get this disease from eating uncooked or poorly cooked foods that contain the *Vibrio cholerae* bacteria. The signs and symptoms of cholera include severe watery diarrhea and vomiting. This happens because the cholera bacteria make a molecule called a toxin that causes the small intestine to secrete water and salts. The water and salts are lost in diarrhea, resulting in severe dehydration, a great loss of water in the body. Cholera is a common disease for people living in areas where the water supply is not always clean.

Epidemics have occurred in South America, Bangladesh, India, Democratic Republic of the Congo, and South Africa. The main way to treat cholera is by increasing the amount of fluids and salts in the body.

COMPREHENSION CHECK

1. *Work with a partner to label each statement true (T) or false (F). **If the statement is false, correct it so that it is true.***

   _____ 1. Disease is caused by microorganisms.

   _____ 2. You can see microorganisms with your naked eye.

   _____ 3. Infections can occur when microorganisms enter your body.

   _____ 4. Viruses and bacteria are only found on dirty things.

   _____ 5. Viruses can reproduce without any help from other cells.

   _____ 6. A bacterium is considered to be alive.

   _____ 7. A bacterium contains a nucleus.

   _____ 8. A microorganism can be a pathogen.

2. *Work with a partner. If the information is correct, put a check mark (✓) in the appropriate box.*

Characteristic	Bacterium	Virus
Alive	☐	☐
Has nucleic acid	☐	☐
Single-celled organism	☐	☐
Pathogen	☐	☐
Causes cholera	☐	☐
Causes influenza	☐	☐

BUILDING LANGUAGE AND STUDY SKILLS

Defining Terms

When you study anatomy and physiology, you come across many new words and medical terminology. You will need to give definitions of these words and phrases so your teacher can check your comprehension. You will also need to define terms on tests and when you give presentations. You can find definitions of words in dictionaries or on the Internet. There are also medical dictionaries that have the meanings of medical terms, but sometimes these definitions are too short with not enough detail or are too complex. Being able to give correct and concise definitions is an important skill to have.

Here are some tips when giving definitions:

- Define a term with a synonym—another word that means the same thing. In anatomy and physiology, some terms have two or more names to describe the same concept. For example:

  The *trachea* is commonly known as the *windpipe*.
  Erythrocytes—or *red blood cells*—carry oxygen to all the cells in the body.

  Remember that the synonym and the word it defines must be the same part of speech (noun and noun, verb and verb), so that one term can be substituted for another.

- Give a formal statement of definition. To do this:

  1. Find a larger category in which the word fits.

     For example, a *dog* is part of the category called *animals*.

     A *rose* is part of the category called *flowers*.

  2. Add characteristics that will differentiate this word from other words in the same category.

     A dog is an animal that has *four legs, a tail, fur, and barks*.

     A rose is a flower that has *many petals, thorns on its stem, and is commonly given by lovers on Valentine's Day*.

- Remember to repeat the word in the definition sentence.

  What is the meaning of *a dog*? *A dog is* . . .

Look at these examples of medical terminology:

WORD	CATEGORY	DISTINGUISHING CHARACTERISTICS
Anemia	is a blood disease	caused by a lack of iron in the diet.
An allergy	is a condition	whereby the immune system overreacts to a foreign substance.
A thrombocyte	is a blood cell	that helps the blood to clot.
An immunologist	is a doctor	who specializes in the study of allergies.

PRACTICE

1. *Work with a partner. Read the words and fill in the category and any distinguishing characteristics. Then, on your own, write the definitions of the words. Share your definitions with your partner.*

Word	Category	Distinguishing characteristics
1. basophils	*white blood cells*	*trigger inflammation*
2. lymphocytes		
3. lymphocytic leukemia		
4. bacteria		
5. plasma		

DEFINITIONS

1. basophils: *Basophils are white blood cells that trigger inflammation.*
2. lymphocytes: _____
3. lymphocytic leukemia: _____
4. bacteria: _____
5. plasma: _____

2. *Read the definitions below. Work with a partner. Using the model on page 163, decide which definitions are good and which are not good. Rewrite the definitions that are not good.*

    1. Hemoglobin is a molecule in red blood cells that carries oxygen.

    2. A pathogen causes diseases.

    3. A virus has no organelles.

    4. Cholera is a disease that is caused by a bacterium called *Vibrio cholerae*.

    5. Platelets play an important role in stopping bleeding.

3. *These are authentic questions taken from an anatomy and physiology class. Use the vocabulary and grammar you know to answer these questions.*

Define the following terms:
    a. hemophilia
    b. leukemia
    c. neutrophil

Using Reference Sources

As you continue your studies, you will need to use additional sources to find information about topics, answer questions, prepare presentations, or complete homework. You will find that sometimes it's not enough to just use your textbook. You will need to use other sources to find additional information. Here are a few reference sources you can use to find information.

1. An **encyclopedia** contains information and articles on a variety of subjects. It may also contain diagrams, illustrations, and definitions of terms. A general encyclopedia contains a collection of articles on a great variety of topics. A subject encyclopedia includes more detailed articles on very specific topics, such as medicine or biology.

2. A **dictionary** is a resource if you are looking for the meaning of words you are not familiar with. In addition to meaning, a dictionary will show you how to pronounce and spell words. Just as there are general and subject encyclopedias, there are also general and specialized dictionaries. Specialized dictionaries provide detailed information only about words that apply to a specific subject, such as math, biology, medicine, or psychology.

3. A **thesaurus** contains synonyms for common words. A synonym is a word that has the same or almost the same meaning as another word. For example, the words *difficult* and *complex* are synonyms. A thesaurus can be very useful when you write a paper or prepare a presentation. It can help you express your ideas more clearly.

4. The **Internet** is another good source of information. You can find encyclopedias, dictionaries, and thesauruses on the Internet. You can also find websites that provide information on almost every topic including body systems. You can use a browser to search for information. There are many browsers you can use, such as Google, Yahoo, or Alta Vista. One disadvantage of using the Internet, however, is that you can't always be sure that the information is accurate. Therefore, be sure to check your sources to see that they are reliable. Information from an academic institution is usually more reliable and less biased than information from other sources, such as companies or individuals. If the information is from an academic institution it will have an *edu* at the end of its Internet address (URL).

Look up the word hemophilia *in these different sources. Write down two pieces of information that you find from each source. Then do the activity that follows.*

Source	Information
Encyclopedia	_____
Dictionary	_____
Thesaurus	_____
Internet source 1	_____
Internet source 2	_____

Break up into small groups. Share the information about hemophilia that you found using each source and then discuss the following questions:

1. Was there a difference in the amount of detail you found among the sources?

2. What is the benefit of using each source?

BODY DEFENSES

In English, when people talk about curing a disease, they often use the vocabulary of war, such as: "battling a disease," "beating a disease," "fighting a disease," "winning the war on a disease," or "line of defense against a disease."

Your body has amazing ways to defend itself against bacteria and viruses. In fact, there are so many ways that the body can defend itself that if one defense mechanism doesn't work, there is usually another way for your body to defend itself against disease. The defenses in the body that fight against bacteria and viruses are known as the immune system. These defenses can be grouped into two categories: **innate** (ɪˊneyt) and **adaptive** (əˊdæptɪv) defenses. Most people consider all defenses to be part of the immune system. However, scientists only consider the adaptive defenses to be the immune system.

Innate Defenses

There are several kinds of innate defenses working all of the time to keep you healthy. They work on nearly all invaders such as bacteria and viruses that enter the body and are determined to be foreign. The "first line of defense" includes barriers, hairs, and cilia. The "second line of defense" includes several molecules and cells that can destroy microorganisms.

FIRST LINE OF DEFENSE

Barriers are the most important of your innate defenses. Nearly every organ system has a barrier, like a wall, preventing the entry of microorganisms into that system. For example:

- The **integument (skin)** is an excellent barrier to microorganisms because of its thick layers of cells and its keratin. The only way viruses or bacteria can enter through the skin is if you have a cut or wound. That's why it is always important to clean a break in your skin.

- **Mucous membranes** are another barrier. The thick epithelial layers that *line* the digestive, respiratory, and female reproductive systems are protective for two reasons. For one, their thickness protects the tissues below from the things that might cut or damage the surface. It is difficult for microorganisms to *penetrate* this thick, sticky mucus lining. In fact, they are often captured there. Because mucus is usually alkaline, it is also hard for bacteria to grow there. Most bacteria grow best in neutral (not acidic or alkaline) environments.

- **Wax** inside the ear canal acts as a barrier to trap microorganisms from reaching the internal tissues in the ear. This wax is made by glands within the lining of the ear canal.

- To protect the brain from microorganisms, there is a thickening of cells between blood vessels and the neurons inside the brain. This is called the **blood-brain barrier**.

Meningitis! **Meningitis** (mɛnɪn'dʒaytəs) is one of only a few diseases caused by microorganisms that affect the central nervous system. Meningitis causes the protective coverings around the brain and spinal cord to become inflamed. This puts pressure on the neurons and can cause severe damage and death. There are two types of meningitis: bacterial and viral. The bacterial form is the most serious type of meningitis, and often results in a rapid death. Both forms are highly contagious.

- Hairs inside the nose help to trap bacteria and viruses that may enter through the air. Therefore, when you blow your nose, you are removing mucus that contains these trapped microorganisms. Sometimes, you sneeze when these trapped microorganisms irritate the mucous membranes.

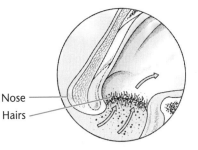

Nose
Hairs

FIGURE 8.6   **Hairs lining the nasal cavity trap particles in the air**

- Deeper in the respiratory system, there are cells along the trachea (the passageway to the lungs) that have tiny hairs called **cilia** ('sɪliyə). These cilia help to sweep any bacteria or viruses upward to the throat where they can be spit out. People who smoke are more likely to get respiratory infections because the nicotine in cigarettes is harmful to their cilia. The only way smokers have to get rid of bacteria is to cough, because their cilia can no longer move the bacteria and viruses upward.

COMPREHENSION CHECK

1. *Read the questions and then scan the text for answers. When you find the answers, underline them. Then work with a partner and take turns asking and answering the questions. Try to remember the answers without looking back at the text.*

    1. Where do you find mucous membranes?

    2. Why is it hard for bacteria to grow in mucus?

    3. Why does the ear produce wax?

    4. Explain what the blood-brain barrier is.

    5. What is the function of the hair in your nose?

    6. Why are smokers more likely to get respiratory infections?

    7. Name four innate defenses that are barriers.

    8. What is meningitis?

2. *Match the terms with their definitions by writing the letters in the correct blanks. Then compare your answers with those of a partner.*

_____ 1. barrier	**a.** barrier that keeps skin waterproof
_____ 2. cilia	**b.** barrier that keeps pathogens out of brain
_____ 3. keratin	**c.** barrier that lines digestive and respiratory tracts
_____ 4. blood-brain barrier	**d.** tiny hairs sweep pathogens up from trachea
_____ 5. wax	**e.** inflammation of protective lining of brain
_____ 6. mucous membrane	**f.** a wall-like structure; keeps pathogens out
_____ 7. meningitis	**g.** barrier found in the ear

SECOND LINE OF DEFENSE

The barrier methods are quite effective in preventing microorganisms from going deeper within the body. However, sometimes microorganisms can penetrate these barriers. When that happens, there are still other types of innate defenses ready to destroy them. These are called "second line" defenses because they act only if the "first line" fails.

Some types of molecules that can kill or weaken microorganisms are:

- **Lysozyme** ('layzəzaym) is found in saliva and tears. This molecule helps to destroy bacteria that might be in the food you eat.

- **Acids**, produced in the stomach, vagina (female reproductive system), the urine, and skin, prevent most bacteria from growing. Most bacteria like to grow in neutral (not acid and not alkaline) conditions. Acid makes it hard for bacteria to multiply.

- **Proteases** ('prowtiyeyzɪz) are molecules found in the digestive system. They help to destroy bacteria and viruses in the food we eat.

- **Interferon** (ɪntər'fɪrɑn), produced by cells that are infected by viruses, helps to prevent that virus from infecting other cells. This molecule has been shown to be effective in treating some viral infections and doctors sometimes prescribe interferon for certain illnesses.

- **Complement**, a group of molecules present in the blood and most tissues, can destroy bacteria. This group of molecules can be *activated* directly by bacteria or by other defense mechanisms. After being activated, complement causes bacteria to *burst*.

Another innate defense is **phagocytes** ('fægəsayts). They are special leukocytes (white blood cells) that help to destroy bacteria and viruses. Phagocytes wander (move randomly) through the body and bloodstream, looking for invaders. These cells actually surround and eat the invading organism. *Phago* means *to eat*. Phagocytes can be found in the blood (neutrophils, monocytes), in the **lymph nodes** (bean-shaped organs that are found throughout the body), and in the fluids surrounding body cells.

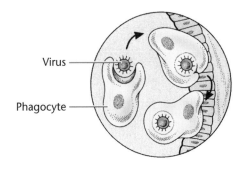

Virus

Phagocyte

FIGURE 8.7   A phagocyte "swallows" a virus

Besides special cells and molecules, another innate defense is a process called **inflammation** (ɪnflə'meyʃən). When you have a wound (such as a cut on your arm), it often appears red and swollen, and feels warm and painful. Redness, swelling, warmth, and pain are called the "four cardinal signs" of inflammation. (The word *cardinal* means *clear* or *distinct*.) Although inflammation is connected to a bad thing (a wound), it actually is your body's way of speeding up the healing process.

What causes inflammation and how does it speed up the healing process? The heat and redness is due to blood vessels in the area becoming wider. Wider blood vessels allow more blood, with its nutrients and disease-fighting cells, to come to the injured area to promote faster healing. The swelling is caused by an increase in fluid going out of the blood into the tissue near the wound. This fluid brings nutrients and disease-fighting cells to the area. The cardinal sign of pain occurs when pain receptors in the damaged area are stimulated to send a message about pain to the brain. Your brain needs this message so that you know something is wrong.

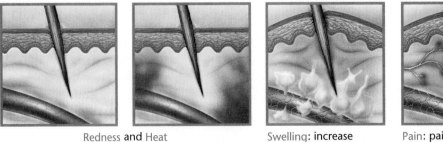
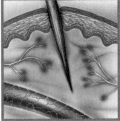

Redness and Heat

Swelling: increase in fluid going out of the blood

Pain: pain receptors stimulated

Result of blood vessels becoming wider

FIGURE 8.8   The four cardinal signs of inflammation

Fever is another innate defense that you may have thought was bad for you. However, just like inflammation, fever is actually your body's way of speeding up the disease-fighting process. Remember from Chapter 6 that homeostasis of body temperature is maintained by an area of the brain called the hypothalamus. When phagocytes are fighting an infection, they send a molecule called a **cytokine** ('saytəkayn) to the hypothalamus. The cytokine tells the hypothalamus to increase the "set point" for the body temperature. The temperature rises, resulting in a fever. An increase of just a few degrees causes the body to speed up its chemical reactions. For example, a fever causes the cells needed to repair an injury to work faster. Also, a fever makes you feel tired—like you need to rest. If you rest, more energy can be used to fight the infection. In addition, the higher temperature makes it more difficult for bacteria to reproduce. So having a low-grade fever is actually good! However, if a fever becomes too high (especially in a child), you need to consult a doctor immediately. Too high a temperature may cause brain damage.

COMPREHENSION CHECK

1. *Complete the chart. Write where the following molecules are found and what they do. Check your answers with the class.*

Innate Defenses	Where?	What do they do?
Acids		
Complement		
Interferon		
Lysozyme		
Proteases		

2. *Circle the letter of the correct answer. Check your answers with those of a partner.*

1. This makes it difficult for bacteria to grow.
   a. complement
   b. acid
   c. interferon

2. This group of molecules causes bacteria to burst.
   a. protease
   b. interferon
   c. complement

3. When one of your cells is infected by a virus, it produces this molecule to prevent other cells from being infected by viruses.
   a. acid
   b. interferon
   c. lysozyme

4. Phagocytes are found _____.
   a. in most body tissues and blood
   b. only in the lymph nodes
   c. only in the blood

5. Inflammation has _____ cardinal signs.
   a. 5
   b. 4
   c. 3

6. Which is NOT a cardinal sign of inflammation?
   a. heat
   b. swelling
   c. sneezing

7. During a fever, what kind of molecule tells the hypothalamus to reset the body's set point?
   a. lysozyme
   b. cytokine
   c. interferon

Adaptive Defenses

Adaptive defenses are produced in response to a microorganism that has escaped the first two lines of defense (barriers and chemical defenses), the innate defenses. Adaptive defenses are very specific to a particular microorganism and will not work against any other bacterium or virus. For example, adaptive defenses produced in response to a measles virus infection won't work against an influenza virus.

The blood cells involved in adaptive defenses are the lymphocytes. There are two major categories of lymphocytes: B cells and T cells. **B cells** develop in bone marrow. Each B cell has the ability to recognize only one particular microorganism. For example, one B cell might be able to recognize the influenza virus, but no other viruses. Another B cell might only be able to recognize a measles virus, but no other viruses. When the B cell meets that microorganism, the B cell makes copies of itself, and some of these B cell copies make a protein called an **antibody**. An antibody is a protein molecule that searches for and collects one particular (specific) microorganism. When the antibody recognizes and attaches to a particular microorganism, it stops the microorganism from attaching to the body's cells. Then phagocytes can destroy it. Antibodies simply find and collect the microorganisms, but they do not kill them.

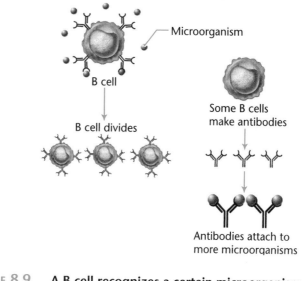

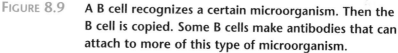

FIGURE 8.9   **A B cell recognizes a certain microorganism. Then the B cell is copied. Some B cells make antibodies that can attach to more of this type of microorganism.**

The other type of lymphocyte is a **T cell**. T cells develop in the **thymus gland** (′θaymǝs ′glænd), which lies just beneath the sternum (breast bone). There are two major types of T cell:

- **Helper T cells** "help" the B cells by giving them a "second opinion" that a microorganism is dangerous. For example, a B cell recognizes the hepatitis A virus. Before the B cell can produce antibodies to collect the hepatitis A viruses, it must get a second opinion from a helper T cell that has also recognized the hepatitis A virus. Only when the helper T cell "agrees" that the hepatitis A virus is dangerous, can the B cell make copies of itself and make antibodies.

- **Cytotoxic** (saytǝ′tɑksɪk) **T cells** are programmed to recognize and kill a cell that has been infected with a particular virus. Each cytotoxic T cell can only recognize human cells that are infected with a single type of virus. It doesn't recognize human cells infected with bacteria. Also, cytotoxic T cells do not kill viruses that are outside your cells—only your cells that contain the particular type of virus.

AIDS! Acquired ImmunoDeficiency Syndrome, or AIDS, is a disease caused by a virus called HIV (Human Immunodeficiency Virus). This virus destroys macrophages, Helper and Cytotoxic T lymphocytes. Without these cells, it is very difficult for the individual to resist disease. AIDS has a long-term progression, often taking up to 10 years before the person is actually diagnosed. HIV infection is treated with a combination of drugs that prevent the virus from making copies of itself. However, there is no cure for AIDS.

COMPREHENSION CHECK

1. *Put the steps in order from 1 to 5 with 1 being the first step.*

   _____ B cell makes copies of itself.

   _____ Phagocytes "eat" and destroy the hepatitis virus.

   __1__ B cell recognizes a hepatitis A virus.

   _____ B cells make antibodies that can recognize the hepatitis A virus.

   _____ Antibodies attach to the hepatitis A viruses, preventing attachment to cells.

2. *Answer the questions below. Then compare your answers with those of a partner.*

   1. Which of the two types of lymphocyte is involved in making antibodies?

   2. What is the function of antibodies? Does a particular antibody work against any microorganism?

   3. After antibodies collect the microorganisms, what kills them?

   4. What are the two types of T cells and what is the function of each?

   5. Do cytotoxic T cells kill viruses inside or outside of cells? Do they work against bacteria?

3. *Circle the correct word(s) to complete each sentence. Take turns reading the correct sentences aloud with a partner.*

   1. Microorganisms can be identified and gathered by proteins called **interferon / antibodies**.

   2. The **cytotoxic T cell / helper T cell** gives a "second opinion" to the B cell.

   3. T-cells develop in the **lymph / thymus** gland.

   4. The general type of leukocyte that is involved in the adaptive defenses is the **neutrophil / lymphocyte**.

   5. The **barrier / adaptive** defenses work after a microorganism escapes the innate defenses.

   6. The **helper T cell / cytotoxic T cell** is able to kill cells that are infected with a virus.

   7. The **B cells / T cells** are lymphocytes that produce antibodies.

   8. HIV destroys **B cells / T cells**.

Lymphatic Organs in Blood and Body Defenses

The **lymphatic** (lɪmˈfætɪk) **system** contains several organs that play a role in fighting disease. The lymphatic system also includes a network of **lymphatic vessels** that help to maintain homeostasis of blood volume. Note in Figure 8.10 that the lymphatic vessels provide circulation between the lymphatic organs.

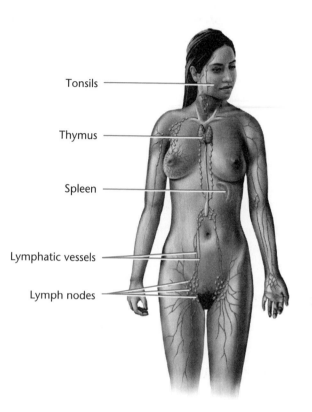

Tonsils

Thymus

Spleen

Lymphatic vessels

Lymph nodes

FIGURE 8.10   **The lymphatic organs and vessels of the body**

The fluid that is brought to the lymphatic organs by lymphatic vessels contains water, dissolved molecules (such as proteins and salts), and sometimes includes microorganisms when you are sick. These microorganisms often come from the fluid-filled areas around the body tissues known as tissue spaces. Lymphatic vessels pick up the extra fluid from these tissue spaces and carry it back to the bloodstream. Before emptying into a blood vessel, these lymphatic vessels pass through one or more lymph nodes.

The **lymph nodes** are kidney-bean-shaped organs that contain phagocytes. Lymph nodes are found throughout the body, often in large clusters in the armpit and groin regions of the body. As lymphatic fluid passes through the lymphatic vessels and lymph nodes, the phagocytes seek out and destroy any foreign microorganisms and molecules that might be carried in the lymphatic fluid. These same phagocytes may also wander into the immediate area around the lymph nodes seeking out microorganisms.

The **spleen** is a lymphatic organ that can be found on the left side of the abdominal cavity, just beneath the diaphragm and near the stomach. The spleen has three important functions:

<table>
<tr><td>

Children used to have their tonsils removed when they were repeatedly infected. Today, doctors are less likely to remove children's tonsils because they realize their important role in immunity.

</td><td>

1. It filters the blood, removing old blood cells, microorganisms, and toxins.
2. It *recycles* iron from old blood cells so it can be reused.
3. It stores platelets.

</td></tr>
</table>

Another lymphatic organ, the thymus, lies just beneath the sternum and plays a role in helping T cells to mature.

Finally, several pairs of lymph organs called **tonsils** ('tɑnsəlz) surround the pharynx. The tonsils' function is to collect microorganisms that pass through this area, preventing them from entering the digestive or respiratory tract. The tonsils also play a role in helping the immune system to remember different types of microorganisms, so you will be immune to them the next time they invade.

COMPREHENSION CHECK

1. *Work with a partner to label each statement true* (T) *or false* (F). *If the statement is false, correct it so that it is true.*

   _____ 1. Lymphatic vessels carry watery fluid.

   _____ 2. One of the spleen's functions is to filter the blood.

   _____ 3. The thymus helps B cells to mature.

   _____ 4. The thymus is located in the neck.

   _____ 5. The tonsils surround the trachea.

   _____ 6. Iron in the red blood cells can be recycled.

   _____ 7. Lymph nodes contain many phagocytes that destroy microorganisms.

   _____ 8. Lymph vessels help to maintain homeostasis of body temperature.

2. *Match the terms with their definitions by writing the letters in the correct blanks. Then compare your answers with those of a partner.*

   _____ 1. lymph node

   _____ 2. lymphatic system

   _____ 3. lymphatic vessels

   _____ 4. spleen

   _____ 5. thymus

   _____ 6. tonsils

   a. collect microorganisms passing through the pharynx

   b. recycles iron from old blood cells

   c. carry lymph fluid

   d. helps T cells to mature

   e. bean-shaped organ that contains phagocytes

   f. contains several organs which play a role in fighting disease

Spiritual Forces in Healing

Some people believe that if they wear a special piece of jewelry or if they carry something such as a rabbit's foot, it will bring them luck and keep them healthy. Many people also believe in the power of prayer to help them get better when they feel sick. Other people prefer to give birth or have surgery only on special dates because they believe some dates are luckier than others.

The following story is about a cultural conflict that people may experience in a health-care setting. Read the story and then discuss the questions in small groups.

Michelle is a nurse in an emergency room. A patient named Gitta was brought into the ER with an irregular heartbeat. Gitta was conscious, but very frantic. Michelle noticed that Gitta was wearing a very interesting and beautiful stone on a cord around her neck. In an effort to calm her patient, Michelle reached to touch the stone and commented on how beautiful it was. This sent Gitta into an absolute panic. She pushed away Michelle's hand and said "NO! Don't touch it!" As a result Gitta's heartbeat became even more irregular.

1. Why do you think Gitta doesn't want Michelle to touch the stone?

2. Do you carry anything with you which you feel helps you to maintain your health and luck?

3. If you had to go to the hospital for an operation, would you want to pray or be careful about the date of the operation?

Check Your Understanding

1. *Answer the following questions about the blood and body defenses.*

1. What are the two major components of blood?

2. Name the three major types of cells in the blood and the major function of each.

3. Which molecule carries oxygen in the blood? In which cell is it found?

4. What isn't working if a person has hemophilia?

5. How do innate and adaptive defenses differ when it comes to body invaders?

6. Name one major difference between a virus and a bacterium.

7. What do phagocytes do?

8. What are the four cardinal signs of inflammation?

9. Is it a T cell or a B cell that kills cells infected by viruses?

10. How do lymph nodes help your immune system?

2. *Label Figure 8.11 with the terms provided.*

lymph nodes	lymphatic vessels	spleen	thymus	tonsils

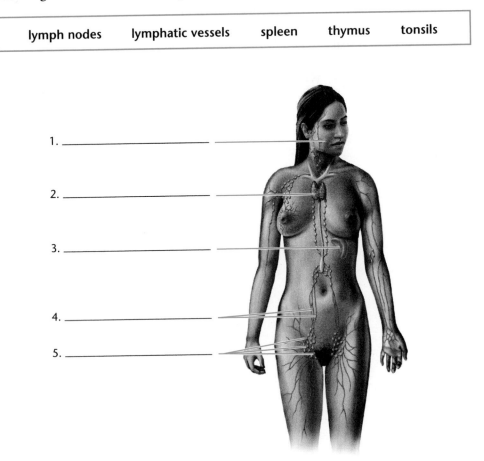

1. _____

2. _____

3. _____

4. _____

5. _____

FIGURE 8.11   **The lymphatic system**

3. *Answer these typical anatomy and physiology quiz questions.*

1. _____ Is this true or false? Anemia is a disease in which there are not enough leukocytes.

2. _____ Is this true or false? The first lines of defense are the adaptive defenses.

3. Which blood cell carries oxygen to cells throughout the body?
   a. lymphocyte   **b.** neutrophil   **c.** erythrocyte   **d.** platelet

4. Which of the following is NOT matched correctly with its function?
   a. Spleen: removes old red blood cells from blood.
   b. T cell: makes antibodies.
   c. Neutrophil: type of leukocyte that does phagocytosis.
   d. Thymus: place where T cells mature.

5. Which of these is NOT a part of the blood plasma?
   a. erythrocytes   **b.** protein   **c.** water   **d.** salts

6. What would happen to the body if the lymphatic vessels were blocked and the fluid couldn't return to the bloodstream from the tissues?

7. Name two functions of the blood.

8. Describe three different innate defenses and explain how each defends against disease.

Think More about It

1. How is the integument system related to the body defense system?

2. The lymphatic vessels branch and form a network throughout the body. What other structures form networks and travel throughout the body?

3. Is blood considered a cell, tissue, or organ? Why?

Word Bank		
activate	disease	overwhelm
adaptive defense	erythrocyte	pathogen
antibody	helper T cell	penetrate
B cell	immune system	phagocytes
bacterium	inflammation	plasma
barrier	innate defenses	platelet
burst	interferon	protease
centrifuge	leukocyte	recycle
cilia	line	tag
coagulate	lymph nodes	thrombocyte
complement	lymphatic system	virus
cytokine	lysozyme	
cytotoxic T cell	microorganism	

CHAPTER 9

The Cardiovascular System

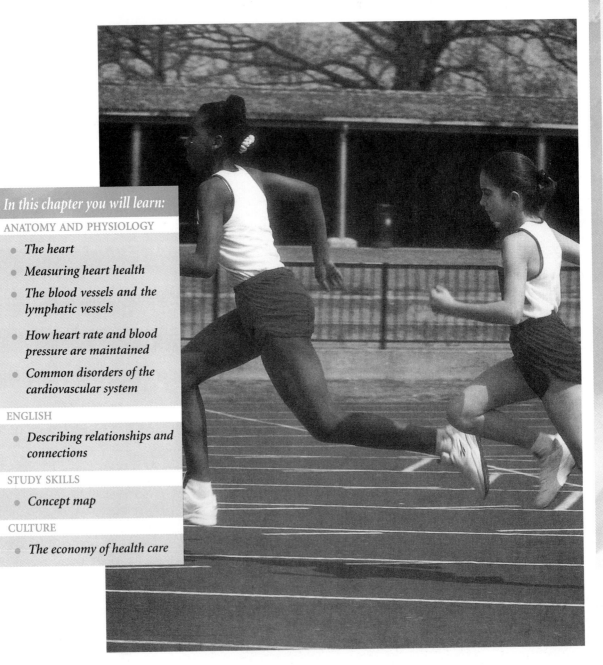

In this chapter you will learn:

ANATOMY AND PHYSIOLOGY

- *The heart*
- *Measuring heart health*
- *The blood vessels and the lymphatic vessels*
- *How heart rate and blood pressure are maintained*
- *Common disorders of the cardiovascular system*

ENGLISH

- *Describing relationships and connections*

STUDY SKILLS

- *Concept map*

CULTURE

- *The economy of health care*

DID YOU KNOW *there are 60,000 miles (96,560 kilometers) of blood vessels in the body? It is enough to reach around the Earth!*

INTRODUCTION

The cardiovascular system is comprised of the heart, blood, and blood vessels. You learned about blood in the previous chapter. In this chapter, you will study how the heart acts as a pump to move blood throughout the body through different types of blood vessels (arteries, veins, and capillaries). Then you will also learn about some common heart problems.

1. *Work with a partner. Look at the diagram of the cardiovascular system. Try to label the parts with the words in the box. Look at Figure 9.2 on page 180 to check your answers.*

artery   heart   lung   vein

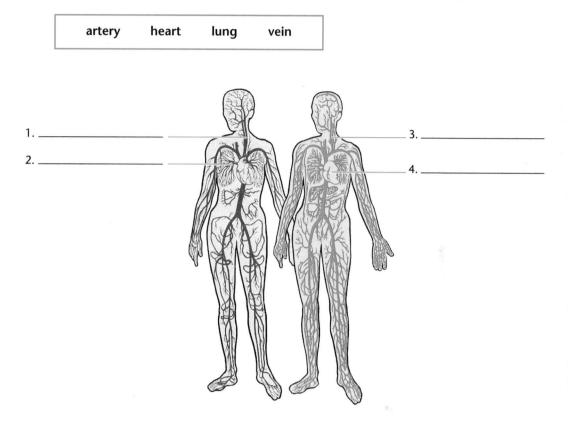

1. _____

2. _____

3. _____

4. _____

FIGURE 9.1   **The cardiovascular system**

2. *With your partner, try to answer these questions. If you do not know the answers, do not worry. You will find the answers as you read through this chapter.*

1. What is the function of the heart?

2. What type of tissue is found in the heart?

3. Where does blood pick up oxygen?

4. What is the difference between arteries, veins, and capillaries?

5. What happens when someone has a heart attack?

6. What is the function of the blood vessels?

7. What is blood pressure, and what happens to the body when blood pressure is too low or too high?

3. *Read each verb, its simple definition, and its passive voice form. Then fill in the verbs in the sentences that follow. Pay attention to verb tense and subject / verb agreement. Compare your answers with those of another student.*

BASE FORM	PASSIVE VOICE FORM	MEANING
branch	be branched	divide into many parts, like a tree
constrict	be constricted	reduce the diameter (width)
dilate	be dilated	increase the diameter (width)
exert	be exerted	to cause, to push
oxygenate	be oxygenated	to add oxygen

1. Poorly oxygenated blood becomes _____ in the lungs.

2. Blood pressure is the pressure _____ by the blood on blood vessel walls.

3. When you enter a dark room, the pupils in your eyes _____, so that you can see.

4. When you go out into the bright sunshine, the pupils in your eyes _____ because you don't need as much light to see.

5. The aorta leaves the heart and then _____ into several other blood vessels that go to different places in the body.

THE HEART

The **cardiovascular** (kɑrdiow'væskyələr) system is comprised of the heart, blood, and blood vessels. *Cardio-* means *heart*; *vascular* means *vessels*. The main job of the cardiovascular system is to transport blood throughout your body. Recall that blood transports nutrients, oxygen, hormones, and waste products.

The Anatomy of the Heart

The heart lies within the **thoracic** (θə'ræsɪk) cavity, also known as the chest cavity. It is located beneath the left lung and lies on its side. The heart is inside a sac, like a sandwich inside a bag. This sac is called the **pericardium** (pɛrə'kɑrdiyəm). *Peri-* means *around*; *cardio-* means *heart*.

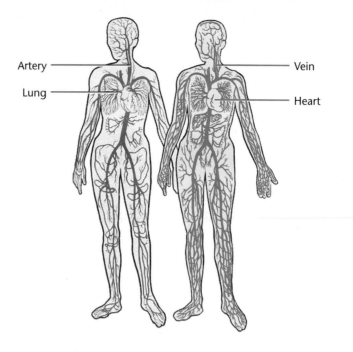

FIGURE 9.2   The cardiovascular system

The Wall of the Heart

The wall of the heart is comprised of three main layers: pericardium, cardiac muscle, and endocardium.

The outermost layer of the heart is one of the two layers of **pericardium**. In between the two layers of pericardium there is a slippery fluid called **pericardial fluid**. The pericardial fluid protects the heart from damage as it beats against the wall of the chest cavity.

The middle layer of the heart is made of cardiac muscle. The middle layer is called the **myocardium** (mayow′kɑrdiyəm). *Myo-* means *muscle*; *cardio-* means *heart*. The myocardium is the thickest of the three layers and is the muscle that contracts when your heart beats.

Finally, the inner layer of the wall of the heart (next to the blood itself) is made of epithelium. Recall that epithelial tissue is also found in the skin. This layer of the heart is called the **endocardium** (ɛndow′kɑrdiyəm). The epithelium in the endocardium provides a smooth layer against which the blood flows.

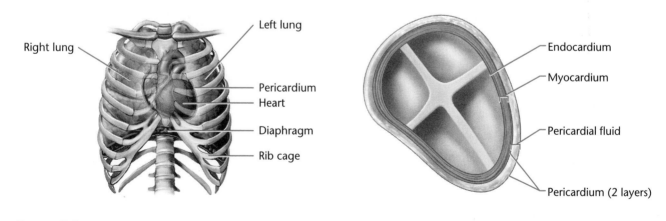

FIGURE 9.3   Position of the heart in the thoracic cavity

FIGURE 9.4   The heart wall

COMPREHENSION CHECK

1. *Answer the questions below. Then compare your answers with those of a partner.*

   1. In what cavity are the lungs and the heart located?
   2. What are the three layers of the heart wall?
   3. Which layer of the heart wall actually does the pumping of blood?
   4. What is the name of the inner layer of the heart wall?
   5. Where do you find the pericardial fluid?
   6. Why does the heart need pericardial fluid?

2. *Match the terms with their definitions by writing the letters in the correct blanks. Then compare your answers with those of a partner.*

   _____ 1. thoracic   **a.** muscle

   _____ 2. endo-   **b.** within

   _____ 3. cardio-   **c.** vessel

   _____ 4. vasc-   **d.** around

   _____ 5. myo-   **e.** chest

   _____ 6. peri-   **f.** heart

The Chambers and Valves of the Heart

The heart has four chambers. The word *chamber* means *room*. The top two smaller chambers are called **atria** (ˈeytriyə) (singular = atrium). The bottom two larger chambers are called **ventricles** (ˈvɛntrɪkəlz). The atria and ventricles are named for the nearest side of that person's body: right or left. Therefore, you have a right atrium and a left atrium, a right ventricle and a left ventricle.

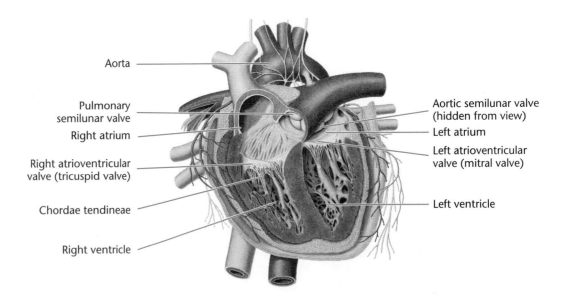

FIGURE 9.5   Chambers and valves of the heart

Blood always flows from the atria to the ventricles. Small door-like structures called **valves** separate each atrium from the ventricle below it. Since there are two atria and two ventricles, there are two **atrioventricular** (eytriyowvən'triykyələr) valves, or **AV valves** for short.

The atrioventricular valve on the right is called the **tricuspid valve** (*tri*- means *three*). This valve has three cusps—flaps or small pieces of tissue that form part of the valve. The AV valve on the left is called the **bicuspid valve** (*bi*- means *two*) or **mitral valve**. This valve has two cusps.

Blood flows easily from the atria through AV valves to the ventricles due to gravity. Liquids naturally flow downhill. When the ventricle is full of blood, the blood pushes the cusps of the AV valves closed. You can see in Figure 9.5 that there are strings that attach the cusps to a muscle in the wall of the ventricle. These strings, called **chordae tendineae** ('kɔrdey tɛn'dɪney), hold the cusps in the closed position so they don't push into the atria.

There are two more valves in the heart. These valves are called **semilunar** (sɛmiy'luwnər) **valves** (*semi*- means *half*; *lunar* means *moon*). These two valves look like half moons. One semilunar valve is between the right ventricle and the pulmonary artery (*pulm*- means *lungs*). This valve is called the **pulmonary semilunar valve**. As blood travels through the heart, it is pumped from the right ventricle to the pulmonary artery and then to the lungs to be *oxygenated*. The pulmonary semilunar valve closes to make sure that blood doesn't flow back into the ventricle after it enters the pulmonary artery.

The other semilunar valve, called the **aortic semilunar valve**, separates the left ventricle from the aorta which is the largest artery in the body. When oxygenated blood leaves the left ventricle, it passes through the aortic semilunar valve and enters the aorta to travel throughout the body. The aortic semilunar valve closes to prevent the blood from falling back into the left ventricle.

Comprehension Check

1. *Work with a partner to label each statement true* (T) *or false* (F). *If the statement is false, correct it so that it is true.*

    _____ 1. The semilunar valves connect the ventricles with the atria.

    _____ 2. The atria are smaller than the ventricles.

    _____ 3. Blood flows from the ventricles to the atria.

    _____ 4. The tricuspid valve is on the right side of the heart.

    _____ 5. The aortic semilunar valve connects the aorta with the left ventricle.

    _____ 6. The bicuspid valve is between the left ventricle and the left atrium.

    _____ 7. Blood flows from the right ventricle through the pulmonary semilunar valve to the pulmonary artery.

    _____ 8. When the atria are contracting, the AV valves are closed.

2. *Circle the correct word(s) to complete each sentence. Take turns reading the correct sentences aloud with a partner.*

1. The vessel that takes blood to the lungs is the **aorta / pulmonary artery**.

2. The smaller chambers at the "top" of the heart are called **ventricles / atria**.

3. A "door" between two chambers of the heart is called a **valve / ventricle**.

4. The strings that keep valves from opening in the wrong direction are called **semilunars / chordae tendineae**.

5. A valve with three flaps is the **tricuspid / bicuspid**.

6. A valve that has flaps that look like half-moons is the **mitral / semilunar** valve.

Tracing the Path of Blood through the Heart

You've just learned the basic anatomy of the heart. Now let's trace the path of blood as it moves through the heart, from where it first enters the heart from the body to where it exits the heart to return to the body.

First, two large vessels carry poorly oxygenated blood from the body to the right atrium of the heart. One vessel, the **superior vena cava** (suw′pɪriyər ′viynə ′keyvə), brings blood to the heart from the areas of the body above the heart, such as the shoulders, head, and upper chest. The **inferior vena cava**, the other large vessel, brings blood to the heart from the areas below the heart, such as the digestive system and the legs.

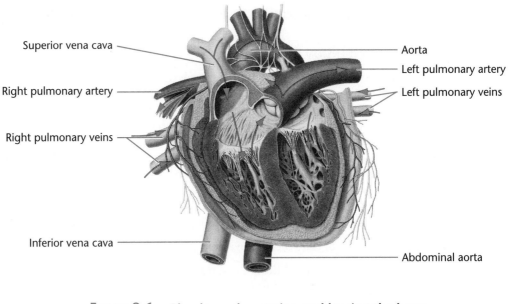

Superior vena cava
Right pulmonary artery
Right pulmonary veins
Inferior vena cava
Aorta
Left pulmonary artery
Left pulmonary veins
Abdominal aorta

FIGURE 9.6 **Blood vessels entering and leaving the heart. Arrows indicate direction of blood flow.**

The blood is now in the right atrium. Most of the blood simply falls through the tricuspid valve and enters the right ventricle. The right atrium then contracts to make sure that almost all of the blood gets into the right ventricle. Then the tricuspid valve closes. Nearly all of the blood is now in the right ventricle.

Next, the right ventricle contracts to push the blood upward through the pulmonary semilunar valve into the **pulmonary artery**. The pulmonary artery splits into right and left branches. One branch goes into each lung. Blood goes to the lungs via pulmonary arteries to become oxygenated.

In the lungs, the pulmonary arteries *branch* repeatedly until they become **pulmonary capillaries** (ˈkæpəlɛriyz). Capillaries are the smallest vessels in the body. The blood gets rid of its carbon dioxide (waste) in the lungs. The carbon dioxide passes through the thin capillary walls and when you breathe out, you remove this carbon dioxide from your body. At the same time the blood gets rid of carbon dioxide, oxygen enters the thin capillary walls from the lungs. The blood is now oxygenated and most of the carbon dioxide is gone (see Figure 9.7).

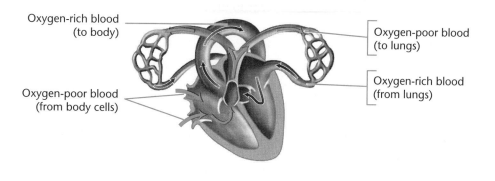

Oxygen-rich blood
(to body)

Oxygen-poor blood
(to lungs)

Oxygen-rich blood
(from lungs)

Oxygen-poor blood
(from body cells)

FIGURE 9.7   **Gas exchange in the lungs. Black arrows indicate oxygen-rich blood. Blue arrows indicate oxygen-poor blood.**

Once the blood has picked up more oxygen, it returns to the left atrium of the heart via **pulmonary veins**. Then blood in the left atrium simply falls through the bicuspid valve to enter the left ventricle. The left atrium then contracts to make sure that all of the blood gets into the left ventricle.

Finally, to complete the path of blood through the heart, the left ventricle contracts (and the bicuspid valve closes), sending blood upward through the aortic semilunar valve to the aorta, the biggest vessel in the body. Oxygenated blood leaves the aorta to travel via arteries throughout the body.

You now understand the step-by-step path of blood as it flows through the heart. However, there is one more very important fact to learn. There are two flows of blood moving through the heart at the same time. The right side of the heart is pushing poorly oxygenated blood to the lungs at the same time as the left side is sending oxygenated blood to the aorta. These two processes happen simultaneously, which means that they happen at the same time.

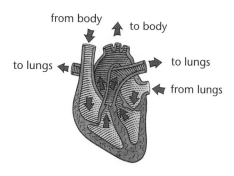

from body   to body

to lungs   to lungs

from lungs

FIGURE 9.8   **The simultaneous path of blood in the heart**

1. *Put the steps of blood flow in order from 1 to 7. The first step is labeled for you.*

   _____ Blood from the right ventricle is pushed through the semilunar valve into the pulmonary artery that carries it to the lungs.

   _____ The left ventricle sends blood through the aortic semilunar valve into the aorta.

   __1__ Blood enters the right atrium.

   _____ Blood picks up oxygen in the lungs.

   _____ Blood passes through the bicuspid valve into the left ventricle.

   _____ Blood returns to the left atrium via the pulmonary veins.

   _____ Blood passes through the tricuspid valve into the right ventricle.

2. *Work with a partner. If the information is correct, put a check mark (✓) in the appropriate box.*

	Blood high in oxygen	**Blood low in oxygen**
The right ventricle	☐	☐
The left ventricle	☐	☐
The left atrium	☐	☐
The right atrium	☐	☐

How the Heart Pumps Blood

The heart is like a mechanical pump that forces blood through your blood vessels. The heart needs to *exert* enough pressure so that blood can get to the farthest parts of your body. Obviously, it is much easier for blood to flow below the heart to your legs and feet because of the pull of gravity. Going uphill is more difficult, and your heart works very hard to pump blood uphill to your brain. Getting blood to your brain is very important, and luckily your heart muscle is very strong and doesn't tire easily. Amazingly, your heart pumps over 15,000 liters (4,000 gallons) of blood per day.

People often refer to the heart as a big muscle. Recall that the heart is comprised of a large amount of myocardium. Cardiac muscle differs from skeletal muscle in one important way. While skeletal muscle must receive a message from the nervous system to contract, cardiac muscle contracts on its own. All cardiac muscle fibers are **autorhythmic** (atow′rıðmık), meaning they contract on their own without any neural messages. In fact, if you took the heart out of the body, it would continue to beat on its own until it ran out of oxygen.

How is the heart able to contract on its own? The heart can contract because it has a special area of cardiac muscle in the right atrium called the **pacemaker** or **sinoatrial** (saynow′eytriyəl) **node** (**SA node**). The SA node is responsible for making the cardiac muscle fibers in the atria or ventricles contract as a group. In effect, the SA node is the control center for heart contractions. Obviously, it would not be good for each fiber to have its own "rhythm" or pace. The cardiac muscle fibers in each chamber must work together to contract at the same time to pump blood efficiently. The coordination of these contractions is the job of the SA node.

To make sure that cardiac muscle fibers in each chamber contract at the same time, the SA node sends signals along a **conduction system**. The conduction system of the heart is comprised of special cardiac muscle fibers that begin at the SA node. The function of these conducting fibers is to send electrical messages to the four chambers of the heart. Because the SA node is in the right atrium, the atria get the message first and contract first. When the signal reaches the ventricles, they contract. Because the conducting fibers are tightly connected to one another, an electrical signal is sent very rapidly.

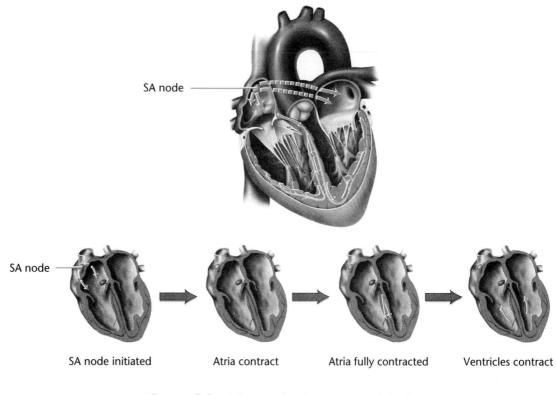

SA node

SA node

SA node initiated   Atria contract   Atria fully contracted   Ventricles contract

FIGURE 9.9   **The conduction system of the heart**

Heart Attack! The obvious function of the heart is to pump blood through the body. However, the heart muscle has to have its own blood supply in order to get nutrients and oxygen needed for muscle contractions. Recall that highly oxygenated blood leaves the heart through the aorta. Some of this blood enters the coronary arteries to nourish the heart. If there is a blockage of one or more of these coronary arteries, the heart muscle supplied by that area may experience pain called **angina pectoris** (æn'dʒaynə 'pɛktərɪs). Because the cardiac muscle is denied nutrients, the muscle may actually die. When heart muscle dies, it cannot help the heart pump. This usually leads to a **myocardial infarction** (mayə'kardiyəl ɪn'farkʃən) or heart attack. Muscle tissue, in the case of myocardial infarction, does not grow back. Connective tissue replaces the dead muscle and this weakens the heart. The more heart attacks a person has, the less likely he will be able to recover.

1. *Read the questions and then scan the text for answers. When you find the answers, underline them. Then work with a partner and take turns asking and answering the questions. Try to remember the answers without looking back at the text.*

   1. Is it harder for your heart to pump blood to your brain or to your feet? Why?

   2. How is cardiac muscle different from skeletal muscle?

   3. Which structure in the heart sets the rate at which cardiac muscle contracts?

   4. What makes all cardiac muscle fibers contract in a coordinated way?

   5. Describe the connections between cardiac muscle fibers.

   6. What two things are brought to the cardiac muscle fibers by blood vessels?

   7. What happens if the blood supply to a part of the heart is blocked?

2. *Complete the sentences using the words in the box. Take turns reading the correct sentences aloud with a partner.*

angina pectoris	conduction	pacemaker
autorhythmic	myocardial infarction	sinoatrial node

   1. Cardiac muscle fibers are able to contract without outside stimulation. They are said to be _____.

   2. The _____ system of the heart sends signals to all the cardiac muscle fibers.

   3. The rate of contraction is determined by the _____ (also called the _____).

   4. When the blood supply to a part of the heart is blocked, the person may feel pain in that area. This pain is called _____.

   5. When cardiac muscle cells die from lack of oxygen, the person may experience a heart attack or _____.

MEASURING HEART HEALTH

When you visit the doctor, he or she takes important measurements of your heart. These measurements tell the doctor information about your heart's health.

Heart Rate

The **heart rate** is the number of contractions (or beats) your heart makes per minute. The heart rate tells the doctor whether a person's heart is working too hard or too little. Heart rate is typically measured by taking the **pulse rate**. When the ventricles contract in a rhythmic fashion, this sends blood into the arteries in bursts. So when you put a little pressure on a blood vessel near the skin, you can feel the pulse.

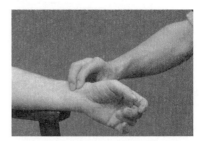

Heart Rate

The normal resting heart rate is about 72 beats per minute. This rate is adequate for getting enough blood (and therefore nutrients) to the tissues of the body when the person is resting. However, there are times when the heart rate must change. Recall that the sympathetic division ("fight or flight") of the autonomic nervous system causes an increase in heart rate when you are scared or stressed out. The heart rate also increases in the following situations:

- During exercise
- If you have been drinking caffeine or smoking (nicotine)
- Increased body temperature (for example, fever)

If the heart were not able to beat faster during stress or exercise, the body would use oxygen and nutrients faster than they could be supplied. Eventually, there would not be enough oxygen to the brain and the person could lose consciousness.

Age also affects heart rate. The average heart rate in a fetus (an unborn baby) is 150 beats per minute! As we get older, our heart rate gradually decreases.

COMPREHENSION CHECK

1. *Circle the correct word(s) to complete each sentence. Take turns reading the correct sentences aloud with a partner.*

    1. Heart rate is measured with **breathing rate / pulse rate**.

    2. Normal resting heart rate is **72 / 52** beats per minute.

    3. The sympathetic nervous system causes the heart rate to **increase / decrease**.

    4. Your heart rate increases during **exercise / meals**.

    5. Heart rate increases during **hypothermia (cold) / fever**.

    6. Resting heart rate **increases / decreases** with age.

    7. Heart rate **increases / decreases** during stress.

2. *Measuring Pulse Rate. While seated, measure your pulse rate by placing your middle finger on the blood vessel at the inside of your wrist (the radial artery) or in your neck (the carotid artery). Apply enough pressure to feel the pulse, but not enough to block the blood flow. Use a clock or watch with a second hand and count the number of beats for 15 seconds. Multiply this number by 4 to arrive at the beats per minute (bpm).*

    My resting pulse rate is _____ bpm.

    Compare your resting pulse rate with your pulse rate:
    a. when you are standing.
    b. when you are lying down.
    c. right after you have exercised.

Heart Sounds

By listening to the sounds the heart makes, a doctor can tell if the heart is pumping efficiently and if valves are working properly. If you listen to the heart with a **stethoscope** (ˈstɛθəskowp), you can hear two distinct heart sounds. These heart sounds are actually caused by the closing of heart valves. The first sound is long, loud, and low-pitched. We sometimes say it sounds like "lub." This is caused by the closing of the AV (bicuspid and tricuspid) valves as the blood fills the ventricles. The second sound is shorter and more high-pitched. We sometimes say it sounds like "dup." The second sound is caused by the closing of the semilunar (aortic and pulmonary) valves as the blood moves out from the ventricles.

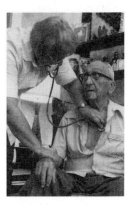

Heart Murmur! A heart murmur is an unusual sound a physician may hear when listening to heart sounds. Sometimes, this may be an extra swishing sound. This may indicate a problem with one or more of the heart valves. One common heart valve problem is having a **stenotic** (stəˈnɑtɪk) **valve**. A stenotic valve is one that is not flexible and therefore does not open as easily as it should. Therefore, not as much blood can be pumped through the valve (and thus out to the body). Another common heart valve problem is an **incompetent valve**. An incompetent valve doesn't close as tightly as it should. Therefore, blood may leak back into the previous chamber instead of being pumped to the next location. In both of these cases, the heart has to pump harder to deliver the same amount of blood to the body.

COMPREHENSION CHECK

Complete the sentences using the words in the box. Take turns reading the correct sentences aloud with a partner.

AV valves	incompetent	second	stenotic
first	murmur	semilunar valves	stethoscope

1. The doctor listens to heart sounds with a _____.

2. The first heart sound is caused by the closing of the _____.

3. The second heart sound is caused by the closing of the _____.

4. The _____ heart sound is shorter and more high-pitched.

5. An unusual sound in the heart is called a heart _____.

6. A(n) _____ valve is not as flexible, doesn't open as easily, and allows less blood through it.

7. A(n) _____ valve doesn't close very well and thus blood leaks through it.

8. The _____ heart sound is longer and more low-pitched.

EKG

Sometimes, the measurement of the heart rate and listening to the heart sounds with a stethoscope are good enough. However, if there seems to be a problem with the heart, the doctor uses an **electrocardiograph** (ɪlɛktrow'kardiyəgræf) or **EKG**. The EKG allows the health-care professional to learn how the heart's electrical signals are being transmitted along the conduction system. When a person gets an EKG, he or she is hooked up to several **electrodes** that measure the change in electrical current between different areas of the body. These measurements produce a particular pattern on the electrocardiograph machine. If the pattern on the EKG is different from what is considered normal, the doctor can usually tell what is wrong with the patient's heart. For example, the doctor can often tell if the patient's conduction system is working properly or if there are areas of the heart that are not contracting.

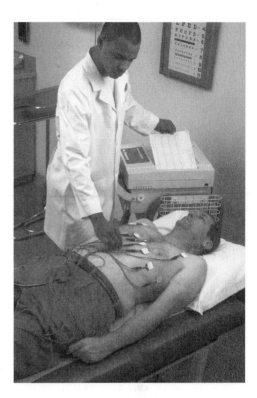

 Arrhythmia! **Arrhythmia** (ə'rɪðmiyə) is an abnormal heart rhythm and can often be detected with an EKG. There are many different types of arrhythmia, each with its own distinct EKG pattern and causes.

Fibrillation (faybrɪ'leyʃən) is an arrhythmia in which the heart muscle does not beat in a coordinated fashion because the conduction system is not controlling the muscle like it should. If this occurs in the ventricles, the ventricles often look like a "bag of worms," with each little part of the ventricle beating in its own rhythm. As a result, little blood is pumped out of the ventricles because there is no coordination of contraction.

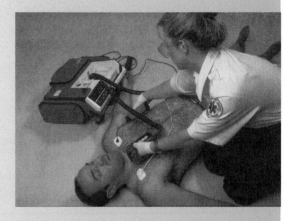

If a patient has ventricular fibrillation, the emergency room personnel will often use a **defibrillator**, a machine that "shocks" the heart muscle into following the directions of the conduction system. In effect, the heart is shocked back into a normal rhythm. The defibrillator is often shown in television programs when a character has a heart attack. The doctor uses a pair of paddles to deliver the electrical shock to the heart area.

Work with a partner to label each statement true (T) or false (F). If the statement is false, correct it so that it is true.

_____ **1.** The EKG helps the doctor listen to heart sounds.

_____ **2.** Electrodes used with the EKG measure the change in electrical current in different areas of the body.

_____ **3.** Problems with the conduction system of the heart can be detected with the EKG.

_____ **4.** Arrhythmia is the normal heart rhythm.

_____ **5.** When heart muscle contractions are not coordinated, it results in a condition called defibrillation.

_____ **6.** The heart muscle must contract in a coordinated way to pump blood efficiently.

_____ **7.** Sometimes, electrical shocks are used to stop heart muscle from beating in an irregular fashion.

Blood Pressure

Nearly every visit to the doctor includes a check of blood pressure. **Blood pressure (BP)** is a measurement of the pressure exerted by blood on the walls of blood vessels. Doctors measure blood pressure because it gives them an idea of how well the cardiovascular system is working.

Blood pressure is recorded with two numbers, such as 110 / 70. The upper number (110, in this case) is called the **systolic** (sɪ′stɑlɪk) **pressure** and indicates the pressure the ventricles exert when they are contracting. The lower number (70) is called the **diastolic** (dayə′stɑlɪk) **pressure** and indicates the pressure when the ventricles are relaxing. If someone has a resting blood pressure of over 120 / 80, it is considered high.

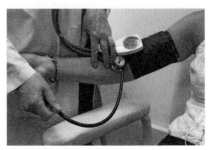

Blood pressure rises or falls, depending on one or more of the following three changes:

1. **Changes in the volume of blood pumped per contraction from the heart**
   When the heart sends out more blood per contraction, this increases blood pressure.

2. **Changes in level of contraction of muscle in the artery walls**
   Changes occur in the level of muscle contraction in arteries when either the sympathetic or parasympathetic part of the autonomic nervous system is activated. For example, if you are frightened, sympathetic nerves cause **vasoconstriction** (the vessels *narrow*) and blood pressure rises. When you lie down to sleep, parasympathetic nerves cause **vasodilation** (the vessels widen) and blood pressure falls.

3. **Changes in blood volume**
   Blood volume decreases due to extreme loss of blood or dehydration. When your blood volume decreases, so does blood pressure. If you have a hormonal imbalance or eat a lot of salty food, you might retain water. If you retain water, your blood volume and blood pressure increase.

What changes blood volume and what changes the level of contraction in the artery walls? Work with a partner. Put a check mark (✓) in the appropriate box.

	Changes blood volume	Changes the level of contraction in the artery walls
Hormonal imbalance	☐	☐
Loss of blood or dehydration	☐	☐
Salt	☐	☐
When you are frightened	☐	☐
When you lie down to sleep	☐	☐

MAINTAINING HOMEOSTASIS

Blood Pressure

It is very important for the body to maintain a constant blood pressure to ensure that an adequate supply of blood gets to the brain. Therefore, blood pressure is monitored by sensory receptors called **baroreceptors** (bærərɪˈsɛptərz). *Baro-* means *pressure*. These receptors are located inside the walls of certain large arteries. They are connected by afferent neurons to the medulla. Recall that the medulla is a small area within the brainstem that regulates heart rate and blood pressure. When blood pressure is too high or too low, a **baroreceptor reflex** occurs. The baroreceptor reflex contains the five components of a reflex that you studied in the nervous system: sensory receptor, afferent neuron, CNS, efferent neuron, and effector organ. The effector organs in this case are the heart and muscles within the blood vessels. Let's look at an example of the baroreceptor reflex.

Marc is sleeping soundly. He suddenly wakes up and looks at the clock. Oh, no! The alarm did not ring and he is late for work. Marc jumps quickly out of bed. He suddenly feels dizzy and sits down quickly. After sitting for minute, he is able to get up without feeling dizzy. Why did Marc get dizzy and have to sit down?

While Marc was sleeping, his blood pressure was low because his horizontal position made it easy for blood to travel all over his body. When he suddenly jumped up, there was not enough pressure to get blood to Marc's brain and that made him feel dizzy.

As soon as Marc jumped out of bed, the baroreceptors in his arteries sent messages to his medulla that his blood pressure was low. The medulla then sent messages along efferent neurons to the heart (causing an increase in heart rate) and to the blood vessel walls causing vasoconstriction. Both of these changes eventually increased Marc's blood pressure back to normal levels. At that time, the baroreceptors sent another message along afferent neurons to the medulla, indicating that the blood pressure had risen.

What happens in the opposite situation where a person's blood pressure becomes too high? The baroreceptors also send messages about this change to the medulla. The medulla sends messages along efferent neurons to the heart (causing a decrease in heart rate) and also the blood vessel walls causing vasodilation. Both of these changes decrease blood pressure to normal levels.

This baroreceptor reflex can only be effective if the change in blood pressure is due to a change in volume pumped by the heart and/or in the amount of muscle contraction in the blood vessel walls. If the change in blood pressure is due to the third possible cause, a change in blood volume, the baroreceptor reflex cannot fix that. Blood volume can only be changed by the kidneys (excreting more or less water), the hypothalamus (causing you to drink more or less water), or hormones such as anti-diuretic hormone (from the pituitary gland) and aldosterone (from the adrenal gland). You will learn more about the role of the kidneys and these hormones in Chapter 11.

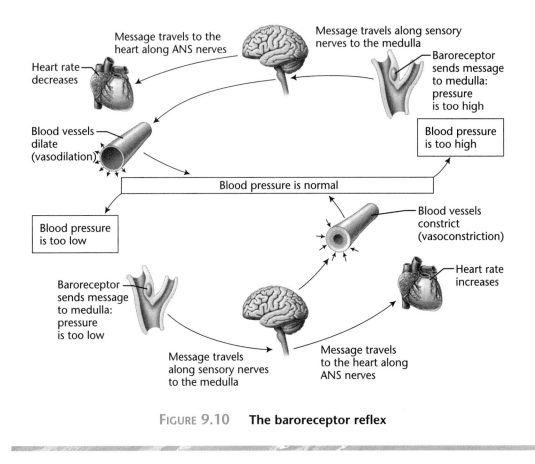

FIGURE 9.10   **The baroreceptor reflex**

These days many packaged foods in grocery stores have "heart healthy" labels. Many of these foods are lower in cholesterol or saturated fats, which contribute to atherosclerosis. Therefore, these foods will be less likely to contribute to hypertension.

Hypertension! Hypertension is a condition in which the blood pressure is consistently high (over 140/80). This may be caused by an accumulation of fatty materials in blood vessels resulting in a condition known as **atherosclerosis** (æθərowsklə′rowsəs), or hardening of the arteries. Hypertension may also be caused by stress, smoking, obesity, heredity, or a diet high in salt and fats.

Hypotension! Hypotension is the opposite of hypertension. The person has low blood pressure. This is usually caused by low blood volume due to diarrhea, kidney problems, or hemorrhage (extreme blood loss).

1. *Circle the correct word(s) to complete each sentence. Take turns reading the correct sentences aloud with a partner.*

    1. Blood pressure is the pressure exerted by blood on the walls of the **heart / blood vessels**.

    2. In a blood pressure reading of 120/80, the 80 represents the **systolic / diastolic** pressure.

    3. The systolic pressure is the pressure when the ventricles are **relaxing / contracting**.

    4. An increase in blood volume **increases / decreases** blood pressure.

    5. When the heart pumps less blood per contraction, this **increases / decreases** blood pressure.

    6. Vasoconstriction **increases / decreases** blood pressure.

    7. If someone has lost a lot of blood, his blood pressure has **increased / decreased**.

2. *Answer the questions below. Then compare your answers with those of a partner.*

    1. Name three things that can cause a change in blood pressure.

    2. Describe the role of baroreceptors. Name the five parts to the baroreceptor reflex.

BUILDING LANGUAGE AND STUDY SKILLS

Describing Relationships and Connections

In your study of anatomy and physiology, you have probably noticed that many structures and processes are connected and relate to one another. Many smaller structures are parts of larger structures and these structures influence each other. In addition, many processes influence these structures, or they may be a result of other processes. Therefore, it is important for you, an anatomy and physiology student, to know how to express connections and relationships between structures and processes.

There are certain verbs and phrases you can use to describe relationships and connections. Study the examples below.

- Blood volume *is influenced by* how much water is in the blood.
- The heart *depends on* the SA node for its ability to contract.
- A heart attack can be *a result of* a lack of nutrients in the heart.
- Cardiac muscle is *a component of* the heart wall.
- Blood *is comprised of* plasma and cells.

Can you think of other verbs or phrases that express relationships and connections?

1. *Fill in the blanks with verbs that express relationships and connections. Compare your answers with those of a partner. There may be more than one correct answer.*

   1. Blood volume _____ blood pressure.

   2. The SA node _____ conduction in the heart.

   3. Plasma _____ blood.

   4. Platelets, leukocytes, and erythrocytes _____ blood.

   5. Stenotic valve _____ heart murmur.

2. *Look at the pairs of words and phrases below. Write sentences expressing their connections and relationships.*

   1. exercise and stress / heart rate

   2. pericardium / heart

   3. heart rate / caffeine and nicotine

   4. baroreceptors / blood pressure

   5. the amount of blood in the blood vessels / blood pressure

3. *These are authentic questions taken from an anatomy and physiology class. Use the vocabulary and grammar you know to answer these questions.*

   1. How is blood volume related to blood pressure?

   2. What comprises the conduction system of the heart?

   3. How is circulation of blood to the heart related to heart attacks?

Concept Map

A concept map is a diagram that consists of shapes and links between the shapes. In a concept map, each shape contains a concept or idea. Related ideas are linked together with lines or "branches." The links show connections between ideas. Look at the concept map below. You can see the word *BLOOD* in the square at the top of the map. This is the main concept or idea of the map. The links coming from the word *blood* are the *components of the blood: Plasma and three types of cells.* Further links and groupings show related ideas. Can you see the relationships?

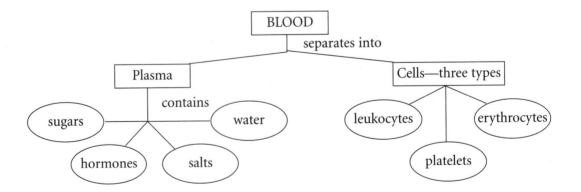

A concept map can be constructed in many different ways. The concept map on page 196 is a hierarchy. It shows relationships from bigger to smaller. Another type of map shows cause and effect or steps in a process. This type of map is sometimes called a flow chart.

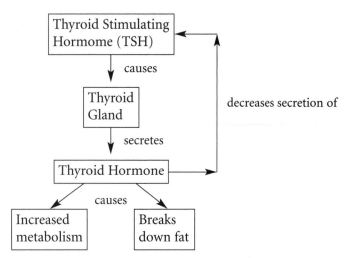

Making a concept map is a good study technique because the maps visualize relationships and connections between concepts. When you study with a concept map, you may have nearly all the information you need on a single page of paper!

PRACTICE

Make a concept map. Use the words below and add more ideas of your own. First, pick out the main idea. Write the word at the top of the page and draw a shape around it. Then decide how and where you will place the other words along with your own ideas.

blood pressure   hypertension   hypotension   baroreceptors

Show your map to a partner. How is your map different from your partner's?

THE BLOOD VESSELS

You've learned the anatomy of the heart, how it pumps blood, and the measurements that we take of the heart. Let's move on to studying the blood vessels which carry blood throughout the body.

Types of Blood Vessels

There are five major types of blood vessels: **arteries, arterioles, capillaries, venules,** and **veins.**

Arteries (ˈɑrtəriyz) are large vessels that carry blood away from the heart. They have thick walls that contain smooth muscle. The smooth muscle is controlled by the autonomic nervous system and, because of this muscle, artery walls can *constrict* (vasoconstriction) or *dilate* (vasodilation), depending on the needs of the body. These arteries branch and gradually get smaller and smaller in diameter until they branch into arterioles.

Many students make the mistake of thinking that all red vessels (in a diagram or a model) are arteries and that all blue vessels are veins. This is true of most arteries, but the pulmonary arteries are one of the exceptions. They contain poorly oxygenated blood (and would appear blue). Instead of relying on color, remember this: <u>A</u>rteries carry blood <u>a</u>way from the heart, while veins bring blood toward the heart.

Arterioles (ɑr′tiyriyowlz) are much smaller in diameter than arteries and have only one to two layers of smooth muscle cells in their wall. This smooth muscle can contract or relax, depending on conditions in the area. For example, if a particular area of the body is low in oxygen, the arteriole dilates (gets wider) so more blood can enter that area. If an arteriole leading to a particular area constricts (gets narrower), then less blood enters that area. Arterioles send blood into very small vessels called **capillaries** (′kæpəlɛriyz).

Capillaries form networks called **capillary beds**. Capillary beds surround tissues and supply them with oxygen and nutrients. They also pick up waste materials such as carbon dioxide and urea. Capillary walls are comprised of only a single layer of epithelium. They have no muscle in their walls. Because capillary walls are so thin, materials in the blood can cross very easily into the tissue spaces that surround them. Sugar, salts, gases (such as oxygen and carbon dioxide), some hormones, and water can cross these walls. However, blood cells and certain proteins are too big to cross capillary walls and are held in the bloodstream.

When nutrients have been delivered to the tissues and waste products have been picked up in the capillaries, it is time for the blood to begin its return to the heart. From the capillary beds, the blood flows into larger vessels called **venules** (′vɛnyuwlz). These are relatively thin-walled vessels, but larger than capillaries. The venules lead into **veins** (veynz), which eventually merge to form either the superior or inferior vena cava. These two vessels bring blood back to the heart. Some veins in the lower parts of the body (for example, the legs) have **valves** that prevent blood from being pulled downward by gravity. This helps to make the return of blood to the heart more efficient.

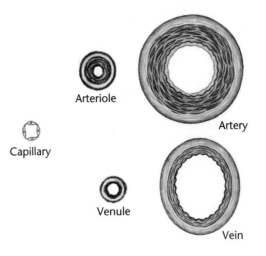

Figure 9.11 **The five major types of blood vessel**

The networks of branching blood vessels form two major circuits (or pathways): the **pulmonary circuit**, which carries blood between the heart and the lungs, and the **systemic circuit** which carries blood from the heart to the rest of the body and back again to the heart.

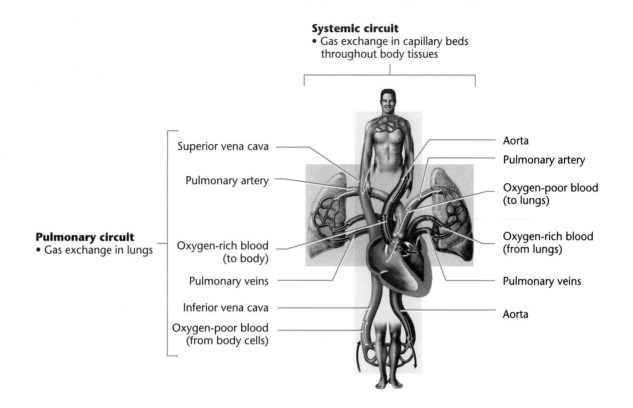

Systemic circuit
• Gas exchange in capillary beds throughout body tissues

Superior vena cava

Pulmonary artery

Pulmonary circuit
• Gas exchange in lungs

Oxygen-rich blood (to body)

Pulmonary veins

Inferior vena cava

Oxygen-poor blood (from body cells)

Aorta

Pulmonary artery

Oxygen-poor blood (to lungs)

Oxygen-rich blood (from lungs)

Pulmonary veins

Aorta

FIGURE 9.12   The pulmonary circuit is shown to the sides of the heart. The systemic circuit is shown above and below the heart.

COMPREHENSION CHECK

1. *Number the vessels in the order that blood passes through them, beginning at the aorta (1). Compare your answers with the class.*

    <u>1</u> aorta   ___ veins   ___ arteries   ___ capillaries   ___ venules   ___ arterioles

2. *What is the function of different blood vessels? Work with a partner. Put a check mark (✓) in the box under each vessel's function.*

	Carry blood to the body	Carry blood to the heart	Carry blood high in oxygen	Carry blood low in oxygen	Gas exchange
Veins	☐	☐	☐	☐	☐
Arteries	☐	☐	☐	☐	☐
Capillaries	☐	☐	☐	☐	☐
Venules	☐	☐	☐	☐	☐
Arterioles	☐	☐	☐	☐	☐

3. *Complete the sentences using the words in the box. Take turns reading the correct sentences aloud with a partner.*

arteries	capillary bed	systemic circuit	venule
arterioles	pulmonary circuit	veins	

1. A _____ is a network of capillaries that supplies a tissue with oxygen and nutrients and removes wastes.

2. The _____ is a network of blood vessels that carries blood from the heart to other areas of the body and back to the heart.

3. _____ are vessels that have muscular walls and deliver blood to capillaries.

4. _____ are small vessels that receive blood from capillaries and deliver it to veins.

5. _____ carry blood directly from the heart. They have thick, muscular walls.

6. _____ carry blood back to the heart and sometimes have valves.

7. The _____ is a network of blood vessels that carry blood between the heart and the lungs.

The Major Blood Vessels of the Body

Your body contains over 60,000 miles (96,560 kilometers) of blood vessels. Figure 9.13 shows the major arteries and the major veins in the body.

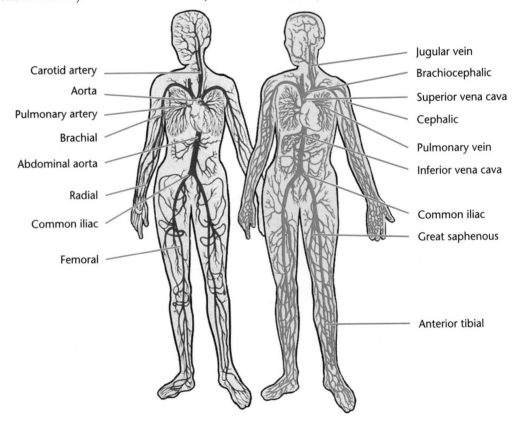

Carotid artery
Aorta
Pulmonary artery
Brachial
Abdominal aorta
Radial
Common iliac
Femoral

Jugular vein
Brachiocephalic
Superior vena cava
Cephalic
Pulmonary vein
Inferior vena cava
Common iliac
Great saphenous
Anterior tibial

FIGURE 9.13   **Major arteries and veins of the body**

1. *Study the diagram of the arteries in Figure 9.13. Then fill in the blanks below with the correct artery names. Compare your answers with the class.*

   1. The _____ artery is located in the upper arm.

   2. The _____ is the main artery that brings blood to the abdomen.

   3. The _____ artery travels through the neck to the head.

   4. The _____ artery is found in the upper leg.

   5. The _____ artery is found in the lower arm and wrist.

   6. The _____ artery takes blood to the lungs.

2. *Study the diagram of the veins in Figure 9.13. Then fill in the blanks below with the correct vein names. Compare your answers with the class.*

   1. The _____ vein is found in the inner thigh.

   2. The _____ vein is located in the upper arm.

   3. The _____ vein delivers blood from the lungs to the heart.

   4. The _____ vein is a main branch of the inferior vena cava.

   5. The _____ vein is a main branch of the superior vena cava.

   6. The _____ is found in the lower leg.

THE LYMPHATIC VESSELS

Recall that in the last chapter you learned about the lymphatic system. You learned that lymph organs (lymph nodes, thymus, tonsils, and spleen) help to defend against disease. You also learned that lymphatic vessels carry fluid back to the bloodstream from spaces around tissues. Now we will look more closely at the lymphatic vessels' role in maintaining blood volume.

Lymphatic capillaries are finger-like vessels that project into tissue spaces. They have thin walls that allow fluid to easily enter, especially if there is an excess amount of fluid in the tissue spaces. An excess amount of fluid occurs because in the capillary beds, a certain amount of fluid leaves the capillaries and enters the tissue spaces. However, less fluid goes back into the blood at the end of the capillary bed. This means that fluid should accumulate in the tissue spaces, but it does not. Instead, the excess fluid passes into the lymphatic capillaries to begin its way back to the bloodstream.

Lymph capillaries join together to form **lymphatic vessels**. Lymphatic vessels carry a milky fluid called **lymph**. Lymph consists of mostly water, along with fats and some dissolved molecules. Eventually, lymphatic vessels empty into the veins in the chest region, and return fluid back to the bloodstream. Thus, homeostasis of blood volume is maintained. (See Figure 9.14.)

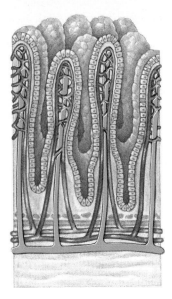

Figure 9.14 Lymph capillaries (in blue) pick up excess fluid from tissue regions such as in the intestine

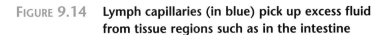

Edema! What would happen if the lymph vessels didn't remove the excess fluids from the spaces within tissues? The tissue spaces would become bloated with fluid (**edema**) and the blood would gradually lose water (resulting in low blood pressure).

COMPREHENSION CHECK

Circle the correct word(s) to complete each sentence. Take turns reading the correct sentences aloud with a partner.

1. Lymphatic vessels return fluid to the **arteries / veins**.
2. **More / Less** fluid leaves the blood capillaries at the tissues than is returned.
3. **Lymph / Plasma** is a milky fluid containing fats, dissolved molecules, and water.
4. **Hypertension / Edema** occurs when the lymphatic vessels fail to do their job.
5. The lymphatic vessels help to maintain homeostasis of **blood volume / blood sugar**.

FOCUS ON CULTURE

The Economy of Health Care

A person can often access health care on many levels. For example, some people who are experiencing chest pain stay home and try to take care of the pain themselves while others go to the hospital emergency room. There are various levels of health care depending on their simplicity and cost. For example, taking care of your health at home is almost free while going to a specialist may cost a great deal of money.

The following story is about a cultural conflict that people may experience in a health-care setting. Read the story and then discuss the questions in small groups.

Kevin is a college student. He is working part-time while going to school. He has had a sore throat for a week. It is very hard for him to even swallow water. At first, he treated it himself by going to the store and getting cough drops. They didn't seem to help so he called his mom, who is a receptionist in a doctor's office. She suspected he might have strep throat and, even worse, that he might be spreading it. She insisted that he go immediately to a clinic. The problem is that Kevin doesn't have any health insurance and has no money to pay for the visit and lab tests.

1. What are Kevin's choices?

2. If you were Kevin, what would you do?

3. Look at the different levels of health care listed below. What would you do if you were sick? Explain your choice.

   _____ Go to a pharmacy and ask a pharmacist.

   _____ Go to the emergency room in a hospital.

   _____ Call a friend or acquaintance.

   _____ Treat yourself.

   _____ Go to a walk-in clinic.

   _____ Get help from a spiritual source.

   _____ Make an appointment to see a doctor.

4. What are the advantages and disadvantages of each of the above choices?

Check Your Understanding

1. *Answer the following questions about the cardiovascular system.*

   1. Which type of valve, semilunar or AV valve, separates the atria from the ventricles?

   2. After blood leaves the right ventricle, does it go to the lungs or to the body?

   3. Do pulmonary arteries or veins go to the lungs?

   4. What's the name of the pacemaker of the heart and where is it located?

   5. What's another word for heart attack?

   6. The first heart sound a doctor listens to is caused by what happening?

   7. Name three things that can make blood pressure change?

   8. Where do you find baroreceptors? What's their purpose?

   9. How do lymph vessels and blood vessels interact?

   10. Which of the five types of vessels is closest to body tissues?

2. *Label Figures 9.15 and 9.16 with the terms provided.*

aorta	left ventricle	right ventricle
aortic semilunar valve	pulmonary artery	superior vena cava
bicuspid valve	pulmonary semilunar valve	tricuspid valve
inferior vena cava	pulmonary veins	
left atrium	right atrium	

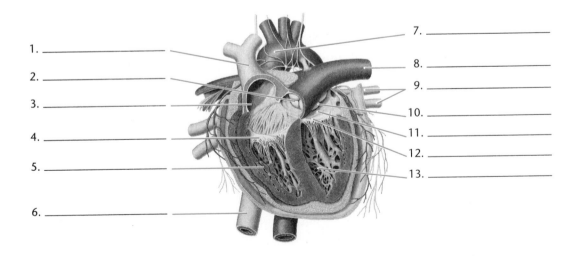

1. _____
2. _____
3. _____
4. _____
5. _____
6. _____

7. _____
8. _____
9. _____
10. _____
11. _____
12. _____
13. _____

FIGURE 9.15   The heart

Arteries:

aorta	carotid	pulmonary
abdominal aorta	common iliac	radial
brachial	femoral	

Veins:

anterior tibial	common iliac	jugular
brachiocephalic	great saphenous	pulmonary
cephalic	inferior vena cava	superior vena cava

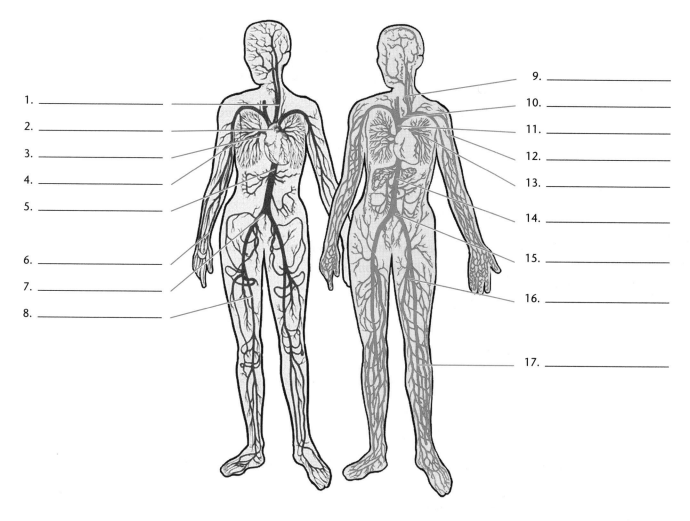

1. _____

2. _____

3. _____

4. _____

5. _____

6. _____

7. _____

8. _____

9. _____

10. _____

11. _____

12. _____

13. _____

14. _____

15. _____

16. _____

17. _____

FIGURE 9.16   Major arteries and veins of the body

CHAPTER 10

The Respiratory System

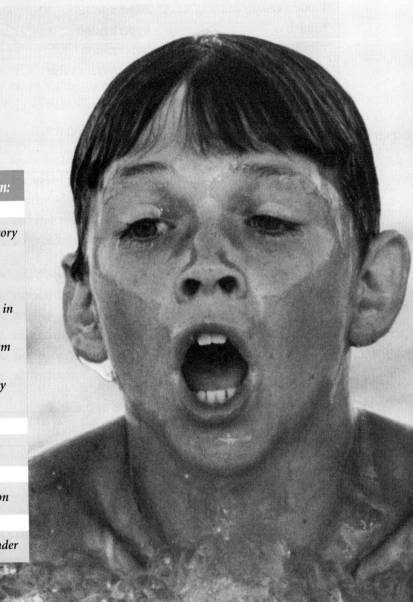

In this chapter you will learn:

ANATOMY AND PHYSIOLOGY

- *The organs of the respiratory tract*
- *How breathing is accomplished*
- *How gases are exchanged in the lungs*
- *How the respiratory system stays healthy*
- *Diseases of the respiratory system*

ENGLISH

- *Describing a process*

STUDY SKILLS

- *Summarizing information*

CULTURE

- *Hierarchy of age and gender*

DID YOU KNOW *that there are about 300 million alveoli (little sacs) in the lungs? If you stretched them out they would cover an entire tennis court!*

INTRODUCTION

The respiratory system includes the lungs, along with the system of tubes that connect the lungs to the nose (nasal cavity) and mouth (oral cavity). These tubes include the pharynx, larynx, trachea, bronchi, and bronchioles. The function of the **respiratory** (ˈrɛsprətɔriy) system is to bring oxygen into the body and to rid the body of waste gases. Your body needs oxygen to survive. Oxygen is necessary for **cellular respiration**, one of the processes used by cells to get energy from food. Your body also needs a way to release waste gases like carbon dioxide, one of the waste products made during cellular respiration. In this chapter, you will learn how air moves within the respiratory system and how these gases are exchanged between the lungs and the bloodstream.

1. *Work with a partner. Look at this diagram of the respiratory system. Try to label the parts with the words in the box. Look at Figures 10.2 and 10.5 on pages 211 and 214 to check your answers.*

bronchi	lungs	nasal cavity	oral cavity	pharynx	trachea

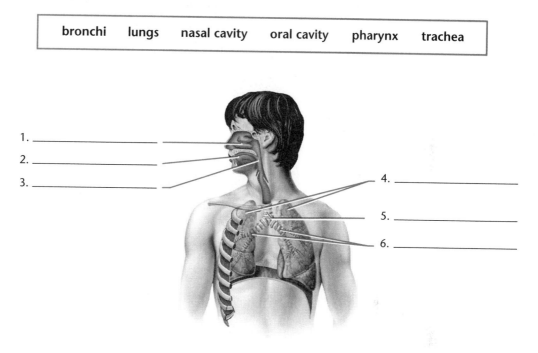

1. _____
2. _____
3. _____
4. _____
5. _____
6. _____

FIGURE 10.1   The respiratory system

2. *With your partner, try to answer these questions. If you do not know the answers, do not worry. You will find the answers as you read through this chapter.*

   1. What is the function of the respiratory system?

   2. Where does air enter the body?

   3. Why does blood have to go to the lungs?

   4. How many lungs do you have?

   5. How does the respiratory system protect itself from disease?

   6. What is emphysema?

   7. How are colds different from influenza (flu)?

3. *Read each verb, its simple definition, and its passive voice form. Then fill in the verbs in the sentences that follow. Pay attention to verb tense and subject / verb agreement. Compare your answers with those of another student.*

BASE FORM	PASSIVE VOICE FORM	MEANING
breathe	—	to bring air in and out of the body
capture	be captured	to trap and hold onto
collapse	be collapsed	to be without air inside
diffuse	be diffused	to move to an area that is less crowded
exhale	be exhaled	to send air out of the body
expand	be expanded	to get larger
expire	be expired	to send air out of the body
filter	be filtered	to remove larger particles
inflate	be inflated	to make larger by filling with air
inhale	be inhaled	to send air into the body
inspire	be inspired	to send air into the body
vibrate	be vibrated	to shake slightly and quickly

1. You _____ before you jump in the water. (Two answers are correct.)

2. You _____ after you take a deep breath. (Two answers are correct.)

3. You have to _____ to stay alive.

4. The hairs in the nose _____ viruses and bacteria.

5. An electric toothbrush has bristles that _____.

6. Oxygen _____ across capillary walls in the lungs.

7. When you inhale, your lungs _____, or fill with air.

8. When you take a deep breath, your lungs and entire chest cavity _____.

9. Hairs, mucus, and cilia help to _____ the air before it reaches the lungs.

10. After she stuck the balloon with a pin, the air escaped and the balloon _____.

ANATOMY OF THE RESPIRATORY SYSTEM

You will learn the anatomy of the respiratory system by studying the path that air takes from the time it first enters the nose or mouth until gas exchange occurs in the lungs.

Upper Respiratory Tract

The respiratory system, or respiratory tract, begins in the **nasal cavity**, the opening within the nose. Air is warmed in the nasal cavity. Particles, which are small things such as dust, bacteria, and viruses, are *captured* by nose hairs, thus helping to prevent diseases because harmful bacteria and viruses are prevented from entering the body. Usually people *breathe* through their noses, but sometimes people breathe through their mouth, or oral cavity.

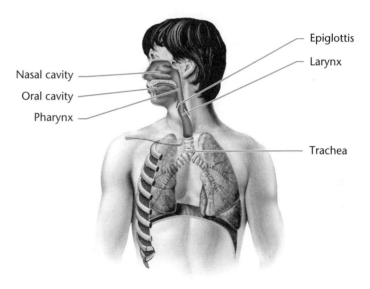

Nasal cavity

Oral cavity

Pharynx

Epiglottis

Larynx

Trachea

FIGURE 10.2   **The upper respiratory tract**

All air entering your respiratory tract passes through the **pharynx** (ˈfærɪŋks). The pharynx begins behind your nasal cavity and extends down past the oral cavity to about the level of your chin. When air reaches the bottom of the pharynx, there are two possible directions it can travel: into the esophagus or the larynx. If air enters the esophagus, it travels to the stomach. Do you want air in your stomach? No. In fact, the presence of air in your stomach can give you the hiccups. Instead, air needs to enter the **larynx** (ˈlærɪŋks). The larynx is the passageway that sends air toward the lungs.

Laryngitis! (lærɪnˈdʒaytəs) Bacterial and viral infections of the larynx can cause the vocal cords to swell (get larger), which makes it difficult to speak. This condition is known as laryngitis. Laryngitis can also be caused by tobacco smoke, alcohol, excessive talking, shouting, coughing, or singing.

Remember from the digestive system chapter that a flap of tissue called the epiglottis closes when you swallow food to prevent the food from entering the larynx. The epiglottis is in the open position when you breathe. Besides being part of the path of air, the larynx is also known as the **voice box**, the place where your voice comes from. **Vocal cords** are attached to the sides of the larynx. When air passes across the vocal cords, they *vibrate* and the voice is produced. The reason that people have different voices is that their vocal cords differ in length and thickness. Because of the effects of the male hormone testosterone, men tend to have thicker and longer vocal cords than women.

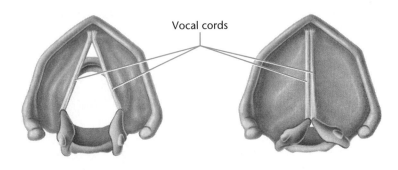

FIGURE 10.3 **Looking down onto the top of the larynx. Vocal cords are stretched across the opening.**

After air passes through the larynx, it enters the **trachea** (ˈtreykiyə). A common word for trachea is "windpipe." The trachea is the fairly rigid tube that carries air from the larynx to the lungs. The trachea is fairly rigid because it is supported by rings of cartilage. (Recall that cartilage is like bone, but is more flexible.) The many rings of cartilage surrounding the trachea keep it open for breathing and hold its shape.

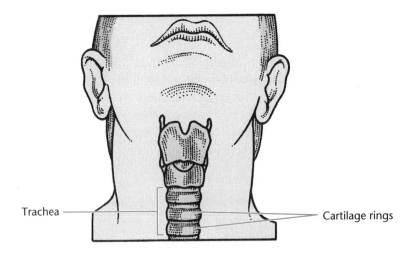

FIGURE 10.4 **Trachea with rings of cartilage**

1. *Read the questions and then scan the text for answers. When you find the answers, underline them. Then work with a partner and take turns asking and answering the questions. Try to remember the answers without looking back at the text.*

    1. What two things happen to air in the nasal cavity?

    2. Where is the pharynx?

    3. What are the two tubes at the end of the pharynx?

    4. What happens when air passes across the vocal cords?

    5. Why do people have different voices?

    6. What is the common word for the trachea?

    7. What is the function of the cartilage surrounding the trachea?

    8. What causes laryngitis? What happens to the vocal cords?

2. *Match the terms with their definitions by writing the letters in the correct blanks. Then compare your answers with those of a partner.*

    _____ 1. epiglottis   **a.** rigid structure that connects larynx with the bronchi

    _____ 2. larynx   **b.** this is where your voice is produced

    _____ 3. nasal cavity   **c.** this covers your trachea when you swallow

    _____ 4. oral cavity   **d.** air goes here after it enters the mouth or nose

    _____ 5. pharynx   **e.** air passes through, hairs capture bacteria and viruses

    _____ 6. trachea   **f.** food enters this area

Entering the Lungs

After air has passed down the trachea to the lungs, it enters two branches: one branch enters the right lung and the other branch enters the left lung. These two branches are called **primary bronchi** (ˈpraymɛɾiy ˈbraŋkay). One branch is called a **bronchus** (ˈbraŋkəs). Bronchi also have cartilage around them, but the amount decreases as the bronchi extend into the lungs. Soon after the primary bronchi enter the lungs, each bronchus branches again. These new branches are called **secondary bronchi**. Each secondary bronchus enters into one of the **lobes** (parts) of the lung. There are three lobes in the right lung and two lobes in the left lung. Thus, there are five secondary bronchi. In the lobes of the lungs, the secondary bronchi branch into **tertiary bronchi** (*tert-* means *three*).

The tertiary bronchi within the lungs branch into smaller tubes called **bronchioles** (ˈbraŋkiyowlz). Although these bronchioles are quite small in diameter, they are very important in regulating the amount of air that enters the lungs. The bronchioles have a thin layer of smooth muscle that constricts when less air is needed and dilates when more air is needed.

Eventually, the air that is carried by the bronchioles enters clusters of **alveoli** (ælˈviyalay). Alveoli are very tiny bubbles with very thin walls. One individual "bubble" is called an **alveolus** (ælˈviyələs). Alveoli cluster around a bronchiole, just like grapes cluster around a stem; therefore, all alveoli in a cluster connect with a single bronchiole. The alveoli are where the blood drops off carbon dioxide and picks up oxygen. Your lungs are packed with them.

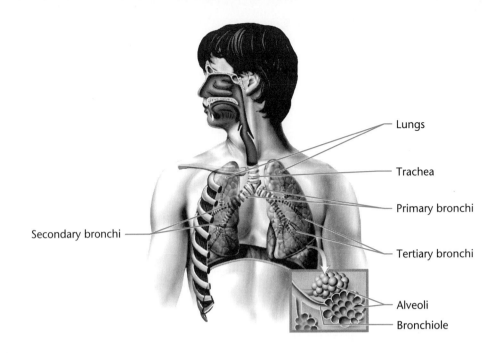

FIGURE 10.5 Airways into the lungs

In fact, each lung contains about 150 million alveoli. Despite all of the tissues your lungs contain, they are very lightweight. They resemble a sponge.

The walls of each alveolus are comprised of elastin fibers. Recall that elastin is also found in skin. Elastin allows skin as well as the wall of each alveolus to stretch when you breathe in and return to its original size when you breathe out.

Emphysema! People usually get **emphysema** (əmfəˈsiymə) as a result of smoking tobacco. The tobacco smoke damages the elastin fibers in the alveoli, making them unable to return to their original shape after they are stretched. (Imagine a pair of stockings that are well worn. They are "baggy" because the elastic is worn.) If the alveoli remain stretched, it is very difficult to *expire* (force air out of the lungs). People with emphysema may use up to 1/4 of their energy just to breathe.

COMPREHENSION CHECK

1. *Work with a partner to label each statement true* (T) *or false* (F). *If the statement is false, correct it so that it is true.*

_____ 1. There are two tracheas, one goes to each lung.

_____ 2. One branch of a bronchus is called a bronchi.

_____ 3. There are five lobes in the lungs.

_____ 4. The function of bronchioles is to regulate the amount of air entering the lungs.

_____ 5. The bronchioles contain cartilage.

_____ 6. There is more cartilage in the trachea than in the bronchi.

_____ **7.** When you need more air, as when you exercise, the bronchioles constrict.

_____ **8.** Alveoli are very tiny bubbles where gas exchange takes place.

_____ **9.** The lungs contain a total of 150 alveoli.

_____ **10.** People with emphysema have more difficulty with inspiration than expiration.

2. *Put the anatomical structures in order from when air first enters the body. Number 1 has been done for you.*

_____ primary bronchi

__1__ nasal or oral cavity

_____ larynx

_____ alveoli

_____ secondary bronchi

_____ pharynx

_____ tertiary bronchi

_____ trachea

3. *Label Figure 10.6 with the terms in the box. Look at Figures 10.2 and 10.5 on pages 211 and 214 to check your answers.*

lungs	oral cavity	primay bronchi	tertiary bronchi
nasal cavity	pharynx	secondary bronchi	trachea

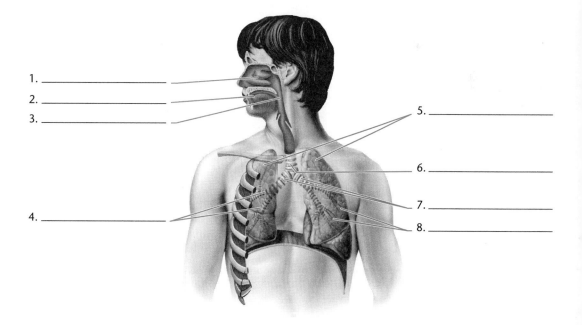

1. _____   _____

2. _____   _____

3. _____   _____

4. _____

5. _____

6. _____

7. _____

8. _____

FIGURE 10.6   **The respiratory tract**

BREATHING

Sometimes, people tell each other to "take a deep breath" before trying to do something difficult or stressful such as asking for a raise at work or jumping off a high dive at a swimming pool. Taking a deep breath can help a person relax.

When air is taken into the lungs, it is called **inspiration** (ɪnspəˈreyʃən). Another word for inspiration is inhalation. Inspiration is controlled by the brain. The brain sends nerve impulses that stimulate the diaphragm, the large muscle that separates the abdominal cavity from the thoracic (chest) cavity, to contract. At the same time the diaphragm is stimulated, other nerve impulses also stimulate the intercostal muscles (the muscles between the ribs) to contract and the rib cage goes up and out. Both of these muscle contractions cause the thoracic cavity to *expand*. Because the lungs are attached to the wall of the thoracic cavity and move with it, the lungs also expand.

When your lungs expand, the pressure inside them decreases to below the pressure of outside air. Air naturally flows from high pressure areas to low pressure areas, so this causes the lungs to fill with air. The person has *inspired* or *inhaled*. So the lungs expand <u>before</u> air enters them, not because they fill with air.

When air goes out of the lungs and out of the body, this is called **expiration** (ɛkspəˈreyʃən). Another word for expiration is *exhalation*. When a person expires (exhales), the diaphragm and intercostal muscles relax. This causes the rib cage to go down and in. Because the thoracic cavity becomes smaller, so do the lungs. The pressure inside the lungs increases, and the difference in pressure between the lungs and outside air forces air out of the lungs.

MAINTAINING HOMEOSTASIS

Regulation of Breathing

Recall that the amount of air that enters the lungs is controlled by smooth muscles in the walls of the bronchioles. This smooth muscle enables the bronchioles to open and close. Bronchioles open wider (dilate) when the body needs more air and become narrower (constrict) if less air is needed. For example, during exercise or stress, the bronchioles open wider to increase the flow of air to the lungs. When a person is resting, the bronchioles close a little because less air is needed when a person is resting.

More children suffer from asthma today in many highly developed countries than they did 25 years ago.

 Asthma! **Asthma** (ˈæzmə) is a common disease of the respiratory system which causes the bronchioles to become inflamed and to constrict. It is characterized by periods of wheezing and difficult breathing. Most cases of asthma are caused by common allergens such as pet dander, eggs, milk, dust, and pollen. One of the most common treatments for asthma is an oral spray (inhalant) containing the hormone **epinephrine** (ɛpəˈnɛfrɪn). Epinephrine is a hormone that stimulates the bronchioles to open.

Another Look at Emphysema! Recall that emphysema patients have damaged elastin fibers in their alveoli. When the alveoli are stretched, they don't return to their original size. The alveoli stay stretched, and therefore, the pressure inside them doesn't change. So expiration doesn't happen unless the patient uses other muscles to make the lungs smaller and force the air out. This is why patients with emphysema have to use so much more energy to breathe and are tired all the time.

1. *Circle the correct answer to complete each sentence. Take turns reading the correct sentences aloud with a partner.*

   1. Breathing is controlled by the _____.
      a. diaphragm   **b.** brain   **c.** intercostal muscles

   2. During inspiration, the diaphragm and the _____ contract.
      a. intercostal muscles   **b.** rib cage   **c.** lungs

   3. The amount of air that enters the lungs is controlled by the
      _____.
      a. bronchi   **b.** bronchioles   **c.** trachea

   4. During inspiration which happens first?
      a. The chest cavity enlarges.
      b. Air comes in.
      c. The chest cavity gets smaller.

   5. When you expire, the rib cage _____.
      a. goes up and out
      b. goes up and in
      c. goes down and in

   6. In which part of breathing do muscles relax?
      a. during inspiration
      b. during expiration

2. *Complete the sentences using the words in the box. Take turns reading the correct sentences aloud with a partner.*

bronchioles	exhalation	inhalation	intercostal
diaphragm	expiration	inspiration	smooth muscle

   1. The two terms for *breathing in* are _____ and _____.

   2. The two terms for *breathing out* are _____ and _____.

   3. The _____ is the muscle that separates the thoracic cavity from the abdominal cavity.

   4. The _____ muscles are located between your ribs.

   5. The amount of air that enters your lungs is controlled by _____ in the walls of the _____.

GAS EXCHANGE

As discussed earlier, the main role of the respiratory system is to provide oxygen for the body and to rid the body of waste gases such as carbon dioxide. Gas exchange takes place between the alveoli and the pulmonary capillaries in the lungs. To understand how gas exchange takes place, let's first look at the basic anatomy of the alveoli and capillaries in the lungs.

Alveoli are comprised of elastin fibers, the same fibers found in your skin that allow your skin to stretch. When you inspire (inhale), each alveolus stretches and when you expire (exhale), it returns to its original size. Each alveolus is closely surrounded by capillaries. The walls of both the alveoli and capillaries are so thin that oxygen and carbon dioxide can travel between the alveoli and capillaries easily.

How do oxygen and carbon dioxide travel between the alveoli and capillaries? Blood low in oxygen is carried from the heart to the lungs by the pulmonary artery (recall what you learned in the cardiovascular chapter). Pulmonary capillaries, the ultimate (final) branches of the pulmonary artery, surround each alveolus. When capillaries bring carbon dioxide to the alveoli, the carbon dioxide easily passes through the alveolar walls. It travels to the center of each alveolus and is then expired out of the lungs. Likewise, when you inspire, oxygen travels down your respiratory tract to your lungs, enters the alveoli, and then passes through both the alveolus wall and the pulmonary capillary wall to enter the capillary. Once inside the capillaries, oxygen enters red blood cells and then attaches to hemoglobin. The blood is now highly oxygenated and travels back to the heart via pulmonary veins. The process of gas exchange takes place simultaneously. In other words, oxygen is entering the capillaries at the same time that carbon dioxide is exiting the capillaries.

Gas Exchange: Oxygen and Carbon Dioxide

The process that allows oxygen and carbon dioxide to move into and out of the bloodstream is called **diffusion** (dɪˈfyuwʒən). *Diffusion* is the net movement of molecules from one area that has a higher concentration (amount) of these molecules toward an area where there is a lower concentration of these molecules. For example, when capillaries bring carbon dioxide to the alveoli, there is more carbon dioxide in the capillaries than there is in the alveoli. Therefore, the carbon dioxide will more likely move into the alveoli than out of them. Likewise, when oxygen molecules enter the alveoli, they are more likely to move into the capillaries where there are fewer oxygen molecules than stay in the alveoli where there are more oxygen molecules.

You might be tempted to think that molecules move to the empty spaces because they are empty. However, this is not so. Net movement is simply the result of the random movement of molecules. Molecules move all of the time and they move to the empty areas because they are not blocked by other molecules. **Net movement** means that the majority of molecules are moving in the direction of emptier space, but not all of them. Here is an example of net movement:

Imagine that the two containers in Figure 10.7 are separated by a membrane, like the outer covering of a cell, and that this membrane has holes big enough for the blue molecules to pass through. Now imagine all the blue molecules are bouncing around inside their containers. The molecules on the left side frequently bounce off one another. Because there are more of them, some of them just happen to, *by chance*, go through the membrane to the other side. The molecules on the right side, however, have lots of empty space in which to move. It is less likely (but still possible) that one of them will move through the membrane to the left side.

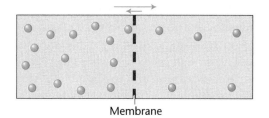

Membrane

FIGURE 10.7   Two containers separated by a membrane. The container on the
left has a higher concentration of molecules (blue) than the one
on the right. Molecules will tend to diffuse from left to right.

Eventually, the two sides will have an equal number of molecules. They will still be moving across the membrane, but there will be no net movement in either direction. Again, net movement only occurs when there are different concentrations (amounts) of molecules in two areas.

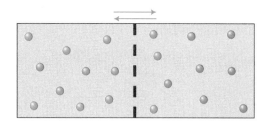

FIGURE 10.8   Eventually, the concentrations on both sides will be
equal. Molecules will tend to move equally in both
directions (no net movement).

Now imagine that the blue molecules represent oxygen molecules. The left container represents the alveolus, filled with oxygen. The right container represents the pulmonary capillary, with very little oxygen. In which direction does diffusion of oxygen occur? Toward the capillary.

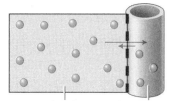

Alveolus   Pulmonary capillary

FIGURE 10.9   In the lungs, the alveolus has a higher concentration of
oxygen molecules than in the capillary. Oxygen will tend
to diffuse into the capillary.

Finally, in order for gas exchange to take place, the alveoli must be *inflated*. If the alveoli are *collapsed*, then no air can flow into them and there will be little oxygen to exchange. Because there is water in the air that you breathe, water ends up in the alveoli. If only water lined the alveoli, the water molecules would be attracted to one another and pull the alveoli closed. They would collapse and you could die. Therefore, alveoli are kept inflated by a molecule called **surfactant** (sɛr'fæktənt). Surfactant is a detergent-like molecule that prevents the alveoli from collapsing by mixing with the water that lines the inside of the alveoli. The surfactant molecules keep the water molecules away from one another and therefore keep the alveoli inflated. Surfactant is produced by large, round cells in the walls of the alveoli.

In many cultures, parents feel more comfortable when their babies sleep with them and they can see their children breathing. However, in other parts of the world, babies sleep in their own room, not with their parents.

Infant Respiratory Distress Syndrome (IRDS)! When babies are premature (born before their due date), they don't yet have the ability to make surfactant. Therefore, their lungs will tend to collapse. These "preemies" are placed on a respirator, a machine that helps to keep the alveoli inflated. Some hospitals also use a nasal spray that actually sprays surfactant into the lungs. Eventually, as the babies get a little older, they develop their own ability to make surfactant and can then be taken off the respirator.

COMPREHENSION CHECK

1. *Answer the questions below. Then compare your answers with those of a partner.*

   1. In what structure does gas exchange take place?

   2. When molecules are in the process of diffusion, what does that mean?

   3. Do the alveoli deliver oxygen (O_2) or carbon dioxide (CO_2) to the capillaries? Does O_2 or CO_2 diffuse from the capillaries to the alveoli?

   4. Describe the walls of capillaries.

   5. What molecule inside of red blood cells carries oxygen?

   6. Why do alveoli need to be inflated?

   7. What is surfactant?

   8. Where is surfactant produced?

2. *Match the terms with their definitions by writing the letters in the correct blanks. Then compare your answers with those of a partner.*

   _____ 1. diffusion

   _____ 2. net movement

   _____ 3. IRDS

   _____ 4. surfactant

   a. movement of molecules to where there are fewer molecules

   b. detergent-like molecule that coats the inside of the alveoli

   c. the direction in which most molecules are moving

   d. occurs when babies don't have enough surfactant and their lungs collapse

Describing a Process

When you study anatomy and physiology, you will hear and read about processes such as how air moves through the respiratory system. You will also need to describe processes when you are called on in class and on tests. The passive voice is often used in describing processes.

Look at the following description of the alveoli. Notice the passive-voice constructions.

> Eventually, the air that **is carried by the bronchioles** enters clusters of alveoli. Alveoli are very tiny bubbles with very thin walls. One individual "bubble" **is called** an alveolus. Alveoli cluster around a bronchiole, just like grapes **are clustered** around a stem; therefore, all alveoli in a cluster **are connected** with a single bronchiole. The alveoli are where the blood drops off carbon dioxide and picks up oxygen. Your lungs **are packed** with them. In fact, each lung contains about 150 million alveoli. Despite all of the tissues and organs your lungs contain, they are very light weight. They resemble a sponge.

As you can see above, passive voice is used along with active voice. The meaning of active and passive sentences is usually similar, but the focus of these sentences changes. The focus in **active sentences** is on the person or thing that performs the action. The focus in **passive sentences** is on the person or thing that receives the action or is affected by the action. In the passive, the object of the active verb becomes the subject of the passive verb. In the examples below, *the baby* is the object in the active sentence. It becomes the subject in the passive sentence. It is important to know that only transitive verbs (verbs that take objects) can be used in the passive.

Active Voice

The doctor placed the baby on a respirator.

  [subject]   [object]

(The focus is on the doctor.)

Passive Voice

The baby was placed on a respirator (by the doctor).

  [subject]   [agent]

(The focus is on the baby.)

Forming the Passive Voice

To form the passive voice, use the correct form of *be* + past participle.

SUBJECT POSITION	BE	PAST PARTICIPLE	(BY + AGENT)
The baby	is	placed on a respirator	by the doctor.
The baby	was	placed on a respirator	by the doctor.
The baby	will be	placed on a respirator	by the doctor.

Using the Passive Voice

In passive voice, it is not always necessary to mention the agent (the person or thing performing the action). In fact, it is more common *not* to mention the agent.

1. Use the passive voice without the agent when:
- It is understood or obvious from the context.

  The patient will be operated on. (It is understood that a doctor is going to operate on the patient.)

- It is unknown or unimportant.

  The injured child was taken to the hospital. (You don't know who took the child to the hospital; it doesn't matter who took the child to the hospital. What is important is that the child was taken to the hospital.)

2. Use the passive voice with the agent when:
- The agent provides new or important information.

  The air is carried by the bronchioles to alveoli. (It is important to know what is carrying the air to alveoli.)

PRACTICE

1. *Work with a partner to label each statement active (A) or passive (P).*

_____ 1. Alveoli cluster around a bronchiole.

_____ 2. People usually get emphysema as a result of smoking tobacco.

_____ 3. The walls of each alveolus are comprised of elastin fibers.

_____ 4. The amount of air that enters the lungs is controlled by smooth muscles in the walls of bronchioles.

_____ 5. During exercise or stress, the bronchioles open wider to increase the flow of air to the lungs.

2. *Complete the paragraph using the active and passive voice. Remember to use the correct tense.*

When air _____ into the lungs, it _____
                    (1. take)   (2. call)
inspiration. Another word for inspiration is inhalation. Inspiration

_____ by the brain. The brain _____ nerve
              (3. control)   (4. send)
impulses that stimulate the diaphragm, the large muscle that _____
                                                                      (5. separate)
the abdominal cavity from the thoracic (chest) cavity, to contract. At the same time the

diaphragm _____, other nerve impulses also stimulate the
                  (6. stimulate)
intercostal muscles (the muscles between the ribs) to contract, and the rib cage goes up

and out. Both of these muscle contractions _____ the thoracic cavity
                                                      (7. cause)
to expand. Because the lungs _____ to the wall of the thoracic cavity
                                      (8. attach)
and _____ with it, the lungs also _____.
        (9. move)   (10. expand)

3. *Work with a partner. Change these active sentences into passive sentences. Decide whether to include the agent. Then discuss why that form is better suited for the context.*

1. Smoking tobacco can cause lung cancer.

2. About 150 million alveoli fill your lungs.

3. Capillaries bring carbon dioxide to the alveoli.

4. The doctors place premature babies on respirators to help them breathe.

5. Large round cells in the walls of the alveoli produce surfactant.

4. *These are authentic questions taken from an anatomy and physiology class. Use the vocabulary and grammar you know to answer these questions. Use the passive voice when it makes sense.*

1. Describe how air moves through the respiratory system.

2. Describe how inspiration occurs.

3. Describe how expiration occurs.

4. Describe how gas exchange occurs in the lungs.

Summarizing Information

A summary is a shorter version of a longer piece of information. It presents the main ideas or the most important information in a brief way. Writing a summary of what you have read is a very good way to study. It helps you remember the important concepts from a reading; the most important information, not the minor details. When you write a summary it is also a good idea to put the information into your own words instead of copying information directly from the text.

While summarizing information, keep these three things in mind:

- The summary is always shorter than the original text.
- The summary includes only the most important concepts and information.
- The summary includes ideas and concepts of the original text in your own words.

Reread the section from this chapter on gas exchange. Notice that the important ideas are underlined. Then read the summary on page 224.

Alveoli are comprised of elastin fibers, the same fibers found in your skin that allow your skin to stretch. *When you inspire (inhale), each alveolus stretches and when you expire (exhale), it returns to its original size. Each alveolus is closely surrounded by capillaries. The walls of both the alveoli and capillaries are so thin that oxygen and carbon dioxide can travel between the alveoli and capillaries easily.*

How do oxygen and carbon dioxide travel between the alveoli and capillaries? Blood low in oxygen is carried from the heart to the lungs by the pulmonary artery (recall what you learned in the cardiovascular chapter). Pulmonary capillaries, the ultimate (final) branches of the pulmonary artery, surround the alveoli. *When capillaries bring carbon dioxide to the alveoli, the carbon dioxide easily passes through the alveolar walls. It travels to the center of each alveolus and is then expired out of the lungs. Likewise, when you inspire, oxygen travels down your respiratory tract to your lungs, enters the alveoli, and then passes through both the alveolus walls and pulmonary capillary walls to enter the capillaries. Once inside the capillaries, oxygen enters red blood cells and attaches to hemoglobin.* The blood is now highly oxygenated and travels back to the heart via pulmonary veins. *This process of gas exchange takes place simultaneously.* In other words, oxygen is entering the alveoli at the same time that carbon dioxide is exiting the alveoli.

Summary:

Gas exchange takes place in the alveoli. Capillaries surround alveoli. The walls of both the capillaries and alveoli are so thin that oxygen and carbon dioxide can easily pass through. When the capillaries bring CO_2 to the alveoli, you breathe it out when you expire. When you breathe in, your alveoli fill with O_2. The O_2 travels to your capillaries and attaches to hemoglobin in your red blood cells. Both gases are exchanged simultaneously.

PRACTICE

With a partner, choose another section of this chapter to summarize. By yourself, underline or highlight the main ideas to be summarized. Write the summary using your own words. Finally, compare your summary with your partner's. Are they the same?

HOW THE RESPIRATORY SYSTEM STAYS HEALTHY

The respiratory system plays an active role in helping us maintain our health. Starting at the beginning of the respiratory system, the upper respiratory system *filters* airborne particles such as dust, bacteria, and viruses. These viruses and bacteria and other particles get trapped in the hairs of the nasal cavity and the mucus of the epithelial linings of the upper respiratory system and thus are prevented from entering our bodies and making us sick. What happens to this virus- and bacteria-laden mucus? We spit out, blow out, or swallow this mucus.

While nasal hairs and upper respiratory mucus trap a lot of particles, some particles still manage to get past these barriers. However, they can still be caught by **cilia** (′sɪliya) along the trachea. Cilia are miniature hair-like structures attached to the cells that line the trachea. This region also has mucous membranes to produce mucus. The mucus traps the particles and the cilia push the mucus upward to the throat to be swallowed or spit out.

Within the lungs, there are two more ways to help us maintain our health. First, there are special cells in the alveoli that eat the dust, bacteria, viruses, and other particles that have escaped filtration. These cells are called **alveolar macrophages** (æl′viyələr ′mækrəfeydʒɪz). *Macro-* means *big*; *phag-* means *to eat*. These "big eaters" wander around freely in each alveolus and eat any particles that have escaped earlier means of filtration.

Second, the respiratory system keeps us healthy because the lungs have the ability to heat and moisten the air we breathe. Near the smallest bronchioles and the alveoli in the lungs is a rich network of capillaries that releases heat and moisture. When air passes through this portion of the lungs, it is warmed and moistened. This prevents the lungs from drying out and makes it easier for gas exchange to occur.

Respiratory Infections! The respiratory system is susceptible to infections linked to airborne bacteria and viruses. The name of an infection is often linked to its location: bronchitis, sinusitis, laryngitis, pharyngitis, pneumonia (*pneumo-* means *lung*). **Influenza** and **colds** are the most common respiratory infections. Even though many of the features of these two infections are similar, they are different. Though both are caused by viruses, the viruses are different. Because they are viral infections, antibiotics do not help to treat these infections. The chart below illustrates some of the differences between these two infections:

	COMMON COLD	INFLUENZA
Caused by	Mostly Rhinovirus	Influenzavirus
Onset	Gradual	Rapid
Length	About 1 week	1–2 weeks
Fever	Rare	Common, high (102–104°F)
Headaches	Rare	Almost always
General aches	Mild	Often severe
Fatigue, exhaustion	Mild	Extreme exhaustion is early and severe; fatigue and weakness can last 2–3 weeks
Nasal symptoms	Usually stuffy and runny nose	Sometimes a stuffy nose
Sneezing	Very common	Sometimes
Sore throat	Common	Sometimes
Cough	Productive with mucus	Sometimes a dry cough
Chest discomfort	Mild to moderate	Common, can be severe

Adapted from the National Institute of Allergy and Infectious Disease
www.niaid.nih.gov/publications/cold/sick.pdf

COMPREHENSION CHECK

1. *Read the questions and then scan the text for the answers. When you find the answers, underline them. Then take turns with a partner asking and answering the questions. Try to remember the answers without looking back at the text.*

   1. What are two ways that the respiratory system helps to filter out dust, bacteria, and viruses?

   2. What are cilia and where are they found?

   3. What is the function of cilia?

   4. Where are macrophages found?

   5. Why is it important that the lungs heat and moisten the air we breathe?

   6. What are three major differences between a cold and the flu?

2. *Match the terms with their definitions by writing the letters in the correct blanks. Then compare your answers with those of a partner.*

_____ 1. airborne particles   **a.** cells that eat particles

_____ 2. cilia   **b.** a sticky substance that traps particles

_____ 3. alveolar macrophage   **c.** dust, bacteria, and viruses are examples

_____ 4. mucus   **d.** little hairs that sweep up particles to be spit out

FOCUS ON CULTURE

Hierarchy of Age and Gender

In different cultures, there are sometimes hierarchies of age and/or gender. Respect is shown to those who are older by addressing them in a more formal fashion, never by their first names. In some cultures, one gender may be more highly respected than the other. For instance, a woman may be required in certain cultures to walk a certain distance behind the man, even if he is her spouse. As a health-care provider, it is important for you to learn as much as you can about your patient's cultural rules regarding age and gender, so that you may treat the patient with respect.

The following stories are about cultural conflicts that people may experience in a health-care setting. Read the stories and then discuss the questions in small groups.

Patty and Maria are both dental office workers. Patty is five years younger than Maria. Patty feels that Maria is rude because she never says "Please" or "Thank you" to Patty. For example, when Maria wants something from Patty, she will say, "Get me the file" or "Sterilize this equipment." Patty feels Maria is disrespectful to her. Patty also thinks Maria is unfriendly because she never calls her older coworkers by their first names, even though they asked her to do so many times.

1. Why do you think Maria refuses to call her coworkers by their first names?

2. Why do you think Maria doesn't say "Please" or "Thank you" to Patty?

3. Do you think Maria is being rude and unfriendly? Why or why not?

4. Do you think either Patty or Maria needs to change? Why or why not?

Mohamed took his wife Khadija to the clinic for her yearly checkup. Mohamed and his wife were told at the reception desk that her regular doctor, a female, was on vacation and that a male doctor would be giving Khadija her checkup. Mohamed asked if there was a female doctor who could see Khadija instead. When the receptionist told him that there wasn't, Mohamed made another appointment for Khadija to see her regular female doctor after she returned from vacation.

1. Why do you think Mohamed didn't want his wife to be seen by a male doctor?

2. Can you imagine a situation where it would be necessary for Khadija to be seen by a male doctor?

3. Do you think that the receptionist should have been sensitive to Mohamed and Khadija and called them to tell them that no female doctor was available before they came to the clinic?

Check Your Understanding

1. *Answer the following questions about the respiratory system.*

    1. What two cavities send air to the pharynx?

    2. What is the purpose of cilia in the respiratory system?

    3. Which structures connect to the alveoli: bronchi or bronchioles?

    4. Where does each of the five secondary bronchi go?

    5. Which two muscles contract to cause inspiration?

    6. In asthma, what two things happen to the bronchioles?

    7. Explain what diffusion is.

    8. How do phagocytes protect the lungs?

2. *Label Figure 10.10 with the terms provided.*

alveolus	oral cavity	secondary bronchi
bronchiole	pharynx	tertiary bronchi
lungs	primary bronchi	trachea
nasal cavity		

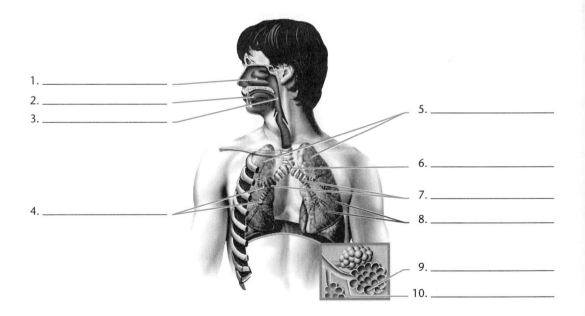

1. _____
2. _____
3. _____
4. _____
5. _____
6. _____
7. _____
8. _____
9. _____
10. _____

FIGURE 10.10   The respiratory system

3. *Answer these typical anatomy and physiology quiz questions.*

1. Which of these disorders involves the inability of alveoli to return to their original shape after inflation?
   - **a.** Infant Respiratory Distress Syndrome
   - **b.** asthma
   - **c.** emphysema
   - **d.** laryngitis

2. When a person exercises, which of these will occur?
   - **a.** dilation of bronchioles
   - **b.** constriction of bronchioles

3. _____ Is this true or false? Your lungs inflate because air has filled them.

4. Circle the correct word. When you speak, your vocal cords **contract / relax / vibrate**.

5. Circle the correct words. Contraction of the **diaphragm / bronchioles** causes the thoracic cavity and lungs to **expand / get smaller**. This causes a difference in **weight / pressure** of the air inside the lungs as compared with outside. Air will **rush into / leave** the lungs.

6. Circle the correct words. Inside the lungs, **oxygen / carbon dioxide** diffuses into the **alveoli / capillaries**.

7. What is the function of the respiratory system?

8. Where does incoming air go after it leaves the trachea?

9. Describe three protective mechanisms in the respiratory system that prevent disease.

10. Describe three ways in which colds differ from influenza.

Think More about It

1. Where in the respiratory system do we find muscle? What type of muscle is it (smooth, cardiac, or skeletal)?

2. In what ways is the nervous system involved with the respiratory system?

3. How are the respiratory and cardiovascular systems linked?

Word Bank		
alveolus	expand	pharynx
breathe	expire, expiration	primary
bronchiole	extend	pulmonary
bronchus	filter	respirator
capture	inflate	secondary
cartilage	inhale	sinus
cellular respiration	inspire, inspiration	surfactant
collapse	larynx	tertiary
diffuse	lobe	trachea
epiglottis	macrophage	vibrate
exhale	nasal cavity	vocal cords

CHAPTER 11

The Urinary System

In this unit you will learn:

ANATOMY AND PHYSIOLOGY

- *The anatomy and physiology of the kidneys*
- *Other organs of the urinary system*
- *Disorders of the urinary system*

ENGLISH

- *Asking hypothetical questions*

STUDY SKILLS

- *Categorizing information*

CULTURE

- *Confidentiality and privacy*

DID YOU KNOW *that each kidney is about the size of a computer mouse?*

INTRODUCTION

The urinary system is a very important system because it has the job of removing waste from the blood and sending it outside the body in the form of urine. Two organs called kidneys produce urine. Two tubes called ureters deliver the urine to the urinary bladder where it is stored until it is excreted from the body through the urethra. In this chapter, you will learn how the kidneys filter molecules from the blood, how urine is formed, and how the other organs of the urinary system help to remove the urine from the body. You will also learn how kidneys play a role in regulating blood volume.

1. *Work with a partner. Look at the diagram of the urinary system. Try to label the parts with the words in the box. Look at Figure 11.2 on page 232 to check your answers.*

kidney	urinary bladder	urethra	ureter

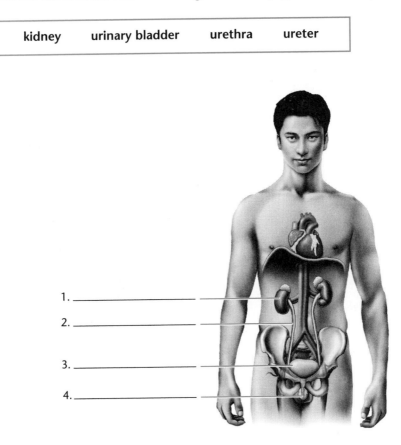

1. _____

2. _____

3. _____

4. _____

FIGURE 11.1   The urinary system

2. *With your partner, try to answer these questions. If you do not know the answers, do not worry. You will find the answers as you read through this chapter.*

   1. What is the function of the urinary system?

   2. What are two things that make a person urinate (go to the bathroom to excrete urine) more often? Less often?

   3. What kinds of disorders can occur in a person's urinary system?

3. *Read each verb, its simple definition, and its passive voice form. Then fill in the verbs in the sentences that follow. Pay attention to verb tense and subject / verb agreement. Compare your answers with those of another student.*

BASE FORM	PASSIVE VOICE FORM	MEANING
crystallize	be crystallized	to change from a dissolved form to a solid form
donate	be donated	to give away for free
inhibit	be inhibited	to prevent
lodge	be lodged	to become stuck
reclaim	be reclaimed	to get back
urinate	—	to send urine outside the body

1. He needed to _____ so he went to the bathroom.

2. She _____ her own blood to her sister after her sister lost a lot of blood.

3. A large piece of food became _____ in his esophagus.

4. She threw away her book, but then realized she needed it for another class and went to _____ it.

5. When a salt solution dries out, the salt molecules will

   _____ .

6. If it is not convenient to go to the bathroom, the brain can
   _____ the feeling to urinate.

THE KIDNEYS

Anatomy of the Kidney

Most people have two kidneys, but a few people are born with only one. The function of the kidneys is to remove wastes from the blood. The kidneys are located toward the back of the body, one on either side of the spinal cord. They are attached to the back wall of the abdomen by a layer of fat. The fat also protects the kidneys from damage. Notice in Figure 11.2 that one kidney sits a little higher than the other.

Also visible in Figure 11.2 are the other organs of the urinary system: the two ureters, the urinary bladder, and the urethra. These organs will be discussed in detail later in the chapter.

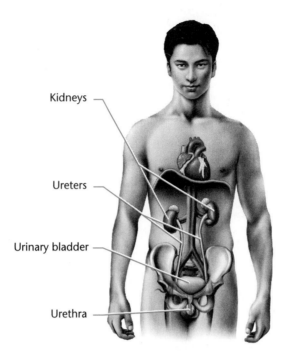

FIGURE 11.2   **The urinary system**

Each kidney consists of three layers, as shown in Figure 11.3,

- The outermost layer is called the **capsule**.
- The next layer inside is called the **cortex**.
- The layer on the inside of the cortex is called the **medulla**. The medulla contains triangular areas called **pyramids**.

The funnel-like region is called the **pelvis**. This is where urine collects before it enters the **ureter**.

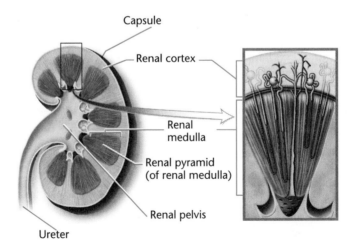

FIGURE 11.3   **Section through the kidney, with enlargement of renal pyramid**

Blood enters the kidney through the **renal artery**, which branches from the abdominal aorta. About 400 gallons (1,500 liters) of blood are pumped through the kidneys each day. Once the renal artery enters the kidney, it branches off many times to eventually enter the **nephrons** (ˈnɛfranz) in the kidneys. Nephrons are the filters where blood goes to be cleaned. Most nephrons are located within the cortex region of the kidney. There are over 1 million nephrons in each kidney! Each very tiny nephron consists of these structures:

- A cluster of capillaries called the **glomerulus** (glowˈmɛruwləs). The glomerulus has the function of filtering the blood. The plural form of glomerulus is glomeruli.

- An **afferent arteriole**, a blood vessel that brings blood to the glomerulus, and an **efferent arteriole** that takes blood away from the glomerulus.

- A cup-shaped structure called the **Bowman's capsule**. The Bowman's capsule surrounds the glomerulus. The Bowman's capsule collects the liquid waste that is filtered out of the blood.

- A **renal tubule**, a tube that carries the waste from the Bowman's capsule to larger tubes called collecting ducts.

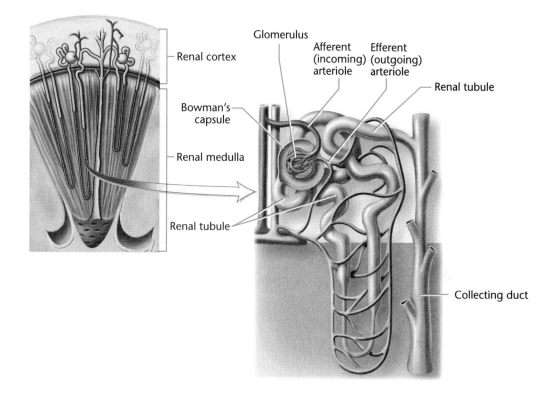

FIGURE 11.4   **Section through a renal pyramid, with enlargement of a single nephron**

1. *Put the layers of the kidney in order from outside to inside. Make 1 the outermost layer.*

   _____ cortex   _____ pelvis   _____ capsule   _____ medulla

2. *Complete the sentences using the words in the box. Take turns reading the correct sentences aloud with a partner.*

afferent arteriole	collecting duct	glomerulus
Bowman's capsule	efferent arteriole	renal tubule

   1. The part of the nephron that filters the blood is called the
      _____.

   2. The _____ is the blood vessel that brings blood to the glomerulus.

   3. The _____ collects urine from many nephrons.

   4. The _____ collects the fluid that is filtered and sends it to the renal tubule.

   5. The blood vessel that takes blood away from the glomerulus is called the
      _____.

   6. The long tube that connects the Bowman's capsule and the collecting duct is called the _____.

Physiology of the Kidney

Each nephron has three main functions: filtration, reabsorption, and secretion. These three processes work together to maintain homeostasis of molecules in the blood. The three functions are explained below.

FILTRATION

A glomerulus is a cluster of capillaries. Things that are small enough to pass through the walls of the glomerulus are filtered out of the blood. These things include: water, sugar, salts, and other dissolved molecules. Proteins and blood cells are too large to exit the walls of the glomerulus and they stay in the blood.

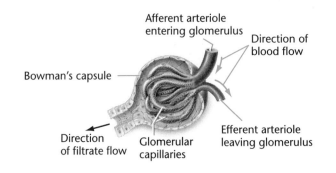

FIGURE 11.5   **The glomerulus and Bowman's capsule. Blue arrows indicate blood flow. Black arrow indicates filtrate flow.**

The amount of blood in the glomerulus determines how much of each type of molecule is filtered. To imagine how the glomerulus functions, think of two balloons with very small holes in them. One balloon is filled to capacity with water, while the second balloon has just a little water in it. The filled balloon has more pressure from all the water inside. Therefore, more fluid is forced out of the small holes of the full balloon than from the one that is nearly empty. The pressure pushes the water out of the small holes. The nearly empty balloon has very little pressure to push the water out. Likewise in the glomerulus, the more blood volume, and therefore blood pressure, the greater the filtration. So, it is very important to maintain adequate blood pressure in the glomerulus for filtration to occur. If a person has severe dehydration (not enough water in her system) and very low blood pressure, there may not be enough pressure for filtration to occur. Renal failure can result.

Renal (Kidney) Failure! When the kidneys don't work properly, the blood is not cleaned. Waste products then accumulate in the blood and cause problems with many normal body functions. These include problems with blood pressure, neural functions, heart function, and muscle contractions. Renal failure can be caused by many different things: physical damage to the kidneys, diabetes, chronic hypertension, or bacterial infections.

All of the molecules that are filtered through the holes of the glomerulus are called **filtrate**. This filtrate is collected in the Bowman's capsule. From the Bowman's capsule, the filtrate flows into the renal tubule. The renal tubule is where the filtrate is altered to eventually become urine. Each renal tubule has three major regions.

- The first region is a coiled area that extends from the Bowman's capsule. This region is called the **proximal convoluted tubule** or PCT. (*Proximal* means *near*; *convoluted* means *coiled*.)

- The second region is a long loop called the **loop of Henle**. The loop of Henle connects the PCT to the third region.

- The third region is called the **distal convoluted tubule** or DCT. (*Distal* means *far*; *convoluted* means *coiled*.)

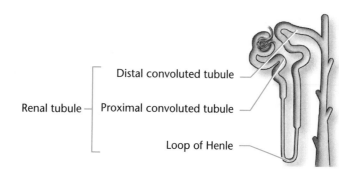

Renal tubule

Distal convoluted tubule

Proximal convoluted tubule

Loop of Henle

FIGURE 11.6   **Parts of the renal tubule**

1. *Read the questions and then scan the text for answers. When you find the answers, underline them. Then work with a partner and take turns asking and answering the questions. Try to remember the answers without looking back at the text.*

   1. What is the function of the glomerulus?

   2. What parts of the blood are too big to be filtered out of the glomerulus?

   3. If pressure is low in the glomerulus, are more or fewer molecules filtered out of the blood?

   4. After filtrate leaves the Bowman's capsule, what is the first region of the renal tubule that it enters?

   5. Draw a picture of a renal tubule and label its parts.

   6. In what structure does filtrate become urine?

2. *Match the terms with their definitions by writing the letters in the correct blanks. Then compare your answers with those of a partner.*

   _____ 1. afferent arteriole

   _____ 2. convoluted

   _____ 3. distal

   _____ 4. filtrate

   _____ 5. glomerulus

   _____ 6. renal tubule

   _____ 7. proximal

   _____ 8. renal artery

   a. blood enters the kidney through this vessel

   b. supplies the glomerulus with blood

   c. the liquid filtered from the glomerulus

   d. far

   e. near

   f. after leaving the Bowman's capsule, filtrate goes here

   g. coiled

   h. a cluster of capillaries

REABSORPTION AND SECRETION

Recall that the function of the glomerulus is filtration. Two other functions occur in various parts of the renal tubule: reabsorption and secretion. Some of the molecules that have been filtered out of the glomerulus (for example, sugar) are needed by the body. Your body needs sugar for energy. The process of returning molecules to the blood is called **reabsorption** (riyəb'sɔrpʃən). Reabsorption primarily occurs in the proximal convoluted tubule (PCT). In healthy people, reabsorption *reclaims* 100 percent of the sugar and about 90 percent of the water from the filtrate and returns it to the blood. Roughly 90 percent of salts such as sodium are also returned to the blood by the process of reabsorption.

There is some evidence to support the idea that a diet high in refined sugars and carbohydrates makes a person more likely to develop diabetes. The number of people with diabetes in highly developed countries is much higher than in less developed countries.

 Diabetes! When someone has a higher than normal amount of sugar in his blood, he has **diabetes mellitus** (dayə'biytəs mə'laytəs). The kidneys of a person with diabetes are not able to reabsorb all this extra sugar. As a result, the urine contains sugar. In fact, the name *mellitus* means *sweet!* People with untreated diabetes often have sweet-smelling urine. In fact, before the start of laboratory testing, some doctors used to actually taste the urine to see if it was sweet!

So far, the steps of cleaning the blood are filtration and reabsorption. The other major function of the renal tubule is **secretion** (sɪ'kriyʃən). Secretion is the opposite of reabsorption. Recall that reabsorption takes molecules from the filtrate and returns them to the blood. Secretion, on the other hand, takes additional molecules from the blood that the body wants to get rid of and adds those molecules to the filtrate. These molecules include wastes such as urea, uric acid, and medications. These wastes could become toxic and therefore dangerous to the body if they were allowed to accumulate. Some of the cells in the renal tubule take these harmful substances out of the blood and add them to the filtrate that is passing through the renal tubule. In addition to removing harmful molecules, secretion is also very important in maintaining the proper pH balance in the blood.

After the processes of reabsorption and secretion, the filtrate that remains is called urine. After exiting the renal tubule, the urine enters a **collecting duct**. Each kidney contains many collecting ducts. One collecting duct collects urine from several nephrons. Collecting ducts transport urine through the medulla of the kidney to the renal pelvis. The renal pelvis becomes the ureter, the tube that carries urine to the urinary bladder.

To summarize, blood is cleaned in a three-step process as follows:

- **Filtration** occurs in the glomerulus. Filtration is the removal of certain molecules and water from the blood.

- **Reabsorption** occurs in the renal tubule. Reabsorption is the return of certain molecules and water that have been filtered back to the blood.

- **Secretion** also occurs in the renal tubule. Secretion is the removal of additional molecules from the blood after it has gone through the glomerulus.

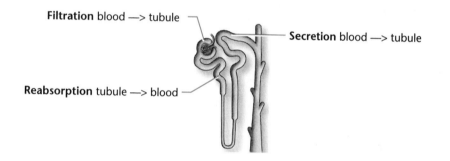

Filtration blood —> tubule

Secretion blood —> tubule

Reabsorption tubule —> blood

FIGURE 11.7   **Comparison of filtration, reabsorption, and secretion**

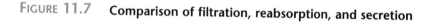

CHARACTERISTICS OF NORMAL URINE:

- Neutral or slightly acid
- About 95 percent water
- 1,200 ml per day is excreted
- Normally is sterile (no microorganisms)

Renal Failure! When someone's kidneys fail, he is often placed on **dialysis** (day′ælɔsɪs). A dialysis machine does the filtering that the kidneys would normally do. In this treatment, the patient's blood is sent through a series of tubes to a machine that filters it. The blood is then returned to the patient's body. The patient must do this for about 15 hours a week. This solution is often temporary until someone can be found to *donate* a kidney to the patient. This procedure is called a **kidney transplant**. The majority of healthy people can donate a kidney and still be able to live with one healthy kidney. However, the kidney being donated must have tissue that is very similar to the person receiving the kidney. Otherwise, the body defenses will attack the donated kidney as something foreign.

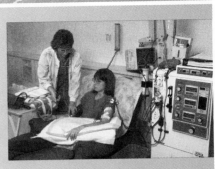

COMPREHENSION CHECK

1. *Work with a partner to label each statement true* (T) *or false* (F). *If the statement is false, correct it so that it is true.*

   _____ 1. Reabsorption reclaims molecules from the filtrate and returns them to the blood.

   _____ 2. Secretion occurs primarily in the glomerulus.

   _____ 3. Reabsorption occurs after filtration.

   _____ 4. The fluid in the renal tubules is called urine.

   _____ 5. Secretion occurs before filtration.

   _____ 6. The proximal convoluted tubules deliver urine to the collecting ducts.

   _____ 7. In a healthy person, almost all of the water and all of the sugar that is filtered becomes reabsorbed.

2. *Filtration, reabsorption, and secretion are the three important processes in the kidney. Work with a partner. If the function primarily occurs at the location, put a check mark* (✓) *in the appropriate box.*

	Filtration	**Reabsorption**	**Secretion**
Glomerulus	☐	☐	☐
Renal tubule	☐	☐	☐

OTHER FUNCTIONS OF THE KIDNEYS

The cleansing of the blood is an important function of the kidneys. However, the kidneys have other important roles in helping the body maintain homeostasis.

First, the kidneys produce **erythropoietin** (iyrɪθrow′powiytən), the hormone that stimulates production of red blood cells. People with kidney diseases often experience anemia. Recall from studying blood that anemia is a condition where a person's blood does not carry enough oxygen. Second, the kidneys convert Vitamin D (which is made in the skin) to its active (useful) form. Vitamin D plays an important role in the absorption of calcium and thus bone formation.

Maintaining Blood Volume

When you drink a lot of water, you have to *urinate* a lot. This is a sign that your body is maintaining homeostasis of body fluids. The kidneys play an important role in maintaining levels of body fluids, salts, and therefore, blood pressure.

Recall that blood pressure is influenced by the volume of blood. The amount of water in the blood determines blood volume. Since it is very important to maintain a constant blood pressure, it is important to control blood volume.

THINGS THAT INCREASE BLOOD VOLUME	THINGS THAT DECREASE BLOOD VOLUME
Rapidly drinking lots of fluids	Low intake of fluids
Stress, trauma, and pain	Hemorrhage (significant blood loss)
Too much sugar or salt in blood	Diarrhea, vomiting
	Excessive sweating

There are a number of ways to maintain homeostasis of blood volume. The kidneys play a large role in this process.

If blood volume is too low:

- The afferent arteriole constricts. Less water enters the glomerulus. Filtration decreases and more water stays in the blood. Thus, blood volume increases.

- The kidneys secrete **renin** (ˈrɛnɪn). Renin causes a series of chemical reactions that ultimately result in increased blood volume.

- The two adrenal glands, one on top of each kidney, secrete **aldosterone** (ælˈdɑstərown) which results in the kidneys' reabsorption of more water. This increases blood volume.

- The pituitary gland secretes a hormone called **anti-diuretic** (æntiydayəˈrɛtɪk) **hormone (or ADH)**. ADH causes the kidneys to reabsorb more water and thus increase blood volume.

If blood volume is too high:

- The afferent arteriole dilates. More water enters the glomerulus to be filtered out. Thus, blood volume decreases.

- The heart secretes a hormone called **atrial natriuretic** (ˈeytriyəl neytryuwˈrɛtɪk) **peptide** (or ANP). ANP ultimately causes less water to be reabsorbed, thus reducing blood volume.

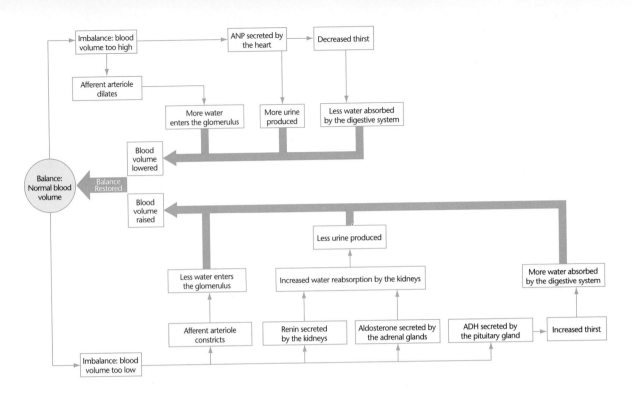

FIGURE 11.8   Homeostasis of blood volume

Alcohol Intoxication! When someone drinks too much alcohol, he has to urinate a lot. This is because the alcohol takes water out of the blood into the urine. A "hangover" often follows the next day. The person has a headache, feels dehydrated, and is sometimes nauseous. This is because the alcohol has *inhibited* the production of ADH. Recall that ADH causes blood volume to increase. So alcohol makes a person feel more dehydrated. If a person loses too much water while drinking alcohol, he may actually lose consciousness ("pass out"). The headache from drinking is due to low blood pressure in the brain.

COMPREHENSION CHECK

1. *Circle the correct word(s) to complete each sentence. Take turns reading the correct sentences aloud with a partner.*

   1. **Aldosterone / Erythropoietin** is a hormone made by the kidney that stimulates red blood cell production.

   2. The **kidneys / adrenal gland** convert Vitamin D to its active form.

   3. Renin causes an **increase / decrease** in blood volume.

   4. Aldosterone **increases / decreases** blood volume.

   5. ADH **increases / decreases** water reabsorption.

   6. **Aldosterone / ADH** is secreted by the pituitary gland.

   7. ANP has the **opposite / same** effect on blood volume as aldosterone.

   8. Alcohol **increases / inhibits** ADH production.

2. *Work with a partner. If the information is correct, put a check mark (✓) in the appropriate box.*

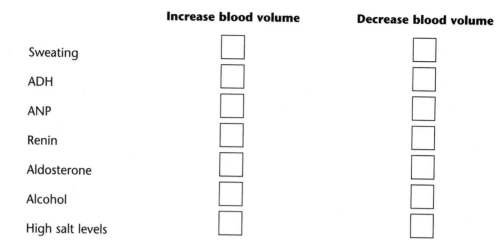

	Increase blood volume	Decrease blood volume
Sweating	☐	☐
ADH	☐	☐
ANP	☐	☐
Renin	☐	☐
Aldosterone	☐	☐
Alcohol	☐	☐
High salt levels	☐	☐

BUILDING LANGUAGE AND STUDY SKILLS

Asking Hypothetical Questions

When you study anatomy and physiology, you learn about many structures and processes in the body. Learning new information often creates new questions in one's mind. For example, after learning about the function of the nephron, a person might wonder, "What happens to a person if only half of their nephrons work properly?" This kind of question, where you consider possible problems or the likelihood of future events, is called a hypothetical question. To hypothesize means to wonder about something and ask "What if?" Hypothetical questions are based on facts you already know. It's good to hypothesize when you study anatomy and physiology because it "stretches" your brain. Don't feel shy about asking hypothetical questions in class. These creative questions are an important part of learning.

Read the following examples of hypothetical questions.

What happens if a person has only one kidney?

What might / could happen to a person's kidneys if he or she drank alcohol every day?

I wonder what happens if a person with diabetes isn't treated?

I wonder what might / could happen if a person with kidney failure couldn't get on dialysis?

If someone is anemic, what can a doctor do for him or her?

PRACTICE

1. *Look at the following facts you have studied in this chapter. Try to think of a hypothetical question for at least five of the items. Then share your questions with a partner. Can he or she answer any of them? Can you answer any of your partner's questions?*

For example:

Kidneys are attached to the back wall of the abdomen by a layer of fat.

Hypothetical question: *I wonder what would happen if a person lost the fat that attaches the kidneys to the back of his or her abdomen.*

1. There are over 1 million nephrons in each kidney.

2. Glomeruli are leaky so molecules can easily pass through.

3. Ninety percent of the water in the filtrate is returned to the blood.

4. The rate of diabetes is higher in developed countries.

5. Urine is normally sterile.

6. Erythropoietin is a hormone that stimulates red blood cell production.

7. Aldosterone has the effect of increasing blood pressure.

2. *Share the questions you and your partner could not answer with the rest of the class. Who can answer the questions?*

3. *These are authentic questions taken from an anatomy and physiology class. Use the vocabulary and grammar you know to answer these questions. Ask your teacher to check your answers.*

1. What would happen to filtration in the kidneys if a person had lost a lot of blood in an automobile accident?

2. What would happen to the kidneys if a person lost all the fat around the kidneys?

3. What would be the result if a person lost half of his nephrons?

4. What would happen if a transplanted kidney did not match the recipient's tissue?

5. What would happen to the kidneys if a large kidney stone blocked each ureter?

Categorizing Information

Sometimes when you are studying anatomy and physiology, you may start to feel overwhelmed. You may start to feel like there is so much to learn that you don't know where to begin. One way to solve that problem is to get into the habit of categorizing information. To categorize information means to group it according to how it is similar to other information. Let's use a familiar example to illustrate how this is done. Remember when you learned the words for food in English? You had to learn words such as beef, milk, orange, beans, broccoli, and rice. If you had studied the names of foods according to categorizing, you might have taken a piece of paper and made five circles or buckets on it. (Many people also find it helpful to create each circle or bucket in a different color.) Each circle or bucket would have been labeled with the name of a food group: fruits, vegetables, meats, grains, and dairy products. In each circle or bucket, you would have then written all of the names of foods according to their category. Doing the same thing with anatomy and physiology structures and concepts is equally helpful. When you categorize information on paper, you are helping your brain to organize the information. Organized information is learned information!

In this chapter, you have learned the following terms. Create categories in which to divide the terms and put the terms into these categories. Share the categories you created with the class. Did everyone come up with the same categories?

afferent arteriole	filtration	reabsorption
Bowman's capsule	glomerulus	renal tubule
capsule	kidney	secretion
collecting duct	loop of Henle	ureter
cortex	medulla	urethra
distal convoluted tubule	nephron	urinary bladder
efferent arteriole	pelvis	urine
filtrate	proximal convoluted tubule	

OTHER ORGANS IN THE URINARY SYSTEM

The Ureters

The **ureters** (ˈyuwrətərz) are tubes that carry urine from the kidneys to the urinary bladder. There are two ureters, one leading from each of your two kidneys. Smooth muscle in the walls of the ureters helps to propel the urine toward the bladder. The ureters connect with the upper posterior portion of the urinary bladder.

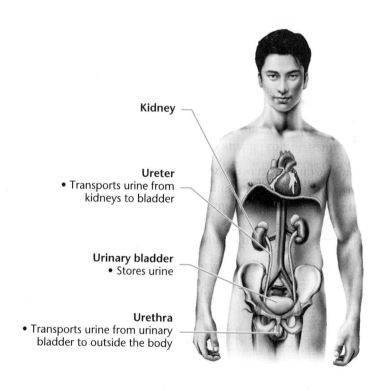

Kidney

Ureter
• Transports urine from kidneys to bladder

Urinary bladder
• Stores urine

Urethra
• Transports urine from urinary bladder to outside the body

FIGURE 11.9   Organs of the urinary system

Kidney Stones (Renal Calculi)! Sometimes, the balance of salts and water in the urine is not correct. If there are too many salts, the salts may *crystallize* and form kidney stones. (Recall how gallstones formed in the same way in the digestive system.) Kidney stones most commonly form in the ureters. However, sometimes kidney stones may form in the kidney itself. Kidney stones have very sharp edges, so they are very painful as they move through the ureter. Most kidney stones pass through the urethra during urination, but sometimes they become *lodged* in a certain location. In those cases, doctors often use ultrasound or a laser to break the stones into small pieces, so they can pass through the ureters more easily.

The Urinary Bladder

The urinary bladder is a muscular sac that collects urine until it can be released from the body. The bladder can hold an average of one liter of urine.

There is a three-step process involved in urination. First, as the bladder fills with urine, its walls stretch. This stretching causes stretch receptors in the bladder's walls to send a message along a neuron to the spinal cord. Second, this message ("the bladder is full") causes the spinal cord to send a neural message to the **internal urethral sphincter**, which is located at the base of the bladder, where the urethra begins. This message tells the internal urethral sphincter to relax. This sphincter is involuntary (not under conscious control). Third, when the internal urethral sphincter relaxes, the spinal cord then sends a message to the brain to tell the person that he needs to urinate. Most people can choose when to urinate because the act of urination is under a person's conscious control. People can control the opening and closing of their **external urethral sphincter**. Babies, however, have not yet developed the neural connections to control urination.

 Incontinence! Incontinence (ɪnˈkɑntənənts) is when a person cannot control urination. Sometimes, this is due to damage to parts of the brain, spinal cord, or to the external urethral sphincter.

The Urethra

The **urethra** (yuwˈriyθrə) is a tube that extends from the base of the bladder to the outside of the body. In females, the urethra is rather short, about 3–5 cm (1–2 inches). In males, the urethra is about 18–20 cm (7–8 inches) in length, and extends through the center of the penis.

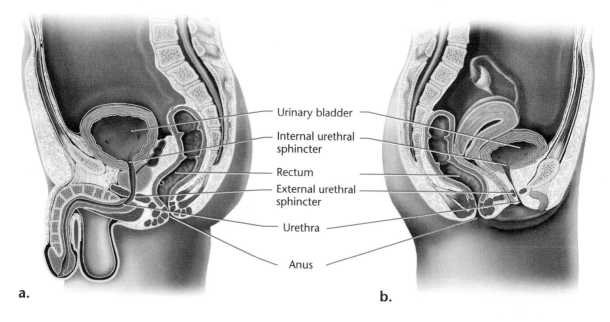

Figure 11.10 Side view of the male urinary system (a). Note the long urethra. Side view of the female urinary system (b). Note the shorter urethra and its closer location to the anus.

The function of the urethra is to carry urine to the outside of the body. In males, the urethra has a second function: to carry sperm to the outside of the body. You will learn more about this function in the next chapter.

Urinary Tract Infection (UTI)! Bacteria can sometimes travel from outside the body up the urethra to the urinary bladder. Sometimes, these bacteria can even travel as far as the kidneys. Most of these infections are caused by *E. coli* bacteria transfered from the anal region to the urethra. Bacteria may also enter the body when a medical instrument (catheter) is inserted in the urethra. If left untreated, these infections can cause serious damage to the kidneys. About 50 percent of the infections that patients contract while in the hospital are UTIs. If a person experiences pain during urination, they should immediately consult their doctor. Women are more likely to contract UTI than men because their urethra is shorter and it is easier for bacteria to be transferred from the anal region to the urethra.

COMPREHENSION CHECK

1. *Circle the correct word(s) to complete each sentence. Take turns reading the correct sentences aloud with a partner.*

   1. The **ureter / urethra** is the tube that carries urine to the outside of the body.

   2. The urinary bladder holds an average of **1 liter / 10 liters** of urine.

   3. The urethra is **longer / shorter** in males than in females.

   4. Kidney stones most often form in the **ureter / urethra**.

5. **Excretion / Secretion** is a term used to describe urination.

6. Pain during urination is most likely a symptom of **incontinence / urinary tract infection**.

2. *Put the steps of how urination occurs in order from 1 to 6. The first thing that happens is already done for you.*

_____ The spinal cord sends message to relax the internal urethral sphincter.

_____ The spinal cord sends message to the brain that the bladder is full.

_____ A neural message is sent to the spinal cord.

_____ The internal urethral sphincter relaxes.

__1__ The stretch receptors detect that the bladder is full.

_____ The person consciously relaxes the external urethral sphincter.

FOCUS ON CULTURE

Confidentiality and Privacy

In different cultures, medical information has different levels of privacy. Another word for privacy is confidentiality. In the United States, it is illegal for a health-care provider to give a patient's medical information to anyone. The patient must give written permission to the doctor to share this information with even family members. In some cultures, however, medical information may be given to the patient's family but not told to the patient.

This commonly happens if the patient has a very serious illness. Some people believe that telling a patient bad news about her condition will prevent her from recovering. As a health-care provider, it is important for you to understand the legal rules and cultural views about the privacy of this information.

> *The following story is about a cultural conflict that people may experience in a health-care setting. Read the story and then discuss the questions in small groups.*

Lai is a student in a nursing program at a college in the United States. She is a native of Laos and often serves as a translator for people from her country who are unable to speak English. She has accompanied a family friend to the hospital for a routine checkup. The doctor suspects that the patient may have a heart condition. The doctor does not want to disclose this information to Lai. Lai's friend wants to know what is going on. She is upset that she doesn't understand their conversation. When Lai tries to explain that she needs permission from her friend to translate what the doctor is saying, her friend becomes angry at Lai and the doctor.

1. Why doesn't the doctor want to tell Lai about his patient's health?

2. Why is Lai's friend becoming angry?

3. How can Lai resolve this situation?

4. Are privacy laws important? Why or why not?

Check Your Understanding

1. *Answer the following questions about the urinary system.*

   1. What are the four main organs in the urinary system? What is the major function of each?

   2. What structure does filtration?

   3. What are the five parts of the nephron?

   4. Does filtration take things out of the blood or put things in the blood?

   5. What homeostatic function do kidneys have?

   6. How do kidneys relate to the production of blood?

   7. Which process, secretion or reabsorption, takes things out of the blood and into the urine?

   8. Which two hormones cause the kidneys to reabsorb more water?

   9. What structure in the urinary bladder causes the urination process to begin?

   10. What are the two functions of the male's urethra?

2. *Label Figures 11.11 and 11.12 with the terms provided.*

kidney   ureter   urethra   urinary bladder

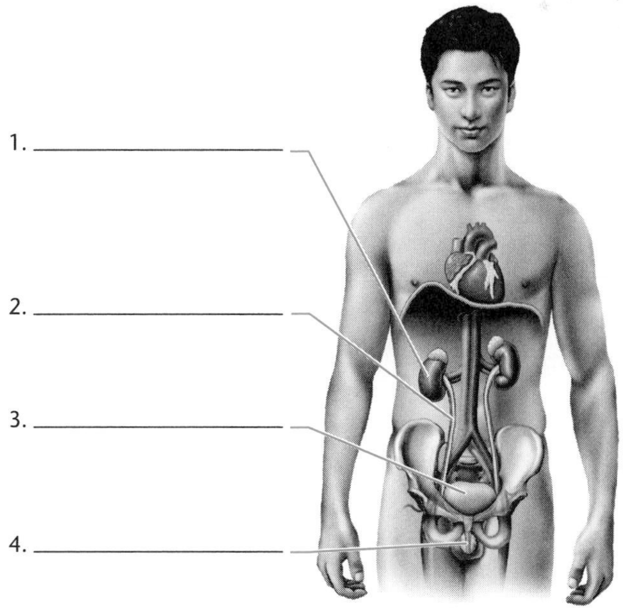

1. _____

2. _____

3. _____

4. _____

FIGURE 11.11   The urinary system

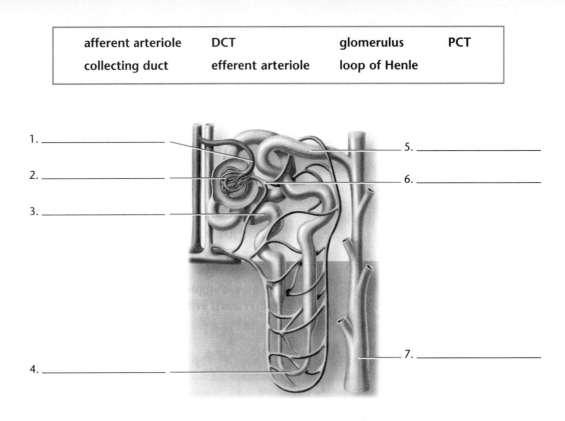

| afferent arteriole | DCT | glomerulus | PCT |
| collecting duct | efferent arteriole | loop of Henle | |

1. _____

2. _____

3. _____

4. _____

5. _____

6. _____

7. _____

FIGURE 11.12   The nephron

3. *Answer these typical anatomy and physiology quiz questions.*

   1. The specific part of the kidney that filters the blood is the _____.
      a. medulla
      b. ureter
      c. collecting duct
      d. glomerulus

   2. Which of these structures is NOT correctly matched with its function?
      a. urethra: carries urine from urinary bladder to outside of body
      b. collecting duct: carries urine from nephron toward renal pelvis
      c. efferent arteriole: carries blood to the glomerulus
      d. proximal convoluted tubule: reabsorption and secretion

   3. Which of these choices is the correct pathway for urine?
      a. kidney ⟶ urinary bladder ⟶ urethra ⟶ ureter
      b. kidney ⟶ urethra ⟶ urinary bladder ⟶ ureter
      c. kidney ⟶ urinary bladder ⟶ ureter ⟶ urethra
      d. kidney ⟶ ureter ⟶ urinary bladder ⟶ urethra

   4. _____ Is it true or false? Too much water in the urine can cause formation of kidney stones.

5. ____ Is it true or false? People with renal failure often require dialysis treatment.

6. ____ Is it true or false? Both ADH and aldosterone are hormones used by the body to increase blood volume by reabsorbing more water.

7. Name three molecules that are normally found in the urine.

8. Describe what causes kidney failure and how it is treated.

9. Name the three processes that occur in the nephron. Tell whether each process returns things to the blood or takes things out of the blood.

Think More about It

1. How does the urinary system help to regulate the cardiovascular system?

2. In what ways does the nervous system help with (control) the urinary system?

3. Where are muscles important in the urinary system located?

Word Bank		
arteriole (afferent and efferent)	excrete	reabsorb
	filter	renal tubule
Bowman's capsule	filtrate	secrete
capsule	glomerulonephritis	ureter
cortex	glomerulus	urethra
diabetes	incontinence	urinate
dialysis	nephron	
erythropoietin	pelvis	

CHAPTER 12

The Reproductive System

In this unit you will learn:

ANATOMY AND PHYSIOLOGY

- *Male reproductive system*
- *Female reproductive system*
- *Fertilization and embryonic development*
- *Common reproductive disorders*

ENGLISH

- *Answering hypothetical questions*

STUDY SKILLS

- *Putting it all together*

CULTURE

- *Discussing the reproductive system with patients*

DID YOU KNOW *that a man can produce up to half a billion sperm per day and females are born with all the eggs they will ever have (about 2 million)?*

INTRODUCTION

The reproductive system includes the organs that are necessary for reproduction, the formation of a new person from two parents. The reproductive system is quite different in males and females. The male reproductive system has more organs than the female reproductive system. However, the homeostasis of hormones is much simpler in males than in females. In this chapter you will first learn about both male and female reproductive systems and how they are affected by hormones. You will then learn the steps involved in the reproduction process.

1. *Work with a partner. Look at the diagrams of male and female reproductive systems. Try to label the parts with the words in the box. One word is used twice. Look at Figures 12.6 and 12.8 on pages 256 and 263 to check your answers.*

ovary	penis	testis	urethra	uterus	vagina

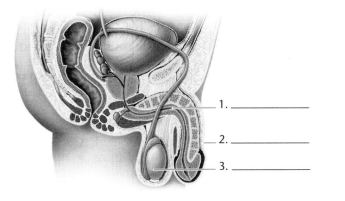

1. _____
2. _____
3. _____

FIGURE 12.1   **The male reproductive system**

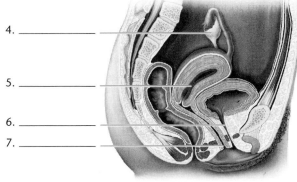

4. _____
5. _____
6. _____
7. _____

FIGURE 12.2   **The female reproductive system**

2. *With a partner, try to answer these questions. If you do not know the answers, do not worry. You will find the answers as you read through this chapter.*

   1. What is the name of the organ in the male that makes sperm?

   2. What is the name of the organ in the female that makes the egg?

   3. What do you think tells the male to make sperm and the woman to produce eggs?

3. *Read each verb, its simple definition, and its passive voice form. Then fill in the verbs in the sentences that follow. Pay attention to verb tense and subject / verb agreement. Compare your answers with those of another student.*

BASE FORM	PASSIVE VOICE FORM	MEANING
circumcise	be circumcised	to remove the foreskin around the tip of the penis
ejaculate	be ejaculated	to send out forcefully
fertilize	be fertilized	the sperm cell unites with the egg
implant	be implanted	to embed, to attach within
lubricate	be lubricated	to make slippery
rupture	be ruptured	to break open

1. Mucus is a slippery substance that helps to _____ passageways within the body such as the vagina and the nostrils.

2. In reproduction, the sperm joins with, or _____, the egg and then a baby begins to grow.

3. An embryo (the start of a baby) must _____ within the walls of the uterus where it will grow and develop.

4. When you stick a pin in a balloon, the balloon _____.

5. Male babies are _____ in some cultures.

6. The male _____ the sperm into the female.

THE MALE REPRODUCTIVE SYSTEM

The organs in the male reproductive system are made to produce sperm and transport sperm into the female. These organs include the testes, which make sperm, and the series of tubes that send sperm out of the body.

Production of Sperm

The male cells that will unite with the female's egg are called **sperm**. Sperm are also called **spermatozoa** (spɛrmətə′zowə). In the male, the organ that produces sperm is called the **testis** (′tɛstɪs). Men have two testes.

The testes are located within a sac called the **scrotum** (′skrowtəm). The scrotum is a pouch of skin that hangs outside a man's body. The location of the scrotum allows it to keep the testes at a temperature that is a few degrees cooler than a man's internal body temperature. Proper temperature is very important for the production of sperm. There are muscles in the wall of the scrotum that contract and relax to change the distance of the scrotum from the body. When it is cold, the scrotum is pulled closer to the body. The body's heat can keep the temperature in the testes ideal for sperm production. When it is hot, the scrotum lies farther away from the body.

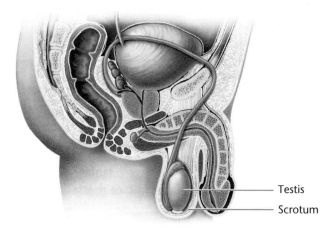

Testis

Scrotum

FIGURE 12.3   Location of testis within scrotum

Sperm are produced inside **seminiferous** (sɛmə′nɪfərəs) **tubules**. There are many seminiferous tubules within each testis. In the lining of seminiferous tubules, there are cells called **spermatocytes** (spɛr′mætəsayts). Spermatocytes are the cells that eventually become sperm.

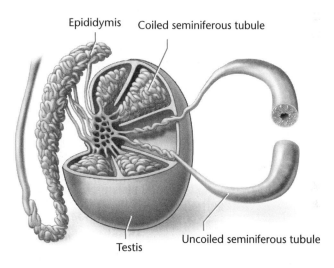

Epididymis   Coiled seminiferous tubule

Uncoiled seminiferous tubule

Testis

FIGURE 12.4   Section through the testis showing seminiferous tubules

Before a spermatocyte can become a sperm, it must undergo a special type of cell division called **meiosis** (may′owsɪs). Meiosis takes one spermatocyte and divides it into four identical cells called **spermatids** (′spɛrmətɪdz). Spermatids have half the number of **chromosomes** (′krowməsowmz) as spermatocytes and other body cells. Chromosomes are the structures within the nucleus of a cell that contain the cell's genetic information. When a sperm and an egg join, a child is produced. The child gets half of its chromosomes from the mother and half from the father. That's why a man's sperm and a woman's egg only need half the number of chromosomes as other cells.

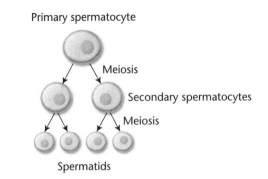

Primary spermatocyte

Meiosis

Secondary spermatocytes

Meiosis

Spermatids

FIGURE 12.5   The process of sperm production

After meiosis occurs, the spermatids are released into the **lumen** (′luwmən), or central opening, of the seminiferous tubule. At this point, spermatids are immature sperm because they are not yet able to swim. Sperm must be able to swim to reach the egg in a woman's body. To mature into sperm, spermatids travel within a liquid in the seminiferous tubule to a long, coiled tube that sits on top of each testis. This tube is called the **epididymis** (ɛpɪ′dɪdəmɪs). The epididymis is the place where sperm become mature. The sperm remain here until a man *ejaculates*, and the sperm exit his body.

COMPREHENSION CHECK

1. *Answer the questions below. Then compare your answers with those of a partner.*

    1. Where are sperm produced?

    2. Where are the testes located?

    3. Do the testes require a temperature higher or lower than body temperature to make sperm?

    4. What happens to the scrotum when it's cold?

    5. In what kind of tubules are sperm made?

    6. Where are these tubules located?

    7. Which has more chromosomes, a spermatocyte or a spermatid?

    8. How do spermatids differ from mature sperm and where do they become mature?

2. *Match the terms with their definitions by writing the letters in the correct blanks. Then compare your answers with those of a partner.*

    _____ 1. scrotum   **a.** a cell that will divide to form sperm

    _____ 2. testes   **b.** the place where sperm mature

    _____ 3. spermatid   **c.** the organ that makes spermatids

    _____ 4. epididymis   **d.** an immature sperm

    _____ 5. spermatocyte   **e.** the place within the testes where spermatids are made

    _____ 6. seminiferous tubules **f.** sperm

    _____ 7. spermatozoa   **g.** a sac that holds the testes

Sexual Arousal in the Male

When the male becomes sexually excited (aroused), several changes occur in his reproductive system:

1. **erection** of the **penis** ('piynəs)
2. secretions of **bulbourethral** (bəlbowyuw'riyθrəl) **glands**
3. **ejaculation**

The penis is the organ that delivers the sperm out of the male's body. Before sperm can exit a man's body, his penis must enlarge and become upright, or erect. This occurs when a man becomes sexually excited. The penis contains **erectile** (ɪ'rɛktayəl) **tissue** separated by many open areas, or channels, that are richly supplied with blood vessels. When the man becomes excited, the blood vessels dilate and the channels fill with blood. When a man's penis is erect, it is commonly said that he has an erection. When the man is not excited, the blood vessels are constricted, the channels are empty, and the penis is **flaccid** ('flæsɪd). It hangs loosely from the body.

As the penis is becoming erect, two small glands located on either side of the urethra secrete fluid into the urethra. These glands are called **bulbourethral glands**. Sometimes, the bulbourethral glands are called "Cowper's glands." The secretion from these glands is like watery mucus. This slippery secretion helps to *lubricate* the penis so that it can enter the female's vagina more easily. The secretion is also alkaline, which helps to neutralize the acid environment inside the female's vagina. Sperm survive better in a neutral environment.

 Impotence! Impotence is the inability to produce or maintain an erection. It may be caused by nerve damage, plaque in the arteries of the penis, alcohol, or emotional anxiety. Recently, drugs such as **Viagra™** (vayægrə) and **Cialis™** (siy'æləs) have become popular in helping men to achieve and maintain erections. These drugs help to keep the blood vessels in the penis in a dilated state, so that the penis maintains an erection.

COMPREHENSION CHECK

Work with a partner to label each statement true (T) *or false* (F). *If the statement is false, correct it so that it is true.*

_____ **1.** Erectile tissue fills with sperm to make the man's penis become erect.

_____ **2.** Bulbourethral glands secrete watery mucus into the urethra.

_____ **3.** Lubrication makes passage of the penis into the vagina more difficult.

_____ **4.** Sperm survive better in an alkaline environment.

_____ **5.** Ejaculation happens before an erection.

_____ **6.** Drugs exist to help a man achieve and maintain an erection.

_____ **7.** Circumcisions are often done at birth.

_____ **8.** Impotence is the failure to ejaculate.

Many male babies throughout the world are circumcised. Circumcision is a surgical procedure in which the doctor removes a flap of tissue that surrounds the tip of the penis. This flap of tissue is called the foreskin or prepuce. Although circumcision was originally done for religious reasons, there are some medical reasons for doing it. Men who are not circumcised tend to have a greater chance of infections because bacteria grow easily in the foreskin.

The Path of Sperm

When the man reaches the peak of excitement, he ejaculates. Ejaculation is the forceful release of sperm from the penis. Just prior to ejaculation, the sperm move from the epididymis upward through a tube called the **vas deferens** (væs ˈdɛfərɛnz). Sometimes, scientists prefer to use the term **ductus deferens** instead of vas deferens. The vas deferens is about 45 cm (18") long. Muscle in the wall of the vas deferens contracts in peristaltic waves to push the sperm along its length.

Once the vas deferens has passed inside the body wall, it joins with a duct from the **seminal vesicles** (ˈsɛmɪnəl ˈvɛsɪkəlz). The seminal vesicles are sac-like glands that produce an alkaline fluid containing sugar and clotting enzymes. The fluid is alkaline to help neutralize the acid conditions inside the female's reproductive tract. The sugar serves as an energy source for the sperm. The sperm use the sugar to help them swim within the female. The clotting enzymes help this fluid to coagulate so that it does not easily leave the female's body once it is deposited. The combination of the fluid from the seminal vesicles and the sperm is called **semen** (ˈsiymən).

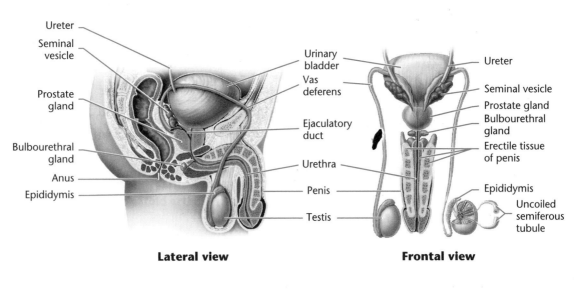

Lateral view　　　　**Frontal view**

FIGURE 12.6　The male reproductive system. Lateral view is on left, frontal view is on right.

The vas deferens transports semen toward the urethra. Near the urethra, the vas deferens and the duct from the seminal vesicle join together to form a short tube called the **ejaculatory duct** (ɪˈdʒækyələtoriy dəkt). The ejaculatory duct empties into the urethra which carries semen to the outside of the body. However, before the ejaculatory duct empties into the urethra, it passes through the **prostate gland** (ˈprɑsteyt glænd), a walnut-sized gland that lies just below the urinary bladder. The prostate gland adds a milky fluid to the semen. This milky fluid contains additional enzymes that help with clotting of the semen once it enters the woman's body. The milky fluid also contains anti-bacterial molecules to kill bacteria.

 Prostatic Hypertrophy! Men who are over 60 years old often experience **prostatic hypertrophy** (prɑˈstætɪk hayˈpɛrtrəfiy), meaning an enlarged prostate gland. When the prostate enlarges, it pushes upward against the urinary bladder. The enlarged prostate prevents the urinary bladder from holding the normal amount of urine. This means the man has to urinate more frequently, often in the middle of the night.

1. *Put the life of sperm in order from 1 to 6. The first thing that happens is already done for you.*

   _____ The sperm are in the urethra.

   _____ The sperm are in the vas deferens where fluid is added from the seminal vesicles.

   _____ The spermatids are in the lumen of seminiferous tubule.

   __1__ Spermatocytes undergo meiosis.

   _____ The sperm are in the epididymis.

   _____ The sperm are in the ejaculatory duct where the prostate adds a milky fluid to semen.

2. *Match the organs with their secretions by writing the letters in the correct blanks. Then compare your answers with those of a partner.*

   _____ **1.** seminal vesicles   **a.** milky fluid containing antibacterial molecules

   _____ **2.** prostate gland   **b.** watery alkaline mucus

   _____ **3.** bulbourethral glands   **c.** alkaline fluid containing sugar and clotting enzymes

3. *Label Figure 12.7 with the terms in the box. Look at Figure 12.6 on page 256 to check your answers.*

bulbourethral gland	**seminal vesicle**	**vas deferens**
epididymis	**testis**	
prostate gland	**urethra**	

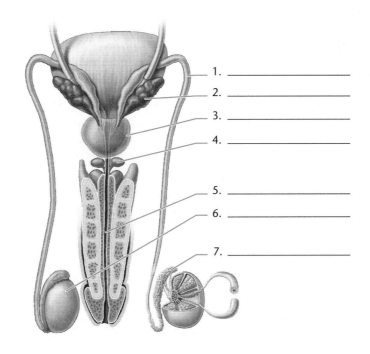

1. _____

2. _____

3. _____

4. _____

5. _____

6. _____

7. _____

FIGURE 12.7   **The male reproductive system**

Male Reproductive Hormones

Two hormones from the pituitary gland are important in controlling male reproductive function.

1. **Follicle stimulating hormone (FSH)** gets the testes ready to produce sperm.

2. **Luteinizing hormone (LH)** is responsible for telling the testes to make **testosterone** (tɛ'stɑstərown), the main male reproductive hormone.

Testosterone has many functions, as shown in the table below. The most important job of testosterone is to stimulate sperm production. Testosterone is produced in small groups of cells in the testes called **interstitial** (ɪntər'stɪʃəl) **cells.** Interstitial means *in between.* Interstitial cells are located in the seminiferous tubules between the spermatocytes. Interstitial cells make testosterone when they receive a signal from LH.

EFFECTS OF TESTOSTERONE		
PRIMARY SEXUAL EFFECTS	**SECONDARY SEXUAL EFFECTS**	**NON-SEXUAL EFFECTS**
Sperm production	Growth of facial hair	Increase muscle mass
Sex drive	Thickening of vocal cords (deeper voice)	Stimulate metabolism
Maturation and maintenance of accessory glands and organs	Increased sebum in skin (pre-adult)	Bone growth (pre-adult)

During puberty, ages 11 to 16, the pituitary gland releases increasing amounts of LH. This results in gradually increasing levels of testosterone. In teenage boys, these increasing levels of testosterone have effects such as the changing of the voice, growth of facial hair, and acne. When a man reaches adulthood, the levels of testosterone become relatively steady.

In many countries, parents expect to see many physical and behavioral changes in their children during puberty. Parents sometimes have difficulty getting along with their teenagers.

MAINTAINING HOMEOSTASIS

Testosterone and Sperm Production

The male reproductive system regulates production of sperm and testosterone by processes involving negative feedback. Recall that negative feedback occurs when the body detects a problem or an imbalance and then sets out to correct the problem. For example, when both the sperm count and testosterone levels are high, the testes make a hormone called **inhibin** (ɪn'hɪbɪn). Can you guess whether this hormone stimulates or inhibits (stops or slows down) sperm production? Inhibin slows down sperm production. When inhibin enters the bloodstream and travels to the pituitary gland, it inhibits the release of both LH and FSH. If sperm count and testosterone are already high in a man, he doesn't need more LH (which stimulates testosterone production) or FSH (which stimulates sperm production). Therefore, when the sperm count and/or testosterone levels are low, the testes stop making inhibin. This means that there is nothing to inhibit the pituitary gland from releasing both LH and FSH until adequate levels of testosterone and sperm are reached again.

Infertility! In males, infertility means that the man is unable to *fertilize* an egg. There can be many causes of this condition: too few sperm produced, sperm that cannot swim, or too little testosterone.

COMPREHENSION CHECK

1. *Answer the questions below. Then compare your answers with those of a partner.*

   1. Name the organ that produces both sperm and testosterone.

   2. What are the functions of testosterone?

   3. Which of these situations will cause inhibin to be produced?

      Low LH   Low FSH   Low testosterone   Few sperm

      High LH   High FSH   High testosterone   Lots of sperm

   4. How do boys' bodies change during puberty?

   5. What is one cause of male infertility?

2. *Work with a partner. Put a check mark (✓) in the box which describes each hormone's function.*

Hormones	Stimulate sperm production	Stimulate testosterone production
Testosterone	☐	☐
LH	☐	☐
FSH	☐	☐

BUILDING LANGUAGE AND STUDY SKILLS

Answering Hypothetical Questions

In this final chapter, instead of learning a specific language skill, you will learn how to understand and answer hypothetical questions. This will require that you apply the language skills you have learned thus far in this text.

When you study anatomy and physiology, you will have to be able to answer two different kinds of questions. The first kind of question is a **direct question**, such as "*Why does the scrotum change positions in relation to a male's body?*" Direct questions are easy to answer because you have already read and studied the exact information in your textbook. Therefore, to answer direct questions, all you have to do is remember what you read: "*The scrotum changes position depending on the outside temperature. If it's cold, the scrotum moves closer to the male's body. If it's hot, the scrotum moves further from the male's body.*"

The other kind of question you'll have to be able to answer is a **hypothetical** question. A hypothetical question presents an imaginary situation that is based on factual information. Hypothetical questions are more difficult to answer than direct questions because they require you to think about the information you've studied and apply the information you know to a situation that wasn't discussed in your textbook. Solving hypothetical questions in class helps you to develop the critical thinking skills you'll need as a health-care worker. Health-care workers use critical thinking skills to solve problems by combining the information they know about a patient with the information they learned in their training. An example of a hypothetical question that a health-care worker might face is: "*A man has a pituitary tumor that causes excessive production of LH. What would be some of the effects of this tumor on the man's reproductive system?*" The following critical thinking process will help you to understand and answer hypothetical questions that you'll be asked in class.

1. Identify the situation.
   A man has a pituitary tumor, and as a result too much LH, which is affecting his reproductive system.

2. Define the terms.
   LH: Luteinizing hormone
   Reproductive system: penis, sex drive, erection, sperm, ejaculate, etc.

3. Analyze the question.
   How does LH affect a man's reproductive system?

4. Evaluate the information you need to answer the question.
   I need to know how LH affects a man's reproductive system.

5. Hypothesize a possible answer to the question. Figure out what you have to do to answer the question.
   I have to describe what LH does and then explain the effects of too much LH on the man's reproductive system.

Re-read the hypothetical question above and then read a possible answer.

The pituitary tumor that is causing an excessive production of LH would have some effects on the man's reproductive system. First, because LH stimulates testosterone production, the man would have an increase in sperm production. An increase in testosterone would also result in an increase in the man's sex drive.

To answer a hypothetical question, follow these rules:

1. Restate the question.
   The pituitary tumor that is causing an excessive production of LH would have some effects on the man's reproductive system.

2. Define necessary terms.
   LH stimulates testosterone production.

3. Develop an answer.
   The man would have an increase in sperm production. An increase in testosterone would also result in an increase in the man's sex drive.

1. *Follow the critical-thinking process described on page 260 and fill in the charts to answer the hypothetical question below. Compare your completed charts with a partner.*

   A man has to have his prostate gland removed. What effects would this have on his reproductive function?

Identify the situation.	
Define the terms.	
Analyze the question.	
Evaluate the information you need to answer the question.	
Hypothesize a possible answer.	

Restate the question.	
Define necessary terms.	
Develop an answer.	

2. *These are authentic questions taken from an anatomy and physiology class. Work with a partner. Use the vocabulary and grammar you know to answer these questions. You may use the charts from Exercise 1 to help you answer these questions.*

   1. Mary has been trying to get pregnant for six months. She is 42 years old and her husband John has hypertension (high blood pressure). What are two possible reasons that Mary is having difficulty getting pregnant?

   2. How could you stimulate sperm production in a man who has a low sperm count?

Study Skills: Putting It All Together

In this text you have learned ten study skills.

CHAPTER	STUDY SKILL
2	Using index cards
3	Studying with diagrams
4	Mnemonic devices
5	Active reading
6	Forming a study group
7	Imagining a process
8	Using reference sources
9	Concept maps
10	Summary writing
11	Categorizing information

1. Work in groups of three or four. Review the study skills in the list above. If you can not recall a particular study skill, refer back to the chapter indicated.

2. Work individually. Look at the activities below. Decide what study skills you might use to complete each task. Then share your answers with your group.

ACTIVITY	STUDY SKILL(S)
Memorize the anatomy of the male reproductive system	
Explain the ovarian cycle	
Describe the pathway of blood through the heart	
Define the body's innate defenses	
Explain how the accessory organs aid in digestion	
Explain the five-step reflex process	
Memorize the muscles of the arms and legs	
Describe the function of different parts of the brain	

3. Answer these questions in your group.

- Did the members of your group share the same study skill preferences for each learning task?

- What three study skills do you prefer using?

- Is there a study skill that you don't really like using?

4. What have you discovered about the way you learn that you hadn't known before taking this course? What?

FEMALE REPRODUCTIVE SYSTEM

The Organs of the Female Reproductive System

The organs of the female reproductive system are specialized for three things: production of **ova** (eggs), **fertilization** (the union of egg and sperm), and the growth of the new individual before it is born. The female reproductive system consists of four different kinds of organ: two ovaries, two Fallopian tubes, the uterus, and the vagina.

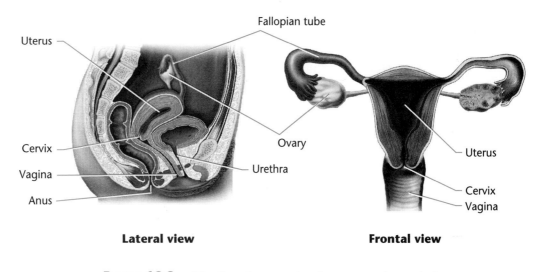

Uterus

Cervix

Vagina

Anus

Lateral view

Fallopian tube

Ovary

Urethra

Uterus

Cervix

Vagina

Frontal view

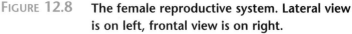

FIGURE 12.8   **The female reproductive system. Lateral view is on left, frontal view is on right.**

Like the testes, the **ovaries** ('owvəriyz) are oval-shaped organs that produce ova and hormones. Unlike the male who makes sperm daily, females are born with all of the **oocytes** ('owəsayts)—cells that ultimately form ova—that they will ever have.

Fertilization (the union of ovum and sperm) usually happens in the **Fallopian tubes** (fə'lowpiyən tuwbz). The Fallopian tubes connect to the **uterus** ('yuwtərəs) at the upper corners of the uterus. The uterus is a pear-shaped organ, about the size of a fist. Its function is to nourish a developing **fetus** ('fiytəs) (the term given to the baby before it is born). The uterus has a thick muscular wall. The inner lining (during child-bearing years) is richly supplied with blood vessels to nourish the fetus.

In the United States, children learn about reproductive organs in school at about age 12.

In the lower portion of the uterus is a channel called the **cervix** ('sɛrvɪks) The cervix is the connection between the main part of the uterus and the **vagina** (vəˈdʒaynə) below. The vagina is where semen is deposited by the penis. The vagina leads to the outside of the body and is the canal through which the baby passes in order to be born.

C-Section! C-Section is the short name of a medical procedure called Caesarean section. Sometimes, there are problems when the baby begins to move down the vagina. If those problems cannot be resolved, the doctor may need to make a cut in the mother's uterus to remove the baby. This type of delivery is risky because it involves cutting into the mother's body. It is estimated that about 25 percent of all births in the United States are by Caesarean section.

Yeast Infection! Most women experience yeast infections at some time during their lives. The symptoms include itchiness and burning. Yeasts are a type of fungus that lives naturally on our skin, in our oral cavity, and in the vagina. Most of the time, we don't have a negative reaction to yeasts because they live in balance with the bacteria that naturally occur in those regions. Usually, yeast infections occur when those bacteria are somehow killed and the yeasts multiply to fill those "empty spaces." This can happen when a person takes an antibiotic. Antibiotics kill bacteria, even our good bacteria, but do not affect yeasts. Yeast infections may also occur if there is something that prevents the immune system from operating properly, such as in the case of AIDS.

COMPREHENSION CHECK

1. *Read the questions and then scan the text for answers. When you find the answers, underline them. Then work with a partner and take turns asking and answering the questions. Try to remember the answers without looking back at the text.*

   1. Which organ produces oocytes?

   2. Which organ is the place where the baby develops inside the mother?

   3. When the baby is ready to be born, which area does it move through just before it leaves the mother's body?

2. *Place these openings in the proper order, with 1 being the one that is closest to the anterior (front) of the body:*

   _____ vaginal opening

   _____ anal opening

   _____ urethral opening

3. *Label Figure 12.9 with the terms in the box. Look at Figure 12.8 on page 263 to check your answers.*

| cervix | Fallopian tube | ovary | uterus | vagina |

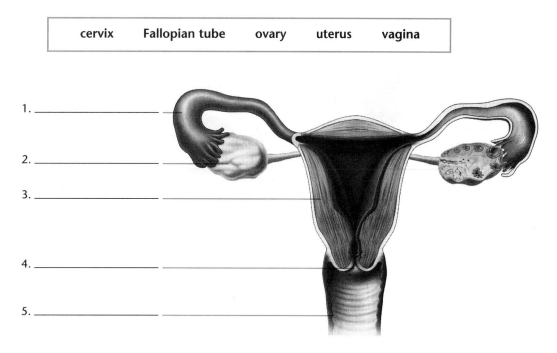

1. _____

2. _____

3. _____

4. _____

5. _____

Figure 12.9   **The female reproductive system**

The Ovarian Cycle: To Produce an Ovum

In the female, there are two different cycles:

- The ovarian cycle, which occurs in the ovary.
- The menstrual (uterine) cycle, which occurs in the uterus.

While these cycles occur in different organs, they are closely related. These two cycles occur at the same time. In other words, day 1 of the ovarian cycle is the same day as day 1 of the uterine cycle. The hormones produced in the ovarian cycle control the events of the uterine cycle.

The **ovarian cycle** is the process by which an ovum (egg) is produced. The ovarian cycle is designed mostly to produce eggs for fertilization. The ovarian cycle begins approximately every 28 days throughout a woman's child-bearing years. Day 1 of the ovarian cycle is the same day as the first day of a woman's **menstruation** (mɛnstruw'eyʃən) (blood exiting the woman's vagina).

Recall that a female baby's ovaries have all the **oocytes** she will ever have. Recall that oocytes are the cells that will produce the ova. Each month after puberty begins, several of these oocytes begin to develop. At this initial stage of development, each oocyte is surrounded by a layer of cells. This entire structure is called a **follicle** ('fɑlɪkəl).

In the United States as well as some other cultures, the average age when a girl begins to have an ovarian cycle is 11 years old. This coincides with her first menstrual period. Some scientists suggest that diet may cause this early onset of menstruation.

2. *Put the steps of the ovarian cycle in order from 1 (first step) to 6 (last step).*

_____ The follicle turns into a corpus luteum which produces progesterone.

_____ Most follicles stop growing, but one continues to grow and produce estrogen.

_____ If fertilization doesn't occur, corpus luteum disintegrates.

_____ Ovulation occurs.

_____ The primary oocyte continues meiosis to produce a polar body and a secondary oocyte.

_____ Follicles begin to develop.

The Menstrual Cycle: Preparing for Fetal Development

You just read about the ovarian cycle, which occurs in the ovary and causes the production of the ovum. The next cycle to learn about is the **menstrual (uterine) cycle**. It occurs in the uterus and its job is to prepare the uterus first for the arrival of sperm and then for the arrival of the embryo. The menstrual cycle is closely linked with the ovarian cycle and occurs during the same time period. The menstrual cycle is also influenced by the ovarian hormones, estrogen and progesterone.

The menstrual cycle involves two layers of the wall of the uterus: the endometrium and myometrium. These two layers are important for the development of the embryo and during childbirth. The **endometrium** (ɛndow′miytriyəm) is the layer that is closest to the lumen (cavity) of the uterus. (*Endo-* means *within*.) This layer will change its appearance during the menstrual cycle. The **myometrium** (mayow′miytriyəm) lies beneath the endometrium. The myometrium is a thick layer of smooth muscle. (*Myo-* means *muscle*.)

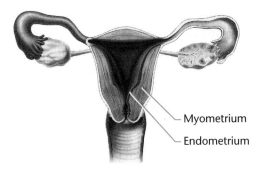

Myometrium
Endometrium

FIGURE 12.11   **The layers of the uterus**

Day 1 of the menstrual cycle begins with the loss of blood and cells from the endometrium. These things pass out of the body through the vagina. This bleeding is called **menstruation**. Menstruation usually lasts about 5 days, but this can vary from woman to woman. Some women menstruate for only 3 days, while others may menstruate for longer than a week.

At about day 5 of the menstrual cycle, estrogen enters the bloodstream. Recall that estrogen is produced in the first half of the ovarian cycle. In the uterus, the estrogen causes the endometrium to thicken gradually. More layers of cells are produced, and new blood vessels grow into this area. This thickening process is called **proliferation** (prəlıfə′reyʃən). Proliferation continues until the time of ovulation (about day 14).

After the midpoint of the cycle (about day 14), estrogen no longer is the dominant hormone affecting the uterus. Progesterone is now being secreted by the corpus luteum in the ovary.

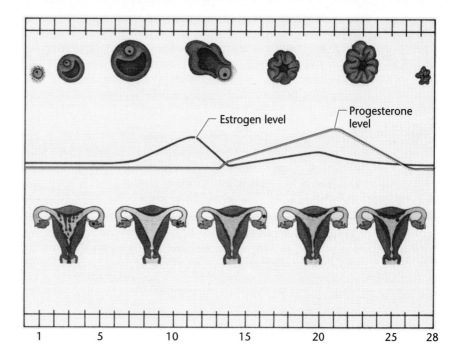

FIGURE 12.12   Timing of the ovarian (top) and menstrual (bottom) cycles

Progesterone causes the inner layer of endometrium to store nutrients in the form of a carbohydrate called **glycogen**. Glycogen is stored in preparation for the arrival of an embryo, which will *implant* or embed in the endometrium for protection and nourishment.

If fertilization occurs, progesterone continues to cause the endometrium to store food. Recall that the corpus luteum controls progesterone production. The endometrium is therefore preparing ideal conditions for the nourishment of an embryo.

However, if fertilization does not occur, progesterone levels drop as the corpus luteum disintegrates. Without progesterone to maintain them, the blood vessels in the endometrium bend and cut off the flow of blood to the outer endometrium. Imagine a garden hose that is bent. Water does not flow out of the hose if the bend is too tight. When blood doesn't reach the cells in the endometrium, the cells die. Cells that make up the walls of the blood vessels also die. This causes blood and dead cells to enter the lumen of the uterus. Menstruation begins, marking day 1 of another menstrual cycle.

Review the following events in the menstrual (uterine) cycle:

1. Days 1–5: Blood is released from broken blood vessels and this washes out the dead cells of the inner endometrial lining. This is called menstruation.
2. Days 6–13: Bleeding stops. Estrogen causes the endometrium to grow in thickness. Blood vessels grow into these new layers of endometrium.
3. Days 14–28: Progesterone becomes the dominant hormone. It causes the endometrium to store large amounts of glycogen.

    If fertilization occurs, progesterone continues to cause glycogen storage for about another month.

    If fertilization does not occur, progesterone levels decrease at about day 25. This causes the blood vessels to bend, cutting off blood supply to the inner endometrium. Cells die and eventually the blood vessels break. A new cycle begins with menstruation.

Endometriosis! Endometriosis (ɛndowmiytriy′owsəs) occurs when some of the endometrial tissue that lines the uterus begins to grow in an area outside the uterus, usually in the abdominal cavity. These growths can cause severe pain, bleeding, and even infertility. This disorder can be treated with hormones or by surgically removing the growth.

PMS and Menstrual Cramps! Many women experience symptoms a few days before menstruation begins. These symptoms include headaches, bloating (fluid retention), breast enlargement, and irritability. This collection of symptoms is called **premenstrual syndrome, or PMS**. It is believed that PMS is caused by hormonal changes just before the end of a cycle. Once menstruation begins, many women experience **menstrual cramps**. Menstrual cramps are painful muscle contractions in the myometrium of the uterus. These contractions are caused by a change in hormone levels and are made worse in some women by secretion of local hormones called **prostaglandins** (prastə′glændɪnz). Prostaglandins make the pain feel much worse in these women.

COMPREHENSION CHECK

1. *Circle the correct word(s) to complete each sentence. Take turns reading the correct sentences aloud with a partner.*

   1. The layer of the uterus that is closest to the inside is the **myometrium / endometrium**.

   2. **Estrogen / Progesterone** causes the endometrium to get thicker.

   3. The menstrual cycle prepares the woman's body for **fertilization / development of the embryo**.

   4. When endometrial tissue grows outside the uterus, this is called **menstruation / endometriosis**.

   5. If fertilization does not occur, progesterone levels **drop / stay the same**.

   6. In preparation for implantation of the embryo, the endometrium begins to store **protein / glycogen**.

2. *Put the steps of the menstrual (uterine) cycle in order from 1 to 7. Assume fertilization does not occur. The first thing that happens is already done for you.*

   _____ Walls of blood vessels die and blood begins to flow out of the uterus.

   _____ Estrogen causes endometrium to increase in thickness.

   __1__ Menstruation (flow of blood and dead cells out of the body).

   _____ Endometrial cells die.

   _____ Falling progesterone levels cause blood vessels to bend, cutting off blood supply.

   _____ Progesterone causes endometrium to store food.

   _____ Blood vessels grow into endometrium.

Regulating Female Hormones

What keeps the ovarian and menstrual cycles working? Homeostasis of these cycles is maintained by hormones from the hypothalamus and the pituitary gland. However, the homeostasis mechanism is not simply a negative feedback mechanism as in the male reproductive system. Homeostasis of the female cycles is much more complex. In this text, we will simply summarize the role of two hormones that regulate the ovarian and menstrual cycles. These two hormones are secreted from the pituitary gland.

- **Follicle stimulating hormone (FSH)** stimulates the ovaries to begin an ovarian cycle. It causes follicular cells to begin to divide and oocytes to mature. FSH levels are highest at the beginning of the ovarian cycle and again just before ovulation. FSH plays a minor role in stimulating ovulation.

- **Luteinizing hormone (LH)** stimulates ovulation. After ovulation, it causes the corpus luteum to develop and to produce progesterone. LH levels are highest just before ovulation. In fact, LH causes ovulation to occur.

Effects of the Female Hormones: A Summary

Estrogen and progesterone are considered the primary female hormones. However, like males, females also make testosterone which is responsible for the sex drive in females as well as in males. Testosterone is also the molecule which is used to make estrogen and progesterone. The table below summarizes the effects of estrogen and progesterone.

COMPARISON OF ESTROGEN AND PROGESTERONE	
EFFECTS OF ESTROGEN	**EFFECTS OF PROGESTERONE**
Development and maintenance of female reproductive organs	Stimulate storage of glycogen in uterus—maintain the endometrium
Development of secondary sexual characteristics (breast development, body hair, distribution of fat)	Increase blood vessel growth into the endometrium
Causes growth in thickness of endometrium	Prevent contractions of the uterus

Menopause! **Menopause** ('mɛnəpɑz) is technically defined as the time when a woman's menstrual cycles stop. Usually menopause occurs between the ages of 45 and 55. It was once believed that menopause occurred when there were no more follicles remaining in the ovary to develop. However, scientists now know that the beginning of menopause is signaled by high levels of the pituitary hormones FSH and LH.

After menopause, estrogen levels are almost zero. Given what you now know about estrogen, list some things that might happen to the body of a post-menopausal woman (a woman who has already gone through menopause).

Answer the questions below. Then compare your answers with those of a partner.

1. Which pituitary hormone causes ovulation and the corpus luteum to develop?

2. Which pituitary hormone causes the follicles to begin to develop?

3. Which pituitary hormone causes oocytes to mature?

4. Which ovarian hormone is responsible for causing breast development and other secondary sexual characteristics?

5. Which ovarian hormone is responsible for maintenance of the endometrium?

6. What causes menopause?

FERTILIZATION AND EMBRYONIC DEVELOPMENT

Sexual intercourse is the act of depositing sperm inside the female. Fertilization occurs when the sperm combines with the ovum to form a single cell. The single cell that results from fertilization is called a **zygote** (′zaygowt).

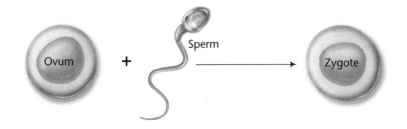

FIGURE 12.13   Fertilization: an ovum and sperm unite to form a zygote

Obstacles to Fertilization

When sperm are ejaculated into the woman's vagina, they encounter several obstacles to fertilization. However, for every obstacle presented in the woman's body, there is also a solution. First, because the semen is liquid, there is a chance that it can simply flow back out of the vagina. However, recall that the semen contains clotting enzymes that cause the semen to coagulate. This makes it more likely that the semen can remain inside the woman's vagina long enough for the sperm to travel through the vagina, cervix, uterus, and to the Fallopian tubes where fertilization occurs.

An additional obstacle in the vagina is the acidic nature of vaginal fluids. Sperm do not survive well in acidic conditions. They prefer neutral or slightly alkaline conditions. Fortunately, the semen is alkaline due to secretions from the seminal vesicles, the prostate, and the bulbourethral glands. The alkaline fluids in the semen neutralize the acidity in the vagina, making it easier for the sperm to survive.

Another obstacle to fertilization is that the sperm must swim uphill from the lower vagina toward the Fallopian tubes. This requires a great deal of energy. Of the several hundred million sperm that are ejaculated, only a few thousand actually make it to the Fallopian tubes. Fortunately, only one sperm is needed to fertilize the egg. Also, while the uterus looks like a hollow organ, it is actually filled with mucus. Most of the time, this mucus is very thick. Most sperm cannot swim all the way through this mucus before they run out of energy. However, around the time of ovulation, the mucus in the uterus becomes very watery for a couple of days. This makes it easier for the sperm to swim toward the Fallopian tubes at the time when it is most likely that an ovum will be available for fertilization. Women are said to be especially fertile during this time.

Another barrier to fertilization is that the uterus moves. The uterus has thick layers of muscle in its wall. This muscle contracts in a motion similar to a washing machine. Sperm get pushed all around the uterus, and therefore don't have a straight path to the entrance of the Fallopian tubes.

Finally, the sperm that do reach the Fallopian tubes must swim against one more obstacle. The Fallopian tubes are lined with cilia. Recall from the respiratory system unit that cilia are hair-like structures that are on the outside of a cell. Cilia beat (wave) in a particular direction to move things toward or away from a particular location. In the Fallopian tubes, most of the cilia beat toward the entrance to the uterus. They move in that downward direction to move the zygote (fertilized egg) toward the place where it can implant in the uterus. However, this same beating tends to push the sperm out of the Fallopian tubes, back toward the uterus and away from the ovum.

Many sperm do overcome these obstacles, but only one sperm is needed to fertilize the ovum. When the first sperm breaks through the outer membrane of the ovum, a chemical is produced that prevents other sperm from entering the ovum. This makes it very unlikely that a single ovum will be fertilized by more than one sperm. The remaining sperm die.

Ectopic Pregnancy! An **ectopic** (ɛkˈtɑpɪk) pregnancy occurs when the ovum enters the abdominal cavity, instead of the Fallopian tube, and is fertilized there. The term "ectopic" means an unusual or unexpected place. An ectopic pregnancy is possible because the ovary and the Fallopian tube do not connect directly to one another. They are separated by a space that is open to the abdominal cavity. If an ovum enters the abdominal cavity and a sperm is able to fertilize this ovum, the embryo can attach to some of the tissues inside the abdominal cavity. It is possible that this type of pregnancy can go to full term (9 months), but sometimes delivery is very complicated.

A similar type of condition called a **tubal pregnancy** occurs when an embryo does not move to the uterus for development, but remains in the Fallopian tube. Since this tube does not have an adequate blood supply to nourish the embryo, these pregnancies are not successful. They often cause the mother great pain, and the physician usually has to remove the embryo for the mother to survive.

Twins! You might wonder what events lead to the birth of twins and why some twins look alike while others don't. There are two types of twins: **identical** and **fraternal**. Identical twins occur when the zygote (fertilized egg) divides into two completely separate cells. Each cell develops into a separate embryo. Because each embryo came from the same fertilized egg, they have identical genetic material. Identical twins are always the same sex and look very much alike. Fraternal twins, on the other hand, happen when two sperm fertilize two separate ova. Each ovum has its unique genetic material, as does each sperm. Thus, these two individual zygotes do not have the exact same genetics. Fraternal twins may be different sexes and may not look alike at all. Multiple births (triplets, quadruplets, and so on) are usually the result of fertilization of separate ova and are thus considered to be fraternal.

COMPREHENSION CHECK

Read the questions and then scan the text for answers. When you find the answers, underline them. Then work with a partner and take turns asking and answering the questions. Try to remember the answers without looking back at the text.

1. What two things does semen contain which help sperm to survive in a woman's body?

2. Where does fertilization typically occur in a woman's body?

3. How is the uterus similar to the stomach?

4. What other body structure contains cilia?

5. What happens to the sperm that don't fertilize the egg?

6. Where does an ectopic pregnancy occur? Where does a tubal pregnancy occur?

7. What is the difference between fraternal and identical twins?

Embryonic Development

Once the zygote begins to divide into many cells, it is called an **embryo**. The embryo eventually implants itself in the lining of the female's uterus (womb). In the uterus, it will continue to develop.

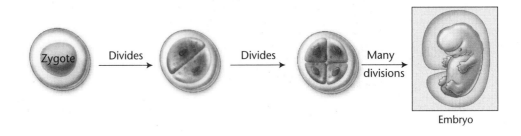

FIGURE 12.14   **A zygote divides repeatedly to form an embryo**

After 9 weeks, the embryo is called a fetus until the baby is born. Soon after the embryo implants in the wall of the uterus, a complex network of blood vessels forms. This network is called the **placenta** (plə′sɛntə). This is how the mother nourishes the fetus and gets rid of waste products. The urinary and respiratory systems of the fetus do not function until the baby is born. Some highlights of the fetal development are shown in Figure 12.15.

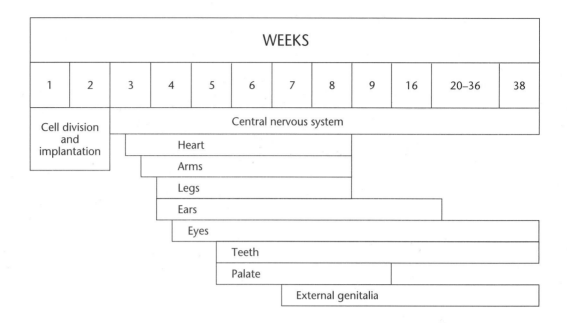

FIGURE 12.15   **Fetal development**

The child that is produced has a unique mixture of his or her parents' characteristics. The word **inheritance** (ɪn′hɛrɪtənts) means the passing of information found in cells from the parents to the child. Eye color, skin color, and height are examples of information that is inherited. Information is passed from parent to child in the form of chromosomes. Recall that the chromosomes are located in the nucleus of cells.

COMPREHENSION CHECK

1. *Read the questions and then scan the text for answers. When you find the answers, underline them. Then work with a partner and take turns asking and answering the questions. Try to remember the answers without looking back at the text.*

   1. When a sperm combines with an egg, what is the resulting cell called?

   2. Which develops first: a fetus or an embryo?

   3. What are two examples of inherited information?

   4. Where are chromosomes found?

2. *Complete the sentences using the words in the box. Take turns reading the correct sentences aloud with a partner.*

embryo	fetus	meiosis	zygote
fertilization	inheritance	sperm	

1. The passing of eye color from parents to a child is an example of _____.

2. _____ occurs when a sperm enters an egg.

3. The male "sex cell" is called the _____.

4. The single cell that results from fertilization is called a _____.

5. _____ is the process that reduces chromosome numbers.

6. Once the zygote begins to multiply into many cells, it's called an _____.

7. Before a baby is born, it is called a _____.

FOCUS ON CULTURE

Discussing the Reproductive System with Patients

In some cultures, the reproductive system and sexual intercourse are not openly discussed. It may be appropriate only to talk about such things with one's spouse or with a doctor of the same sex. Many people do not feel comfortable going to a doctor who is not the same sex as they are. However, as a future health-care professional, you will encounter situations where you may have to ask questions of or give advice to strangers about matters that may seem uncomfortable, including sexually transmitted diseases. (See the table on page 277.) It is important for a health-care professional to be able to speak openly with a patient so that the patient can make wise choices and important decisions concerning sexual matters.

1. *Work in small groups of three or four students. Your teacher will assign your group one of the following topics for discussion. Report on your discussion to the class.*

   1. You are a nurse working in a family medicine clinic where people of many different cultures are treated. You are assisting a doctor who is doing a physical exam on a 16-year-old unmarried boy. The boy appears to have genital herpes. How would you and the doctor proceed with informing the boy and advising him about his disease? Would you do anything differently if the boy were from a culture that does not allow extramarital sex? What if the boy's parents refuse to permit you to advise him about how to protect himself against sexually transmitted diseases?

   2. You are in the same situation as in number 1 above, except the patient is a 16-year-old unmarried girl who appears to have gonorrhea. How would you proceed?

   3. You are a nurse working in a hospital emergency room. A woman is brought in and looks like she has been beaten and sexually assaulted. What is your role in this situation?

2. *As a class, discuss the following topics.*

   1. In your culture(s), when and where are people educated about reproduction? What things are discussed? What things are not to be discussed? What things do you think should be taught to people as they reach sexual maturity, and by whom?

   2. What role do you think health-care workers have in educating their patients about birth control? Sexually transmitted diseases?

COMMON SEXUALLY TRANSMITTED DISEASES (STDs)

DISEASE	CAUSED BY	INCUBATION PERIOD (TIME UNTIL ONSET OF SYMPTOMS)	SYMPTOMS	CONSEQUENCES
AIDS	Human immunodeficiency virus (HIV)	6 days–6 weeks First symptoms often not noticed.	Initial flu-like symptoms	Increased susceptibility to infection; usually results in death from one of those infections
Chancroid	*Haemophilus ducreyi,* a bacterium	3–10 days	Soft red ulcer on penis or on / near vagina, painful lymph nodes	Lymph nodes burst, releasing pus
Chlamydial infection	*Chlamydia trachomatis,* a bacterium	7–14 days Many have no symptoms.	Male: runny gray discharge from penis, painful testes Female: vaginal discharge, painful urination, abdominal pain, vaginal bleeding	Male: inflammation in testes and urethra, possible sterility Female: Infection and scarring of Fallopian tubes, liver infection, sterility, ectopic pregnancy
Genital herpes	Human herpes virus (HHV) 2	2–20 days	Small blisters on / near penis or vagina. Itching and pain near blisters.	May be passed on to newborn from infected mother.
Gonorrhea	*Neisseria gonorrhoeae,* a bacterium	2–5 days Some may have no symptoms.	Male: thick discharge from penis, pain with urination Female: minimal, some pain with urination and vaginal discharge	Male: sterility, urinary tract infections Female: infection and scarring of Fallopian tubes (infertility), peritonitis, ectopic pregnancy Blindness in newborns of infected mother
Papillomavirus Infections	Human papillomavirus (HPV)	3 weeks–8 months	Often no symptoms. Warts on penis or vagina.	Increased risk of cervical cancer in women. May be transmitted to newborn, causing respiratory failure.
Syphilis	*Treponema pallidum,* a bacterium	10–90 days	Painless hard red ulcer on penis or in vagina (often unnoticed in females). Later, flu-like symptoms appear.	Sterility, blindness, nervous system disorders (stroke, mental illness), miscarriage and stillbirth. Mother may pass disease onto babies that survive.
Trichomoniasis	*Trichomonas vaginalis,* a single-celled parasite	4–20 days	Males: Most have no symptoms. Some discharge from penis, painful urination. Females: burning / itching in vaginal region, yellow discharge, painful urination	May be passed on to newborn from infected mother.

Check Your Understanding

1. *Answer the following questions about the reproductive system.*

    1. Name the organ that produces both sperm and testosterone.

    2. List the places that sperm travel, from the time they are made to the time they leave the male body.

    3. What glands produce secretions that become part of the semen?

    4. Which has more chromosomes: spermatids or spermatocytes?

    5. Which hormone, LH or FSH, stimulates production of testosterone?

    6. List the jobs of testosterone.

    7. Which cycle, ovarian or uterine, produces estrogen?

    8. What two pituitary hormones influence the ovarian cycle? Which one causes the follicle to begin to grow?

    9. What is the name of the cell that is released during ovulation?

    10. What is the job of the uterus?

    11. Define menopause.

    12. Where does fertilization usually take place?

    13. Which hormone causes the development of the female's secondary sexual characteristics?

    14. How does sperm production differ from production of the ovum?

2. *Label Figures 12.16 and 12.17 with the terms provided.*

bulbourethral gland	seminal vesicle	urethra
epididymis	testis	vas deferens
prostate gland		

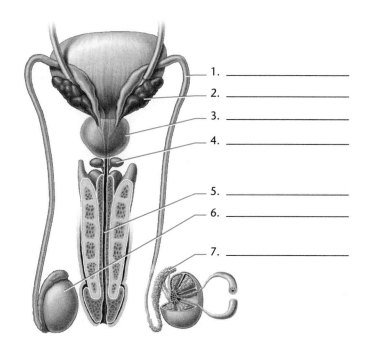

1. _____

2. _____

3. _____

4. _____

5. _____

6. _____

7. _____

FIGURE 12.16   The male reproductive system

Fallopian tube	ovary	uterus	vagina

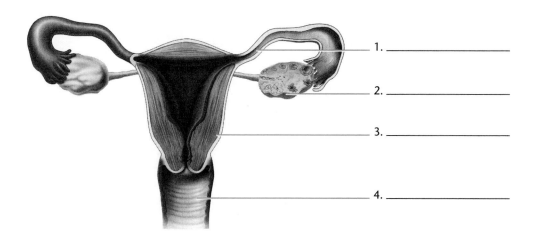

1. _____

2. _____

3. _____

4. _____

FIGURE 12.17   The female reproductive system

3. *Answer these typical anatomy and physiology quiz questions.*

1. Which of the following is NOT true about the ovarian cycle?
   a. The first day of the cycle is the day when ovulation occurs.
   b. Amounts of progesterone are higher after ovulation than before.
   c. Estrogen is produced in the follicles; progesterone in the corpus luteum.
   d. FSH helps to stimulate growth of the follicle.

2. Which male organ is NOT correctly matched with its function?
   a. seminal vesicles: sperm production
   b. epididymis: storage and maturation of sperm
   c. prostate gland: secretion of portion of the seminal fluid
   d. urethra: transport of sperm and urine

3. The sperm travel through ALL BUT ONE of the following structures on the way out of the male reproductive tract. Which structure is NOT a passageway for sperm?
   a. ejaculatory duct
   b. vas deferens
   c. epididymis
   d. urethra
   e. seminiferous tubule
   f. seminal vesicle

4. _____ Is this true or false? Progesterone stimulates secretion of glycogen by the endometrium during the uterine (menstrual) cycle.

5. _____ Is this true or false? The uterus is the main source of estrogen and progesterone in females, while the seminal vesicles are the main source of testosterone in males.

6. _____ Is this true or false? Identical twins result from a division of the zygote AFTER fertilization.

7. _____ Is this true or false? Decreasing levels of progesterone at the end of the uterine cycle cause arteries to kink and cells of the endometrium die, resulting in menstruation.

8. _____ Is this true or false? The purpose of meiosis during production of sperm and ovum is to reduce the number of chromosomes.

Think More about It

1. Where in the reproductive system do muscles play an important role? Are they smooth muscle or skeletal muscle or both?

2. What hormones from outside the reproductive organs play a role in regulating those reproductive organs?

3. How does the female reproductive system relate to the skeletal system?

chromosome	glycogen	placenta
circumcision	impotence	polar body
ectopic	infertility	proliferation
ejaculation	interstitial	reproduction
embryo	meiosis	semen
endometrium	menopause	spermatids
erect	menstruation	spermatocyte
erection	myometrium	spermatozoan (sperm)
fertilization	oocyte	yeast
flaccid	ovulation	zygote
follicle	ovum (egg)	

Pronunciation Key

Vowel symbol	Example	Consonant symbol	Example
iy	see, piece	p	pepper, paper
I	sit, give	b	boring, number
ey	say, break	t	time, most
ɛ	get, rest	d	day, hard
æ	map, laugh	k	cat, kind
ə	ago, shut	g	goose, dig
ɑ	hot, father	θ	thumb, tooth
uw	boot, shoe	ð	this, bathe
ʊ	book, could	f	finger, rough
ow	go, road	v	vase, ever
ɔ	law, bought	s	silver, nice
ay	buy, side	z	zebra, reason
aw	now, house	ʃ	shop, nation
oy	toy, voice	ʒ	casual, beige
		h	hot, ahead
		tʃ	chocolate, watch
		dʒ	joke, age
		m	milk, summer
		n	nose, know
		ŋ	sing, tongue
		r	rock, borrow
		l	last, collect
		y	yeast, young
		w	west, away

Metric–English System Conversions

Length

1 inch (in.) = 2.54 centimeters (cm)
1 centimeter (cm) = 0.3937 inch (in.)
1 foot (ft.) = 0.3048 meter (m)
1 meter (m) = 3.2808 feet (ft.)
1 mile (mi.) = 1.6904 kilometers (km)
1 kilometer (km) = 0.6214 mile (mi.)

Mass

1 ounce (oz.) = 28.3496 grams (g)
1 gram (g) = 0.03527 ounce (oz.)
1 pound (lb.) = 0.4536 kilogram (kg)
1 kilogram (kg) = 2.2046 pounds (lb.)
1 ton (tn.), U.S. = 0.91 metric ton (t)
1 metric ton (t) = 1.10 tons (tn.), U.S.

Volume

1 cubic inch (cu. in.) = 16.39 cubic centimeters (cm^3)
1 cubic centimeter (cm^3) = 0.06 cubic inch (cu. in.)
1 cubic foot (cu. ft.) = 0.028 cubic meter (m^3)
1 cubic meter (m^3) = 35.30 cubic feet (cu. ft.) = 1.3079 cubic yards (cu. yd.)
1 fluid ounce (oz.) = 29.6 milliliters (mL) = 0.03 liter (l)
1 milliliter (mL) = 0.03 fluid ounce (oz.) = $1/4$ teaspoon (approximate)
1 pint (pt.) = 473 milliliters (ml) = 0.47 liter (l)
1 quart (qt.) = 946 milliliters (ml) = 0.9463 liter (l)
1 gallon (gal.) = 3.79 liters (l)
1 liter (l) = 1.0567 quarts (qt.) = 0.26 gallon (gal.)

Area

1 square inch (sq. in.) = 6.45 square centimeters (cm^2)
1 square centimeter (cm^2) = 0.155 square inch (sq. in.)
1 square foot (sq. ft.) = 0.0929 square meter (m^2)
1 square meter (m^2) = 10.7639 square feet (sq. ft.) = 1.1960 square yards (sq. yd.)
1 square mile (sq. mi.) = 2.5900 square kilometers (km^2)
1 acre (a.) = 0.4047 hectare (ha)
1 hectare (ha) = 2.4710 acres (a.) = 10.000 square meters (m^2)

Word Parts

Word Part	Meaning	Example
adeno-	glandular	adenosine tri-phosphate
af-	toward	afferent
angi- or angio-	vessel	angina
anterior	in front of	anterior tibial
anti-	against	anti-bacterial
append-	attach to	appendicular
arthr-	joint	arthritis
asth-	weak	asthma
auto-	self	autonomic
ax- or axi-	axle	axial
baro-	pressure	baroreceptor
bi-	two	biceps
brach-	branch	biceps brachii
bronc-	airway	bronchus
cardio-	heart	cardiovascular
cephalo-	head	diencephalon
cervico-	neck	cervical
circum-	around	circumcision
scis-	cut	incisors
coag-	clot	coagulation
costa-	rib	intercostals
crani-	skull	cranial
-crine	to secrete	endocrine
-cyte or cyto-	cell	osteocyte; cytoplasm
dendr-	branch	dendrites
dent-	teeth	dentin
derm-	skin	epidermis
dorso-	back	latissimus dorsi
ef-	away	efferent
-emia	blood	anemia
endo-	within, inside	endometrium
epi-	upon	epithelial
erythr-	red	erythrocytes
ex-	out, out of, away	exhale
-ferent	carry	afferent
gastr-	stomach	gastroesophageal
glom-	ball	glomerulus
glyco-	sugar	glycogen
-gram	mark, tracing	diagram
-graph	writing, description	electrocardiograph
hema- or hemo-	blood	hemoglobin
hepa-	liver	hepatitis
hyper-	above, excessive, too much	hypertension
hypo-	under, beneath, too little	hypotension
im- or in-	not	imbalance
inter-	between	intercostals
-ism	condition	hypothyroidism
-itis	inflammation	appendicitis

Word Part	Meaning	Example
kera-	hard	keratin
laryng-	larynx	laryngitis
latero-	side	lateral
leuco- or *leuko-*	white	leukocytes
-ology	study	physiology
luna-	moon	semilunar
macro-	big	macrophages
mela-	color	melanin
men- or *meno-*	month	menopause
meta-	beyond	metatarsals
metr-	uterus	endometrium
micro-	small	microscope
mono-	one, single	monocytes
-motor	movement	oculomotor
myo-	muscle	myometrium
neur-	nerve	neuron
-nomic	to govern	autonomic
ocul-	eye	orbicularis oculi
-oma	tumor	melanoma
oo- or *ov-*	egg	oocytes; ovary
orb-	around	orbicularis
oro-	mouth	orbicularis oris
-osis	condition, disease	osteoporosis
osteo-	bone	osteocytes
para-	besides, accessory to	parasympathetic
path- or *-pathy*	disease	pathogens
peri-	around	pericardium
-phage or *phago-*	eat, ingest	phagocytes
pneumo-	lungs	pneumonia
pulmo-	lung	pulmonary artery
rheum-	watery discharge	rheumatoid arthritis
-rrhea	flow or discharge	diarrhea
seb-	fat, oily	sebaceous glands
semi-	half	semilunar valve
sclero-	hard, hardening	atherosclerosis
-stasis or *stat-*	stop, fix, remain	homeostasis
steno-	narrowing	stenotic valve
syn- or *sym-*	joined together	synovial
tert-	three	tertiary
thrombo-	clot	thrombocytes
trach-	trachea	trachea
tri-	three	triceps
uro-	urine	urology
vaso-	vessels	vasoconstriction

ACHIEVEMENT TESTS

Achievement Test 1
CHAPTERS 1–3
(50 points total)

A. *Answer the questions below, using complete sentences.* *(2 points)*

1. What is homeostasis?

2. What is the function of hormones?

B. *Match each item with the building block that describes it.* *(5 points)*

_____ 1. the femur bone   **a.** tissue

_____ 2. the epidermis   **b.** molecule

_____ 3. all the bones in the body   **c.** cell

_____ 4. osteocyte   **d.** organ system

_____ 5. keratin   **e.** organ

C. *Circle the correct word(s) to complete each sentence.* *(5 points)*

1. When a bone has a crack or break, this is called a **dislocation / fracture**.

2. Bones are connected to other bones by **tendons / ligaments**.

3. In flat and long bones, the outermost layer of bone is **spongy / compact**.

4. Nerves and blood vessels are found inside the **dermis / epidermis** of the skin.

5. When the cartilage at a joint becomes worn away, the person may experience **rheumatoid arthritis / osteoarthritis**.

D. *Label each statement true* (T) *or false* (F). *(6 points)*

_____ 1. The hypodermis is the outermost layer of skin.

_____ 2. The sebaceous glands are the glands in the skin that help to control body temperature.

_____ 3. Some of the cells in the epidermis are dead.

_____ 4. Blood vessels can be found inside bones.

_____ 5. The cell membrane is permeable.

_____ 6. Calcitonin is a hormone that causes calcium in the blood to be stored in the bones.

E. *Complete the sentences with the correct word(s).* *(6 points)*

1. Bone matrix is made of two molecules: _____ and _____.

2. Bone cells are called _____.

3. One function of the skin is to _____.

4. Another name for a joint is a(n) _____.

5. Another name for the kneecap is the _____.

6. Physiology is the study of the _____ of body parts.

F. *Circle the correct answer.* *(7 points)*

1. The dermis is made of _____ tissue.

    a. epithelial   **b.** bone   **c.** connective   **d.** muscle

2. Which of the following is always found near a hair follicle?

    a. a sebaceous gland   **b.** a sweat gland

3. The part of a cell that contains DNA and controls the rest of the cell is _____.

    a. an organelle   **b.** a nucleus   **c.** a membrane   **d.** cytoplasm

4. Which of the following is NOT TRUE about collagen?

    a. It is found in connective tissue.
    b. It is a protein that forms a fiber.
    c. It is able to stretch a lot.
    d. It is part of the matrix of bone.

5. The structures that are able to detect heat, pressure, or pain are called _____.

    a. nerves   **b.** sensory receptors   **c.** effector organs

6. Which of these is NOT a synovial joint?

    a. a knee joint   **b.** an elbow joint   **c.** wrist joints   **d.** sutures

7. Which of these groups of vertebrae are the ones closest to the head?

    a. cervical   **b.** coccyx   **c.** lumbar   **d.** thoracic

G. *Read the story. Then circle the correct word(s) to complete each sentence.* *(4 points)*

Hawa and Marcela are eating lunch. Hawa tells a joke. This makes Marcela laugh, just as she is swallowing her food. Some of Marcela's food goes down her trachea (windpipe) instead of her esophagus. (It goes down the wrong tube.) Marcela coughs until the food is pushed back up to her throat, and she can swallow it again.

1. The sensors in this reflex are located in Marcela's **brain / trachea.**

2. The effectors in this reflex are located in Marcela's **trachea / spinal cord.**

3. The stimulus in this reflex was the **cough / food in the trachea.**

4. The part that makes the decision in this reflex is Marcela's _____.

    a. trachea   **b.** spinal cord   **c.** muscles

H. *Label the diagram.* *(10 points)*

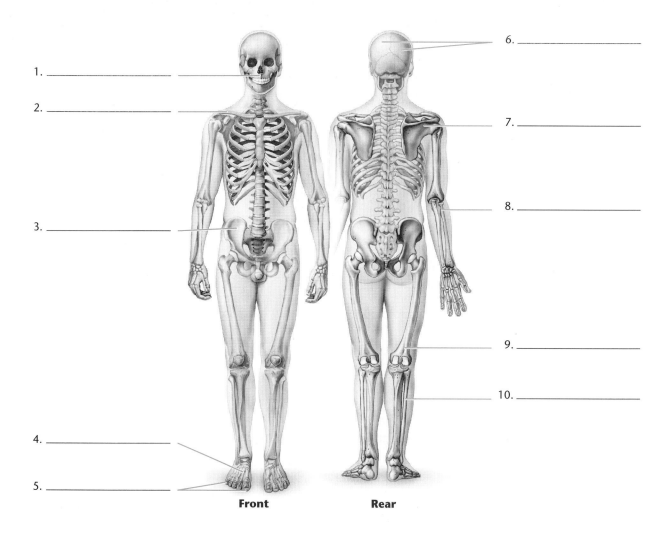

1. _____

2. _____

3. _____

4. _____

5. _____

6. _____

7. _____

8. _____

9. _____

10. _____

Front   **Rear**

I. *Write 4 to 5 sentences to answer each question below.*

1. Describe how homeostasis of calcium is maintained when the levels of calcium in the blood fall <u>below</u> normal. In other words, how does the body raise calcium levels back to normal? Be very specific. (**3 points**)

2. Choose ONE of the following disorders and describe what happens in this disorder. Be very specific. (**2 points**)

OSTEOPOROSIS   **ACNE**

Achievement Test 2

Chapters 4–6

(50 points total)

A. *Answer the questions below, using complete sentences.*

   1. Describe what happens in a reflex. (**2 points**)

   2. What is the function of a neurotransmitter? (**1 point**)

B. *Match each part of the nervous system to its function.* (*6 points*)

   _____ 1. interprets messages coming from the ear   **a.** cerebellum

   _____ 2. controls movement of skeletal muscles   **b.** thalamus

   _____ 3. "relay center" for sensory information   **c.** medulla

   _____ 4. controls heart rate, breathing, blood pressure   **d.** frontal lobe

   _____ 5. helps control position of body and balance   **e.** temporal lobe

   _____ 6. keeps track of the passage of time   **f.** pineal gland

C. *Circle the correct word(s) to complete each sentence.* (*7 points*)

   1. The **effector / receptor** is the part of the reflex that carries out the orders.

   2. The **parasympathetic / sympathetic** part of the autonomic nervous system is the one that is working when you are scared or stressed.

   3. The brain sends a message to the effector along an **afferent / efferent** neuron.

   4. Bundles of actin and myosin that are found inside a muscle fiber are called **myofibril / fascicle**.

   5. A **sensory / motor** neuron releases a neurotransmitter that attaches to a skeletal muscle fiber and causes it to contract.

   6. When a skeletal muscle fiber contracts, it gets **longer / shorter**.

   7. A message sent along the length of an axon is a(n) **electrical current / neurotransmitter**.

D. *Label each statement true* (T) *or false* (F). (*6 points*)

   _____ 1. The lattisimus dorsi muscle is found on your back.

   _____ 2. A protein molecule that looks like a golf club is called actin.

   _____ 3. Smooth and cardiac muscle are controlled by autonomic neurons.

   _____ 4. ATP is the molecule that provides the energy to the myosin molecule.

   _____ 5. Myofibrils are smaller than myofilaments.

   _____ 6. All skeletal muscles are under conscious (voluntary) control.

E. *Complete the sentences with the correct word(s). (5 points)*

1. The gland in the brain that secretes many hormones important for the regulation of water balance, growth, and reproduction is the _____ gland.

2. The _____ is the part of the neuron that receives messages from other neurons.

3. At the beginning of a reflex, the _____ detects a change (for example, pressure or heat).

4. The _____ is the space between the axon of one neuron and the dendrite of another neuron.

5. A _____ is a bundle of axons or muscle fibers.

F. *Circle the correct answer. (7 points)*

1. Myelin _____. (Circle all answers that are correct.)
   a. is found in the gray matter
   b. helps the nervous system to send messages quickly
   c. is found on the cell body of the neuron
   d. is made of fatty molecules

2. Which of these are parts of the peripheral nervous system (PNS)? (Circle all that are correct.)
   a. cranial nerves   e. spinal nerves
   b. thalamus   f. eye and ear
   c. cerebellum   g. brainstem
   d. sensory receptors   h. cerebrum

3. Muscles that mix food in the stomach or control the width of blood vessels are _____ muscles.
   a. cardiac   b. skeletal   c. smooth

4. One function of the parietal lobe is to _____.
   a. coordinate movement
   b. interpret what you hear
   c. control the heart rate
   d. interpret sensory information from all over the skin

5. Two organs that are important in controlling the autonomic nervous system functions are _____.
   a. hypothalamus and thalamus
   b. hypothalamus and medulla
   c. thalamus and medulla
   d. cerebellum and hypothalamus

6. Which one DOES NOT occur when the sympathetic nervous system is in charge?

    a. increased blood pressure

    b. faster breathing

    c. increased digestion

    d. increased heart rate

7. A sarcomere _____.

    a. is comprised of several myofibrils

    b. is a bundle of muscle fibers

    c. contains actin and myosin arranged in a particular pattern

    d. is a disorder where the muscle is no longer able to contract

G. *Read the story. Then circle the correct word(s) to complete each sentence.* *(4 points)*

Isabella woke up late for school. She hurried to get ready and jumped into her car. Her heart was pounding. She got on the freeway and needed to change lanes. Unfortunately, she was in such a hurry that she didn't see the car in the lane next to her, and she almost hit it. The driver in the other car honked his horn. Isabella pushed the gas pedal and sped away. She got to school and sat in the car a few moments to calm down.

1. The part of the brain that controlled Isabella's heart rate was the **pons / medulla**.

2. When Isabella heard the horn, that message was sent by an **afferent / efferent** neuron from her ear to her brain.

3. The **triceps brachii / tibialis anterior** was a muscle in Isabella's leg that received the message to move in order to push the gas pedal.

4. The part of Isabella's brain that stored the message to wake up earlier was the **cerebellum / cerebrum**.

H. Label the diagram. (*7 points*)

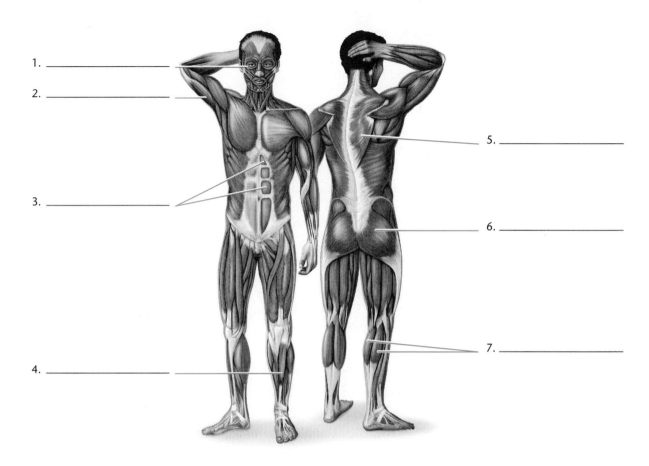

1. _____

2. _____

3. _____

4. _____

5. _____

6. _____

7. _____

I. *Write 4 to 5 sentences to answer each question below.*

1. Using all of the terms below, write a paragraph that describes how someone's nervous system will react after seeing a bear while hiking in the woods. (**3 points**)

afferent neuron	eye	sensory receptors
autonomic neurons	heart	skeletal muscle in the leg
CNS neurons	motor neurons	

2. Choose ONE of the following disorders and describe what happens in this disorder. Be very specific. (**2 points**)

MULTIPLE SCLEROSIS   **STROKE**   **MUSCULAR DYSTROPHY**

Achievement Test 3

CHAPTERS 7–9

(50 points total)

A. *Write the definition of each of these terms. (3 points)*

1. artery

2. absorption

3. inflammation

B. *Match each item to its function. (7 points)*

_____ 1. stores and concentrates bile   **a.** mucus

_____ 2. eats bacteria and viruses   **b.** platelets

_____ 3. makes bile and removes toxins from food   **c.** gall bladder

_____ 4. neutralizes acid; coats the stomach   **d.** bile

_____ 5. breaks apart fat molecules   **e.** phagocyte

_____ 6. liquefies food; begins digestion   **f.** saliva

_____ 7. helps with blood coagulation   **g.** liver

C. *Circle the correct word(s) to complete each sentence. (8 points)*

1. Most of the digestion and absorption of food occurs in the **stomach / small intestine.**

2. As part of the pulmonary circuit, the pulmonary **artery / vein** carries blood from the heart to the lungs.

3. In the lungs, the blood picks up **oxygen / carbon dioxide.**

4. High blood pressure is also called **hypotension / hypertension.**

5. Glucagon causes blood sugar levels to **increase / decrease.**

6. Only **protein / carbohydrate** is digested in the stomach.

7. The left ventricle pumps blood into the pulmonary **artery / aorta.**

8. Vasoconstriction will **increase / decrease** blood pressure.

D. *Label each statement true* (T) *or false* (F). *(5 points)*

_____ 1. The first heart sound is caused by the opening of the semilunar valves.

_____ 2. Diabetes occurs when the pancreas is not able to make insulin.

_____ 3. Ulcers in the stomach are caused by spicy foods.

_____ 4. Saliva contains molecules that help to digest carbohydrates.

_____ 5. Peristalsis means that all the muscle in an organ contracts at once.

E. *Complete the sentences with the correct word(s). (6 points)*

1. The _____ are the type of blood cell involved in body defenses.

2. Another name for red blood cells is _____.

3. The name given to the liquid part of blood is called _____.

4. Two molecules that you could find in blood are _____ and _____.

5. The disorder in which blood does not carry enough oxygen is called _____.

6. The _____ is the pacemaker of the heart.

F. *Circle the correct answer. (6 points)*

1. The _____ closes when you swallow to prevent food from entering the lungs.

    a. trachea   **b.** esophagus   **c.** epiglottis   **d.** vocal cord   **e.** pharynx

2. Which gland makes the hormone that increases general metabolism (getting energy from food)?

    a. pituitary   **b.** thyroid   **c.** adrenal   **d.** pancreas

3. The _____ vessels bring extra fluid back to the cardiovascular system from the tissue spaces.

    a. pulmonary   **b.** cardiac   **c.** lymphatic   **d.** endocrine

4. When the blood supply to an area of cardiac muscle is reduced, this causes a painful sensation called _____.

    a. constipation   **b.** fibrillation   **c.** peristalsis   **d.** angina pectoris

5. Which of these is NOT part of the lymphatic system?

    a. pancreas   **b.** spleen   **c.** tonsils   **d.** lymph nodes

6. When the immune system overreacts to foreign substances that enter the body, this is called an _____.

    a. autoimmune disease
    b. allergy
    c. autorhythmic disease

G. *Read the story. Then circle the correct word to complete each sentence. (3 points)*

While Jason is at the market, someone sneezes in his face. A day later he begins to feel very tired. Soon after that, his throat becomes very sore. He goes to his doctor, and the doctor does some tests. The doctor tells Jason that he has the flu. Since this is caused by a virus, the doctor says that antibiotics will not help, but instead tells him to rest and drink plenty of fluids. After doing what the doctor instructed, Jason feels much better after a few days.

1. Flu viruses that were able to get into Jason's nose might have been captured by **phagocytes / hairs** which are a first-line defense.

2. If a virus escapes the first-line defenses, then perhaps a second type of innate defense called a(n) **phagocyte / antibody** might be able to capture it.

3. If Jason's defense system made antibodies to this virus, the antibodies would be able to **destroy / attach to** the flu viruses.

H. *Label the diagram. (7 points)*

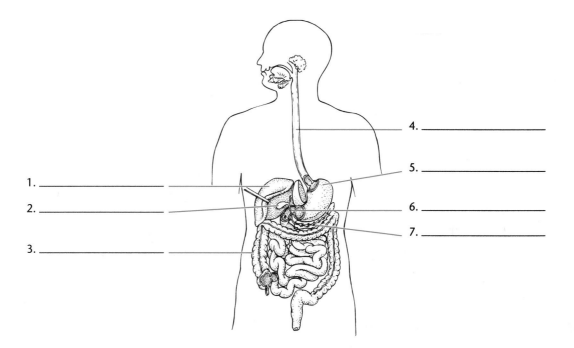

1. _____

2. _____

3. _____

4. _____

5. _____

6. _____

7. _____

I. *Write 4 to 5 sentences to answer each question below.*

1. Masashi has just eaten a meal. His blood sugar levels have risen above normal. Describe how the body maintains homeostasis of blood sugar in this situation. (**3 points**)

2. Choose ONE of the following disorders and describe what happens in this disorder. Be very specific. (**2 points**)

   HEARTBURN   **MYOCARDIAL INFARCTION**   **HEMOPHILIA**

Achievement Test 4
CHAPTERS 10–12
(50 points total)

A. *Write the definition of each of these terms.* *(3 points)*

   1. reabsorption

   2. menopause

   3. impotence

B. *Match each item to its function.* *(7 points)*

   _____ **1.** delivers urine to the outside of the body   **a.** spinal cord

   _____ **2.** secretes lubricant onto penis before ejaculation   **b.** corpus luteum

   _____ **3.** secretes progesterone   **c.** cilia

   _____ **4.** keeps alveoli from collapsing   **d.** surfactant

   _____ **5.** traps bacteria and viruses in the nose   **e.** bulbourethral gland

   _____ **6.** sweeps mucus upward from trachea   **f.** mucus

   _____ **7.** tells internal urethral sphincter to relax   **g.** urethra

C. *Circle the correct word(s) to complete each sentence.* *(6 points)*

   1. Fertilization usually occurs in the **uterus / Fallopian tubes**.

   2. The endometrium is the lining of the **urinary bladder / uterus**.

   3. Menstruation occurs at the **beginning / middle** of the uterine or menstrual cycle.

   4. The cell that results from the union of the sperm and ovum is called the **embryo / zygote**.

   5. The urethra is **longer / shorter** in males than in females.

   6. When a person is not able to control the urge to urinate, it is called **impotence / incontinence**.

D. *Label each statement true* (T) *or false* (F). *(6 points)*

   _____ **1.** About 90 percent of the water that is filtered out of the blood by the kidney will end up in the urine.

   _____ **2.** Females are more likely to contract urinary tract infections than males.

   _____ **3.** Secretion in the kidneys moves molecules from the renal tubule back into the blood.

   _____ **4.** When a woman is pregnant, she continues to menstruate.

   _____ **5.** Identical twins are the result of the fertilization of a single ovum by a single sperm.

   _____ **6.** Semen contains molecules that help it to coagulate once it is inside the female's vagina.

E. *Complete the sentences with the correct word(s).* (6 points)

1. Sperm usually become mature in the _____.

2. The lungs are surrounded by two layers of membrane with fluid in between. The space where the fluid is located is called the _____ cavity.

3. The _____ is the organ that moves urine from the kidney to the urinary bladder.

4. The _____ gland secretes aldosterone, which helps the body to maintain homeostasis of blood volume.

5. The hormone _____ causes development of female sexual characteristics and also causes development of the follicle.

6. The hormone _____ is responsible for the sex drive in both men and women.

F. *Circle the correct answer.* (6 points)

1. The specific part of the kidney that filters the blood is the _____.

   a. medulla   **b.** collecting duct   **c.** renal tubule   **d.** glomerulus

2. In the male, production of both sperm and testosterone occurs in the _____.

   a. prostate gland   **b.** testis   **c.** epididymis   **d.** vas deferens

3. The two hormones that tell the kidneys to increase reabsorption of water are _____.

   a. testosterone and estrogen
   b. ADH and aldosterone
   c. aldosterone and testosterone
   d. ANP and ADH

4. In the ovarian cycle, _____.

   a. several ova are released every month during ovulation
   b. ovulation occurs in the middle of the cycle (about day 14)
   c. the corpus luteum forms at the beginning of the cycle
   d. progesterone is the hormone that is made first in the cycle

5. The fetus grows and develops while attached to the lining of the _____.

   a. Fallopian tube   **b.** vagina   **c.** ovary   **d.** uterus

6. Which of these does NOT occur during expiration?

   a. The diaphragm contracts.
   b. The chest cavity gets smaller.
   c. Pressure inside alveoli increases.
   d. The intercostal muscles relax.

G. *Read the story. Then circle the correct word(s) to complete each sentence.* *(4 points)*

Eduardo has been studying in the United States for a year, and was finally able to return home to Ecuador to visit his family. After traveling on the airplane and arriving at his family's home, he became very ill with food poisoning. It caused him to have severe vomiting and diarrhea, resulting in decreased blood volume. After he fainted, his family took him to the doctor. The doctor prescribed antibiotics and told him to drink lots of fluids. After a few days, Eduardo felt much better.

1. Eduardo's decreased blood volume most likely caused him to have **increased / decreased** blood pressure.

2. One hormone that would attempt to correct this problem is **testosterone / aldosterone**.

3. In order to retain more water, Eduardo's kidneys should **increase / decrease** reabsorption of water and salts.

4. The pituitary gland **would / would not** release ADH in this situation.

H. *Label the diagrams.* *(8 points)*

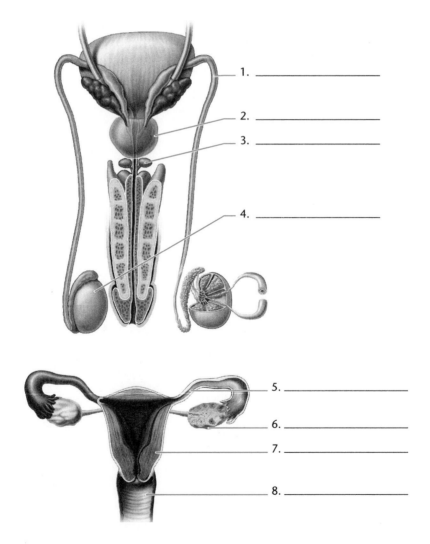

1. _____

2. _____

3. _____

4. _____

5. _____

6. _____

7. _____

8. _____

I. Write 4 to 5 sentences to answer each question below.

1. Describe the process of inspiration. What organs / structures are involved? What causes it to occur? What makes the air come into the lungs? Be very specific. (**2 points**)

2. Choose ONE of the following disorders and describe what happens in this disorder. Be very specific. (**2 points**)

   KIDNEY STONES   ENDOMETRIOSIS   EMPHYSEMA

Answer Key

CHAPTER 1

INTRODUCTION (pages 2–3)

Exercise 1
1. molecule
2. cell
3. tissue
4. organ
5. organ system

Exercise 2
1. Anatomy is the study of the location and organization of the parts of the body.
2. a cell
3. heart, stomach, eye, spleen, lungs, etc.
4. The body sweats. The face gets red.
5. A hormone is a molecule that travels in the bloodstream. It carries messages from one part of the body to another.

Exercise 3
1. take in
2. comprised
3. maintain
4. interprets
5. give off
6. performs
7. secrete
8. forms
9. are arranged
10. monitors

COMPREHENSION CHECK (page 6)

Exercise 1
1. everywhere; in living and nonliving things
2. in nonliving things
3. a microscope
4. to hold the cell parts together
5. things can move through it
6. no
7. in the nucleus
8. a molecule containing information for the cell

Exercise 2
1. d   2. f   3. h   4. b
5. a   6. c   7. e   8. g

COMPREHENSION CHECK (page 8)

Exercise 1
1. groups of cells
2. epithelial, muscle, nerve, connective, bone, blood
3. epithelial, muscle, connective, and blood
4. heart, brain, stomach, liver, lungs
5. An organ system is a group of organs that work together to carry out a function.

Exercise 2
2—cell
5—organ system
4—organ
1—molecule
3—tissue

Exercise 3
1. tissue
2. organs
3. organ system

COMPREHENSION CHECK (page 11)

1. temperature, heart rate, breathing rate, blood sugar, water in the blood
2. Homeostasis is when the body keeps conditions constant.
3. the body sweats; it sends blood to the outer parts of body (face gets red); the person is thirsty
4. a desired level
5. It has a set point and goes on or off when the temperature moves away from that set point.

COMPREHENSION CHECK (page 13)

Exercise 1
1. F—it takes a short time
2. T
3. T
4. F—homeostasis is usually maintained with negative feedback
5. T
6. T

Exercise 2
1. reflex
2. spinal cord
3. muscle
4. negative feedback
5. Nerves

1. neural
2. hormonal
3. hormones
4. bloodstream
5. nerve

REVIEW (pages 16–17)

Check Your Understanding

Exercise 1

1. study of the parts of the body
2. study of the function of body parts
3. molecule, cell, tissue, organ, and organ system
4. cell; organ
5. heart, stomach, eyes, muscle, liver
6. homeostasis
7. jumping when you are frightened; pulling your hand away from a flame; blinking your eyes when something is thrown at you
8. the body sweats; blood rushes to the face; the person is thirsty
9. hormones and nerves

Exercise 2

1. molecule
2. cell
3. tissue
4. organ
5. organ system

Exercise 3

1. c
2. b
3. 5—organ systems
   3—tissues
   2—cells
   4—organs
   1—molecules
4. Sensors detect the stimulus. Nerves send a message. The spinal cord makes decisions.
5. nerves and hormones; nerves; hormones

Think More about It

1. digestive, cardiovascular, skeletal, respiratory, immune, muscular, nervous, endocrine, reproductive, urinary

2. heart rate, breathing rate, sweating, blood pressure, temperature

CHAPTER 2

INTRODUCTION (pages 19–20)

Exercise 1

1. hair
2. nerve
3. oil gland
4. epidermis
5. dermis
6. hypodermis
7. sweat gland
8. blood vessels

Exercise 2

1. protection; to hold body together
2. People with darker skin have more melanin.
3. yes
4. protection; for sensation and filtering air
5. It keeps body temperature the same, and it rids the body of wastes.

Exercise 3

1. are excreted
2. evaporates
3. invade
4. insulate
5. interact
6. varies
7. moisturize

COMPREHENSION CHECK *(page 21)*

Exercise 1

1. keratin
2. keratin
3. It's a barrier protecting you from invading bacteria. It allows you to excrete wastes by sweating.
4. People with darker skin have more melanin than people with lighter skin.
5. He would see a change in a mole.

Exercise 2

1. d	2. i	3. a	4. g	5. h
6. f	7. e	8. c	9. j	10. b

COMPREHENSION CHECK *(page 23)*

Exercise 1
1. connective, adipose
2. cells, protein
3. Elastin
4. callus

Exercise 2
1. Reticular
2. Adipose
3. dermis
4. Elastin
5. epithelial

COMPREHENSION CHECK *(pages 25–26)*

Exercise 1

Allow us to have feeling in our skin: Nerves
Deliver food and oxygen: Blood Vessels
Contain sensory receptors: Nerves
Located in the hypodermis and dermis: Nerves, Blood Vessels
Send messages to our brain: Nerves
You can see them where the epidermis is thin: Blood Vessels

Exercise 2
1. c
2. d
3. a
4. b

COMPREHENSION CHECK *(page 27)*

Exercise 1
1. T
2. F—nails get their hardness from keratin
3. T
4. F—everyone has different amounts of melanin in their hair
5. F—hair starts growing in the dermis

Exercise 2
1. b
2. c
3. d
4. a

COMPREHENSION CHECK *(pages 28–29)*

Exercise 1
1. to lubricate the hair
2. The skin would become dry and cracked.
3. People sweat to maintain temperature homeostasis and to excrete water and wastes.
4. dermis
5. sweating and sending blood to thin-skinned areas

Exercise 2
1. sebaceous
2. temperature
3. Sebum
4. a fever

REVIEW (pages 30–31)

Check Your Understanding

Exercise 1
1. epidermis, dermis, hypodermis
2. dermis
3. to maintain body temperature and excrete wastes
4. keratin, melanin, sebum, water, collagen, elastin
5. epithelium, connective, blood, nervous, adipose
6. they have more melanin
7. yes
8. lubricate, keep water inside, kill bacteria
9. dermis
10. collagen (support), elastin (stretch), reticular (support)
11. sensation, filtering, protection
12. follicle
13. keratin

Exercise 2
1. hair
2. sweat gland
3. nerve
4. sensory receptor
5. blood vessel
6. epidermis
7. dermis
8. hypodermis
9. hair follicle

Exercise 3

1. b
2. c
3. A sweat gland looks like a coiled tube.
4. It excretes water in the process of sweating.
5. Melanin adds color to the skin and protects it from the UV rays of the sun.
6. protection, holding body together, excretion of waste, temperature homeostasis, sensation

Think More about It

1. Clean it regularly. Disinfect all wounds. Keep it moisturized. Clean under the fingernails.
2. Yes. People with lighter skin have less melanin, and thus less protection from the sun's damaging UV rays.

CHAPTER 3

INTRODUCTION (pages 33–34)

Exercise 1

1. mandible
2. clavicle
3. sternum
4. ribs
5. humerus
6. pubis
7. femur

Exercise 2

1. support, movement, protection of organs, storage of calcium and fat, production of blood cells
2. calcium salts, collagen, cells
3. they get soft and break more easily
4. ligaments
5. tendons

Exercise 3

1. is constructed
2. cured
3. attaches
4. fuse
5. is stored
6. classified
7. support
8. located
9. be relieved
10. are embedded

Comprehension Check (page 36)

Exercise 1

1. osteocyte
2. collagen, calcium salts
3. strength and hardness
4. spongy and compact
5. like many onion slices
6. blood vessels

Exercise 2

1. spongy bone
2. compact bone
3. osteocytes
4. matrix
5. collagen
6. calcium salts

Comprehension Check (page 37)

1. T
2. F—the inside of long bones is hollow
3. F—the outer part of both flat bones and long bones is comprised of compact bone
4. T
5. T

Comprehension Check (page 41)

Exercise 1

1. matrix
2. Milk
3. stored in
4. parathyroid hormone
5. parathyroid hormone
6. weak

Exercise 2

1. calcium
2. Calcitonin
3. osteoporosis
4. PTH
5. Parathyroid gland
6. thyroid gland

Comprehension Check (page 47)

Exercise 1

1. cartilage is more flexible
2. ligament; tendon
3. articulation
4. sutures, slightly moveable, synovial
5. Synovial joints have synovial fluid and are able to move more.

6. to cushion the joint

7. bone moving against bone

8. attacking one's own tissues

9. swelling and accumulation of fluid

Exercise 2

1. c	**2.** l	**3.** a	**4.** e	**5.** b
6. i	**7.** d	**8.** f	**9.** j	**10.** h
11. m	**12.** k	**13.** g		

COMPREHENSION CHECK *(page 49)*

Exercise 1

1. T

2. F—there's only one occipital bone

3. T

4. F—the temporal bone covers the side of the head

5. T

Exercise 2

1. zygomatic

2. occipital

3. temporal

4. maxilla

5. occipital

COMPREHENSION CHECK *(page 35)*

Exercise 1

1. to hold up the body

2. backbone

3. 33

4. five

5. lungs, heart

6. 12

7. cartilage

Exercise 2

1. vertebrae; vertebra

2. ribs

3. sternum

Exercise 3

5—coccyx

1—cervical

3—lumbar

4—sacrum

2—thoracic

COMPREHENSION CHECK *(pages 53–54)*

Exercise 1

1. three

2. radius, ulna

3. carpals

4. metacarpals

5. two

6. 28

Exercise 2

1. femur	**4.** phalanges
2. ilium	**5.** tarsals
3. patella	

Exercise 3

Carpals: Wrist and Hand

Clavicle: Shoulder Region

Humerus: Arm

Metacarpals: Wrist and Hand

Phalanges: Wrist and Hand

Radius: Arm

Scapula: Shoulder Region

Ulna: Arm

Exercise 4

1. e	**2.** f	**3.** i	**4.** j	**5.** c
6. a	**7.** d	**8.** g	**9.** b	**10.** h

REVIEW (pages 56–58)

Check Your Understanding

Exercise 1

1. protection, support, storage, blood cell production

2. calcium salts and collagen

3. compact and spongy; yes

4. bones; calcitonin; thyroid gland

5. it takes calcium out of bone; PTH; parathyroid gland

6. They break easily and are too soft.

7. joints

8. ligaments; tendons

9. skull; moveable joints like the elbow and knee

10. Osteoarthritis is caused by the wearing down of cartilage at the joints, while rheumatoid arthritis is caused by an attack of the body defenses on the joint tissue causing inflammation.

Exercise 2

1. frontal
2. zygomatic
3. maxilla
4. mandible
5. clavicle
6. sternum
7. ribs
8. vertebra
9. ilium
10. pubis
11. ischium
12. patella
13. tarsals
14. metatarsals
15. phalanges
16. parietal
17. occipital
18. scapula
19. humerus
20. radius
21. ulna
22. sacrum
23. coccyx
24. carpals
25. metacarpals
26. phalanges
27. femur
28. fibula
29. tibia

Exercise 3

1. support, storage, protection, blood cell production
2. milk, soybeans, tofu, fortified cereals
3. Ligaments connect bones to one another, while tendons connect bones to muscles.
4. movement and flexibility
5. b
6. d

Think More about It

1. collagen
2. hypodermis
3. Yes, because they connect to one another and share locations.

CHAPTER 4

INTRODUCTION (pages 60–61)

Exercise 1

1. triceps brachii
2. pectoralis
3. biceps brachii
4. quadriceps
5. tibialis anterior

Exercise 2

1. to move the bones
2. in bundles
3. actin and myosin
4. neurons
5. heart, stomach, blood vessels, skeletal muscles

Exercise 3

1. flex
2. extend
3. transmit
4. bend
5. contract
6. stimulated
7. inherited

COMPREHENSION CHECK (page 63)

Exercise 1

1. myofibrils
2. inside a myofibril
3. actin and myosin
4. myofilament
5. Fibers comprise fascicles.
6. Myofilaments comprise myofibrils. Myofibrils comprise fibers. Fibers comprise fascicles. Fascicles comprise muscles.

Exercise 2

1. c   2. d   3. f   4. a
5. e   6. b   7. h   8. g

Exercise 3

1. fascicle
2. fiber
3. myofibril
4. myofilaments

Exercise 1

1. F—motor neurons do not touch skeletal muscle fibers
2. F—neurotransmitters are molecules that are sent to the fiber from the motor neuron
3. T
4. T
5. F—motor neurons send messages to the muscle from the brain

Exercise 2

1. b   2. c   3. a

COMPREHENSION CHECK *(page 66)*

Exercise 1

1. Z-lines
2. a twisted string of pearls
3. the Z-line
4. a bundle of golf clubs
5. in the center
6. cocked

Exercise 2

1. Z-line
2. sarcomere
3. Z-line
4. actin
5. myosin

COMPREHENSION CHECK *(page 68)*

1. shorten
2. cocked
3. mitochondria
4. food molecules
5. myosin pushes actin

COMPREHENSION CHECK *(page 69)*

1. Mixing and breaking apart food in the stomach: Smooth
2. Running to catch the bus: Skeletal
3. Making the heart beat: Cardiac
4. Chewing food: Skeletal
5. Making the blood vessels narrower: Smooth
6. Contracting the uterus during childbirth: Smooth

COMPREHENSION CHECK *(page 70)*

Exercise 1

1. c   2. e   3. b   4. a   5. d

Exercise 2

1. "Frontalis" tells you that this muscle is at the front of the head.
2. "Orbicularis" means to go around or to encircle.
3. The term "oculi" refers to the eye.
4. The term "oris" refers to the mouth.

COMPREHENSION CHECK *(page 72)*

Exercise 1

1. T
2. T
3. F—the deltoid muscle covers your shoulder
4. F—the sternocleidomastoid goes from your sternum to your head
5. F—the external oblique is located to the side of your abdomen
6. T
7. T

Exercise 2

1. d   2. i   3. j   4. b   5. h
6. a   7. c   8. e   9. g   10. f

COMPREHENSION CHECK *(page 74)*

Exercise 1

1. a   2. b   3. c   4. b

Exercise 2

1. three attachment places
2. on the back
3. at the side
4. largest
5. branches

COMPREHENSION CHECK *(pages 76–77)*

Exercise 1

1. vastus intermedius
2. vastus intermedius, vastus lateralis, vastus medialis, rectus femoris
3. rectus femoris
4. tibialis anterior

Exercise 2

1. e   2. g   3. a   4. c
5. d   6. f   7. b

REVIEW (pages 81–83)

Check Your Understanding

Exercise 1
1. to move bones
2. A muscle is made of bundles (fascicles) of fibers. Fibers are made of bundles (myofibrils) of myofilaments. Each myofilament is comprised of one of two kinds of protein: actin and myosin.
3. actin, which looks like a twisted string of beads, and myosin, which looks like golf clubs
4. from the nervous system
5. The signal causes myosin heads to attach to actin and push them toward the center of the sarcomere. This causes the fiber to shorten (contract).
6. ATP
7. Cardiac muscles are found only in the heart and are what causes the heart to beat. Smooth muscles are used to move things in other places where conscious control is not necessary (for example, the stomach).
8. stomach, intestines, blood vessel walls, bladder, uterus
9. Cardiac muscles are involuntary while skeletal are voluntary. Cardiac muscles are found only in the heart while skeletal muscles are found in the skeletal muscles.
10. diaphragm, intercostal muscles
11. rectus femoris, biceps femoris, tibialis anterior, sartorius
12. frontalis, mandible, maxilla, temporalis

Exercise 2
1. fiber
2. fascicle
3. myofibril
4. Z-line
5. Z-line
6. sarcomere
7. myosin
8. actin
9. myofilament

Exercise 3
1. frontalis
2. temporalis
3. masseter
4. pectoralis major
5. biceps brachii
6. external oblique
7. rectus abdominis
8. rectus femoris
9. sartorius
10. tibialis anterior
11. triceps brachii
12. deltoid
13. trapezius
14. latissimus dorsi
15. gluteus maximus
16. biceps femoris
17. gastrocnemius
18. Achilles tendon

Exercise 4
1. a
2. c
3. ATP provides energy for movement of the myosin myofilament. If there were no ATP, then muscles couldn't contract or relax.
4. A sprain is tearing or overstretching of the ligaments, while a strain is an overstretching of a muscle.
5. ACh stands for acetylcholine, a neurotransmitter that is made in and released from motor neurons to tell skeletal muscles to contract.

Think More about It
1. Muscle helps us to chew and swallow our food as well as to move and mix it all along the digestive tract.
2. Muscle helps the heart to beat and also helps the blood vessels to change their diameter.
3. digestive, cardiovascular, urinary, respiratory, reproductive

CHAPTER 5

INTRODUCTION (pages 85–86)

Exercise 1
1. brain
2. spinal cord
3. nerves

Exercise 2
1. to control the body's activities
2. Nerves are bundles of neurons. They send messages.
3. They detect changes. Sensory organs include the eye, ear, and nose.
4. neuron

5. A sensory receptor receives a stimulus and sends a message along an afferent neuron. That message is received by a CNS neuron that then sends a message back to the area along an efferent neuron. This message is received by a muscle that carries out the response.

Exercise 3
1. detect
2. excite
3. deaden

COMPREHENSION CHECK *(page 87)*

1. spinal cord
2. CNS
3. Nerves
4. sensory receptor
5. PNS

COMPREHENSION CHECK *(page 88)*

1. sensory receptors
2. CNS
3. spinal cord
4. brain
5. memory

COMPREHENSION CHECK *(page 90)*

1. b   2. c   3. c   4. d   5. a

COMPREHENSION CHECK *(pages 91–92)*

Exercise 1
2—An electrical current forms.
1—Sodium and potassium move in and out of the neuron.
5—The vesicles release a neurotransmitter.
3—An electrical current is sent to the end of the neuron's axon.
6—The neurotransmitter jumps across the synapse and attaches to the receptor molecules of the next neuron.
4—The electrical current stimulates the vesicles.

Exercise 2
1. synaptic end bulb
2. synapse
3. sodium and potassium
4. Vesicles
5. neurotransmitter
6. axon

7. receptor molecules
8. dendrites

COMPREHENSION CHECK *(page 93)*

1. no
2. myelin
3. myelin sheaths
4. yes
5. They jump over it
6. Someone with multiple sclerosis has slower muscle movement.

COMPREHENSION CHECK *(page 99)*

Exercise 1
1. 12
2. head
3. afferent
4. to
5. from
6. efferent
7. one way
8. two ways
9. exit
10. spinal
11. two-way
12. cranial

Exercise 2
1. e   2. b   3. a   4. c   5. d

COMPREHENSION CHECK *(page 101)*

Exercise 1
1. heat, pain, cold, pressure
2. cell or end of neurons
3. on the retina
4. cells
5. two
6. hearing
7. vestibular apparatus
8. no
9. the end of neurons
10. General anesthesia affects the person's consciousness while local anesthesia affects just a small area of the body.

Exercise 2
1. vestibular apparatus
2. rods and cones
3. stimulus
4. sensory receptors
5. cochlea

REVIEW (pages 104–106)

Check Your Understanding

Exercise 1

1. to control body functions
2. CNS: brain and spinal cord; PNS: sensory organs and nerves
3. Sensory receptor detects stimulus. Message sent along afferent neuron to CNS. CNS makes decision. Message sent along efferent neuron to effector. Effector carries out action.
4. A neuron is part of a nerve.
5. Dendrites receive messages. Cell body makes decisions. Axon sends message.
6. It travels via neurotransmitters.
7. It increases the speed of the message.
8. Cranial nerves can be mixed, sensory or motor, while all spinal nerves are mixed. Cranial nerves extend from the head outward. Spinal nerves extend from the spinal cord outward.
9. spinal nerves
10. part of neuron or the entire cell
11. afferent neurons

Exercise 2

Figure 5.16

1. dendrite
2. nucleus
3. axon
4. cell body

Figure 5.17

1. vesicle
2. neurotransmitter
3. synapse
4. synaptic end bulb

Exercise 3

1. F—sensory nerves carry afferent messages
2. T
3. motor
4. d
5. b
6. a
7. Order is: 3—CNS, 5—skeletal muscle fiber, 4—motor neuron, 1—sensory receptor, 2—sensory neuron

Think More about It

1. when digestion starts/stops, bowel movements, appetite

2. controls skeletal muscle function, coordination of muscle movements
3. heart rate, blood pressure

CHAPTER 6

INTRODUCTION (pages 108–109)

Exercise 1

1. cerebrum, cerebellum, hypothalamus, thalamus, pons, medulla, pineal gland, pituitary gland, etc.
2. spinal cord
3. The area that is closest to the ear is the temporal lobe and it is responsible for interpreting what you hear.

Exercise 2

1. to control muscles, thinking, memory; to interpret speech; to make decisions about maintaining homeostasis
2. to send messages; reflexes
3. skull bones
4. It sends messages along neurons.

Exercise 3

1. detect
2. excited
3. deaden
4. sort out

COMPREHENSION CHECK *(page 111)*

Exercise 1

1. inside the central opening in the vertebral column
2. to transmit messages; reflexes
3. Motor neurons have their cell bodies in the spinal cord. If the spinal cord is damaged, muscles won't get messages to contract.
4. very strong
5. The spinal cord is faster.
6. gray matter
7. myelin
8. White matter is for transmitting messages, while gray matter is for making the decisions.

Exercise 2

1. sensory receptor
2. gray matter
3. white matter
4. sensory neuron
5. CNS neuron
6. motor neuron

COMPREHENSION CHECK (page 114)

Exercise 1

Interpret touch: Parietal lobe
Control skeletal muscles: Frontal lobe
Interpret what you hear: Temporal lobe
Interpret what you see: Occipital lobe

Exercise 2

1. frontal lobe
2. temporal lobe
3. parietal lobe
4. occipital lobe
5. cerebellum

COMPREHENSION CHECK (page 116)

Exercise 1

1. b   2. b   3. a   4. c

Exercise 2

	Thalamus	Hypothalamus	Pituitary gland	Pineal gland
Location	Below cerebrum	Below thalamus	Below hypothalamus	Toward the back
Function	Relay station	Homeostasis	Making important hormones	Body clock
Hormone(s) secreted	None	None	Many hormones such as growth hormone	Melatonin

COMPREHENSION CHECK (pages 117–118)

Exercise 1

1. T
2. T
3. T
4. F—the thalamus is a relay station for sensory messages
5. T
6. T

Exercise 2

1. hypothalamus
2. pituitary gland
3. pons
4. medulla
5. thalamus
6. pineal gland
7. midbrain

COMPREHENSION CHECK (page 118)

1. The limbic system is responsible for the emotional part of one's personality.
2. The reticular formation is responsible for maintaining the state of alertness in the brain.
3. The reticular formation shuts down.

COMPREHENSION CHECK (page 122)

Exercise 1

1. Examples of a fight or flight situation include being frightened by something, being in an emergency situation (such as car accident or fire), or being stressed out.
2. When scared, the body increases heart rate and blood pressure, breathing rate increases, pupils dilate, and digestion slows down.

Exercise 2

2—A message is sent along afferent neurons to the CNS.
5—The organs carry out the response. The woman jumps on a chair and screams.
4—Messages are sent along efferent neurons to the different organs needed for a reaction.
1—Sensory receptors in the eyes see a rat.
3—The message is interpreted in the CNS and decisions are made regarding how the woman should react.

Exercise 1

1. "Rest and digest" usually occurs right after mealtime and at bedtime.
2. When relaxing, the heart rate and breathing rate slow, blood pressure decreases, pupils constrict, and digestion increases.

Exercise 2

5—The digestive organs begin the digestive process.

1—Sensory receptors in his stomach detect the presence of food.

4—Messages are sent along efferent neurons to the different digestive organs.

2—Messages about the food are sent along afferent neurons to the CNS.

3—The message is interpreted in the CNS and decisions are made to start the digestive process.

REVIEW (pages 125–127)

Check Your Understanding

Exercise 1

1. brain and spinal cord
2. reflexes and transmission of messages
3. cerebrum, cerebellum, diencephalon, brainstem
4. Gray matter makes decisions, while white matter sends messages.
5. cerebrum
6. Lobes are located under the bone of the same name.
7. frontal (motor control), parietal (general sensory interpretation), temporal (hearing), occipital (vision)
8. Hypothalamus: In the diencephalon
   Medulla oblongata: In the brainstem
   Midbrain: In the brainstem
   Pineal gland: In the diencephalon
   Pituitary gland: In the diencephalon
   Pons: In the brainstem
   Thalamus: In the diencephalon
9. emotions
10. reticular formation
11. parasympathetic and sympathetic
12. no
13. sympathetic
14. Afferent goes toward the CNS, and efferent goes from the CNS.
15. Sensory receptors in eye detect the vision of the snake. Messages sent along afferent neurons to the CNS. Decision made by CNS. CNS sends messages along efferent neurons to the skeletal muscles. Your muscles would move to cause you to jump or run away.

Exercise 2

1. cerebrum
2. hypothalamus
3. pituitary gland
4. pons
5. medulla
6. thalamus
7. midbrain
8. cerebellum
9. spinal cord

Exercise 3

1. F—the area of the brain that interprets hearing is the temporal lobe of the cerebrum
2. T
3. c
4. d
5. b, d
6. pineal
7. occipital
8. d

CHAPTER 7

INTRODUCTION (pages 129–130)

Exercise 1

1. mouth
2. liver
3. large intestine
4. esophagus
5. stomach
6. small intestine

Exercise 2

1. The digestive system takes in food and breaks it down into smaller molecules. Then the smaller molecules are placed into the bloodstream.

2. mouth, pharynx, esophagus, stomach, small intestine, large intestine
3. The tongue mixes and helps to break apart large pieces of food.
4. After leaving the stomach, food goes to the small intestine.
5. ulcers, cavities in the teeth, heartburn, diarrhea, constipation, indigestion

Exercise 3
1. absorbs
2. neutralized
3. eliminated
4. liquefies
5. regulate
6. grinding
7. accumulates
8. dissolve
9. converted
10. digested

COMPREHENSION CHECK (pages 134–135)

Exercise 1
1. Saliva starts to digest starch. Starch is a large molecule.
2. sweet, sour, bitter, salty, umami
3. Saliva liquefies food.
4. 32
5. Listed from front to back: incisors, canines, premolars, molars
6. Listed from the outside to the inside: enamel, dentin, pulp
7. Bacteria produce acids that break apart the enamel, leading to decay of the tooth. You can prevent cavities by brushing frequently.

Exercise 2
1. c   2. b   3. d
4. a   5. c   6. b

COMPREHENSION CHECK (pages 136–137)

Exercise 1
1. The epiglottis keeps food from entering the respiratory tract.
2. The trachea leads toward the lungs and carries air.
3. The esophagus leads toward the stomach and carries food.
4. choking
5. Peristalsis moves food with wave-like contractions in the esophagus.
6. The gastroesophageal sphincter is comprised of smooth muscle tissue.

Exercise 2
1. esophagus
2. epiglottis
3. Peristalsis
4. heartburn
5. larynx, trachea
6. sphincter

COMPREHENSION CHECK (page 139)

Exercise 1
1. oral cavity
2. pharynx
3. small intestine
4. salivary glands
5. esophagus
6. gastroesophageal sphincter
7. stomach
8. pyloric sphincter

Exercise 2
1. Protein
2. pyloric
3. a bacterium
4. Mucus
5. alkaline

COMPREHENSION CHECK (page 143)

Exercise 1

Molecule	Where is it made?	Where does it go?	Function
Sodium bicarbonate	Pancreas	Small intestine	Neutralize acid
Digestive enzymes	Pancreas	Small intestine	Digest food
Bile	Liver	Gall bladder to small intestine	Break up fat

Exercise 2

1. stores
2. small tube
3. cholesterol
4. ultrasound
5. fat

COMPREHENSION CHECK (page 145)

Exercise 1

1. T
2. T
3. T
4. F—right after a big meal, the pancreas is releasing insulin
5. T

Exercise 2

1. c   2. a   3. b   4. b   5. b

COMPREHENSION CHECK (page 147)

Exercise 1

1. c   2. b   3. c   4. d

Exercise 2

1. d   2. f   3. e
4. a   5. b   6. c

COMPREHENSION CHECK (page 148)

1. T
2. F—TSH causes more thyroid hormone to be secreted
3. F—someone with hypothyroidism has too little thyroid hormone
4. T
5. F—hypothyroidism leads to cretinism
6. T

COMPREHENSION CHECK (page 149)

1. Constipation
2. anus
3. external
4. Peritonitis
5. Appendicitis
6. rectum
7. water

REVIEW (pages 151–153)

Check Your Understanding

Exercise 1

1. to break down starch, liquefy food, kill bacteria
2. oral and nasal cavities (mouth and nose)
3. The esophagus leads to the stomach and carries food, while the trachea leads to the lungs and carries air.
4. the larynx
5. three
6. to neutralize the acid produced there and protect the lining of the stomach
7. Bile breaks apart large fat molecules. It's made in the liver and stored in the gall bladder.
8. insulin and glucagon
9. small intestine
10. Their thyroid gland produces a lot of thyroid hormone and it causes them to use food very rapidly for energy.
11. to stimulate the body to use food for energy
12. water, salts, and vitamins

Exercise 2

1. liver
2. gall bladder
3. large intestine
4. appendix
5. esophagus
6. pyloric sphincter
7. pancreas
8. small intestine
9. rectum

Exercise 3

1. epiglottis
2. F—peristalsis means that all the muscle in an organ contracts in a wave-like fashion
3. b
4. b
5. b and c
6. Mucus is important because it helps to protect the stomach lining from the acid made there.

Think More about It

1. The nervous system controls muscle movement in the digestive system.
2. Skeletal muscle is found at the upper end of the digestive tract (mouth, tongue, pharynx, upper esophagus) and at the very end (external anal sphincter). Smooth muscle is found in the middle regions (lower esophagus, stomach, intestines).
3. insulin, glucagon, thyroid hormone

CHAPTER 8
INTRODUCTION (pages 155–156)

Exercise 1
1. plasma
2. cells

Exercise 2
1. Blood carries nutrients, water, and hormones to all areas of the body. Cells in the blood help to carry oxygen, fight disease, and help blood to clot.
2. cells, water, nutrients, hormones, wastes
3. yes
4. influenza, colds, AIDS, strep throat, hepatitis

Exercise 3
1. centrifuged
2. penetrate
3. coagulate
4. lines
5. burst
6. tag
7. activated
8. recycled
9. overwhelmed

COMPREHENSION CHECK (page 160)

Exercise 1
1. plasma and cells
2. erythrocytes, leukocytes, platelets
3. carry oxygen
4. four
5. to help blood clot
6. The unusual erythrocytes clog blood vessels.
7. The person will not stop bleeding unless he has taken the drugs that replace their coagulation factors.
8. It is inherited from one's parents.

Exercise 2
Basophils: Trigger inflamation
Eosinophils: Trigger inflamation
Lymphocytes: Produce antibodies
Monocytes: Eat bacteria
Neutrophils: Eat bacteria

COMPREHENSION CHECK (pages 161–162)

Exercise 1
1. T
2. F—you can't see microorganisms with your naked eye
3. T
4. F—viruses and bacteria are found everywhere
5. F—viruses need help to reproduce from host cells
6. T
7. F—a bacterium does not contain a nucleus
8. T

Exercise 2
Alive: Bacterium
Has nucleic acid: Bacterium; Virus
Single-celled organism: Bacterium
Pathogen: Bacterium; Virus
Causes cholera: Bacterium
Causes influenza: Virus

COMPREHENSION CHECK (page 167)

Exercise 1
1. in the linings of all body openings
2. Mucus is very thick and usually alkaline.
3. to trap bacteria, viruses, and other debris in the air
4. The blood-brain barrier is a special barrier of thicker cells that exists between the bloodstream and the brain tissue. It prevents most microorganisms from infecting the brain.
5. to trap microorganisms and debris
6. The cilia of smokers are not working, so they can't remove microorganisms away from the lungs.
7. skin, mucus, wax, blood-brain barrier
8. Meningitis is an inflammation of the coverings of the brain and spinal cord.

Exercise 2
1. f   2. d   3. a   4. b
5. g   6. c   7. e

Exercise 1

Innate Defenses	Where?	What do they do?
Acids	Skin, stomach, vagina, urine	Prevent bacteria from growing
Complement	Bloodstream and tissue spaces	Causes bacteria to burst
Interferon	Virus-infected cells	Protects nearby cells from virus
Lysozyme	Saliva, tears	Kills bacteria
Proteases	Digestive system	Destroys viruses and bacteria

Exercise 2

1. b   2. c   3. b   4. a
5. b   6. c   7. b

COMPREHENSION CHECK *(page 172)*

Exercise 1

2—B cell makes copies of itself.
5—Phagocytes "eat" and destroy the hepatitis virus.
1—B cell recognizes a hepatitis A virus.
3—B cells make antibodies that can recognize the hepatitis A virus.
4—Antibodies attach to the hepatitis A viruses, preventing attachment to cells.

Exercise 2

1. B cells
2. to attach to microorganisms; they are very specific
3. phagocytes or complement
4. helper and cytotoxic
5. inside cells; they do not work against bacteria

Exercise 3

1. antibodies
2. helper T cell
3. thymus
4. lymphocyte
5. adaptive defenses
6. cytotoxic T cell
7. B cells
8. T cells

COMPREHENSION CHECK *(page 174)*

Exercise 1

1. T
2. T
3. F—the thymus helps T cells to mature
4. F—the thymus is located in the upper chest
5. F—the tonsils surround the pharynx

6. T
7. T
8. F—Hypothalamus helps to maintain homeostasis of body temperature. Lymph vessels remove excess water from tissues.

Exercise 2

1. e   2. f   3. c
4. b   5. d   6. a

REVIEW (pages 176–177)

Check Your Understanding

Exercise 1

1. plasma and cells
2. Erythrocytes carry oxygen and carbon dioxide. Leukocytes help with body defenses. Platelets help blood to clot.
3. Hemoglobin carries oxygen in the blood. It is found in erythrocytes.
4. blood clotting
5. Innate defenses are not specific to a single pathogen. Adaptive defenses are very specific and only work after you're exposed to the pathogen.
6. Viruses are not cells and use host cells to reproduce. Bacteria are cells and can reproduce by themselves.
7. They "eat" pathogens.
8. heat, swelling, redness, and pain
9. T cell
10. They contain phagocytes that can "eat" microorganisms.

Exercise 2

1. tonsils
2. thymus
3. spleen
4. lymphatic vessels
5. lymph nodes

Exercise 3

1. F—anemia is a disease in which there is not enough oxygen in blood
2. F—the first lines of defense are the innate defenses
3. c
4. b
5. a
6. The fluid would accumulate in that tissue region, causing swelling.
7. It carries nutrients, wastes, and hormones. It helps with temperature regulation.
8. The skin helps to act as a barrier to prevent microorganisms from entering the body. The mucous membranes trap bacteria and viruses in the mucus, preventing them from going deeper into the body. Inflammation helps to bring more nutrients, as well as repair- and disease-fighting cells to an injured area.

Think More about It

1. The integument (skin) is itself a barrier to disease. It is also acidic, which prevents many bacteria from growing there. Also sebum from sebaceous glands prevents many microorganisms from growing on the skin.
2. blood vessels, nerves
3. Blood is a tissue because it contains different types of cells, and all of the parts of blood work together to carry out several functions.

CHAPTER 9

INTRODUCTION (pages 179–180)

Exercise 1

1. artery
2. lung
3. vein
4. heart

Exercise 2

1. The heart pumps blood throughout the body.
2. cardiac muscle, epithelium, connective, blood
3. in the lungs
4. Arteries carry blood away from the heart and veins carry blood toward the heart. Capillaries are the smallest vessels and are where exchange of nutrients and waste occurs.

5. Blood to a part of the heart is blocked and the muscle in that area dies. This prevents that part of the heart from pumping blood.
6. Blood vessels carry nutrients and waste products from one area to another in the body.
7. Blood pressure is the pressure of the blood on the walls of the blood vessels. If it's too low, not enough nutrients get to the body tissues. If it's too high, this can cause problems with the heart and also damage blood vessel walls.

Exercise 3

1. oxygenated
2. exerted
3. dilate
4. constrict
5. branches

COMPREHENSION CHECK (page 182)

Exercise 1

1. thoracic
2. pericardium, myocardium, and endocardium
3. myocardium
4. endocardium
5. between the two layers of pericardium
6. to cushion it as it contracts and to prevent damage to the wall

Exercise 2

1. e	2. b	3. f
4. c	5. a	6. d

COMPREHENSION CHECK (pages 183–184)

Exercise 1

1. F—the AV valves connect the ventricles with the atria
2. T
3. F—blood flows from atria to ventricles
4. T
5. T
6. T
7. T
8. F—when atria are contracting, the AV valves are open

Exercise 2

1. pulmonary artery
2. atria
3. valve
4. chordae tendineae
5. tricuspid
6. semilunar

Exercise 1

3—Blood from the right ventricle is pushed through the semilunar valve into the pulmonary artery that carries it to the lungs.

7—The left ventricle sends blood through the aortic semilunar valve into the aorta.

1—Blood enters the right atrium.

4—Blood picks up oxygen in the lungs.

6—Blood passes through the bicuspid valve into the left ventricle.

5—Blood returns to the left atrium via the pulmonary veins.

2—Blood passes through the tricuspid valve into the right ventricle.

Exercise 2

The right ventricle: blood low in oxygen

The left ventricle: blood high in oxygen

The left atrium: blood high in oxygen

The right atrium: blood low in oxygen

COMPREHENSION CHECK *(page 188)*

Exercise 1

1. It's harder for the heart to pump blood to your brain because it is uphill.
2. Cardiac muscle contracts without stimulation from a neuron.
3. the pacemaker or SA node
4. the conduction system of the heart
5. Cardiac muscle fibers are very closely connected so that they can send electrical messages from one cell to the other.
6. nutrients and oxygen
7. heart attack

Exercise 2

1. autorrhythmic
2. conduction
3. sinoatrial node, pacemaker
4. angina pectoris
5. myocardial infarction

COMPREHENSION CHECK *(page 189)*

1. pulse rate
2. 72
3. increase
4. exercise

5. fever
6. decreases
7. increases

COMPREHENSION CHECK *(page 190)*

1. stethoscope
2. AV valves
3. semilunar valves
4. second
5. murmur
6. stenotic
7. incompetent
8. first

COMPREHENSION CHECK *(page 192)*

1. F—the stethoscope helps the doctor listen to heart sounds
2. T
3. T
4. F—arrhythmia an is abnormal heart rhythm
5. F—when heart muscle contractions are not coordinated, it results in a condition called fibrillation
6. T
7. T

COMPREHENSION CHECK *(page 193)*

Changes blood volume: Hormonal imbalance; Loss of blood or dehydration; Salt

Changes the level of contraction in the artery walls: When you are frightened; When you lie down to sleep

COMPREHENSION CHECK *(page 195)*

Exercise 1

1. blood vessels
2. diastolic
3. contracting
4. increases
5. decreases
6. increases
7. decreased

Exercise 2

1. change in volume of blood pumped from heart, changes in contraction of blood vessel walls, changes in blood volume

2. Baroreceptors monitor blood pressure.
Baroreceptors detect change in blood pressure.
Afferent message sent to medulla (brain).
Medulla makes a decision. Medulla sends
efferent messages to heart and muscle in wall of
blood vessels. Heart and blood vessels adjust to
fix the problem.

COMPREHENSION CHECK (pages 199–200)

Exercise 1
1—aorta
6—veins
2—arteries
4—capillaries
5—venules
3—arterioles

Exercise 2
Vein: Carry blood to the heart; Carry blood low
in oxygen
Artery: Carry blood to the body; Carry blood
high in oxygen
Capillary: Carry blood to the body; gas exchange
Venule: Carry blood to the heart; Carry blood
low in oxygen
Arteriole: Carry blood to the body; Carry blood
high in oxygen

Exercise 3
1. capillary bed
2. systemic circuit
3. Arterioles
4. Venules
5. Arteries
6. Veins
7. pulmonary circuit

COMPREHENSION CHECK (page 201)

Exercise 1
1. brachial
2. abdominal aorta
3. carotid
4. femoral
5. radial
6. pulmonary

Exercise 2
1. great saphenous
2. cephalic
3. pulmonary
4. common iliac

5. brachiocephalic
6. anterior tibial

COMPREHENSION CHECK (page 202)

1. veins
2. More
3. Lymph
4. Edema
5. blood volume

REVIEW (pages 204–207)

Check Your Understanding

Exercise 1
1. AV valve
2. lungs
3. arteries
4. SA node, located in right atrium
5. myocardial infarction
6. closing of the AV valves
7. change in blood volume pumped by the heart in
   a contraction, change in contraction of arteries,
   change in blood volume
8. Baroreceptors are located in the walls of the
   larger arteries. They monitor blood pressure.
9. lymph vessels return fluid to veins
10. capillaries

Exercise 2
Figure 9.15
1. superior vena cava
2. pulmonary semilunar valve
3. right atrium
4. tricuspid valve
5. right ventricle
6. inferior vena cava
7. aorta
8. pulmonary artery
9. pulmonary veins
10. aortic semilunar valve
11. left atrium
12. bicuspid valve
13. left ventricle

Figure 9.16
1. carotid
2. aorta
3. pulmonary
4. brachial

5. abdominal aorta
6. radial
7. common iliac
8. femoral
9. jugular
10. brachiocephalic
11. superior vena cava
12. cephalic
13. pulmonary
14. inferior vena cava
15. common iliac
16. great saphenous
17. anterior tibial

Exercise 3

1. artery; oxygen
2. medulla
3. increase
4. myocardial infarction
5. c
6. b, c, and d
7. c
8. F—arteries have more smooth muscle
9. F—the heart sounds ("lub-dup") occur when the heart valves close
10. T

Think More about It

1. Lungs provide oxygen for blood arriving from the heart.
2. The nervous system helps to control the heart rate and blood pressure. The cardiovascular system helps to provide nutrients and oxygen for the tissues in the nervous system.
3. The cardiovascular system provides oxygen and nutrients to the muscles.

CHAPTER 10

INTRODUCTION (pages 209–210)

Exercise 1

1. nasal cavity
2. oral cavity
3. pharynx
4. lungs
5. trachea
6. bronchi

Exercise 2

1. to provide oxygen to the bloodstream
2. Air enters the body through nasal and oral cavities.
3. to pick up oxygen and get rid of carbon dioxide
4. two
5. mucus, cilia, hairs, phagocytes
6. In emphysema, the alveoli fail to return to their original size after stretching. This makes it very hard for the patient to exhale.
7. Colds: gradual onset; last about one week; fever is rare; headaches are rare; mild aches; mild fatigue; usually stuffy nose; sneezing is common; cough with mucus
   Flu: rapid onset; lasts 1–2 weeks; high fever; headaches; severe aches; extreme exhaustion; sometimes stuffy nose; sneezing only sometimes; dry cough

Exercise 3

1. inspire, inhale
2. exhale, expire
3. breathe
4. capture
5. vibrate
6. diffuses
7. inflate
8. expand
9. filter
10. collapsed

COMPREHENSION CHECK (page 213)

Exercise 1

1. The air is filtered and warmed.
2. The pharynx is located where the nasal and oral cavities meet at the back of the oral cavity.
3. larynx and esophagus
4. They vibrate.
5. People have different voices because they have different thicknesses and lengths of vocal cords.
6. windpipe
7. to keep the trachea open and protect it
8. Laryngitis is caused by an inflammation of larynx caused by bacterial or viral infections. Vocal cords may become swollen.

Exercise 2

| 1. c | 2. b | 3. e |
| 4. f | 5. d | 6. a |

Exercise 1

1. F—there is one trachea and two primary bronchi
2. F—singular is *bronchus*; plural is *bronchi*
3. T
4. T
5. F—trachea and bronchi have cartilage
6. T
7. F—the bronchioles dilate when you need more air
8. T
9. F—each lung contains 150 million alveoli
10. F—people with emphysema have more difficulty with expiration than inspiration

Exercise 2

5—primary bronchi
1—nasal or oral cavity
3—larynx
8—alveoli
6—secondary bronchi
2—pharynx
7—tertiary bronchi
4—trachea

Exercise 3

1. nasal cavity
2. oral cavity
3. pharynx
4. secondary bronchi
5. lungs
6. trachea
7. primary bronchi
8. tertiary bronchi

Exercise 1

1. b   2. a   3. b
4. a   5. c   6. b

Exercise 2

1. inhalation, inspiration
2. expiration, exhalation
3. diaphragm
4. intercostal
5. smooth muscle, bronchioles

Exercise 1

1. alveolus
2. There is a net movement toward the area where there are fewer of the molecules.
3. Alveoli deliver oxygen to the capillaries. CO_2 diffuses from the capillaries to the alveoli.
4. Capillary walls are very thin, only one cell layer thick.
5. hemoglobin
6. Alveoli need to be inflated to allow proper pressure for inspiration and expiration.
7. Surfactant is a detergent-like molecule that prevents alveoli from collapsing by separating water molecules from one another.
8. Surfactant is produced by cells lining the alveolus.

Exercise 2

1. a   2. c   3. d   4. b

Exercise 1

1. nose hairs, cilia, mucus
2. Cilia are small hair-like structures in the lining of the trachea.
3. Cilia help to sweep mucus and debris upward, away from the lungs.
4. Macrophages are found in the alveoli.
5. It makes gas exchange easier.
6. Colds have gradual onset, flu has rapid onset; fever and headaches are common with flu and not with colds; sore throats are more common with colds than flu.

Exercise 2

1. c   2. d   3. a   4. b

REVIEW (pages 227–228)

Check Your Understanding

Exercise 1

1. oral and nasal
2. to sweep mucus and debris upward
3. bronchioles

4. one to each lobe of the lungs
5. diaphragm and intercostals
6. The bronchioles constrict, become inflated and fill with mucus.
7. Diffusion is the net movement of molecules toward areas where they are in lower concentration.
8. They "eat" bacteria and viruses.

Exercise 2
1. nasal cavity
2. oral cavity
3. pharynx
4. secondary bronchi
5. lungs
6. trachea
7. primary bronchi
8. tertiary bronchi
9. alveolus
10. bronchiole

Exercise 3
1. c
2. a
3. F—lungs are already inflated when air comes in
4. vibrate
5. diaphragm; expand; pressure; rush into
6. oxygen; capillaries / carbon dioxide; alveoli
7. to provide oxygen to the bloodstream and remove carbon dioxide from the blood
8. primary bronchi
9. mucus, cilia, nose hairs, macrophages
10. Colds have gradual onset, flu has rapid onset; fever and headaches are common with flu and not with colds; sore throats are more common with colds than flu.

Think More about It
1. Skeletal muscle is found in the wall of the pharynx, and smooth muscle is found in the walls of the bronchioles. Also, the diaphragm and intercostal muscles (skeletal muscles) help with breathing.
2. The nervous system controls the rate and depth of breathing by communicating with the diaphragm and intercostal muscles.
3. The respiratory system provides oxygen and removes carbon dioxide from the blood. This blood is part of the cardiovascular system.

CHAPTER 11
INTRODUCTION (pages 230–231)

Exercise 1
1. kidney
2. ureter
3. urinary bladder
4. urethra

Exercise 2
1. The urinary system helps to clean the blood and remove wastes. It also helps in regulating blood volume.
2. more often: drinking more water / drinking alcohol, and high blood pressure; less often: dehydration and low blood pressure
3. urinary tract infections, kidney stones, renal failure

Exercise 3
1. urinate
2. donated
3. lodged
4. reclaim
5. crystallize
6. inhibit

COMPREHENSION CHECK (page 234)

Exercise 1
2—cortex
4—pelvis
1—capsule
3—medulla

Exercise 2
1. glomerulus
2. afferent arteriole
3. collecting duct
4. Bowman's capsule
5. efferent arteriole
6. renal tubule

COMPREHENSION CHECK (page 236)

Exercise 1
1. to filter the blood
2. proteins and cells
3. fewer molecules are filtered

4. proximal convoluted tubule

5. Check your answer with Figure 11.6.

6. the collecting ducts

Exercise 2

1. b   **2.** g   **3.** d   **4.** c

5. h   **6.** f   **7.** e   **8.** a

COMPREHENSION CHECK *(page 238)*

Exercise 1

1. T

2. F—filtration occurs primarily in the glomerulus

3. T

4. F—the fluid in the renal tubules is called filtrate

5. F—secretion occurs after filtration

6. F—the distal convoluted tubules deliver urine to the collecting ducts

7. T

Exercise 2

Glomerulus: Filtration

Renal tubule: Reabsorption; Secretion

COMPREHENSION CHECK *(pages 240–241)*

Exercise 1

1. Erythropoietin

2. kidneys

3. increase

4. increases

5. increases

6. ADH

7. opposite

8. inhibits

Exercise 2

Sweating: Decrease blood volume

ADH: Increase blood volume

ANP: Decrease blood volume

Renin: Increase blood volume

Aldosterone: Increase blood volume

Alcohol: Decrease blood volume

High salt levels: Increase blood volume

COMPREHENSION CHECK *(pages 245–246)*

Exercise 1

1. urethra

2. 1 liter

3. longer

4. ureter

5. Excretion

6. urinary tract infection

Exercise 2

4—The spinal cord sends message to relax internal urethral sphincter.

3—The spinal cord sends a message to brain that bladder is full.

2—A neural message is sent to the spinal cord.

5—The internal urethral sphincter relaxes.

1—Stretch receptors detect that the bladder is full.

6—The person consciously relaxes the external urethral sphincter.

REVIEW (pages 247–249)

Check Your Understanding

Exercise 1

1. Kidneys cleanse the blood. Ureters transport urine to the bladder. Urinary bladder stores urine. Urethra sends urine outside the body.

2. glomerulus

3. glomerulus, Bowman's capsule, renal tubule (PCT, loop of Henle, DCT), afferent arteriole, efferent arteriole

4. Filtration takes things out of the blood.

5. maintaining blood volume

6. Kidneys secrete erythropoietin which causes bone marrow to make blood cells.

7. secretion

8. ADH and aldosterone

9. internal urethral sphincter

10. to excrete urine and send sperm out of body

Exercise 2

Figure 11.11

1. kidney

2. ureter

3. urethra

4. urinary bladder

Figure 11.12

1. afferent arteriole

2. glomerulus

3. PCT

4. loop of Henle

5. DCT

6. efferent arteriole

7. collecting duct

Exercise 3

1. d
2. c
3. d
4. F—too little water in the urine can cause formation of kidney stones
5. T
6. T
7. urea, water, uric acid
8. Kidney failure is caused by physical damage to kidneys, diabetes, chronic hypertension, or bacterial infections.
9. Filtration takes things out of the blood. Reabsorption returns things into the blood. Secretion takes things out of the blood.

Think More about It

1. The kidneys help with regulation of blood volume. This, in turn, can affect blood pressure. They also secrete erythropoietin to cause synthesis of blood cells.
2. The nervous system can control the constriction of blood vessels, including those leading to the kidneys. It also plays an important role in the urination process.
3. Smooth muscle is found in the walls of the ureters and the urinary bladder. This will help the bladder to contract when it is emptied.

CHAPTER 12

INTRODUCTION (pages 251–252)

Exercise 1

1. urethra
2. penis
3. testis
4. ovary
5. uterus
6. urethra
7. vagina

Exercise 2

1. testis
2. ovary
3. hormones

Exercise 3

1. lubricate
2. fertilizes
3. implant

4. ruptures
5. circumcised
6. ejaculates

COMPREHENSION CHECK (page 254)

Exercise 1

1. in the testes
2. inside the scrotum
3. lower than body temperature
4. It moves closer to the body.
5. seminiferous tubules
6. inside the testes
7. spermatocytes
8. Spermatids aren't yet able to swim. They become mature in the epididymis.

Exercise 2

1. g   2. c   3. d   4. b
5. a   6. e   7. f

COMPREHENSION CHECK (page 255)

1. F—erectile tissue fills with blood to make the man's penis become erect
2. T
3. F—lubrication makes passage of the penis into the vagina easier
4. F—sperm survive better in a neutral environment
5. F—ejaculation happens after an erection
6. T
7. T
8. F—impotence is the failure to maintain an erection

COMPREHENSION CHECK (page 257)

Exercise 1

6—The sperm are in the urethra.

4—The sperm are in the vas deferens where fluid is added from the seminal vesicles.

2—The spermatids are in the lumen of seminiferous tubule.

1—Spermatocytes undergo meiosis.

3—The sperm are in the epididymis.

5—The sperm are in the ejaculatory duct where the prostate adds a milky fluid to semen.

Exercise 2

1. b   2. c   3. a

Exercise 3

1. vas deferens
2. seminal vesicles
3. prostate gland
4. bulbourethral gland
5. urethra
6. testis
7. epididymis

COMPREHENSION CHECK *(page 259)*

Exercise 1

1. testis
2. to cause sperm production, development of male organs, and secondary sexual characteristics
3. high LH, high FSH, high testosterone, lots of sperm
4. increased muscle, growth in height, acne, thickening of vocal cords
5. low testosterone, inability of sperm to swim, too few sperm

Exercise 2

Testosterone: Stimulate sperm production
LH: Stimulate testosterone production
FSH: Stimulate sperm production

COMPREHENSION CHECK *(pages 264–265)*

Exercise 1

1. ovary
2. uterus
3. vagina

Exercise 2

2—vaginal opening
3—anal opening
1—urethral opening

Exercise 3

1. Fallopian tube
2. ovary
3. uterus
4. cervix
5. vagina

COMPREHENSION CHECK *(pages 267–268)*

Exercise 1

1. secondary oocyte
2. estrogen
3. progesterone
4. after

5. does not
6. 28 days

Exercise 2

5—The follicle turns into a corpus luteum which produces progesterone.
2—Most follicles stop growing, but one continues to grow.
6—If fertilization doesn't occur, corpus luteum disintegrates.
4—Ovulation occurs.
3—The primary oocyte continues meiosis to produce a polar body and a secondary oocyte.
1—Follicles begin to develop.

COMPREHENSION CHECK *(page 270)*

Exercise 1

1. endometrium
2. Estrogen
3. development of the embryo
4. endometriosis
5. drop
6. glycogen

Exercise 2

7—Walls of blood vessels die and blood begins to be released.
2—Estrogen causes endometrium to increase in thickness.
1—Menstruation (flow of blood and dead cells out of the body).
6—Endometrial cells die.
5—Falling progesterone levels cause blood vessels to bend, cutting off blood supply.
4—Progesterone causes endometrium to store food.
3—Blood vessels grow into endometrium.

COMPREHENSION CHECK *(page 272)*

1. LH
2. FSH
3. FSH
4. estrogen
5. progesterone
6. lack of available follicles and/or high levels of LH and FSH

COMPREHENSION CHECK *(page 274)*

1. clotting factors, alkaline fluid
2. in the Fallopian tubes

3. The uterus has smooth muscle and can stretch a great deal.
4. trachea
5. The sperm that don't fertilize the egg die.
6. Ectopic pregnancy occurs in the abdominal cavity. Tubal pregnancy occurs in the Fallopian tubes.
7. Fraternal twins come from two separate zygotes (two eggs fertilized by two sperm), while identical twins come from one original zygote that separates into two separate individuals.

COMPREHENSION CHECK *(pages 275–276)*

Exercise 1
1. zygote
2. embryo
3. eye color, hair color
4. in the nucleus of cells

Exercise 2
1. inheritance
2. Fertilization
3. sperm
4. zygote
5. Meiosis
6. embryo
7. fetus

REVIEW (pages 278–281)

Check Your Understanding

Exercise 1
1. testis
2. testis, epididymis, vas deferens, ejaculatory duct, urethra, outside the body
3. seminal vesicles, prostate gland, and bulbourethral gland
4. spermatocytes
5. LH
6. stimulate sperm production, development of male organs, secondary sexual characteristics, sex drive
7. ovarian
8. LH and FSH; FSH
9. secondary oocyte
10. development of embryo and fetus
11. Menopause starts when the menstrual cycles cease.
12. in the Fallopian tubes
13. estrogen
14. one spermatocyte produces four sperm; one oocyte produces just one egg

Exercise 2
Figure 12.16
1. vas deferens
2. seminal vesicle
3. prostate gland
4. bulbourethral gland
5. urethra
6. testis
7. epididymis

Figure 12.17
1. Fallopian tube
2. ovary
3. uterus
4. vagina

Exercise 3
1. a
2. a
3. f
4. T
5. F—the ovary is the main source of estrogen and progesterone in females, while the testes are the main source of testosterone in males
6. T
7. T
8. T

Think More about It
1. Muscles help to move the sperm along its path out of the male. They also are important in the uterus, especially during childbirth. These muscles are all smooth muscle.
2. pituitary hormones LH and FSH
3. Estrogen helps females to retain calcium in their bones. When a woman reaches menopause, there is a danger of osteoporosis because there is less estrogen to help with this.

ACHIEVEMENT TEST 1 (pages 288–290)

Exercise A
1. Homeostasis is when the body maintains conditions such as temperature, blood pressure, or heart rate at a constant level.
2. Hormones are molecules produced by endocrine glands and secreted into the bloodstream. These molecules are used as messengers to deliver information from one part of the body to another.

Exercise B
1. e   **2.** a   **3.** d   **4.** c   **5.** b

Exercise C
1. fracture
2. ligaments
3. compact
4. dermis
5. osteoarthritis

Exercise D
1. F
2. F
3. T
4. T
5. T
6. T

Exercise E
1. calcium salts; collagen
2. osteocytes
3. hold the body contents inside, maintain temperature, protect the internal organs
4. articulation
5. patella
6. function

Exercise F
1. c   **2.** a   **3.** b   **4.** c
5. b   **6.** d   **7.** a

Exercise G
1. trachea
2. trachea
3. food in the trachea
4. spinal cord

Exercise H
1. maxilla
2. clavicle
3. ilium
4. metatarsals
5. phalanges
6. parietal bones
7. scapula
8. radius
9. femur
10. fibula

Exercise I
1. When calcium levels in the blood fall below normal, the parathyroid gland secretes parathyroid hormone (PTH) into the blood.

PTH causes calcium to be released from the bone matrix into the blood until blood calcium reaches normal levels again.

2. OSTEOPOROSIS is a disorder in which there is not enough calcium in the bone matrix. This causes the matrix to be weaker and less dense. A person with osteoporosis is more likely to break a bone.

ACNE is a disorder in which there is too much sebum produced and bacteria infect the pores of the sebaceous glands. This leads to inflamed areas called pimples.

ACHIEVEMENT TEST 2 (pages 291–294)

Exercise A
1. A sensory receptor detects a change in a condition. A message is sent along afferent (sensory) neurons to the central nervous system, which makes a decision. The CNS sends a message along an efferent neuron to an effector which does something to correct the situation.
2. A neurotransmitter is a molecule that carries a message across the synaptic cleft between two neurons (or a neuron and a muscle fiber).

Exercise B
1. e   **2.** d   **3.** b
4. c   **5.** a   **6.** f

Exercise C
1. effector
2. sympathetic
3. efferent
4. myofibril
5. motor
6. shorter
7. electrical current

Exercise D
1. T
2. F
3. T
4. T
5. F
6. F

Exercise E
1. pituitary
2. dendrite

3. sensory receptor
4. synapse
5. fascicle

Exercise F
1. b and d
2. a, d, e, and f
3. c
4. d
5. b
6. c
7. c

Exercise G
1. medulla
2. afferent
3. tibialis anterior
4. cerebrum

Exercise H
1. orbicularis oculi
2. triceps brachii
3. rectus abdominis
4. tibialis anterior
5. trapezius
6. gluteus maximus
7. gastrocnemius

Exercise I
1. My friend was hiking in the woods when she saw a bear. **Sensory receptors** in her **eye** noticed the bear and sent a message along an **afferent neuron** to her brain. **CNS neurons** in the brain made a decision to run and sent a message along **motor neurons** to the **skeletal muscle in her leg**. Also, other **CNS neurons** decided that she would need more blood pumped to her body, so they sent a message along **autonomic neurons** to her **heart** to increase the heart rate. With her heart pounding, she ran away from the bear.

2. MULTIPLE SCLEROSIS is a disorder in which the myelin sheath around neurons is destroyed by the body's own immune system. As the myelin breaks down, messages are not sent as quickly along the neural pathways and the person may have difficulty with coordination of movement or rapid movement.

   A STROKE occurs when a blood clot or injury causes a blockage of blood flow to certain areas of the brain. Without enough oxygen or sugar, the neurons die. The person may lose feeling in parts of his or her body and may be unable to speak.

MUSCULAR DYSTROPHY is a disorder in which connective tissue replaces muscle tissue in skeletal muscles. The muscles become weaker and may eventually not contract at all, leading to paralysis and even death.

ACHIEVEMENT TEST 3 (pages 295–297)

Exercise A
1. An artery is a blood vessel that carries blood in the direction away from the heart.
2. Absorption is the process that moves food molecules from the lumen of the small intestine to the bloodstream.
3. Inflammation is an innate defense mechanism that occurs after an injury or infection. The four cardinal signs of inflammation are heat, swelling, redness, and pain.

Exercise B
1. c	2. e	3. g	4. a
5. d	6. f	7. b	

Exercise C
1. small intestine
2. artery
3. oxygen
4. hypertension
5. increase
6. protein
7. aorta
8. increase

Exercise D
1. F
2. T
3. F
4. T
5. F

Exercise E
1. leukocytes
2. erythrocytes
3. plasma
4. water, sugar, hormones, salts
5. anemia
6. sinoatrial (SA) node

Exercise F
1. c	2. b	3. c
4. d	5. a	6. b

Exercise G
1. hairs
2. phagocyte
3. attach to

Exercise H
1. liver
2. gallbladder
3. large intestine
4. esophagus
5. stomach
6. pyloric sphincter
7. pancreas

Exercise I
1. When Masashi's blood sugar levels rise above normal, the pancreas secretes insulin into the bloodstream. Insulin causes the body's cells to take sugar out of the blood and use it or store it. This reduces the blood sugar levels back to normal.

2. HEARTBURN is a disorder of the digestive system in which food mixed with stomach acid moves back into the esophagus. This creates a burning feeling in the lower esophagus region. This may be caused by a defective gastroesophageal sphincter, lying down too soon after a meal, or too large a meal.

   MYOCARDIAL INFARCTION occurs when blood flow to some of the cardiac muscles is blocked. When the muscles don't get enough oxygen, they begin to die and cannot help the heart to pump blood. The heart may actually stop or go into fibrillation (uncoordinated contractions).

   HEMOPHILIA is an inherited disorder of the blood in which certain proteins necessary for blood coagulation are missing in a person. Without these clotting proteins, the person will lose a large amount of blood if he or she is injured.

ACHIEVEMENT TEST 4 (pages 298–301)

Exercise A
1. Reabsorption is a process, occurring in the nephron, where molecules in the filtrate are returned to the bloodstream.
2. Menopause is an occurrence when a woman no longer has menstrual cycles.

3. Impotence is the inability of a man to have or sustain an erection of the penis.

Exercise B
1. g   2. e   3. b   4. d
5. f   6. c   7. a

Exercise C
1. Fallopian tubes
2. uterus
3. beginning
4. zygote
5. longer
6. incontinence

Exercise D
1. F
2. T
3. F
4. F
5. T
6. T

Exercise E
1. epididymis
2. pleural
3. ureter
4. adrenal
5. estrogen
6. testosterone

Exercise F
1. d   2. b   3. b
4. b   5. d   6. a

Exercise G
1. decreased
2. aldosterone
3. increase
4. would

Exercise H
1. vas deferens
2. prostate gland
3. bulbourethral gland
4. testis
5. Fallopian tube
6. ovary
7. uterus
8. vagina

Exercise I

1. Inspiration is the intake of air into the lungs. First, the diaphragm and intercostal muscles contract, causing the thoracic cavity to increase in size. This stretches the alveoli and decreases the pressure inside them. The decreased pressure in the alveoli causes air to flow into the lungs from the outside of the body.

2. KIDNEY STONES are most often found inside the ureters, but can also be found in the urethra or the kidney. They are crystals of salt that form because there is too little water in the urine (or too much salt). These crystals lodge inside the ureter and cause the person to experience pain. They may also block or impair the movement of urine to the bladder.

ENDOMETRIOSIS is a disorder in women where the endometrium begins to grow outside the uterus, typically in the abdominal cavity. This can cause severe pain and even infertility. EMPHYSEMA is a disorder of the respiratory system in which the alveoli become over-stretched and fail to return to their original size. It is most often caused by smoking. In this disorder, the person must use a large amount of his or her energy to exhale, making him or her very tired.

Index

Absorption, 146
Accessory organs in digestive system, 142–145
    liver, 146
    pancreas, 14
Accessory structures in integument, 19, 25–29
    sebaceous (oil) glands and sweat glands, 20
Accessory structures of bones, 44–47
Acetylcholine (ACh), 64
Achilles or calcaneal tendon, 75
Acid(s)
    as second line of defense, 167
    stomach, 136, 137, 143
Acne, 27
Acquired immunodeficiency syndrome (AIDS), 172, 264, 277
Actin, 62, 64, 65, 66, 67
Active reading, 95
Active sentences, 221
Active voice, 221
Acupuncture, 64, 103
Adaptive defenses, 171–172
Address, forms of, 55
Adenosine tri-phosphate (ATP), 67
ADH, 194, 239, 240
Adipose tissue, 23
Adrenal glands, 14, 239
Afferent arteriole, 233, 235, 239
Afferent nerve. See Sensory (afferent) neurons
African-Americans
    life expectance among, 123
    sickle cell anemia among, 158
Age, heart rate and, 189
AIDS, 172, 264, 277
Air in stomach, 211
Alcohol intoxication, 240
Aldosterone, 194, 239
Alkaline mucus, 137
Alternative medicine, 64, 80
Alveolar macrophages, 224
Alveoli, 213–214, 216
    in gas exchange, 218, 219–220
Alzheimer's disease, 113
Anatomy, defined, 2
Anemia, 158, 238
Anesthesia, 101
Angina pectoris, 187
ANP, 239
Anterior, defined, 71
Anterior trunk, muscles of, 71–72
Antibodies, 158, 171
Anti-diuretic hormone (ADH), 194, 239, 240
Anus, 244, 256, 263
Aorta, 183, 185

Aortic semilunar valve, 183, 185, 190
Appendicitis, 149
Appendicular skeleton, 48, 52–54
Arm
    bones of, 52
    muscles of upper, 71–74
Arousal, sexual, 255
Arrhythmia, 191
Arteriole(s), 198
    afferent, 233, 235, 239
    efferent, 233, 235
Artery(ies), 197–198
    coronary, 187
    major, 200
    pulmonary, 183, 185, 198
    renal, 233
    vasodilation and vasoconstriction in, 192, 193, 194, 197
Arthritis, rheumatoid, 46
Articulation (joint), 45
Asthma, 216
Atherosclerosis, 194
ATP, 67
Atria, 182, 183
    contraction of, 187
    path of blood through heart and, 184–185
Atrial natriuretic peptide (ANP), 239
Atrio-ventricular valves, 182, 183
Autoimmune disorder, 46
Autonomic nervous system (ANS), 121–123
    heart rate increased by, 189
Autorhythmic fibers of cardiac muscle, 186
AV valves, 182, 183, 190
Axial skeleton, 48, 50–51
Axons, 89, 96
    myelinated, 92–93, 110, 112
    unmyelinated part of, 93

Babies
    cultural differences in sleeping arrangements for, 221
    premature, 220
Backbone, 50
Bacterial meningitis, 166
Bacterium/bacteria, 26, 160, 161
    body defenses against. See Body defenses
    in large intestine, 149
    peptic ulcers caused by, 138
    resident, 21
    tagged by antibodies, 158
Balance, cerebellum and maintaining, 113
Baroreceptor reflex, 193–194
Baroreceptors, 193
Barriers, defensive, 165–166
Basophils, 158

B cells, 171
Biceps brachii, 69, 71
Biceps femoris, 75
Bicuspid valve, 182, 183, 185, 190
Bile, 142
Bladder, urinary, 230, 232, 244
Bleeding, clot to stop, 159
Blindness, color, 100
Blister, 23
Blood, 155–160
    cells, 38, 168, 171
    glomerular filtration of, 234–236, 237
    heart as mechanical pump for, 186–188
    lymphatic organs in, 173–174
    oxygenated, 183, 185
    path through the heart, 184–186
    pH balance in, 237
    reabsorption by, 236–238
    secretion by, 236–238
Blood banks, 157
Blood-brain barrier, 166
Blood pressure (BP), 192–195, 239
Blood sugar, regulation of, 144
Blood vessels, 197–201
    inflammation and widened, 168
    in integument, 25–26
Blood volume
    changes in, 192, 194
    homeostasis of, 173, 202
    maintaining, 239
Body defenses, 165–174
Body temperature
    maintaining, 11, 28
    set point, 169
    sweat glands and, 28
Bone(s), 33, 35–47
    accessory structures of, 44, 49, 50, 76, 212
    of appendicular skeleton, 48, 52–54
    of axial skeleton, 48, 50–51
    dislocation of, 53
    fracture (break) of, 53
    of skull, 48, 49
    types of, 48
Bone marrow, 37, 38
    transplant, 159
Bowel movement, 149
Bowman's capsule, 233, 235
BP. See Blood pressure (BP)
Brain, 86, 87, 88, 112
    brainstem, 116–118
    cerebellum, 113–114
    cerebrum, 112–113
    diencephalon, 114–116
    inspiration control by, 216
    limbic system, 118

muscle movement and, 64
reticular formation, 118
Breathing, 211, 216–218
epiglottis raised in, 135
Bronchioles, 209, 213, 214, 216
Bronchus/bronchi, 209, 213, 214
Browsers, Internet, 164
Building blocks of body, 4–7
Bulbourethral glands (Cowper's glands),
255, 256

Caesarean section (C-Section), 264
Calcaneal tendon, 75
Calcitonin, 39
Calcium
bone matrix as storage location
for, 38, 39
dietary sources of, 38
homeostasis of, 39–40
osteoporosis and, 40
Calcium salts, 35
Calculi, renal, 243
Calf muscle (gastrocnemius), 76
Callus, 23
Cancer
leukemia, 159
prostate, 256
skin, 21
Canines, 132, 133
Capillaries, 198
lymphatic, 202
pulmonary, 185, 218
transport of food molecules by, 146
Capillary beds, 198, 202
Capsule, renal, 232
Carbon dioxide, 185, 218–220
Cardiac muscle, 68, 181
autorhythmic fibers of, 186
Cardiovascular system, 178–207. See
also Heart
blood vessels, 25–26, 168
Carpals, 52
Cartilage, 44, 50, 212
Categorizing information, 242
Catheter, 245
Cause and effect
explaining, 140–141
structure words, 140
Cause clause, 140
Cavities in teeth, 134
Cavity, 37
Cell(s), 4–6
B, 171
blood, 157–159, 168, 171
interstitial, 258
muscle, 62
of nervous system, 89–90
T, 171, 172
tissues formed by, 6, 7
Cell body, 89
Cell membrane, 5
Cellular metabolism, regulation of, 148
Cellular respiration, 209

Central nervous system (CNS), 109–118
brain, 86, 87, 88
"fight or flight" response and, 121
meningitis affecting, 166
in "rest and digest" situation, 122
spinal cord, 86, 87, 88
Centrifuge, 157
Cerebellum, 113–114
Cerebrum, 112–113
Cervical vertebrae, 50
Cervix, 263, 264
Chambers of heart, 182–183
Chancroid, 277
Cheekbones, 49
Chest cavity, 181
Chinese medicine, 102
Chlamydial infection, 277
Chlamydia trachomatis, 277
Choking, 136
Cholera, 161
Cholesterol, gallstones and high, 143
Chordae tendineae, 183
Chromosomes, 253
Cialis™, 255
Cilia, 166
along trachea, 224
in Fallopian tubes, 273
Circulatory system, 7
Circumcision, 255
Clarification, asking for, 23–24
Clavicle, 52
Clot, platelets and formation of, 159
CNS. *See* Central nervous system (CNS)
Coagulation factors, 159
Coccyx, 50
Cochlea, 100
Colds, 225
Collagen, 22, 35, 44
Collecting ducts, renal, 237
Color blindness, 100
Color vision, 99
Coma, 118
Communication, cultural differences
in direct, 150
Compact bone, 35, 37
Complement, 168
Comprise, use of, 9
Concept map, 196–197
Conduction system of heart, 187, 191
Cones, 99
Confidentiality, cultural differences in, 246
Connections, describing, 195–196
Connective tissue, 22, 44
Conscious thought in brain, 112
Constipation, 149
Constriction of artery walls. *See*
Vasoconstriction
Contraction(s)
of heart muscle, 186–187, 188–189, 191
in myofibril, 66–68
Coronary arteries, 187
Corpus luteum, 266, 267, 269
Cortex, renal, 232, 233

Cough reflex, 136
Cowper's glands (bulbourethral glands),
255, 256
Cramps, menstrual, 270
Cranial nerves, 96–97
Cretinism, 148
Crystals, gallstone, 143
C-Section (Caesarean), 264
Cultural differences
age and gender hierarchy, 226
alternative medicine and, 80
in baby sleeping arrangements, 220
in confidentiality and privacy, 246
in direct communication, 150
in discussing reproductive system
with patients, 276
economy of health care and, 203
folk medicine and, 102–103
in forms of address, 55
making progress in health care and,
123–124
preparing for future and, 15
spiritual forces in healing and, 175
in use of touch to comfort, 29
Cusps, valve, 183
Cytokine, 169
Cytoplasm, 5
Cytotoxic T cells, 171, 172

Dandruff, 27
DCT, 235
Defecation, 149
Defenses, body, 165–174
Defibrillator, 191
Definitions of terms, 162–164
Deltoid muscles, 71
Dendrites, 89, 91, 96
Dentin, 133, 134
Deoxyribonucleic acid (DNA), 5
Dermis, 20, 22–23, 25
Describing organization and function, 9
Development, embryonic, 274–276
Diabetes mellitus, 145, 236
Diagrams, studying, 43
Dialysis, 238
Diaphragm, 71, 216
Diarrhea, cholera and, 161
Diastolic pressure, 192
Dictionaries, 162, 164
Diencephalon, 114–116
Diet, diabetes and, 236
Differences, stating and asking about, 118–120
Diffusion, 218
Digestion
accessory organs helping in, 142–145
of fats, 142
of protein, 137
of starches, 131
Digestive enzymes, 143
Digestive system, 128–153
oral cavity, 209, 211
pancreas, 14
small intestine, 7

Dilation of artery walls. *See* Vasodilation
Direct communication, cultural differences in, 150
Direct question, 259
Disease(s)
  body defenses against, 165–174
  infectious, 160–162
  sexually transmitted (STDs), 277
Dislocation, 53
Distal convoluted tubule (DCT), 235
DNA, 5
Duct, 28
  bile, 142
  ejaculatory, 256
Ductus deferens (vas deferens), 256

Ear, 100
  wax in, 166
Economy of health care, 203
Ectopic pregnancy, 273
Edema, 202
Effect clause, 140
Efferent arteriole, 233, 235
Efferent neurons, 97
  "fight or flight" situation and, 121
  in "rest and digest" situation, 122
Egg (ovum), 263, 265, 266, 272
Ejaculation, 256
Ejaculatory duct, 256
Elastin, 22, 44, 214, 218
Electrocardiograph (EKG), 191–192
Embryo, 267
Embryonic development, 274–276
Emphysema, 214, 216
Enamel, tooth, 133, 134
Encyclopedia, 164
Endocardium, 181
Endocrine glands, 13, 144
Endometriosis, 270
Endometrium, 268, 269
Enzyme(s), 138
  digestive, 143
  protein digestion and, 138
Eosinophils, 158
Epidermis, 20, 21, 25
Epididymis, 253, 254, 256
Epiglottis, 135, 136, 211, 212
Epinephrine, 216
Epithelial tissue, 21, 181
Epithelium of capillary walls, 198
Erectile tissue, 255, 256
Erection of penis, 255
Erythrocytes (red blood cells), 157, 238
Erythropoietin, 238
Esophagus, 135, 211
  peristalsis of, 136
Estrogen, 266
  menstrual cycle and, 268
  progesterone compared with, 271
Evil eye (folk remedy), 103
Expiration (exhalation), 216
External anal sphincter, 149

External oblique, 72
External urethral sphincter, 244
Eye, 99

Facial muscles, 69–70
Facial nerve, 97
Fallopian tubes, 263, 266, 273
Fascicles
  in muscles, 62
  in nerves, 96
Fat(s)
  adipose tissue, 23
  digestion of, 142
  glucagon and, 144
  stored in yellow bone marrow, 38
Feces, 147, 149
Feedback, negative, 12–13, 258
  regulation of cellular metabolism as form of, 148
Female reproductive system, 251, 263–272
  Fallopian tubes, 273
  ovaries, 14
  urethra, 230, 232
Femur, 52, 53
Fertilization, 263, 272–274
  progesterone production and, 267
Fetal development, 275
Fetus, 263, 275
Fever, 28
  as innate defense, 169
Fiber, 62
Fibrillation, 191
Fibula, 52, 53
"Fight or flight" situations, 121–122
  heart rate increased in, 189
Figures (diagrams), studying, 43
Filament, 62
Filtrate, 235
Filtration, renal, 234–236, 237
First line of defense, 165–167
Flaccid penis, 255
Flat bone, 36
Flow chart, 197
Folk medicine, 102–103
Follicle(s), 265, 266
  hair, 20, 26
Follicle stimulating hormone (FSH), 258
Follicular cells, 266–267
Food
  absorption in small intestine, 146
  digestion of. *See* Digestion; Digestive system
  swallowing, 135–136
  tastes of, 132
Food waste, elimination of, 149
Foreskin (prepuce), 255
Form, use of, 9
Fracture, 53
Fraternal twins, 274
Frontal bone, 49
Frontalis muscles, 69

Frontal lobe, 113
Function of structure, describing, 9
Fungi, 26

Gall bladder, 142–143
Gallstones, 143, 243
Gas exchange, 185, 218–220
Gastrocnemius, 75
Gastroesophageal sphincter, 136
General anesthesia, 101
Genital herpes, 277
Gland(s)
  adrenal, 13, 239
  endocrine, 13, 144
  parathyroid, 14, 39, 40
  pineal, 115
  pituitary, 14, 115, 148, 239, 258
  prostate, 256, 257
  salivary, 131
  sebaceous, 27
  sweat, 28
  thymus, 171
  thyroid, 14, 39, 148
Glomerulus, 233, 234, 235, 236
Glucagon, 144
Gluteus maximus, 73
Glycogen, 269
Gonorrhea, 277
Gravity, blood flow through AV valves due to, 183
Gray matter, 110, 112

Haemophilus ducreyi, 277
Hair(s), 20, 26–27
  nose, 166, 211, 224
Hair follicle, 20
Hamstrings (biceps femoris), 75
Hand, bones of, 52
Hard keratin, 26
Head, muscles of, 69–70
Healing
  inflammation and, 168
  spiritual forces in, 175
Health care
  differences in accessing, 124
  economy of, 203
  making progress in, 123
Health insurance, 203
Healthy People 2010, 123
Heart, 7, 180–195
  blood pressure, 239
  cardiac muscle of, 68
Heart attack, 187
Heartburn, 136
Heart murmur, 190
Heimlich maneuver, 136
Helper T cells, 171, 172
Hemoglobin, 157, 158
Hemophilia, 159
Herpes, genital, 277
HHV 2, 277
Hierarchy, 197

Highlighting, 95
Hip bones, 52, 53
HIV, 172, 277
Homeostasis, 11–14
  autonomic nervous system and, 121
  of blood pressure, 193–194
  of blood sugar, 144
  of blood volume, 173, 202
  of calcium, 39–40
  heart rate and, 189
  of kidneys, 238–239
  maintaining, 12–13, 251, 271
Hormone(s), 14
  for blood sugar homeostasis, 144
  blood volume changed by, 194
  homeostasis of calcium and, 39
  homeostatic maintenance of, 251, 271
  pituitary, 115
  regulation of, 271
  reproductive, 258, 271–272
  thyroid, 148
Hot/old/wet/dry balance, 103
Human herpes virus (HHV) 2, 277
Human immunodeficiency virus (HIV),
      172, 277
Human papillomavirus (HPV), 277
Humerus, 52
Hypertension, 194
Hyperthyroidism, 148
Hypertrophy, prostatic, 256
Hypodermis, 20, 23, 25
Hypotension, 194
Hypothalamus, 115
  blood volume changed by, 194
  body temperature regulation and,
      28, 169
  functions of, 115
Hypothetical questions, 241–242, 259–261

Identical twins, 274
Ilium, 52, 53
Imagining a process, 141–142
Immune system, 165, 174. *See also*
      Innate defenses
  adaptive defenses as, 171–172
Impotence, 255
Incisors, 132, 133
Incompetent valve, 190
Incontinence, 244
Index cards, using, 24–25
Infant Respiratory Distress Syndrome
      (IRDS), 220
Infection(s), 160
  chlamydial, 277
  papillomavirus, 277
  respiratory, 166, 225
  urinary tract (UTI), 245
  viral, 225
  yeast, 264
Infectious disease, 160–162
Inferior vena cava, 184, 198
Infertility, 259

Inflammation, 27, 46, 158
  "four cardinal signs" of, 168
  heartburn, 136
  as innate defense, 168
Influenza, 225
Influenzavirus, 225
Information, categorizing, 242
Inhalation, 216
Inheritance, 275
Inhibin, 258
Innate defenses, 165–170
Inspiration, 216
Insulin, 14, 144, 146
Insulin-dependent (Type I) diabetes, 145
Integumentary system, 18–31
  as barrier, 165
Intercostal muscles, 71, 216
Interferon, 167
Internal anal sphincter, 149
Internal urethral sphincter, 244
Internet, 164
Interstitial cells, 258
Intervertebral disks, 45, 50
Intestine
  large, 149
  small, 7, 142–147
Involuntary muscles, 68
Iodine, 148
IRDS, 220
Ischium, 52, 53

Jet lag, 115
Joints, 45–46, 49
Juvenile diabetes, 145

Keratin, 21, 26
Kidney (renal) failure, 234, 235, 238
Kidneys, 229, 230, 231–240, 243
  blood volume changed by, 194
Kidney stones (renal calculi), 244
Kidney transplant, 238
Kneecap (patella), 52, 53
Knee joint, 44

Language and study skills
  active reading, 95
  active voice, 221
  asking for clarification, 23–24
  categorizing information, 242–243
  concept map, 196–197
  creating good study habits, 10
  defining terms, 162–164
  describing a process, 221–223
  describing a sequence, 94–95
  describing location, 77–79
  describing organization and function, 9
  describing relationships and connections,
      195–196
  explaining cause and effect, 140–141
  forming a study group, 120–121
  hypothetical questions, 241–242, 259–261
  imagining a process, 141–142

passive voice, 221–223
  stating and asking about differences,
      118–120
  stating degree of understanding, 42–43
  studying diagrams, 43
  summarizing information, 223–224
  using index cards, 24–25
  using mnemonics, 79
  using reference sources, 164–165
Large intestine, 149
Laryngitis, 211
Larynx, 135, 209, 211–212
Latissimus dorsi, 73
Leg
  bones of, 52, 53
  muscles of, 75–77
Leukemia, 159
Leukocytes, 157, 158
  phagocytes, 168
Life expectancy, 123
Ligaments, 44
Limbic system, 118
Liver, 142, 146
Lobes
  in cerebrum, 112–113
  of lung, 213
Local anesthesia, 101
Location of various structures, describing,
      77–79
Long bone, 37
Loop of Henle, 235
Lumbar vertebrae, 50
Lumen, 254
Lung(s), 209
  alveoli of, 213–214, 216, 218, 219–220
  capillaries in, 218
  gas exchange in, 185
  lobes of, 213
Luteinizing hormone (LH), 258
Lymph, 201
Lymphatic capillaries, 202
Lymphatic system, 173–174
Lymphatic vessels, 173, 201–202
Lymph nodes, 168, 173
Lymphocytes, 158, 171
Lymphocytic leukemia, 159
Lymph organs, 202
Lysozyme, 167

Macrophages, alveolar, 224
Male reproductive system, 251, 252–259
  ureter, 230, 232, 237, 243
  urethra, 243, 244–245
Mandibles, 49
Marrow cavity, 37
Masseter muscles, 70
Matrix, bone, 35, 38, 39
Maxilla, 49
Medical dictionaries, 162
Medication(s)
  over-the-counter, 225
  secretion of, 237

Medicine
    alternative, 64, 80
    Chinese, 102
    folk, 102–103
Medulla, renal, 232, 233
Medulla oblongata, 117
    baroreceptor reflex and, 193–194
Meiosis, 253, 266
Melanin, 21, 26
Melatonin, 115
Meningitis, 166
Menopause, 271
Menstrual cramps, 270
Menstrual (uterine) cycle, 268–270
Menstruation, 265, 268
Metacarpals, 52
Metatarsals, 53
Microorganisms, infectious disease caused
        by, 160–162
Microscope, 5
Midbrain, 117
Mitochondria, 67
Mitral valve, 182, 183
Mixed nerves, 97–98
Mnemonics, using, 79
Molars, 132, 133
Mole, 21
Molecule, 4, 5
Monocytes, 158, 168
Motor neurons, 64, 89, 97, 110
Mouth (oral cavity), 131–135, 209, 211
Movement
    bones and, 33, 52
    muscles for, 60, 64–68
    net, 218–219
Mucus, 224
    alkaline, 137
    in uterus, 273
Mucous membranes, 166
Multiple sclerosis (MS), 93
Murmur, heart, 190
Muscle(s), 59–83
    attached to bones, 33
    cardiac, 181, 186
    stomach wall, 137, 138
Muscle tissue, 7, 62
Muscular dystrophy, 68
Mycosis, 26
Myelinated axons, 92–93, 110, 112
Myelin sheath, 92, 93
Myocardial infarction, 187
Myocardium, 181, 186
Myofibril, 62
    contraction in, 66–68
    at rest, 65–66
Myofilaments, 62, 64, 65
Myometrium, 268
Myosin, 62, 64, 65, 66, 67

Nail fungus, 26
Nails, 26–27
Nasal cavity (nose), 209, 211

Nasal hairs, 224
Negative feedback, 12–13, 258
    regulation of cellular metabolism as
        form of, 148
Neisseria gonorrhoeae, 277
Nephrons, 233–238
Nerve(s), 96–99. See also Neuron(s)
    as accessory structure in integument, 20
    as homeostatic messengers, 13, 14
    in integument, 25–26
    motor, 64, 89, 110
Nervous system, 84–127
    autonomic (ANS), 189
    brain, 112
    meningitis affecting, 166
Net movement, 218–219
Neuron(s). See also Nerve(s)
    afferent (sensory), 89, 90, 96, 97, 110,
        121, 122
    in brain gray matter, 112
    efferent, 97, 121, 122
    message sending by, 90–93
    motor, 64, 89, 97, 110
    parts of, 89
Neurotransmitter, 64, 90, 91
Neutrophils, 158, 168
Nicotine, 166
Non-insulin dependent (Type II)
        diabetes, 145
Nose hairs, 166, 211, 224
Nose (nasal cavity), 209, 211
Note taking, 95
Nucleic acid, 160
Nucleus, 5
Nutrients, capillary delivery of, 198

Occipital bone, 49
Occipital lobe, 113
Oculomotor nerve, 97
Oocyte, 263, 265
    secondary, 266
Optic nerve, 96
Oral cavity (mouth), 131–135, 209, 211
Orbicularis oculi muscles, 70
Orbicularis oris muscles, 70
Organ(s), 6. See also specific organs
    accessory, in digestion, 142–145
    bones as, 35
    of female reproductive system, 263–265
    "fight or flight" response and, 121
    lymph, 202
    lymphatic, 173–174
    nerves as, 96
    in "rest and digest" situation, 122
    sensory, 86, 99–100
Organelles, 5, 160
Organization of structure, describing, 9
Organ system, 7
Osteoarthritis, 46
Osteocytes, 35
Osteoporosis, 40
Ovarian cycle, 265–268, 269

Ovaries, 14, 263
Over-the-counter medication, 225
Ovulation, 266
Ovum (egg), 263, 265, 266, 272
Oxygen, 209
    in gas exchange, 185, 218–220
    hemoglobin and transport of, 157
Oxygenated blood, 183, 185

Pacemaker, 186
Pain
    anesthesia to prevent, 101
    of inflammation, 168
Pancreas, 14, 143–144
Papillomavirus infections, 277
Paralysis, 93
Parasympathetic division, 122–123
Parathyroid glands, 14, 39, 40
Parathyroid hormone (PTH), 39, 40
Parietal bone, 49
Parietal lobe, 113
Passive sentences, 221
Passive voice, 221–223
Patella, 52, 53
Pathogens, 160
PCT, 235, 236
Pectoralis major, 71
Pelvis, renal, 232, 237
Penis, 255, 256
Peptic ulcers, 137
Pericardial fluid, 181
Pericardium, 181
Peripheral nervous system (PNS), 86–88,
        96–101
Peristalsis, 136, 146
Peritonitis, 149
Permeable membrane, 5
Phagocytes, 168, 169, 173
Phalanges, 52, 53
Pharynx, 135, 209, 211
pH of blood, 237
Physiology, defined, 2
Pimples, 27
Pineal gland, 115
Pituitary gland, 14, 115, 148, 239, 258
Placenta, 275
Plasma, 157
Platelets, 157, 159
PNS. See Peripheral nervous system (PNS)
Polar body, 266
Pons, 117
Posterior, defined, 73
Posterior of trunk, muscles of, 73–74
Potassium
    absorbed in large intestine, 149
    electrical current in neuron and, 90
Pregnancy, 273
Premature babies, 220
Pre menstrual syndrome (PMS), 270
Premolars, 132, 133
Prepuce (foreskin), 255
Primary bronchi, 213, 214

Privacy, cultural differences in, 246
Process(es)
    describing, 221–223
    imagining, 141–142
Progesterone, 267
    estrogen compared with, 271
    fertilization and, 267
    menstrual cycle and, 268–269
Proliferation, 268
Prostaglandins, 270
Prostate gland, 256, 257
Prostatic hypertrophy, 256
Proteases, 167
Protein(s)
    actin, 62, 64, 65, 66, 67
    antibodies, 158, 171
    digestion of, 137
    hemoglobin, 157, 158
    myosin, 62, 64, 65, 66, 67
Protein fibers, types of, 22
Proximal convoluted tubule (PCT), 235, 236
PTH, 39, 40
Puberty, 258, 264
Pubis, 52, 53
Pulmonary artery, 183, 185, 198
Pulmonary capillaries, 185, 218
Pulmonary circuit, 198, 199
Pulmonary semilunar valve, 182, 183, 185, 190
Pulmonary veins, 185, 218
Pulp, tooth, 133, 134
Pulse rate, 188
Pyloric sphincter, 138
Pyramids, renal, 232

Quadriceps femoris, 74
Question(s)
    clarification, 23–24
    about differences, 119–120
    direct, 259
    hypothetical, 241–242, 259–261

Radius, 52
Reabsorption, renal, 236–238
Reading and reciting, 95
Receptor molecules, 91
Rectum, 149, 244
Rectus abdominis, 72
Rectus femoris, 69, 75
Red blood cells (erythrocytes), 157, 238
Red bone marrow, 37, 38
Reference sources, using, 164–165
Reflex(es), 12–13, 86
    baroreceptor, 193–194
    cough, 136
    "fight or flight" response and, 121
    midbrain and, 117
    pathway, 110
    speed of, 92
    steps in, 88, 94
Relationships
    in concept map, 196–197
    describing, 195–196

Relaxation, deep breathing for, 216
Remedies, folk, 102–103
Renal artery, 233
Renal calculi (kidney stones), 244
Renal (kidney) failure, 234, 235, 238
Renal tubule, 233, 235
Renin, 239
Reproductive system, 250–281
Resident bacteria, 21
Resignation (folk remedy), 103
Respiration, cellular, 209
Respiratory system, 208–228
    epiglottis, 135, 136
    gas exchange, 185
    infections of, 166
    larynx, 135
    mouth (oral cavity), 131–135
    pharynx, 135
    trachea, 135, 166
"Rest and digest" situation, 122
Resting heart rate, 189
Reticular fibers, 22
Reticular formation, 118
Retina, 99
Rheumatoid arthritis, 46
Rhinovirus, 225
Ribs, 50
Rods, 99

Sacrum, 50
Saliva, 131
    lysozyme in, 167
Salivary glands, 131
Salts, crystallized, 243
SA node, 186–187
Sarcomere, 66, 67
Sartorius, 75
Scapula, 52
Scrotum, 252, 253
Sebaceous glands, 27–29
Sebum, 27
Secondary bronchi, 213, 214
Secondary oocyte, 266
Second line of defense, 167–170
Secretion, renal, 236–238
Secretion of hormones, 14
Semen, 256, 272
Semilunar valves, 183, 190
Seminal vesicles, 256
Seminiferous tubules, 253–254, 256
Sensory (afferent) neurons, 89, 90, 96, 97
    "fight or flight" situation and, 121
    in reflex pathway, 110
    in "rest and digest" situation, 122
Sensory organ, 86, 99–100
Sensory receptors, 25, 28, 86, 87, 88, 99–101
    baroreceptors, 193
    "fight or flight" situation and, 121
    in reflex pathway, 110
    in "rest and digest" situation, 122
Sentences, active vs. passive, 221
Sequence, describing, 94–95

Set point, 11
    fever as raised, 28, 169
Sex drive, 271
Sexual arousal, 255
Sexual intercourse, 272, 276
Sexually transmitted diseases (STDs), 277
Shivering, 11
Sickle cell anemia, 158
Sinoatrial node (SA node), 186–187
Skeletal muscle, 68, 69–77
    of anterior trunk and upper arm, 216
    organization of, 61–63
Skeleton and skeletal system, 32–58
Skin, 20–29. See also Integumentary system
    accessory structures in, 19
    as barrier, 165
    regions of, 19
    as sensory organ, 100
Skull, 48, 49
    sutures in, 45
Slightly moveable joints, 45
Small intestine, 7, 142–147
Smoking
    effect on cilia, 166
    emphysema from, 214
Smooth muscle, 68
    in arterioles, 198
    of artery walls, 197
Sodium
    absorbed in large intestine, 149
    electrical current in neuron and, 90
Sodium bicarbonate, 143
Sperm (spermatozoa), 272–273
    path of, 256
    production of, 252–254, 258
Spermatids, 253
Spermatocytes, 253
Sphincter
    anal, 149
    gastroesophageal, 136
    pyloric, 138
    urethral, 244
Spinal cord, 86, 87, 88, 109–111
Spinal nerves, 98
Spine, 50
    articulations in, 45
Spiritual forces in healing, 175
Spleen, 174
Spongy bone, 35, 36
Starches, digestion of, 131
STDs, 277
Stenotic valve, 190
Sternocleidomastoid muscle, 69, 71
Sternum, 50
Steroids, 75
Stethoscope, 190
Stomach, 135–139
    acids in, 143
    air in, 211
Storage organ, bone as, 38
Strong emotional state (folk remedy), 103
Study group, forming, 120–121